T0351062

Combatting Cyberbullying in Digital Media with Artificial Intelligence

Rapid advancements in mobile computing and communication technology and recent technological progress have opened up a plethora of opportunities. These advancements have expanded knowledge, facilitated global business, enhanced collaboration, and connected people through various digital media platforms. While these virtual platforms have provided new avenues for communication and self-expression, they also pose significant threats to our privacy. As a result, we must remain vigilant against the propagation of electronic violence through social networks. Cyberbullying has emerged as a particularly concerning form of online harassment and bullying, with instances of racism, terrorism, and various types of trolling becoming increasingly prevalent worldwide.

Addressing the issue of cyberbullying to find effective solutions is a challenge for the web mining community, particularly within the realm of social media. In this context, artificial intelligence (AI) can serve as a valuable tool in combating the diverse manifestations of cyberbullying on the Internet and social networks. This book presents the latest cutting-edge research, theoretical methods, and novel applications in AI techniques to combat cyberbullying. Discussing new models, practical solutions, and technological advances related to detecting and analyzing cyberbullying is based on AI models and other related techniques. Furthermore, this book helps readers understand AI techniques to combat cyberbullying systematically and forthrightly, as well as future insights and the societal and technical aspects of natural language processing (NLP)-based cyberbullying research efforts.

Key Features:

- Proposes new models, practical solutions, and technological advances related to machine intelligence techniques for detecting cyberbullying across multiple social media platforms.
- Combines both theory and practice so that readers (beginners or experts) of this book can find both a description of the concepts and context related to machine intelligence.
- Includes many case studies and applications of machine intelligence for combating cyberbullying.

Mohamed Lahby is Associate Professor at the Higher Normal School (ENS) University Hassan II of Casablanca, Morocco. He received a PhD in Computer Science from the University Hassan II of Casablanca in 2013. His research interests are smart cities and machine learning. He has published more than 50 papers.

Al-Sakib Khan Pathan is currently a Professor at the CSE department, United International University (UIU), Bangladesh. He received a Ph.D. in Computer Engineering (2009) from Kyung Hee University, South Korea, and B.Sc. in Computer Science and Information Technology (2003) from the Islamic University of Technology (IUT), Bangladesh. He has served as a Chair and Committee Member in numerous top-ranked conferences and performed editorial roles in several renowned journals. He is a Senior Member of IEEE.

Yassine Maleh is a cybersecurity professor and practitioner with industry and academic experience. He received a Ph.D. degree in Computer Sciences. Since 2019, he has been working as a professor of cybersecurity at Sultan Moulay Slimane University, Morocco. He was a Former CISO at the National Port Agency, Morocco, between 2012 and 2019. His research interests include information security and privacy, Internet of Things, networks security, information system, and IT governance.

Combatting Cyberbullying in Digital Media with Artificial Intelligence

Edited by
Mohamed Lahby, Al-Sakib Khan Pathan,
and Yassine Maleh

CRC Press
Taylor & Francis Group
Boca Raton London New York

CRC Press is an imprint of the
Taylor & Francis Group, an **informa** business
A CHAPMAN & HALL BOOK

Designed cover image: © Shutterstock ID 1654562416, Vector Image Contributor anttoniart

First edition published 2024
by CRC Press
2385 NW Executive Center Drive, Suite 320, Boca Raton FL 33431

and by CRC Press
4 Park Square, Milton Park, Abingdon, Oxon, OX14 4RN

CRC Press is an imprint of Taylor & Francis Group, LLC

Library of Congress Cataloging-in-Publication Data
Names: Lahby, Mohamed, editor. | Pathan, Al-Sakib Khan, editor. | Maleh, Yassine, 1987- editor.
Title: Combatting cyberbullying in digital media with artificial
intelligence / edited by Mohamed Lahby, Al-Sakib Khan Pathan and Yassine Maleh.
Description: First edition. | Boca Raton, FL : CRC Press, 2024. | Includes bibliographical references and index. | Summary: "Rapid advancements in mobile computing and communication technology and recent technological progress have opened up a plethora of opportunities. These advancements have expanded knowledge, facilitated global business, enhanced collaboration, and connected people through various digital media platforms. While these virtual platforms have provided new avenues for communication and self-expression, they also pose significant threats to our privacy. As a result, we must remain vigilant against the propagation of electronic violence through social networks. Cyberbullying has emerged as a particularly concerning form of online harassment and bullying, with instances of racism, terrorism, and various types of trolling becoming increasingly prevalent worldwide. Addressing the issue of Cyberbullying to find effective solutions is a challenge for the web mining community, particularly within the realm of social media. In this context, artificial intelligence (AI) can serve as a valuable tool in combating the diverse manifestations of Cyberbullying on the internet and social networks. This book presents the latest cutting-edge research, theoretical methods, and novel applications in artificial intelligence techniques to combat cyberbullying. Discussing new models, practical solutions, and technological advances related to detecting and analyzing Cyberbullying is based on artificial intelligence models and other related techniques. Furthermore, the book helps readers understand artificial intelligence techniques to combat cyberbullying systematically and forthrightly, as well as future insights and the societal and technical aspects of NLP-based cyberbullying research efforts"—Provided by publisher.
Identifiers: LCCN 2023032928 (print) | LCCN 2023032929 (ebook) |
ISBN 9781032491882 (hardback) | ISBN 9781032493015 (paperback) |
ISBN 9781003393061 (ebook)
Subjects: LCSH: Cyberbullying—Technological innovations. | Artificial intelligence—Computer programs.
Classification: LCC HV6773.15.C92 C66 2024 (print) | LCC HV6773.15.C92
(ebook) | DDC 302.34/302854678—dc23/eng/20230829
LC record available at https://lccn.loc.gov/2023032928
LC ebook record available at https://lccn.loc.gov/2023032929

ISBN: 9781032491882 (hbk)
ISBN: 9781032493015 (pbk)
ISBN: 9781003393061 (ebk)

DOI: 10.1201/9781003393061

Typeset in Times
by codeMantra

Contents

PART 1 Background

PART 2 Machine Learning Techniques and Cyberbullying Detection

PART 3   *Natural Language Processing (NLP) and Cyberbullying Detection*

PART 4   Case Studies and Future Trends

Chapter 13 Cyberbullying and Social Media: Implications for African
Digital Space 243

Basil Osayin Daudu, Goddy Uwa Osimen, and
Kennedy Shuaibu

Chapter 14 A Study on the Impact of Social Media and Cyberbullying
on Teen Girls in India 254

Swapna M. P. and G. Satyavathy

Preface

Thanks to rapid advancements in mobile computing and communication technology, it is evident that recent technological progress has opened up a plethora of opportunities. These advancements have expanded knowledge, facilitated global business, enhanced collaboration, and connected people through various digital media platforms. While these virtual platforms have provided new avenues for communication and self-expression, they have also posed significant threats to our privacy. As a result, it is crucial for us to remain vigilant against the propagation of electronic violence through social networks. Cyberbullying has emerged as a particularly concerning form of online harassment and bullying, with instances of racism, terrorism, and various types of trolling becoming increasingly prevalent worldwide.

Addressing the issue of cyberbullying to find effective solutions is indeed a great challenge for the web mining community, particularly within the realm of social media. In this context, AI can serve as a valuable tool in combating the diverse manifestations of cyberbullying on the Internet and social networks. AI has the capability to detect and prevent instances of cyberbullying across digital platforms by analyzing patterns, language use, and user behavior. Through advanced algorithms, AI can identify harmful content, offensive language, and potentially harmful interactions.

This book presents the latest cutting-edge research, theoretical methods, and novel applications in AI techniques to combat cyberbullying. The discussion of new models, practical solutions, and technological advances related to detecting and analyzing cyberbullying is based on AI models and other related techniques. These help decision-makers, managers, professionals, and researchers design new paradigms with unique opportunities associated with computational intelligence techniques overall. Furthermore, this book helps readers understand AI techniques to combat cyberbullying systematically and forthrightly.

This book contains 14 chapters classified into four main sections. The first section provides an overview of three key concepts: AI techniques, machine learning (ML) techniques, and deep learning techniques. These concepts are employed to combat cyberbullying. The second section covers various ML solutions that can be utilized to detect and prevent cyberbullying in digital media. The third section includes some chapters that can contribute to combating cyberbullying by using NLP. Finally, the last section provides some case studies and futures trends related to cyberbullying.

Contributors

Wilson C. Ahiara
Department of Computer Engineering
Michael Okpara University of
    Agriculture Umudike
Umudike, Nigeria

Segun Michael Akintunde
Department of Computer Science
Federal University of Agriculture
    Abeokuta
Abeokuta, Nigeria

Brian Chero Arana
Scientific Research Department
Despertar Cientifico editorial
Perú

Biodoumoye George Bokolo
Department of Computer Science
Sam Houston State University
Huntsville, Texas

Ridhika Chatterjee
Department of Management
IILM Academy of Higher Learning
Lucknow, India

Karim Darban
ENCG
University of Hassan II of Casablanca
Casablanca, Morocco

Basil Osayin Daudu
Department of Philosophy
Kogi State University
Anyigba, Nigeria

Ilham
Public Administration Study Program
University of Cenderawasih
Jayapura, Indonesia

Indu V.
Faculty of Engineering and Technology
University of Kerala
Kerala, India

Radha Srinivasan Iyer
Depatment of Neuro-Physiotherapis
SEC Centre for Independent Living
Naigaon, Pune, India

Smail Kabbaj
ENCG
University of Hassan II of Casablanca
Casablanca, Morocco

A. Krishnakumar
Department of Computer Science
NGM College
Pollachi, India

Mohamed Lahby
University Hassan II
Higher Normal School Casablanca
Casablanca, Morocco

Qingzhong Liu
Department of Computer Science
Sam Houston State University
Huntsville, Texas

Sajan Muhammad
School of Computer Science and
    Engineering
Kerala University of Digital Science
    Innovation & Technology
Kerala, India

M. Zaenul Muttaqin
Public Administration Study Program
University of Cenderawasih
Jayapura, Indonesia

Neha M. V.
School of Computer Science and
    Engineering
Kerala University of Digital Science
    Innovation & Technology
Kerala, India

Yosephina Ohoiwutun
Public Administration Study Program
University of Cenderawasih
Jayapura, Indonesia

Olalekan Akinbosoye Okewale
Pan African University for Life & Earth
    Sciences Institute
University of Ibadan
Ibadan, Nigeria

Ogobuchi Daniel Okey
Department of Systems Engineering
    and Automation
Universidade Federal de Lavras MG
Lavras, Brazil

Taiwo Olapeju Olaleye
Department of Computer Science,
Federal University of Agriculture
    Abeokuta
Abeokuta, Nigeria

Goddy Uwa Osimen
Department of Political Science and
    International Relations
Covenant University
Ota, Nigeria

Miguel Ángel Cortez Oyola
Professional School of Biological
    Sciences,
National University of Piura
Piura, Perú

M. Pradeepa
Department of ECE
SNS College of Technology
Coimbatore, India

Santhosh Kumar Rajamani
Department of Otorhinolaryngology
    MAEER MIT Pune's MIMER
    Medical College and DR. BSTR
    Hospital
Pune, India

G. Satyavathy
Department of Computer Science with
    Data Analytics
KPR College of Arts Science and
    Research
Coimbatore, India

Renzo Seminario-Córdova
Training and Teaching Research
    Program,
North Lima Campus
Cesar Vallejo University
Trujillo, Peru

Rejuwan Shamim
Department of Computer Science and
    Engineering with Data Science
Maharishi University of Information
    Technology
Noida, India

Sheetal Sharma
Department of Management
IILM Academy of Higher Learning
Lucknow, India

Kennedy Shuaibu
Department of Social Science Education
Kogi State University
Anyigba, Nigeria

Kalimuthu Sivanantham
Department of Software Development
    Service
Crapersoft
Coimbatore, India

Made Selly Dwi Suryanti
Cardiff School of Technologies
University of Cenderawasih
Cardiff, Indonesia

Swapna M. P.
Department of Cyber Security and
  Networks
Amrita Vishwa Vidyapeetham
Kollam, India

Vince Tebay
Cardiff School of Technologies
University of Cenderawasih
Cardiff, Indonesia

Nipuna Sankalpa Thalpage
Cardiff School of Technologies
Cardiff Metropolitan University
Cardiff, United Kingdom

Sabu M. Thampi
School of Computer Science and
  Engineering,
Kerala University of Digital Science
  Innovation & Technology
Kerala, India

Ibtissam Touahri
Department of Computer Science
University Moulay Ismail
Meknes, Morocco

V. R. Vijaykumar
Department of ECE
Anna University Regional Campus
Coimbatore, India

Part 1

Background

1 Deep Learning as a Digital Tool for the Detection and Prevention of Cyberbullying

Renzo Seminario-Córdova
Cesar Vallejo University

Miguel Ángel Cortez Oyola
National University of Piura

Brian Chero Arana
Despertar Científico editorial

1.1 INTRODUCTION

1.1.1 BACKGROUND

School harassment, also known as school violence or bullying, represents one of the most important social problems nowadays due to heavy consequences it generates for students worldwide. Data provided by the United Nations show that one out of every three students in the world has suffered from bullying at some point in their life. Generally, this issue is characterized by intentional and repetitive intimidation, verbal, physical, social, or psychological, produced by one student toward another. Victims are generally unable to defend themselves against these attacks (Masabanda & Gaibor, 2022; Said et al., 2021). Research on this topic has determined that it mainly occurs among children and young people aged between 7 and 16 years and that it is usually defined by a considerable inequality of power between the aggressor and the victim (Ruiz et al., 2020).

With the progress achieved in the technological field, information and communication technologies (ICT) have allowed, on one hand, the evolution of interpersonal relationships through platforms that enable people to communicate using virtual environments in real time (Ochoa et al., 2022). However, the widespread adoption of electronic devices and platforms, such as social networks and instant messaging applications, by new generations has, in turn, led to the creation of a new form of aggression known as cyberbullying (Pereira et al., 2022). This new issue, conceived during the digital era, maintains most of the elements that define traditional bullying,

DOI: 10.1201/9781003393061-2

with the distinction that now aggressors can use electronic or digital media to carry out their aggressions in new ways (Tozzo et al., 2022).

Since the 1970s, this has been a topic of interest that has generated widespread research aimed at studying this phenomenon in greater depth and finding ways to stop it (Said et al., 2021). The importance of combating this problem lies in the adverse impact it has on the victims, affecting them physically, psychologically, and emotionally, as well as on the school climate itself, not to mention the greater impact and extent that aggressions via Internet can have, compared to what is observed in traditional bullying. As a result, preventing cyberbullying in schools has become a priority over the years, with strategies proposed to promote a healthier coexistence in digital environments (Vásquez et al., 2020; Ojeda & Del Rey, 2021).

The use of digital media in the academic environment has always posed a challenge for educational institutions. In this context, the prevention of virtual dangers, such as cyberbullying, is considered an extremely complex task by both teachers and parents (Martín et al., 2021). A technological advance that could contribute to the achievement of this goal consists of the concept known as artificial intelligence (AI), a novel branch of programming that grants machines an ability to think and learn comparable to that shown by human beings, and even allows them to outperform their data processing capacity (Uyen et al., 2022). Thanks to its online detection capabilities, this field and its branches present unique characteristics that make them useful for developing intervention and prevention measures against cyberbullying (Milosevic et al., 2022). Therefore, the objective of this chapter was to explore the application of artificial intelligence as a novel alternative for the prevention of cyberbullying in schools.

1.1.2 METHODOLOGY

For the elaboration of this chapter, a general literature review was conducted regarding its main topic, in this case, focused mainly on cyberbullying and the application of artificial intelligence as a novel approach to combat this problem. As a result of this search, the most important aspects were identified and the present work was focused more specifically on DL techniques and the current state of research regarding their use for the prevention of cyberbullying in virtual spaces. To this end, the bibliographic research was carried out using scientific databases such as SCOPUS or EBSCO, using keywords such as "Deep learning", "cyberbullying", "research", and "algorithms".

With the purpose of gathering updated information, the bibliographic search focused mainly on articles published since 2019, especially regarding research conducted with this type of algorithms. On the other hand, there was no time restriction regarding information about definitions or previous information required, given the topic reviewed. The large number of articles initially collected from the search performed in the mentioned databases went through a subsequent selection process in order to select the most appropriate information. After a first filtering process based on an abstract review, and a second one based on a full review, 46 references were finally selected to be included in this book chapter.

1.1.3 Chapter Organization

The rest of the chapter is organized as follows: Section 1.2 presents background regarding cyberbullying and DL. Section 1.3 discusses the challenges of an effective control against cyberbullying, while Section 1.4 explores the automatic detection of cyberbullying practices, as well as the advantages that DL presents for this task. Section 1.5 presents some of the most commonly used DL algorithms for detecting cyberbullying. Section 1.6 explores the current state of studies focused on detecting cyberbullying using DL algorithms, while Section 1.7 explores future research on this topic. Section 1.8 discusses the results found in relation to similar studies, while Section 1.9 concludes the chapter.

1.2 RELATED WORK

1.2.1 Cyberbullying

Cyberbullying can be defined as the use of digital media by a person or group in order to generate harm or discomfort in other people by repeatedly sending aggressive or hostile messages. Through these, aggressors are able to use text messages and videos and even impersonate the identity of the assaulted person on the Internet, acquiring new ways to inflict harm to the other person (Pyżalski et al., 2022). This social issue is born from the evolution of traditional bullying, which widens its range of action by adopting the technological advances introduced by the digital era, without losing the objective that has always defined this problem, which is to harm and humiliate a victim through intimidatory behaviors (Bastidas et al., 2021). Table 1.1 shows the main differences between the concept of bullying and cyberbullying.

In a cyberbullying scenario, the following participants can be defined: Aggressors, victims who are usually solitary, accomplices who may participate or merely observe,

TABLE 1.1

Differences between Bullying and Cyberbullying

Traditional Bullying	Cyberbullying
Direct and personal.	Carried out by means of a digital medium.
The aggressor is a person known to others.	The aggressor is able to remain anonymous and hard to identify.
The bullying usually occurs over a period of weeks or months.	Harassment becomes timeless, occurring again at any time.
The bullying occurs within the educational institution, in a defined space.	Harassment can occur in any place or space through digital media.
It is possible to find the aggressor guilty in front of the authorities.	It is difficult to accuse the aggressor of his or her actions.
Bullying manifests itself in several types of specific forms.	Harassment becomes intimate and occurs in multiple forms supported by new technologies.

Source: Adapted from Bastidas (2021).

and family members or teachers who may detect the problem (Said et al., 2021). It is worth highlighting that bullies present similar characteristics among them, related to belonging to dysfunctional homes and lacking values, as well as unrestricted access to technological media, low academic performance, and a higher chance of committing crimes when growing up (Vásquez et al., 2020; Zhang et al., 2021). On the other hand, victims are characterized as people with low self-esteem, which is why they often present a passive and shy personality. Accomplices, in turn, are characterized by being aware of the abuse, although they are not always directly involved (Vásquez et al., 2020).

Children or young people affected by this issue have their physical and mental health significantly affected and may even develop symptoms of aggression and depression. As a result, their bonds with their peers and the healthy coexistence within their families are damaged (Bastidas et al., 2021). Among the main psychological problems that victims of cyberbullying usually show as a result of the attacks received are feelings of worry, fear, depression, terror, and anxiety among others (Alhujailli et al., 2020). Regarding the most serious consequences, victims can go to the extreme of hurting themselves or even be driven to suicide as a result of the abuse that they experience. Therefore, the prevention of cyberbullying has become a fundamental task in recent times (Pyżalski et al., 2022).

Cyberbullying has proven to be much more challenging to control than traditional bullying, as what happens in virtual environments is often beyond the reach of parents or teachers (Milosevic et al., 2022). Some prevention measures have focused on conducting workshops or debates that properly inform children and young people about the risks to their privacy when using the Internet, as well as the impact that practices such as cyberbullying can have on their peers (Pyżalski et al., 2022). More modern measures are betting on the addition of technological advances such as artificial intelligence, but without replacing cybersecurity experts, as some consider that human presence is still required to regulate the use of any technology (Iwendi et al., 2023).

1.2.2 Artificial Intelligence and DL

Artificial intelligence, also called AI by its acronym, is a branch of computer science responsible for the design of computational systems capable of simulating the capabilities of the human brain in order to solve complex problems in a similar way as a regular person would (Ocaña et al., 2019). Artificial intelligence systems have the ability to analyze large amounts of data, identify patterns and trends, formulate predictions, among other functions, faster and more accurately than humans (Margarita, 2020). To do so, AI makes use of two fundamental elements: physical computational systems for data processing and other operations, and big data, large volumes of data from different sources that will be processed by this program (Martínez, 2019).

Currently, artificial intelligence is applied in a wide variety of work fields, being implemented mainly in tasks that require automation, such as data analysis, simulations, linguistic pattern recognition, among others (Moreno, 2019). In recent years, its use has transcended the fields of computer science and robotics, increasingly extending its potential to areas, such as social or business sciences, through the implementation of more advanced systems, such as artificial neural networks (Ocaña et al., 2019). Faced with problems such as cyberbullying, the greatest advantage of artificial intelligence and its branches is its ability to process large amounts of data. Through this tool, researchers hope to be able to automate moderation processes to improve the regulation of online content (Milosevic et al., 2022).

More specifically, the potential of AI regarding this issue is found in its branches, such as machine learning, and more recently DL. In general terms, these branches focus on creating programs capable of recognizing relationships and patterns automatically based on the observations made, highlighting the enhanced ability of DL to learn, thanks to the implementation of deep neural networks (Janiesch et al., 2021). This particular type of neural network is known for not operating with analytical approximations, which is a great advantage for working in situations where the analytical model is not known or is very complex. However, it is also known for lacking flexibility and versatility in comparison with other techniques used (Shlezinger et al., 2022).

DL has positioned itself as an extremely useful tool thanks to its high accuracy in a wide variety of tasks, such as computer vision, natural language processing, among others. Given the potential of such algorithms, these have found significant applications in complex fields, such as facial, image, or voice recognition, as well as being implemented in virtual assistants and chatbots, or even in more advanced machines like robots (Moshayedi et al., 2022). However, it should be noted that the accuracy potential of these algorithms involves high memory and computational power requirements. To properly train one of these models requires an enormous number of parameters that must be thoroughly refined in order for it to work correctly (Chen & Ran, 2019).

1.3   CYBERBULLYING: WHY IS IT SO HARD TO CONTROL?

In current times, it is practically impossible for a person to avoid using social platforms on the Internet, as these are a fundamental part of their social, academic, and even professional development (Byrne, 2021). In the United States, 88% of adolescents have a smartphone, and 92% of them report surfing the Internet daily. This situation is similarly reported in many other countries around the world (Redmond et al., 2020). On the other hand, it should be noted that digital devices such as cell phones, tablets, computers, virtual or augmented reality, and wearable technologies are increasingly gaining a greater presence in the educational environment. As a result, students have been increasingly exposed to cyberbullying within their educational institutions (Tosun & Akcay, 2022).

The increasing massification of digital devices experienced in recent years has contributed to increase this problem, regardless of the level of development of different countries and affecting a large number of children and young people worldwide (Bozyiğit et al., 2021). The widespread use and popularity of social networks, although it managed to revolutionize interpersonal relationships, greatly facilitated the dissemination of offensive content through the internet within social interactions (Rosa et al., 2019). It is estimated that 15%–35% of young people have suffered cyberbullying at some point, while between 10% and 20% of people have admitted to having assaulted others virtually (Gencoglu, 2020).

Bullying through digital media has proven to be very difficult to control, given the freedom people have to protect their identity on the Internet by using multiple identities, false information, or pseudonyms. In turn, educational institutions have a limited capacity for action against this issue, since cyberbullying tends to manifest itself mostly at home, although out of sight of the parents themselves (Helfrich et al., 2020; Tosun & Akcay, 2022). In this context, fast and accurate detection of online bullying is not yet possible, and monitoring the enormous amount of content shared through social networks results in an impossible task for human moderators. For this reason, it has become an important goal to automate this task by using the latest computational advances (Gencoglu, 2020; Milosevic et al., 2022).

1.4   DL AGAINST CYBERBULLYING

Regarding the automatic detection of cyberbullying behaviors, this concept is a very complex one to identify in an automatic way, requiring very well-defined criteria for the development of appropriate detection tools (Rosa et al., 2019). This is mainly due to the large number of forms in which this problem can present itself, for researchers have been able to track the evolution of cyberbullying over the years. Recent investigations found out that this issue can range from aggressive and intense online discussions to more harmful practices such as harassment, stalking, trolling, doxing, masquerading, exclusion, or even online hate crimes (Azumah et al., 2023).

Based on this, there is a wide variety of means of transmitting harmful content through social networks, a characteristic that makes it extremely challenging to detect. Among the main considerations when trying to automatically detect these behaviors are the following (Milosevic et al., 2022):

- Apart from abusive texts that can be easily detected, there are others that use irony or sarcasm, which still remain hard to identify even with the most recent progress in the field of algorithmic learning.
- Some offensive words can be used in a friendly way, which can sometimes result in false positives.
- Offensive content that is posted may contain both text and images or videos, in which sometimes only one of these components is harmful, or they only become harmful when viewed together.
- Properly identifying situations of online exclusion remains a complex task, for it requires a deeper analysis of the social interactions within a group of people, which can lead to possible false positives.

In recent years, given this problem, there has been great interest in addressing this complex problem using AI techniques like machine learning and DL. These techniques are used to develop cyberbullying text detection techniques instead of filtering techniques (Azumah et al., 2023). In this context, studies conducted in this regard determined that DL algorithms are more effective for this task compared to Machine Learning algorithms. DL stands out for its ability to discover complex structures based on the analyzed data and to find the most significant features from a general

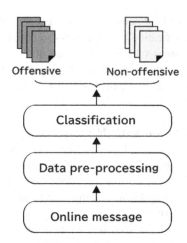

FIGURE 1.1 Online text classification process. Adapted from Alotaibi et al. (2021).

procedure, in addition to providing greater automation than machine learning algorithms (Al-Harigy et al., 2022; Milosevic et al., 2022).

In simplified terms, the strategies encompassed by these techniques first need to simplify the representation of the text and subsequently classify it through algorithms (Alotaibi et al., 2021). In other words, a process known as data labeling is performed, a process in which sentences, messages, or posts are classified into different categories according to the intended classification (Al-Harigy et al., 2022). The process of classifying online texts in terms of cyberbullying can be seen in a simplified way in Figure 1.1.

In general terms, approaches aimed at detecting cyberbullying use a database for training purposes, focus on a specific style of cyberbullying as a target, choose one of several DL algorithms, and finally evaluate the accuracy of the developed method through metrics (Mahat, 2021). In order to train these algorithms, a series of datasets with examples of cyberbullying situations, hate speech, and offensive language are available. Among the best-known are datasets such as the Twitter dataset, the Chinese Sina Weibo dataset, and the Kaggle dataset (Raj et al., 2021). Pre-processing generally includes text cleaning, tokenization, stemming, lemmatization, and stopword identification tasks (Iwendi et al., 2023).

1.5 DL ALGORITHMS

DL has a wide variety of neural networks that can be used to detect cyberbullying behaviors, among which are variants of deep neural networks, such as the recursive neural network, the convolutional neural network, among others (Al-Harigy et al., 2022). Artificial neural networks (ANN) are actually machine learning algorithms based on the functioning of biological neural networks, simulating the synapses between neurons to obtain a desired result. Within the DL branch, this concept was deepened to give rise to new ANNs with better performance and higher accuracy (Choi et al., 2020).

In general, DNNs are types of neural networks capable of achieving near-human performance in object classification tasks. Thanks to this, it is able to defeat professional human players in games such as Go, poker, or Starcraft or to perform tasks such as detecting cancer from X-rays or translating texts from various languages (Geirhos et al., 2020). The following are the most widely used DL algorithms for cyberbullying detection:

Convolutional Neural Network (CNN): A special type of ANNs that get their name from the use of what is known as convolutional filters are useful for extracting specific features from an analyzed image. Thanks to this, they are generally used in the field of image processing, presenting the potential for image segmentation tasks, and being able to identify objects within an image (Choi et al., 2020).

Recursive Neural Network (RNN): It is a type of neural network that has the ability to use previous outputs as inputs, creating a loop. It is known for having mostly short-term memory, being unable to work with long-term dependencies. RNNs are mainly used in natural language processing tasks (Arif, 2021).

Long-Short Term Memory (LSTM): It is an RNN model developed to overcome the exploding/vanishing gradient problems by working with long-term dependencies. The LSTM model has a high applicability and popularity, being used by major companies such as Google or Amazon, and even present in the world of video games (Van Houdt et al., 2020).

1.6   CURRENT RESEARCH

Initially, studies aimed at detecting cyberbullying focused heavily on the application of machine learning techniques for tasks like text detection in social networks. It is in more recent years that interest in using DL algorithms for this same task has increased considerably, in search of developing more effective proposals (Azumah et al., 2023). However, despite the progress made in this field, the detection of cyberbullying in social networks continues to be an active field that remains an active area of research (Hezam et al., 2022).

Currently, there is a great interest in studying mainly CNNs and LSTMs, with comparative analyses such as those by Ahuja et al. (2021) and Ghosh et al. (2021), focused on determining the most effective algorithm for this task, as well as its performance together with other support tools. Multiple proposals for models to combat online bullying are also being developed, such as the studies conducted by Ben (2020), Gada et al. (2021), and Kumari et al. (2021), based on the use of these two types of neural networks. While other algorithms have also been explored to a lesser extent, such as the study by Hezam et al. (2022) proposing a model based on RNNs, they still offer potential for cyberbullying detection (Table 1.2).

Based on this, a good performance of the proposed methods that make use of DL algorithms is observed. However, it is highlighted that most of the models developed so far that use these tools for the detection of offensive behavior on the Internet still require further development in order to become reliable proposals capable of performing this task accurately and efficiently (Iwendi et al., 2023).

TABLE 1.2

Recent Research on Cyberbullying Detection with DL

Algorithm	Objective	Results	Reference
CNN-LSTM	Development of a CNN-LSTM architecture for detecting verbal offenses in social network comments.	• The joint use of CNN with LSTM allowed a better analysis of the evaluated comments. • The results show that this CNN-LSTM architecture outperforms existing proposals.	Ben (2020)
CNN, LSTM	Comparative analysis between CNN and LSTM with different classification algorithms and Word embedding.	• The joint use of CNN with LSTM allowed a better analysis of the evaluated comments. • The results show that this CNN-LSTM architecture outperforms existing proposals. • Better performance is observed when merging CNN with LSTM for this task. • The use of Word embedding proved useful in improving the performance of the models.	Ahuja et al. (2021)
LSTM-CNN	Development of an LSTM-CNN proposal for cyberbullying detection in social networks.	• The model successfully detects offensive content and classifies it into various categories. • The proposed model proved to be effective with content on Twitter and Telegram using a bot.	Gada et al. (2021)
1D-CNN, LSTM, BiLSTM	Comparative analysis between DL techniques regarding their performance in cyberbullying detection.	• The BiLSTM model was superior to the other models in terms of accuracy. • The 1D-CNN model showed the shortest computation time required, as well as good performance in detecting tokenized words.	Ghosh et al. (2021)
LSTM	Development of an LSTM autoencoder to detect cyber aggressions automatically.	• Use of Facebook and Twitter test sets shows a 17% and 11% increase, respectively, compared to the current state-of-the-art in English. • Use of the same test sets shows a 6% and 8% increase, respectively, compared to the current state-of-the-art in Hindi.	Kumari et al. (2021)

(Continued)

TABLE 1.2 (*Continued*)
Recent Research on Cyberbullying Detection with DL

Algorithm	Objective	Results	Reference
DEA-RNN	Development of a DEA (dolphin ecolocation algorithm)-RNN model for cyberbullying detection on Twitter.	• The proposed model performed better than existing BiLSTM or RNN models. • The model showed optimal performance in metrics such as accuracy, F-measure, recall, precision, and specificity.	Hezam et al. (2022)

1.7   FUTURE DIRECTIONS

Despite significant progress achieved in this field, the cyberbullying detection models developed so far have shown issues when attempting to generalize to other languages or social networks not included in the experimental sessions (Iwendi et al., 2023), among other problems. In addition to limitations associated with DL algorithms, there are currently still other limitations of a technical nature, such as the availability of effective databases for training tasks, or even of a legal nature, such as privacy issues regarding the users of social networks (De Angelis & Perasso, 2020).

In the first place, future research aims to improve the work done so far and generalize its use in order to achieve greater effectiveness in detecting cyberbullying (Arif, 2021). Among the improvements that are aimed at, an important one seeks the training of the developed models for the detection of offensive text in a greater number of social networks other than those already evaluated, including the most currently used such as Facebook, Twitter, Youtube, etc. (Hezam et al., 2022; Gada et al., 2021; Kumari et al., 2021). In addition, the vast majority of current research focuses on the detection of offensive text in social networks, being an important goal to seek to extend this capability for detecting multimedia, such as images or videos (Gada et al., 2021; Hezam et al., 2022).

Finally, another type of future research aims to extend the impact of these tools on cyberbullying, seeking to generate intervention proposals that allow mitigating these offensive behaviors once they have been detected by the implemented methods. At this point, a joint work between computer and social sciences is required in order to work on the implementation of psychosocial interventions that will allow dealing with this problem (De Angelis & Perasso, 2020). On the other hand, the analysis in greater detail of the information collected by these DL models can be useful to study other aspects of cyberbullying and boost the development of efficient preventive policies (Arif, 2021).

1.8   DISCUSSION

In general, studies focused on the automatic detection of cyberbullying emphasize the importance of this kind of work in today's society, given the strong emotional impact that these practices can have on innocent people, potentially leading to depression or suicide (Iwendi et al., 2023). As expressed by Gongane et al. (2022), detecting and moderating harmful content is an urgent need nowadays, given the enormous amount of abuse and hate that can be found on social media. Other research, such as that of Alrehili (2019), also highlights the complexity of studying this offensive behavior on the Internet, as it requires social knowledge and constant updates in order to be able to recognize new insults that may appear.

In this context, DL has shown to be a useful instrument for the analysis and detection of cyberbullying behaviors in social interactions that occur on the Internet. Studies, such as the one by Arif (2021), also highlight the popularity that DL algorithms are gaining as a useful tool against cyberbullying, especially for detecting the intentions of an aggressor toward a victim through natural language processing. Table 1.1 has also shown the effectiveness of the methods developed so far, even compared to other alternatives such as machine learning, although it is generally agreed that there is still work to be done.

Taking this into account, comparisons such as those made by Suleiman et al. (2022) have also considered DL as a superior alternative to machine learning in this field. Mainly, they emphasize its ability to process large amounts of information and detect offensive content more effectively, functions that prove difficult for machine learning algorithms. Similar to what is observed in the present work, more specifically in Table 1.1, Bayari and Bensefia (2021) also highlight CNN as the most widely used DL method for cyberbullying detection, thanks to its optimal performance, especially when working with English-language texts.

In addition, an important limitation that currently exists regarding this type of research should be highlighted. From the review in this chapter, it can be observed that it is more accessible to conduct studies aimed at detecting cyberbullying practices in English, given that there is a great variety of information and datasets available. However, this situation is somewhat different when it comes to detecting such practices in other languages. In this regard, the study by ALBayari et al. (2021), for example, points out the limited amount of research in this field conducted with Arabic texts, as well as the limited number of datasets available in this language. Similarly, the study by Suleiman et al. (2022) presents a similar situation regarding languages such as Turkish.

1.9 CONCLUSION

This chapter explores the issue of cyberbullying and the current interest in combating this problem through technological approaches based on DL. The massification of digital devices has greatly increased the dissemination of offensive content through the large number of existing social networks, in the form of text, images, or videos and generating new ways to harass and hurt other people online. As a consequence, considering the strong negative impact it has on the affected people and the academic environment, it is essential to develop more efficient detection and prevention measures to combat harmful practices such as cyberbullying.

As a result of the growing interest in combating cyberbullying, a large number of methods for automatic detection of this problem have been studied, going through machine learning algorithms and finally focusing on the use of DL. The latter has proven to be an effective tool, with powerful and accurate algorithms for a successful detection of harmful behavior on the Internet that considerably outperforms the results shown by other types of algorithms. Based on the promising results obtained in several studies, there is a potential for DL technology to be extended to the detection of harmful multimedia content, and even participating in tasks of prevention or mitigation of cyberbullying.

However, while DL has proven to be a powerful tool for this task, there is still a long way to go before it becomes a solid and reliable solution against cyberbullying. This chapter presented some limitations, mainly by focusing on studies conducted with text in English, emphasizing the small number of existing studies in other languages. Therefore, the results obtained using DL algorithms show that further research and massification are still required in order to exploit their full potential. Despite these limitations, the potential shown so far indicates that it will become a valuable resource in the future for preventing offensive behavior on the Internet.

REFERENCES

Ahuja, R., Banga, A., & Sharma, S. C. (2021). Detecting Abusive Comments Using Ensemble Deep Learning Algorithms. In: Stamp, M., Alazab, M., & Shalaginov, A. (eds) *Malware Analysis Using Artificial Intelligence and Deep Learning* (pp. 515–534). Springer, Cham. https://doi.org/10.1007/978-3-030-62582-5_20

ALBayari, R., Abdullah, S., & Salloum, S. A. (2021). Cyberbullying Classification Methods for Arabic: A Systematic Review. In: *Proceedings of the International Conference on Artificial Intelligence and Computer Vision (AICV2021)* (pp. 375–385). Springer International Publishing, Cham. https://doi.org/10.1007/978-3-030-76346-6_35

Al-Harigy, L. M., Al-Nuaim, H. A., Moradpoor, N., & Tan, Z. (2022). Building towards automated cyberbullying detection: A comparative analysis. *Computational Intelligence and Neuroscience*, 2022, 4794227. https://doi.org/10.1155/2022/4794227

Alhujailli, A., Karwowski, W., Wan, T. T., & Hancock, P. (2020). Affective and stress consequences of cyberbullying. *Symmetry*, 12(9), 1536. https://doi.org/10.3390/sym12091536

Alotaibi, M., Alotaibi, B., & Razaque, A. (2021). A multichannel deep learning framework for cyberbullying detection on social media. *Electronics*, 10(21), 2664. https://doi.org/10.3390/electronics10212664

Alrehili, A. (2019). Automatic Hate Speech Detection on Social Media: A Brief Survey. In: *2019 IEEE/ACS 16th International Conference on Computer Systems and Applications (AICCSA)* (pp. 1–6). IEEE, Abu Dhabi. https://doi.org/10.1109/AICCSA47632.2019.9035228

Arif, M. (2021). A systematic review of machine learning algorithms in cyberbullying detection: Future directions and challenges. *Journal of Information Security and Cybercrimes Research*, 4(1), 1–26. https://doi.org/10.26735/GBTV9013

Azumah, S. W., Elsayed, N., ElSayed, Z., & Ozer, M. (2023). Cyberbullying in text content detection: An analytical review. arXiv preprint arXiv:2303.10502. https://doi.org/10.48550/arXiv.2303.10502

Bastidas, M. A., Bazurto, S., Bedoya, N., Barrionuevo, N., & Artos, S. (2021). Cyberbullying in adolescents and its increase due to new technologies. *Kronos - The Language Teaching Journal*, 2(1), 50–59. https://doi.org/10.29166/kronos.v2i1.3023

Bayari, R., & Bensefia, A. (2021). Text mining techniques for cyberbullying detection: State of the art. *Advances in Science, Technology and Engineering Systems Journal*, 6, 783–790. https://dx.doi.org/10.25046/aj060187

Ben, M. M. (2020). Insult detection using a partitional CNN-LSTM model. *Computer Science and Information Technologies*, 1(2), 84–92. https://doi.org/10.11591/csit.v1i2.p84-92

Bozyiğit, A., Utku, S., & Nasibov, E. (2021). Cyberbullying detection: Utilizing social media features. *Expert Systems with Applications*, 179, 115001. https://doi.org/10.1016/j.eswa.2021.115001

Byrne, V. L. (2021). Blocking and self-silencing: Undergraduate students' cyberbullying victimization and coping strategies. *TechTrends*, 65(2), 164–173. https://doi.org/10.1007/s11528-020-00560-x

Chen, J., & Ran, X. (2019). Deep learning with edge computing: A review. *Proceedings of the IEEE*, 107(8), 1655–1674. https://doi.org/10.1109/JPROC.2019.2921977

Choi, R. Y., Coyner, A. S., Kalpathy-Cramer, J., Chiang, M. F., & Campbell, J. P. (2020). Introduction to machine learning, neural networks, and deep learning. *Translational Vision Science & Technology*, 9(2), 14–14. https://doi.org/10.1167/tvst.9.2.14

De Angelis, J., & Perasso, G. (2020). Cyberbullying detection through machine learning: Can technology help to prevent internet bullying? *International Journal of Management and Humanities*, 4(11), 57–69. https://dx.doi.org/10.35940/ijmh.K1056.0741120

Gada, M., Damania, K., & Sankhe, S. (2021). Cyberbullying Detection Using LSTM-CNN Architecture and Its Applications. In: *2021 International Conference on Computer Communication and Informatics (ICCCI)* (pp. 1–6). IEEE, Coimbatore. https://doi.org/10.1109/ICCCI50826.2021.9402412

Geirhos, R., Jacobsen, J. H., Michaelis, C., Zemel, R., Brendel, W., Bethge, M., & Wichmann, F. A. (2020). Shortcut learning in deep neural networks. *Nature Machine Intelligence*, 2(11), 665–673. https://doi.org/10.1038/s42256-020-00257-z

Gencoglu, O. (2020). Cyberbullying detection with fairness constraints. *IEEE Internet Computing*, 25(1), 20–29. https://doi.org/10.1109/MIC.2020.3032461

Ghosh, S., Chaki, A., & Kudeshia, A. (2021). Cyberbully Detection Using 1D-CNN and LSTM. In: Sabut, S. K., Ray, A. K., Pati, B., & Acharya, U. R. (eds) *Proceedings of International Conference on Communication, Circuits, and Systems*. Lecture Notes in Electrical Engineering, vol 728 (pp. 295–301). Springer, Singapore. https://doi.org/10.1007/978-981-33-4866-0_37

Gongane, V. U., Munot, M. V., & Anuse, A. D. (2022). Detection and moderation of detrimental content on social media platforms: Current status and future directions. *Social Network Analysis and Mining*, 12(1), 129. https://doi.org/10.1007/s13278-022-00951-3

Helfrich, E. L., Doty, J. L., Su, Y. W., Yourell, J. L., & Gabrielli, J. (2020). Parental views on preventing and minimizing negative effects of cyberbullying. *Children and Youth Services Review*, 118, 105377. https://doi.org/10.1016/j.childyouth.2020.105377

Hezam, B. A. H., Abawajy, J., Mallappa, S., Naji, M. A., & Esmail, H. D. (2022). DEA-RNN: A hybrid deep learning approach for cyberbullying detection in Twitter social media platform. *IEEE Access*, 10, 25857–25871. https://doi.org/10.1109/ACCESS.2022.3153675

Iwendi, C., Srivastava, G., Khan, S., & Maddikunta, P. K. R. (2023). Cyberbullying detection solutions based on deep learning architectures. *Multimedia Systems*, 29, 1839–1852. https://doi.org/10.1007/s00530-020-00701-5

Janiesch, C., Zschech, P., & Heinrich, K. (2021). Machine learning and deep learning. *Electronic Markets*, 31(3), 685–695. https://doi.org/10.1007/s12525-021-00475-2

Kumari, K., Singh, J. P., Dwivedi, Y. K., & Rana, N. P. (2021). Bilingual cyber-aggression detection on social media using LSTM autoencoder. *Soft Computing*, 25, 8999–9012. https://doi.org/10.1007/s00500-021-05817-y

Mahat, M. (2021). Detecting Cyberbullying across Multiple Social Media Platforms Using Deep Learning. In: *2021 International Conference on Advance Computing and Innovative Technologies in Engineering (ICACITE)* (pp. 299–301). IEEE. https://doi.org/10.1109/ICACITE51222.2021.9404736

Margarita, A. (2020). Artificial intelligence and robotics: Its social, ethical and legal dilemmas. Derecho global. Estudios sobre derecho y justicia, 6(16), 49–105. https://doi.org/10.32870/dgedj.v6i16.286

Martín, J. M., Casas, J. A., & Ortega, R. (2021). Parental supervision: Predictive variables of positive involvement in cyberbullying prevention. *International Journal of Environmental Research and Public Health*, 18(4), 1562. https://doi.org/10.3390/ijerph18041562

Martínez, A. (2019). Artificial Intelligence Big Data and Digital Era: A Threat To Personal Data?. *Revista La Propiedad Inmaterial*, (27), 5–23. https://doi.org/10.18601/16571959.n27.01

Masabanda, M. J., & Gaibor, I. A. (2022). School harassment and its relationship with social skills in adolescents. Ciencia Latina Revista Científica Multidisciplinar, 6(6), 10775–10792. https://doi.org/10.37811/cl_rcm.v6i6.4164

Milosevic, T., Van Royen, K., & Davis, B. (2022). Artificial intelligence to address cyberbullying, harassment and abuse: New directions in the midst of complexity. *International Journal of Bullying Prevention*, 4(1), 1–5. https://doi.org/10.1007/s42380-022-00117-x

Moreno, R. D. (2019). The arrival of artificial intelligence to education. Revista De Investigación En Tecnologías De La Información, 7(14), 260–270. https://doi.org/10.36825/RITI.07.14.022

Moshayedi, A. J., Roy, A. S., Kolahdooz, A., & Shuxin, Y. (2022). Deep learning application pros and cons over algorithm. *EAI Endorsed Transactions on AI and Robotics*, 1(1), e7. https://dx.doi.org/10.4108/airo.v1i.19

Ocaña, Y., Valenzuela, L. A., & Garro, L. L. (2019). Artificial intelligence and its implications in higher education. Propósitos y Representaciones, 7(2), 536–568. https://dx.doi.org/10.20511/pyr2019.v7n2.274

Ochoa, L. M., Hernández, V. J., & Maldonado, R. L. (2022). Impact on child development, influence of cyberbullying in social networks. Dilemas Contemporáneos: Educación, Política y Valores, 10(1). https://doi.org/10.46377/dilemas.v10i1.3287

Ojeda, M., & Del Rey, R. (2021). Preventing and intervening in risks associatedwith information and communication technologies: The case of cyberbullying. Revista Tecnología, Ciencia Y Educación, 19, 53–80. https://doi.org/10.51302/tce.2021.612

Pereira, M. P., Sales, S. M., & Vieira, C. L. (2022). Virtual bullying: Psycho-emotional causes and consequences in adolescent's victims of cyberbullying. *Research, Society and Development*, 11(5), e55011528686. https://doi.org/10.33448/rsd-v11i5.28686

Pyżalski, J., Plichta, P., Szuster, A., & Barlińska, J. (2022). Cyberbullying characteristics and prevention-what can we learn from narratives provided by adolescents and their teachers? *International Journal of Environmental Research and Public Health*, 19(18), 11589. https://doi.org/10.3390/ijerph191811589

Raj, C., Agarwal, A., Bharathy, G., Narayan, B., & Prasad, M. (2021). Cyberbullying detection: Hybrid models based on machine learning and natural language processing techniques. *Electronics*, 10(22), 2810. https://doi.org/10.3390/electronics10222810

Redmond, P., Lock, J. V., & Smart, V. (2020). Developing a cyberbullying conceptual framework for educators. Technology in Society, 60, 101223. https://doi.org/10.1016/j.techsoc.2019.101223

Rosa, H., Pereira, N., Ribeiro, R., Ferreira, P. C., Carvalho, J. P., Oliveira, S., Coheur, L., Paulino, P., Veiga, A. M., & Trancoso, I. (2019). Automatic cyberbullying detection: A systematic review. *Computers in Human Behavior*, 93, 333–345. https://doi.org/10.1016/j.chb.2018.12.021

Ruiz, M., Santibáñez, R., & Laespada, T. (2020). Bullying: Adolescent victims and aggressors. Implication in cycles of violence. Bordón. Revista De Pedagogía, 72(1), 117–132. https://doi.org/10.13042/Bordon.2020.71909

Said, E., Gonzalez, E., & Pallarès, M. (2021). Preventing cyberbullying through ICT-centric education: A case study. *Technology, Pedagogy and Education*, 30(3), 459–472. https://doi.org/10.1080/1475939X.2021.1908415

Shlezinger, N., Eldar, Y. C., & Boyd, S. P. (2022). Model-based deep learning: On the intersection of deep learning and optimization. *IEEE Access*, 10, 115384–115398. https://doi.org/10.1109/ACCESS.2022.3218802

Suleiman, S., Taneja, P., & Nainwal, A. (2022). Cyberbullying detection on Twitter using machine learning: A review. *International Journal of Innovative Science and Research Technology*, 7(6), 258–262. https://doi.org/10.5281/zenodo.6757912

Tosun, N., & Akcay, H. (2022). Cyberbullying/cyber-victimization status, cyberbullying awareness, and combat strategies of administrators and teachers of pre-school education institutions. *International Journal of Technology in Education and Science (IJTES)*, 6(1), 44–73. https://doi.org/10.46328/ijtes.336

Tozzo, P., Cuman, O., Moratto, E., & Caenazzo, L. (2022). Family and educational strategies for cyberbullying prevention: A systematic review. *International Journal of Environmental Research and Public Health*, 19(16), 10452. https://doi.org/10.3390/ijerph191610452

Uyen, T. T., Thi, H., & Kieu, T. T. (2022). Applying Artificial Intelligence (AI) to Enhance Teaching Quality at FPT High School. In: *Proceedings of the 4th International Conference on Modern Educational Technology* (pp. 7–12). Association for Computing Machinery, New York. https://doi.org/10.1145/3543407.3543409

Van Houdt, G., Mosquera, C., & Nápoles, G. (2020). A review on the long short-term memory model. *Artificial Intelligence Review*, 53, 5929–5955. https://doi.org/10.1007/s10462-020-09838-1

Vásquez, J. H., García, D. G., Ochoa, S. C., & Erazo, J. C. (2020). Cyberbullying and risk factors. *Episteme Koinonia*, 3(1), 577–597. https://doi.org/10.35381/e.k.v3i1.1028

Zhang, Y., Li, Z., Tan, Y., Zhang, X., Zhao, Q., & Chen, X. (2021). The influence of personality traits on school bullying: A moderated mediation model. *Frontiers in Psychology*, 12, 650070. https://doi.org/10.3389/fpsyg.2021.650070

2 Detection and Prevention of Cyberbullying in Social Media Using Cognitive Computational Analysis

Neha M. V. and Sajan Muhammad
Kerala University of Digital Science Innovation & Technology

Indu V.
University of Kerala

Sabu M. Thampi
Kerala University of Digital Science Innovation & Technology

Words have the power to both destroy and heal. When words are both true and kind, they can change the world.

—Buddha

2.1 INTRODUCTION

In today's digital age, the concept of a smart city has emerged, utilizing interconnected information to optimize the use of limited resources and improve the quality of life. Smart city technology can enhance citizen and government engagement, facilitate flexible and intelligent learning systems, and improve transportation and communication safety. While technology has brought us closer together, it has also presented challenges in managing online content and addressing issues like cybercrimes. One of the most concerning issues in today's digital age is cyberbullying, particularly on social media platforms.

Cyberbullying is a form of repeated behavior that utilizes digital technologies to scare, anger, or shame individuals, often occurring on social media, messaging platforms, gaming platforms, or mobile phones. Examples of cyberbullying include spreading lies, posting embarrassing photos or videos, sending abusive or threatening messages or images, and impersonating someone through fake accounts. Unlike face-to-face bullying, cyberbullying leaves a digital footprint that can serve as evidence to help stop the abuse. However, the consequences of cyberbullying can be severe, including anxiety, depression, and even suicide, making it crucial to raise

DOI: 10.1201/9781003393061-3

awareness about cyberbullying and take steps to prevent and address this harmful behavior.

Despite the growing need for effective detection and prevention strategies, the prevention of cyberbullying remains largely unexplored. Social media platforms have provided users with new ways to communicate and connect with others, but they have also become breeding grounds for online harassment and abuse. Therefore, it is essential to create a safe and secure online environment that promotes positive communication while also ensuring user privacy and security. By increasing awareness and promoting responsible digital citizenship, we can combat cyberbullying and promote a more positive and inclusive online community.

The following are the primary objectives of this book chapter:

1. Provide a comparative analysis of various automated cyberbullying detection techniques.
2. Recommend a comprehensive strategy for cyberbullying prevention.
3. Focus on the significance of dynamical prediction algorithms in detecting cyberbullying.
4. Highlight technical challenges associated with cyberbullying detection.
5. Identify areas of research that require attention to improve cyberbullying prevention in the future.

2.1.1   An Overview of Techniques Leveraged in Detection of Cyberbullying

Cyberbullying is a complex and challenging issue that requires a multi-faceted approach to be effectively addressed. One key component of managing cyberbullying is using detection techniques to identify and prevent online harassment and abuse.

Various methods are leveraged to detect cyberbullying, from manual monitoring and analysis to advanced machine-learning algorithms. This overview explores some of the most common and effective techniques to detect cyberbullying.

By understanding the strengths and limitations of each method, we can develop a more comprehensive and practical approach to detecting and preventing cyberbullying in online environments. Cyberbullying in online social networks can be of different forms like textual, image, or video. There are several fields of computer science that can be used to detect cyberbullying, some of the fields are:

- **Soft Computing:** Soft computing is a branch of computer science that integrates machine learning and artificial intelligence techniques for the analysis of large data sets. Cyberbullying can be detected using soft computing methods, such as fuzzy logic and neural networks.
- **Natural Language Processing:** The study of natural language data, such as text messages and social media posts, is a vital component of the subject of computer science known as natural language processing (NLP). By examining the content of communications and spotting patterns of behavior

connected to cyberbullying, NLP techniques have always been a successful approach.

- **Social Network Analysis:** A branch of computer science that examines the composition and operation of social networks, including online forums and social media sites. These techniques have been used to detect cyberbullying by analyzing the interactions between users and identifying patterns of behavior associated with cyberbullying.

- **Cognitive Computing:** A branch of computer science that blends cognitive psychology, machine learning, and artificial intelligence in order to build intelligent computers that can reason, pick up new information, and adapt to changing circumstances. By examining the psychological elements that contribute to cyberbullying as well as the substance of the messages, cognitive computing approaches have been utilized to detect cyberbullying.

2.2 DIFFERENT MODALITIES OF CYBERBULLYING

Several modalities of online social data can be used for cyberbullying via social media. Some of the most common modalities include text-based messages, image or videograms, memes, and other infographic-related content. The modalities are explored on the basis of techniques used, and these techniques are represented as taxonomy shown in Figure 2.1.

2.2.1 TEXT-BASED MESSAGES

Cyberbullies may use social media platforms to send abusive or threatening messages to their targets. This can take the form of direct messages, comments on posts or photos, or public posts targeting the victim.

Detecting textual cyberbullying can be challenging, as it often involves subtle forms of harassment that may not be immediately obvious or explicit. Some of the techniques used for detection of text-based cyberbullying are as follows:

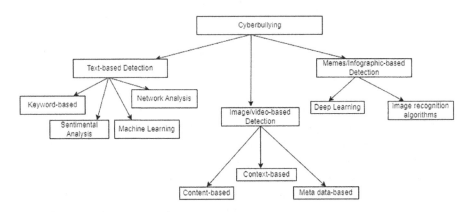

FIGURE 2.1 Taxonomy for the detection of cyberbullying considering different modalities.

- **Keyword-Based Detection:** This technique for recognizing text-based cyberbullying entails identifying particular words or phrases that are frequently used in cyberbullying. Using a list of terms and phrases that are signs of cyberbullying, this technique searches internet content for instances of the words and phrases in question. Keyword-based detection uses expressions like "kill yourself," "dumb," "ugly," "slut," "faggot," and "loser" for the detection.
- **Sentiment Analysis:** By recognizing text that exhibits negative emotional tones like anger, frustration, or hostility, sentiment analysis can be used to detect text-based cyberbullying. It involves analyzing the emotive tone of online text to identify text-based cyberbullying. Using machine learning techniques, this technique identifies the emotional tone of online material as positive, neutral, and negative.
- **Machine Learning:** This technique for identifying text-based cyberbullying examines patterns and trends in online text by employing algorithms. With this technique, machine learning algorithms are trained to spot patterns of cyberbullying behavior, such as the usage of specific words or phrases or the repetition of derogatory language. Then, cyberbullying can be identified in online text using machine learning techniques.
- **Network Analysis:** Network analysis is a method of detecting text-based cyberbullying that involves analyzing the connections between online users. This method involves identifying the relationships between users, such as who communicates with whom and the frequency of their communication.

The above techniques are explained as a review of research works in the coming section. The review highlights the works in the area of textual form of cyberbullying detection by machine learning, sentimental analysis, and social network analysis.

2.2.1.1 Machine Learning for Detection of Textual Cyberbullying

Cyberbullying detection is a challenging issue in the field of online social networks, and from studies, there are multiple machine learning algorithms for detection and prediction of the same. Some of the works in detection of textual cyberbullying in machine learning are reviewed here. Most of the studies on cyberbullying detection uses supervised algorithms as it is a widely used one. SVM (support vector machine), NB (naïve bayes), RF (random forest), DT (decision tree), KNN (K-nearest neighbor), and logistics regression are the classifiers which are widely used for the detection.

The work proposed in [1] uses a machine learning approach for detecting cyber-aggressive comments on social media platforms. The authors used a dataset of user comments collected from social media platforms and manually labeled them as cyber-aggressive or not. They then extracted various features such as the frequency of negative words, the length of the comment, and the presence of slang and emoticons. These features were then used to train various machine learning models such as SVM and Logistic Regression.

The research also highlighted the importance of feature selection in improving the performance of the model. Another recent work mentioned in [2] developed an

SVM model that uses a combination of lexical, syntactic, and semantic features to identify offensive language in social media posts.

The system was trained on a dataset of tweets manually annotated as offensive or non-offensive and evaluated on a separate dataset of tweets. Dinakar et al. [3] used a dataset of labeled social media posts and extracted a set of features, including word n-grams, part-of-speech tags, sentiment, and contextual features. They used these features to train various machine learning models, including naive bayes, SVM, and random forest, and SVM outperformed other models.

Mangaonkar et al. [4] developed a system that combines machine-learning algorithms and crowd-sourcing to identify and classify cyberbullying behavior in tweets.

2.2.1.2   Social Network Analysis

Social network analysis (SNA) is a multidisciplinary field that studies social networks and the patterns of relationships between individuals or groups. SNA involves visualizing and analyzing social networks using mathematical and statistical models. It typically involves identifying actors or nodes in a network, relationships or ties between them, and measuring the strength and direction of those ties. SNA can also identify subgroups or communities within a network and analyze the flow of information or resources between them.

There are several categories of SNA. The work [5] proposes a system to detect and monitor cyberbullying in online social networks. The system uses a combination of message classification and social network analysis techniques to identify and track instances of cyberbullying. The message classification component uses natural language processing techniques to analyze the content of messages and classify them as either cyberbullying or non-cyberbullying.

The social network analysis component analyzes the relationships between users in the network to identify patterns of cyberbullying behavior.

A new approach in [6] takes into account the socio-linguistic features of the messages exchanged in social media. The authors argue that previous studies have focused primarily on syntactic and semantic features of messages, but have not fully considered the social context in which the messages are exchanged. The proposed model analyzes messages exchanged between users in social media and identifies the socio-linguistic features that are indicative of cyberbullying behavior. These features include the use of profanity, personal attacks, and the use of derogatory language.

The model also considers the social relationships between users, such as power dynamics and social status, which may influence cyberbullying behavior. It can also be used to identify influential actors in a network, detect network vulnerabilities, and inform the design of social interventions and policies.

Choi et al. [7] focus on identifying the key cyberbullies in an online social network using text mining and social network analysis techniques. The study analyzes a large dataset of messages exchanged in a social network to identify instances of cyberbullying and identify the most active and influential bullies. It uses NLP techniques to identify instances of cyberbullying and SNA to identify the most active and influential bullies based on their social connections and network centrality measures. The work also identifies several keys to cyberbullying and shows that they exhibit distinct linguistic and behavioral patterns. The study also highlights the importance of identifying key cyberbullies for effective prevention and intervention strategies and provides insights into the nature of cyberbullying dynamics in online communities.

2.2.1.3 Sentimental Analysis

Another method for detecting bullying in the textual data is through sentimental analysis, which classifies them as positive, negative, and neutral concerning cyberbullying. Research on the detection of cyberbullying through sentimental analysis employs machine learning algorithms for accurate and precise results. Some of the research works are discussed in this section.

Leung et al. [8] evaluate an innovative six-session constructivist-based anti-cyberbullying e-course to raise Hong Kong college students' awareness of cyberbullying and increase their intention to help cyberbullied victims. The objective of Sarifa and Mahanani [9] was to examine the association between callous-unemotional traits and cyberbullying in adolescents at State Senior High School of Semarang City. Kiruthika et al. [10] apply rule-based characteristic language processing and content analysis procedures to recognize and extricate subjective data from content of social media and centering on extremity such as positive, negative, unbiased conjointly on sentiments and feelings as irate, upbeat, pitiful. Ferreira et al. [11] aim to investigate the role of emotions and beliefs of perceived severity about cyberbullying behavior in the relationship between bystanders' personal moral beliefs and their behavioral intentions in cyberbullying.

2.2.2 IMAGES AND VIDEOS

Cyberbully may share embarrassing or inappropriate images or videos of their target, often with the intent of publicly shaming or humiliating them. Cyberbullying with images and videos can create adverse effects on the victim, and thus, this harassment must be detected and prevented. Recently, memes, infographics, online images, and videos have become a considerable part of social networks. Only limited computational models are proposed for cyberbullying which focuses on image or video. Some of the techniques leveraged for the detection of image-based cyberbullying are:

- **Content-Based Detection:** A method of detecting image-based cyberbullying that requires examining the visual content of photographs to identify instances of cyberbullying. This method uses computer vision algorithms to detect photos with insulting, threatening, or degrading content. Analyzing the content of photographs for the presence of hate symbols, nudity, or violent imagery are examples of content-based detection.
- **User-Based Detection:** A method of detecting image-based cyberbullying that requires examining the behavior of individual users to identify instances of cyberbullying. This strategy entails constructing a profile for each user based on their online activity, such as the photographs they publish, the captions they use, and the comments they receive. Image-based cyberbullying can be detected via user-based detection by identifying the patterns in the text.

- **Metadata-Based Detection:** A method of detecting image-based cyberbullying that requires evaluating the metadata associated with photographs to identify instances of cyberbullying. It examines the metadata of photos, such as the time and date of production, location data, and camera information, to discover patterns of behavior suggestive of cyberbullying. Identifying photographs that are posted repeatedly or by the same user is an example of metadata-based detection.
- **Machine Learning:** Machine learning is a way of detecting image-based cyberbullying that involves analyzing patterns and trends in photos using algorithms. This strategy entails teaching machine learning algorithms to spot patterns of cyberbullying activity, such as insulting or threatening images. It also helps to find the instances of bullying images.
- **Context-Based Detection:** It is a method of detecting image-based cyberbullying that involves analyzing the context in which images are shared to identify instances of cyberbullying. It also examines the social and cultural context in which images are shared to identify patterns of behavior that are signs of cyberbullying. Examples of context-based detection include analyzing the social network of the user who shared the image and examining the social and cultural norms of the community in which the image was shared.

2.2.3 MEMES AND OTHER INFOGRAPHIC-RELATED CONTENT

Infographics and memes can be used as tools for cyberbullying, as they can be easily shared on social media and have the potential to reach a large audience. Infographics are visual representations of information or data, and they can be used to spread false information or negative stereotypes about a person or group. Memes, on the other hand, are images or videos that are accompanied by humorous or sarcastic captions, and they can be used to mock or ridicule someone. Both infographics and memes can be used to target individuals or groups and can have a significant impact on the victim's emotional well-being.

Cyberbullies can create or share infographics and memes that contain derogatory or harmful content and can use them to harass or intimidate their target. It's important to remember that the impact of cyberbullying can be significant and long-lasting and that infographics and memes are just a few of the many tools that cyberbullies can use to harm their targets. Some of the works under memes and infographic content are showcased here. A recent work proposed in [12] uses a model which detects cyberbullying in three different modalities namely, textual, info-graphic, and image. CapsNet-ConvNet is an all-in-one architecture that consists of a capsule network (CapsNet), deep neural network with dynamic routing for predicting textual bullying material, and a Convolution Neural Network (ConvNet) for predicting visual bullying content.

The infographic content is separated from the image using Google Lens of the Google Photos app. Ramadevi et al. [13] considered both textual and infographic modalities and proposed a DLCNN which detects the bully content and infographic is discretized using google-photo-app, and/or operation is carried out for the detection of content.

There is a lack of research on identifying offensive and hate content in memes, but several studies have attempted to address this issue. Some studies created the multi-modal (Image+Text) meme dataset (MultiOFF) to identify offensive content in memes, using an early fusion approach to merge the image and text modalities.

They compared its performance with respect to a text-only and an image-only baseline.

In a recent study [14], the researchers developed a benchmark dataset called HarMeme, consisting of thousands of memes, to detect harmful memes and their target (individual, organization, community, or society/general public/other) and rated the memes as very harmful, partially harmful, or harmless. While these studies have made significant contributions to the detection of harmful memes and offensive content, there is still much work to be done to improve the accuracy of these models and develop more comprehensive datasets. Some examples of bully content are depicted as Figure 2.2.

Some of the above techniques are summarized as a Table 2.1 showing the methodology used and the type of dataset they have taken for their research work.

The majority-used technique is machine learning, along with some other methodologies using sentimental analysis, NLP, or text mining. The works leverage typically used evaluation metrics. Some are Accuracy, F1-score, Precision, Recall, and ROC.

FIGURE 2.2 Some examples of memes with negative and harmful content.

TABLE 2.1

Summary of Existing Techniques Used for Cyberbullying Detection

Title of the Paper	Methodology	Dataset Used
Machine learning approach for detection of cyber-aggressive comments by peers on social media network [1]	NLP Machine Learning	Kaggle-labeled comments from OSNs
Detecting offensive language in social media to protect adolescent online safety [2]	NLP Advanced Text Mining	YouTube user comments
Modeling the detection of textual cyberbullying [3]	NLP Machine Learning	YouTube user comments
A system to monitor cyberbullying based on message classification and social network analysis [5]	NLP Social Network Analysis	Labeled tweets dataset
Identification of key cyberbullies: A text mining and social network analysis approach [7]	Text Mining Social Network Analysis	Posts and comments via web crawling
Multimodal cyberbullying detection using capsule network with dynamic routing and deep convolutional neural network [12]	ELMo Deep Neural Networks	Kaggle toxic comments dataset
Predicting cyberbullying on social media [13]	NLP Deep Neural Networks	OLID dataset

2.3   ROLE OF EMOJIS IN CYBERBULLYING DETECTION

Emojis have become a popular way of expressing emotions and ideas in digital communication, especially on social media platforms. They provide a strong connection between the symbols and their semantic meaning, which can help users to express sentiments or opinions that cannot be conveyed through text alone. Emojis can also be used to model the underlying semantics of social media messages, including mood, food, or sports. They are interesting because they succinctly encode meaning that otherwise would require more than one word to convey. The use of emojis can be essential in preventing misunderstandings since sentences without them can sometimes be misinterpreted, leading to different meanings. However, negative emojis can be particularly harmful, and they can be categorized into two main types: passive-aggressive emojis and active-aggressive emojis. Passive-aggressive emojis, such as eye-rolls and sarcastic faces, are typically used to convey irritation, irony, or annoyance. On the other hand, active-aggressive emojis, such as angry faces and clenched fists, express more intense emotions such as anger, fury, and violence toward someone.

Moreover, negative emojis are not limited to these emotions alone. They can also convey feelings of egoism, egocentrism, and dominance. Negative emojis are used not only to release negative emotions but also to humiliate, threaten, terrorize, scare, and degrade others. Therefore, it is crucial to be aware of the potential harm that negative emojis can cause, particularly in the context of cyberbullying. We can say that while emojis can enhance online communication, they can also be used as a weapon to hurt, offend, and bully others. As responsible netizens, it is our duty to use emojis appropriately and refrain from using negative emojis that can cause harm to others.

The use of emojis in cyberbullying detection has been explored by a few researchers. The research-based study mentioned in [15] incorporated emojis for detecting offensive content by using separate embeddings in addition to character embedding. They utilized emoji2vec, which consists of pre-trained embeddings for all Unicode emojis using their descriptions in the Unicode emoji standard. Samghabadi et al. [16] proposed an emotion-aware attention mechanism that found the most important words in the text by incorporating emotional information from the text. They created an emoji vector using a DeepMoji model to capture the emotion from the text. They then prepared an emoji vector by tokenizing it into sentences and made an emoji vector as a binary representation by assigning 1 to the five most probable emojis and 0 to the others. They found that angry emojis were highly correlated with the offensive class, while happy and love faces appeared more frequently in the neutral class.

Recent work by Singh et al. [17] also incorporated emojis for cyberbullying detection and sentiment analysis by replacing all emojis with their textual descriptions. These studies suggest that the use of emojis can provide valuable information for detecting cyberbullying and analyzing sentiment in social media messages.

The above-discussed technologies lack the study of human behavior and recognition of the emotional and cognitive human thinking in the current cyberbullying detections, which made a way to rise of new technology which corporates human cognition along with artificial intelligence termed cognitive AI or cognitive computation. The importance of cognitive computation and its significance in cyberbullying is discussed in the next section.

2.4 COGNITIVE COMPUTATION

Cognitive computation deals with the computational modeling of cognitive processes such as perception, thinking, and decision-making. The two main objectives of cognitive computation are learning more about human cognition and creating useful applications in fields like artificial intelligence, robotics, and human-computer interaction. Researchers can build more sophisticated and intelligent systems that interact with people more naturally and effectively by developing computer models of human cognition.

It can also be described as a subfield of artificial intelligence (AI) that seeks to imitate human cognitive functions like learning, reasoning, and decision-making. It integrates cutting-edge methods, including neural networks, machine learning, and natural language processing. These methods might be more effective in capturing the intricate and delicate social dynamics present in cyberbullying, such as figuring out the objectives and motivations of cyberbullies based on their actions and interactions online.

To uncover patterns and behaviors connected to cyberbullying, typical AI techniques like machine learning can also be successful, especially when massive datasets are available. Machine learning algorithms can take primary data to learn from and then use that information to categorize new material as cyberbullying or not.

2.4.1 HOW COGNITIVE COMPUTATION IS APPLIED IN THE AREA OF CYBERBULLYING

In the area of cyberbullying, cognitive computation can be applied to develop tools and techniques that can detect and mitigate instances of cyberbullying. The work proposed by Ang and Goh [18] is an investigation into the prevalence and factors associated with cyberbullying among university students. The study employed a social cognitive perspective, which posits that individual characteristics, social influences, and situational factors interact to influence behavior.

The research was conducted through a survey of University students in China. The results showed that 23.3% of the students had experienced cyberbullying in the past year. Females were more likely to experience cyberbullying than males, and students who spent more time online and had a lower self-esteem were also more likely to be victims of cyberbullying. Furthermore, the study found that students who perceived higher levels of social support were less likely to engage in cyberbullying. Additionally, students who had higher levels of empathy were less likely to engage in cyberbullying, while those with higher levels of aggression were more likely to engage in cyberbullying (Figure 2.3).

The paper concludes that cyberbullying is a prevalent issue among university students and highlights the importance of addressing individual and social factors that contribute to cyberbullying. It is recommended that universities develop prevention and intervention programs that address these factors to reduce the incidence of cyberbullying and its negative effects on students' well-being.

The work in [18] aims to investigate the role of affective and cognitive empathy, as well as gender, in cyberbullying behavior among adolescents. The study used self-reported measures of empathy and cyberbullying behavior. The results showed that affective empathy was negatively related to cyberbullying behavior, while cognitive empathy was positively related to cyberbullying behavior. The research provides valuable insights into the complex relationship between empathy and cyberbullying behavior. Balakrishnan et al. [19] proposed a method to improve the accuracy of

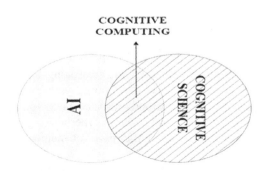

FIGURE 2.3   Venn diagram depicting cognitive computing.

cyberbullying detection on Twitter by incorporating users' psychological features. The authors argue that traditional approaches to cyberbullying detection, which rely solely on linguistic features, are not effective in identifying cyberbullying cases because they often fail to capture the subtle nuances of language that are used to convey negative intentions.

To address this limitation, the authors propose a two-stage machine learning approach that first classifies Twitter users based on their psychological features and then uses this information to improve the accuracy of cyberbullying detection. Specifically, the authors use a twitter user dataset and extract psychological features using the Big Five personality traits and the Dark Triad traits. The authors then use these features to train a binary classifier to distinguish between cyberbullies and non-cyberbullies. Mohan et al. [20] proposed a novel approach to limiting bullying in social media based on cognitive psychology principles. The authors argue that many instances of cyberbullying occur because individuals do not engage in sufficient cognitive processing before posting hurtful messages on social media. To address this issue, they propose a two-pronged intervention strategy based on cognitive psychology principles.

The first prong of the intervention involves providing individuals with cognitive tools and training to help them engage in more thoughtful and reflective decision-making before posting messages on social media. This could include techniques such as perspective-taking, considering the consequences of one's actions, and practicing empathy.

The second prong of the intervention involves changing the social norms around cyberbullying by promoting positive messages and social support for victims of bullying. The authors argue that by creating a culture of empathy and support, individuals will be less likely to engage in bullying behavior on social media.

The authors present several examples of successful interventions based on cognitive psychology principles in other domains, such as reducing prejudice and increasing pro-environmental behavior. They also discuss the potential challenges and limitations of their proposed approach.

Whatever we have discussed so far includes a range of strategies that incorporate ideas from natural language processing, machine learning, and human behavioral aspects. We understand that supervised approaches have been popular and effective for the datasets they have been trained on, but they have limitations. One major issue is that these models rely on predefined lists and combinations of words, which can cause them to fail while encountering newer words or phrases, not in the training data. These challenges can be addressed by analyzing the dynamic nature of the content using dynamic prediction algorithms, which will be discussed further.

2.5 RELEVANCE OF DYNAMIC PREDICTION ALGORITHM IN CYBERBULLYING

Social interaction and language are constantly evolving with the emergence of new slang words, intentional misspellings, and the use of new emojis and emoticons. This evolution creates challenges for monitoring systems, which need to keep up with the changing patterns of communication. As a result, it is becoming increasingly difficult to monitor online conversations and detect potentially harmful or inappropriate content.

Moreover, some supervised approaches use keywords and part-of-speech analysis, which may not fully capture the essence of a sentence or phrase. Furthermore, some instances of cyberbullying may not involve the direct use of specific offensive words but instead rely on the overall tone and feel of the message. This can make it difficult for supervised learning methods to identify instances of cyberbullying accurately.

Additionally, many supervised approaches utilize sampling, which can reduce their performance when encountering new words or phrases. The language corpus should be dynamic and constantly updated to keep up with these changes. To address the challenges posed by the constantly evolving language and social interactions, a system that does not rely solely on training or supervision is needed. Reinforcement learning is an appropriate solution for this. Reinforcement learning [24] involves:

- The system learning by trial and error,
- Receiving feedback on its actions, and
- Adjusting its behavior accordingly.

This approach allows the system to adapt to the constantly changing language and social interaction patterns and improve its accuracy without requiring constant human supervision or training. Aind et al. [21] introduced a new approach called Q-Bully for detecting cyberbullying in online comments.

Q-Bully uses reinforcement learning, which is not limited to a fixed corpus, and combines it with NLP techniques to guide the detection process. The model uses delayed rewards to consider the overall essence of a sentence instead of flagging individual words. The NLP-based optimization improves the convergence rate of Reinforcement Learning. Q-Bully outperforms other models when the dataset is dynamic and contains newer words and slangs.

Yuvaraj et al. [22] proposed an integrated model to detect cyberbullying through a combination of a feature extraction engine and a classification engine using an artificial neural network (ANN) and deep reinforcement learning (DRL) for evaluation. The model considers psychological features, user comments, and context for cyberbullying (CB) detection. The simulation shows that the ANN-DRL model outperforms conventional machine learning classifiers in terms of accuracy, precision, recall, and f-measure. The proposed model has the potential to improve CB detection using automated tools. Reinforcement Learning has proved its mettle in various problem domains, including Cyberbullying. Q-Bully, in particular, has shown remarkable performance by outpacing several baseline models when dealing with a dynamic dataset populated with novel words and intentionally misspelled terms. This success can be attributed to the advantage of using binary classification to identify offensive and non-offensive comments.

Cyberbullying presents unique challenges as language comprehension cannot rely solely on linguistic rules, NLP, and traditional supervised learning algorithms cannot always handle linguistic terms. Reinforcement learning, on the other hand, takes a more human-like approach by incorporating trial and error to learn and achieve its assigned objective. This approach proves beneficial in understanding language, allowing the model to learn through experience and interactions with the environment.

2.6 CYBERBULLYING IN METAVERSE

The Metaverse is a term used to describe a virtual world where users can interact with each other in real time, often using virtual reality or augmented reality technologies. As the use of the Metaverse becomes more widespread, there is growing concern about the potential for cyberbullying in this environment.

Cyberbullying in the Metaverse [23] can take many forms, such as harassment, humiliation, and exclusion. In a virtual world, users may feel encouraged to engage in behavior they would not normally engage in face-to-face interactions. The Metaverse's anonymity and distance can also make it difficult for victims to identify their bullies or seek help. To address the problem of cyberbullying in the Metaverse, developers and policymakers should consider a range of strategies. One approach incorporates tools and technologies to detect and prevent cyberbullying, such as real-time monitoring of user interactions, chat filters, and reporting mechanisms.

Educational programs can also play an essential role in preventing cyberbullying in the Metaverse. These programs can teach users about the potential harms of cyberbullying and provide them with strategies for recognizing and responding to this behavior.

Anecdotal accounts shared on Reddit and narratives from targets and witnesses in news articles describe the harm caused by cyberbullying in the Metaverse. Insults, racial slurs, and other forms of toxicity are reported regardless of whether they manifest orally (voice chat), textually (group chat or private message), or behaviorally (specific actions or inactions). The harm reported is similar to what is seen in other online environments, such as multiplayer games, social apps, Web 2.0 environments, and schools. However, cyberbullying in the Metaverse has the potential to be more insidious and impactful due to the realism of VR(virtual reality) experiences. This realism can translate to emotional, psychological, and physiological fear when individuals are targeted or threatened.

Finally, community-driven approaches can also effectively prevent cyberbullying in the Metaverse. Developers and policymakers can work with users to establish social norms and rules of conduct that promote positive interactions and discourage cyberbullying.

2.7 CHALLENGES AND FUTURE SCOPE

Cyberbullying continues to pose a significant challenge to online communities, making it essential to focus on future research areas that can lead to better detection and prevention. One of the most critical areas of focus is the dynamic nature of language usage and social networks, which can render current data annotation guidelines irrelevant in the future. Reinforcement learning techniques show promise in addressing this challenge, but further exploration is needed.

Anonymity is a key factor contributing to the rise in online crime rates, making it challenging to identify the real identity and number of aggressors behind a cyberbullying incident. To overcome this anonymity challenge and improve the accuracy of cyberbullying detection and prevention, researchers can consider incorporating additional data sources, such as social network metadata and user behavior patterns.

Moreover, the potential of cognitive psychology could be exploited more in this area to understand better the underlying psychological and behavioral factors contributing to cyberbullying. Overall, a multi-disciplinary approach that combines technical, psychological, and social perspectives can lead to better solutions for tackling the issue of cyberbullying.

2.8   CONCLUSION

Online social networks (OSNs) have unlocked a way for communication between online users to interact and share opinion dissemination and text. The rise in these communication media also leads to increased harassment or aggressive behavior by individuals or groups of people against targets, referred to as cyberbullying. This chapter covers the techniques leveraged in detecting different modalities of cyberbullying and unfolds the relevance of cognitive computing in cyberbullying with prevention strategies. The chapter also outlines the analysis of dynamic algorithms for predicting new slang and abbreviations in cyberbullying and how cyberbullying becomes an emerging issue in the digital world metaverse. Nowadays, the world is entirely in a digital system, and there is a chance for security issues. These issues have a negative impact on a person's mental health, resulting in poorer self-esteem, higher anxiety, and a significant alteration in a person's capacity to live peacefully. Therefore, proposing new ideas to secure the users will be of great insights in the future.

REFERENCES

[1] V. S. Chavan and S. S. Shylaja, "Machine learning approach for detection of cyberaggressive comments by peers on social media network," In 2015 International Conference on Advances in Computing, Communications and Informatics (ICACCI), Kochi, India, September 28, 2015.

[2] Y. Chen, Y. Zhou, S. Zhu and H. Xu, "Detecting offensive language in social media to protect adolescent online safety," In 2012 International Conference on Privacy, Security, Risk and Trust and 2012 International Conference on Social Computing, Amsterdam, Netherlands, September 3–5, 2012.

[3] K. Dinakar, R. Reichart and H. Lieberman, "Modeling the detection of textual cyberbullying," In Proceedings of the International AAAI Conference on Web and Social Media, Palo Alto, California, July 17–21, 2011.

[4] A. Mangaonkar, A. Hayrapetian and R. Raje, "Collaborative detection of cyberbullying behavior in Twitter data," In 2015 IEEE International Conference on Electro/ Information Technology (EIT), Dekalb, IL, USA, May 21, 2015.

[5] S. Menini, G. Moretti, M. Corazza, E. Cabrio, S. Tonelli and S. Villata, "A system to monitor cyberbullying based on message classification and social network analysis," In Proceedings of the Third Workshop on Abusive Language Online, Florence, Italy, August 1, 2019.

[6] S. Tomkins, L. Getoor, Y. Chen and Y. Zhang, "A socio-linguistic model for cyberbullying detection," In 2018 IEEE/ACM International Conference on Advances in Social Networks Analysis and Mining (ASONAM), Barcelona, Spain, August 28–31, 2018.

[7] Y.-J. Choi, B.-J. Jeon and H.-W. Kim, "Identification of key cyberbullies: A text mining and social network analysis approach," *Telematics and Informatics*, vol. 56, p. 101504, 2021.

[8] A. N. M. Leung, N. Wong and J. M. Farver, "Testing the effectiveness of an e-course to combat cyberbullying," *Cyberpsychology, Behavior, and Social Networking*, vol. 22, pp. 569–577, 2019.

[9] A. W. Sarifa and F. K. Mahanani, "Callous unemotional traits dan perundungan maya pada remaja (Callous unemotional traits and cyberbullying in adolescents)," *Intuisi: Jurnal Psikologi Ilmiah*, vol. 12, pp. 103–112, 2020.

[10] J. K. Kiruthika, A. P. Janani, M. Sudha and T. Yawanikha, "Fine grained sentimental analysis of social network chat using R," *Journal of Physics: Conference Series*, vol. 1916, p. 012210, 2021.

[11] P. da Costa Ferreira, A. M. V. Simão, V. Martinho and N. Pereira, "How beliefs and unpleasant emotions direct cyberbullying intentions," *Heliyon*, vol. 8, p. e12163, 2022.

[12] A. Kumar and N. Sachdeva, "Multimodal cyberbullying detection using capsule network with dynamic routing and deep convolutional neural network," *Multimedia Systems*, vol. 28, pp. 1–10, 2021.

[13] R. Ramadevi, C. Gouthami and M. R. Babu, "Predicting cyberbullying on social media," *Turkish Journal of Computer and Mathematics Education (TURCOMAT)*, vol. 10, pp. 828–836, 2019.

[14] S. Pramanick, D. Dimitrov, R. Mukherjee, S. Sharma, M. Akhtar, P. Nakov, T. Chakraborty, "Detecting harmful memes and their targets," *arXiv preprint arXiv:2110.00413*, 2021.

[15] T. Ranasinghe and H. Hettiarachchi, "Emoji powered capsule network to detect type and target of offensive posts in social media," In Proceedings of the International Conference on Recent Advances in Natural Language Processing (RANLP 2019), Varna, Bulgaria, September, 2–4 2019.

[16] N. S. Samghabadi, A. Hatami, M. Shafaei, S. Kar and T. Solorio, "Attending the emotions to detect online abusive language," *arXiv preprint arXiv:1909.03100*, 2019.

[17] A. Singh, E. Blanco and W. Jin, "Incorporating emoji descriptions improves tweet classification," In Proceedings of the 2019 Conference of the North American Chapter of the Association for Computational Linguistics: Human Language Technologies, Volume 1 (Long and Short Papers), Minneapolis, Minnesota, June 2–7, 2019.

[18] R. P. Ang and D. H. Goh, "Cyberbullying among adolescents: The role of affective and cognitive empathy, and gender," *Child Psychiatry & Human Development*, vol. 41, pp. 387–397, 2010.

[19] V. Balakrishnan, S. Khan and H. R. Arabnia, "Improving cyberbullying detection using Twitter users' psychological features and machine learning," *Computers & Security*, vol. 90, p. 101710, 2020.

[20] S. Mohan, I. Valsaladevi and S. M. Thampi, "'Think before you post': A cognitive psychological approach for limiting bullying in social media," In Proceedings of the Smart City and Informatization: 7th International Conference, iSCI 2019, Guangzhou, China, November 12–15, 2019.

[21] A. T. Aind, A. Ramnaney and D. Sethia, "Q-bully: A reinforcement learning based cyberbullying detection framework," In 2020 International Conference for Emerging Technology (INCET), Belgaum, India, August 3, 2020.

[22] N. Yuvaraj, K. Srihari, G. Dhiman, K. Somasundaram, A. Sharma, S. M. G. S. M. A. Rajeskannan, M. Soni, G. S. Gaba, M. A. AlZain and M. Masud, "Nature-inspired-based approach for automated cyberbullying classification on multimedia social networking," *Mathematical Problems in Engineering*, vol. 2021, pp. 1–12, 2021.

[23] Z. Qasem, H. Y. Hmoud, D. Hajawi and J. Z. Al Zoubi, "The effect of technostress on cyberbullying in Metaverse social platforms," In Proceedings of Co-creating for Context in the Transfer and Diffusion of IT: IFIP WG 8.6 International Working Conference on Transfer and Diffusion of IT, TDIT 2022, Maynooth, Ireland, June 15–16, 2022.

[24] Richard S. Sutton and Andrew G. Barto, Reinforcement Learning: An Introduction, second edition, Adaptive Computation and Machine Learning series, ISBN:978-0-262-19398-6, The MIT Press Cambridge, 1998.

3 Combating Cyberbullying in Social Networks
An Artificial Intelligence Approach

Sheetal Sharma and Ridhika Chatterjee
IILM Academy of Higher Learning

3.1 INTRODUCTION

3.1.1 BACKGROUND

Digital platforms have sharply escalated and gained popularity at a global level in the last one and a half decades (Azeez et al., 2021). Various platforms like YouTube, Telegram, Facebook, Snapchat, Instagram, Twitter, etc., have proved to be effective and worthy for real-time communication, connecting people across the globe virtually (Whittaker and Kowalski, 2015). According to a report published by Digital Around the World in July 2021, approximately 4.80 billion population across the globe were found to be actively engaged on various social media platforms to communicate, and this accounted for almost 61% of the entire population of the world with the yearly growth of roughly 5.7% new users joining per day (Kemp, 2021). But along with this glorious side of social media, the grey side also affects human behavior. The proliferation of the internet has caused major security concerns. On one hand, wider and easier access to the Web has helped us as individuals in many ways but has also provided a wider room for cybercrimes. Most social media platforms witness aggressive, violent, sexist, and other discriminatory comments, posts, and exchanges of messages toward other members of the platform. This phenomenon is referred to as cyberbullying (Azeez et al., 2021). Bullying refers to the systematic abuse of power and an act of repetitive aggressive behavior or intentional harm to cause emotional, physical, and mental damage to an individual (Wolke and Lereya, 2015). The concept of bullying behavior was introduced by Olweus (1994) and was explained as an intentional act of aggression, conducted by an individual or group of people to cause harm to the victim who is not able to safeguard himself or herself. One of the crucial forms of bullying which is prevalent these days is cyberbullying. The concept of cyberbullying can be explained as an act of repetitive inhuman and aggressive behavior shown by online users to other individuals using digital media (Wright, 2017). It is an offensive and derogatory online behavior where a series of aggressive and harmful messages are sent from a bully to a victim for a period which leads to potential detrimental effects on the victim (Yao et al., 2019).

DOI: 10.1201/9781003393061-4

The term cyberbullying grabbed attention during the year 2000 when the inception of digital platforms happened and provided the scope of bullying in an online environment (Englander et al., 2017). In an online inter-communications environment, any social interaction that involves cruel and offensive content is called cyberbullying or cyber harassment (Rosa et al., 2019). The impact of cyberbullying is far more destructive than a customary form of traditional bullying as it negatively impacts the emotional component of the victim (Hani et al., 2019).

Cyber-aggression, cyberstalking, and cyberbullying are a few major growing concerns. Among them, cyberbullying is growing at the fastest pace and is detrimental to the sustainable growth of our society (Kumari et al., 2019). The consequences of cyberbullying are very traumatic given the fact that it even leads to a state of emotional dysregulation in the victim's children (Chen and Zhu, 2023). Cyberbullying is an increasing public health concern, the young generation i.e., children and youth are mainly victimized and undergo a range of health and mental issues including maladaptive behavior, psychosomatic problems, and an increased level of suicidal tendencies (Mishna et al., 2012). Further research findings indicate 68.5% of adolescents experience effects like anger, stress, fear, and depressive feelings (Ortega et al., 2012). Sabella et al. (2013) advocated that cyberbullying is augmented by technology and happens at the speed of light causing more cruelty. Extensive research conducted on the consequences of cyberbullying behavior on work-life by Muhonen et al. (2017) explains the mediating role of culture and climate of an organization between employee well-being, work engagement, intention to quit, and cyberbullying behavior. There are various forms of cyberbullying as discussed in the literature. Seven popular forms of cyberbullying are discussed and depicted in Figure 3.1.

Let us understand the concept of fake profile creation as a form of cyberbullying with the help of an example. A fake profile of a female victim nearly 15 years old is created and the victim's name, family member's name, nude and obscene photographs, and derogatory comments are posted online to harass the victims which caused her mental disturbance and hampered her academic growth.

Similarly, online harassment can be understood with an example of a 12-year-old boy, who, in due course of time, has become introverted and withdrawn himself from day-to-day activities. One day after school is over, he comes home and goes off to sleep; the boy's parents who were very worried about their son's behavior then accessed his mobile and found that their son is added to different online groups, and he is being bullied by his classmates with offensive comments regarding his clothes and grades.

As a remedial in this case, the parents should immediately report to the school authorities and seek an investigation under the provision of the Juvenile Justice Act, 2000 (Joseph and Jain, 2020).

Further, an example to understand cyberstalking: A manager of a well-known firm Ms Y was stalked online by Z who may be a female or a male member. Initially, Z had sent an email seeking an appointment to meet Ms. Y regarding an investment; subsequently, Ms. Y politely refused to meet. As a result, Z stalker then started sending obscene, vulgar, and aggressive emails with derogatory remarks and threatening calls. As a remedial measure, Ms Y can file a complaint against Z, which can be imposed on the stalker (Joseph and Jain, 2020).

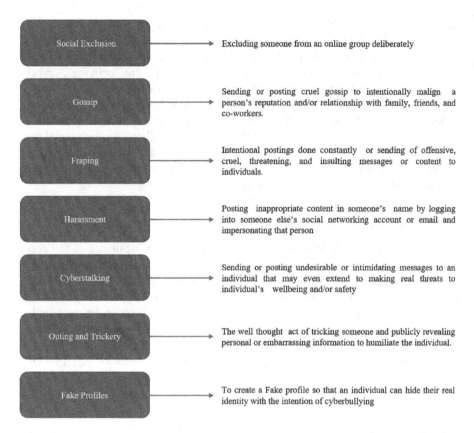

FIGURE 3.1 Forms of cyberbullying.

Source: Al-Marghilani (2022).

The above-mentioned hypothetical illustrations explain that cyberbullying on social media platforms is harmful and problematic causing permanent damage to the victim's well-being. In today's era of technological advancements, AI has contributed immensely and will continue to have a primary role in countless aspects of life, liberty, and livelihood. AI or algorithmic tools intend to automate the task of identifying abusive or offensive language, posts, chat messages, photos, etc. by leveraging various tools, such as machine learning (ML), deep learning (DL), convolutional neural networks (CNN), and natural language processing (NLP) (Gorwa et al., 2020). This chapter further provides insights into how the use of AI helps in the effective management of cyberbullying.

3.1.2 RESEARCH METHODOLOGY

To conduct the extensive literature review, various popular databases (e.g., Google Scholar, Scopus, EBSCO, ProQuest, etc.) were used to assess the available literature on cyberbullying and the use of artificial intelligence in combating cyberbullying.

Almost 50 plus research papers from the year 2010 onwards till date were downloaded. In addition to this, various reports, news items, and blogs from relevant sources were also downloaded and thoroughly read for reviewing the latest updates on the topic of research. The keywords used for the search were "bullying", "cyberbullying", "Artificial Intelligence", "AI models to combat cyberbullying", "Legal framework for cyberbullying", "AI applications for cyberbullying", "challenges", "effects of cyberbullying", and "outcomes." After an extensive review of the literature, the chapter presents a summary of the rise in cyberbullying through social networks and discusses various AI models that have been used to predict cyberbullying incidents. The chapter critically assesses the dark side of cyberbullying and describes the role of AI in combating cyberbullying.

3.1.3 CHAPTER ORGANIZATION

The chapter is further divided into various sections: Section 3.2 discusses and presents reviews of the related work to comprehend how cyberbullying soared with the rise in social media and the major challenges posed by cyberbullying. Section 3.3 explains the role of AI in combating cyberbullying with the help of relevant real-life examples and also presents scenarios to explain the AI intervention for cyberbullying. Section 3.4 discusses the application of various AI models used for early detection and effective management of cyberbullying incidences. Section 3.5 throws light on the legal framework for cyberbullying in the Indian context. Section 3.6 provides the future scope of research in the field of AI applications in managing cyberbullying, and Section 3.7 concludes the chapter.

3.2   RELATED WORK

3.2.1 SOCIAL MEDIA & RISE OF CYBERBULLYING

Social media sites and applications are more prone to various digital forms of cyberbullying. Cyberbullying statistics for 2023 (Security.Org, 2023) say children using YouTube were more prone to be the victims of cyberbullying with 79%, second most by Snapchat at 69%, followed by TikTok at 64%, and Facebook at 49%. According to a report by McAfee, almost 85% of Indian children are victims of cyberbullying which is the highest number globally (Sangani, 2022).

To examine the psyche of online users a model called the identity bubble reinforcement model was conceived and proposed by Keipi et al. (2017). The model explains that the users who interact on social media platforms form an identity bubble with three types of characteristics: (I) A tendency to interact with like-minded individuals, (II) To develop closeness to online social networks, and (III) To have a strong reliance on the information received from others in an online environment. These characteristics of social media users make them more vulnerable to cyberbullying incidents as they are not capable of distinguishing between fake and genuine scenarios.

With the growing social media networks and online communication, cyberbullying has emerged as a prominent concern and is considered a nationwide health issue

(Al-Garadi et al., 2019) The cases of cyberbullying witnessed a significant rise across the globe during the COVID-19 lockdown as children and youth spent most of their time on online platforms for schooling and other purposes, and this problem requires strict interventions (Lobe et al., 2021). The COVID-19 pandemic has largely changed the nuances of social media giving rise to crimes and cyber threats. Not only did it affect our social life, but a great hindrance was also caused to our work and education sector. Children and youth were more likely to be engaged on online platforms for studying, browsing, and playing online games and so did the bullying activities. The pandemic has largely influenced cyberbullying activities and has made youth vulnerable to cyber threats (Kee et al., 2022).

With the rise of technology, various online social networks like chat messengers and online games have been the driving force toward cyberbullying. A cyberbullying game and event named "The Momo Challenge" gained popularity, especially on social media and chat messenger platforms like WhatsApp, Twitter, and Instagram, forcing and motivating teens to commit acts of violence and suicide. Momo is a fictional identity that plays the role of an administrator or cyberbully and sends the victim ominous and offensive messages and a list of orders that are meant to be excessively horrifying and violent. As previously noted, curators are the people who oversee this kind of activity (Khattar et al., 2018). Individuals who engage in this type of activity have troubled and anxious minds with a higher level of sensitivity. As per parents and media reports, Momo Challenge is popular among urban youth and is also considered as a viral counterfeit, or a myth (Sakuma, 2019).

Another online suicide game that emerged as a form of cyberbullying that led to serious implications on teenagers' mental well-being was "The Blue Whale Challenge" (BBC, 2017). It is a "game" where the players play and complete sequential tasks provided by the administrators over 50 days. The tasks start naively before incorporating self-harm and the ultimate challenge, which calls for the player to commit suicide (Radio Free Europe, 2017). Another form of cyberbullying that grabbed attention was girls bullying each other by posting photos of themselves on social media platforms like Instagram and further tagging the girls who were not invited, thus stating a message to bully them and show them that they were excluded (Davis, 2019).

3.2.2 Challenges in Fighting Cyberbullying

Reducing or cutting down cases of cyberbullying needs dedicated efforts by the change agents of society (Vats, 2019). These change agents can be friends, peers, guardians, colleagues, and regulatory bodies, but cyberbullying incidents must get reported to the change agents. It is of paramount importance to have early detection of cyberbullying and mitigate the negative risk that causes permanent damage to the victim. There are a few challenges related to fighting cyberbullying. One of the major challenges in dealing with cyberbullying incidences is timely reporting and corrective actions against the perpetrator. According to a survey of adults conducted by Ipsos International in 28 countries, it revealed that parents or guardians usually do not find confidence in accepting that their children might have faced cyberbullying (Newall, 2018). In the year 2018, India reported that only 37% of parents expressed their concerns and reported cases of cyberbullying to the legal body (Cook, 2023). Children/Youth explicate the complex dynamics of cyberbullying incidents and contribute to the existing body of literature on cyberbullying scenarios. Previous research findings indicate that most children and youth do not disclose their experiences with cyberbullying incidents to their parents or guardians (DePaolis and Wiiliford, 2015). The consequences of cyberbullying are very traumatic given the fact that children are reluctant to share these incidents with their family members or guardians, driven by the fear of losing their mobile phones/or internet access and privilege (Cao et al., 2020).

The lack of disclosure thus generates an immediate need for intervention and prevention to promote disclosure and mitigate cyberbullying incidents.

Another major challenge with cyberbullying is that perpetrators remain hidden or anonymous during their cyberbullying act which harms the emotional, mental, and physical well-being of the victim, and in most cases, it leads to suicide (Khine et al., 2020). Considering various challenges related to cyberbullying, the next section throws light on how AI interventions help combat cyberbullying.

3.3   CONCEPTUALIZING AI IN COMBATING CYBER BULLYING

Considering cyberbullying is a major problem, organizations have spelt out the community guidelines/terms of service, and their policies are also intact regarding cyberbullying on social media (Gillespie, 2018). Research studies suggest that incidences of cyberbullying have sharply increased during the COVID-19 lockdown as most users were engaged in online activities including schools, classes, assignments, games, etc. (Lobe et al., 2021). As per the available literature, there are two types of moderation approaches to combat cyberbullying: reactive and proactive moderation. Reactive moderation means responding to harmful content after users share it on the platform. This method relies on human moderators to monitor chat channels, and user reports to be actioned by moderators of the forum. In proactive moderation, the goal is to prevent bad content from ever appearing on public platforms. This technique uses AI to screen the content before it gets reflected on the platforms. Reactive moderation is done by the users/victims of cyberbullying, and proactive moderation is done by social media platforms bolstered by AI techniques (Milosevic et al., 2022).

There is a high degree of automation required to optimize the detection of cyberbullying content and incidence (Gorwa et al., 2020). Several researchers also confirmed that content removal is the first step where, after reporting, the cyberbullying content is blocked or removed (Milosevic, 2018).

With advancements in technology, a revolutionary change in information generated by users and online human networks has taken place. The data created from social media platforms can be used/ misused by cyber bullies either in structured or unstructured form. Bullies only need internet connectivity and access to any digital gadget like a laptop or a cell phone to perform such malicious acts with the victim. Most researchers support using electronic ways to combat cyberbullying because the traditional way of coping with cyberbullies is insufficient and will not fetch effective results.

It is imperative to detect cyberbullying incidents at the inception stage on online social networks. To detect the initial signs of cyberbullying, a model was developed by Samghabadi et al. (2020) where a simple set of semantic, stylistic, and lexical features were used to train a Support Vector Machine classifier to detect cyberbullying cases. This approach uses a repetitive evaluation of the user's interactions with other users to find out potential abusive words, and rather than chunk-by-chunk evaluation, it adopts post-by-post evaluation to closely examine the real case scenarios. It is advised that cyberbullying can be mitigated through human moderation using simple steps by the users as most social media platforms offer a variety of setting options in which users can choose whom to allow and whom to restrict for commenting or viewing any post; the friend list; and options for blocking, muting, and even reporting cyberbullying.

Facebook and Instagram platforms have extensively upgraded over the years and use AI to the maximum capacity to identify high-suicide-risk cases that happen because of cyberbullies by understanding the patterns of the posts, likes, and related comments. This information is processed repeatedly with other related information such as time; date; and other posts that include images, videos, and texts. Once an item is flagged, it is transferred to Facebook's 1,000-plus team of community standard guidelines for further review. DeepText is the algorithm used by the Facebook platform to understand textual content with "near-human" accuracy. Instagram uses ML techniques to detect bullying in photos, videos, and captions (Zubair et al., 2023).

Another service called Guardio was developed by IBM with the aim of a not-for-profit startup that uses AI to identify any social media activity that is problematic and send a message to the child's parent. Guardio uses IBM Watson technology that enables NLP and NLC to decipher, label, and categorize words and messages. It is a cutting-edge AI that helps parents protect their children from cyberbullying (IBM, n.d.).

An artificial intelligence platform named Emma designed by STOP Out Bullying Company is another technological breakthrough which helps in combating cyberbullying. Emma is an innovative educational tool which processes and analyses thousands of cyberbullying posts using ML and can simulate the emotional, psychological, and physical effects of cyberbullying on the teenager's brain. Emma assists teenagers, educators, and parents in visualizing how cyberbullying affects the developing brain, so they may take appropriate action and promote change (Cision PR Newswire, 2019).

3.3.1 SCENARIOS OF CYBERBULLYING AND AI INTERVENTION

Scenario 1

A female child who was a TikTok user received derogatory and mean remarks on her video. She immediately received notification of cyberbullying being detected. She has the option to see the comment if she wants, or else, she can ignore it to avoid re-traumatization. Thereafter, help is extended from the support desk. This study is of original work and has been tested by (Milosevic et al., 2023).

Scenario 2

Another scenario is from schools in Ireland where AI was used to report cyber-bullying content using AI. Under this scheme, the school had an authorized official account on Instagram, which was managed and supervised by a counselor appointed by the school. The victim child may directly report the incident on the platform. It was also mandatory for schools to have a counselor to guide the students on cyber-bullying incidents and their implications.

3.4   APPLICATION OF AI-BASED MODELS AND TECHNIQUES TO MITIGATE CYBERBULLYING

This section discusses the use of various AI-based models to detect and mitigate cyberbullying incidents. There are various models/approaches in use for detecting cyberbullying incidents automatically and with high precision and accuracy.

A model adopted from the fundamentals of DL was proposed by Kargutkar and Chitre (2020). DL refers to a class of neural networks having several layers of neurons that can learn themselves. As proposed by the authors Kargutkar and Chitre (2020), a model has been developed with CNN implementation with multiple layers that uses iterative analysis to fetch accurate data for analysis. The technique utilizes the fundamental principles of the DL model and proposed a system with better precision as illustrated in Figure 3.2. The DL model has three layers: input, hidden, and output layer. The model preprocesses the dataset and removes unwanted texts and abusive phrases.

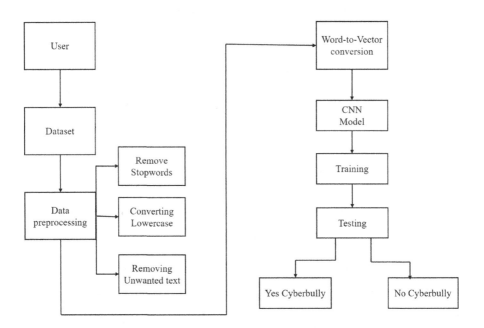

FIGURE 3.2   Deep learning model.

Source: Kargutkar and Chitre (2020).

Another model was developed and proposed by Lowry et al. (2017) which aimed at examining the factors like a non-linear influence on the control imbalance of cyberbullying and understanding the concept of accountability and deindividuation that affect control imbalance. An approach called control balance theory has been used to implement a model that examines cyberbullying from different angles. The approach of the model is to understand the opportunity of the individual who perceives that they are controlled by others and gives them a sense of vulnerability inducing them to engage in cyberbullying activities. This model was proved with a survey conducted on 507 adults.

A model was developed by Nandhini and Sheeba (2015) based on the application of the naïve bayes ML approach and worked on datasets that provided results with 91% accuracy. In the proposed framework, a step-by-step procedure is followed to detect cyberbullying as depicted in Figure 3.3.

Input------Data Preprocessing-------Feature Extraction-----Cyberbully Detection----Naïve Bayes Classifier

The above-proposed framework illustrates the application of the naïve bayes classifier to identify the wrong/abusive data set from the input set of data.

AI can build up a ML model to recognize or identify the tormenting activities on social media. To understand the menace that is caused by tweets, posts, etc., a model was proposed on the concept of ML by Jaithunbi et al. (2021), which discusses the stages involved in identifying and analyzing the tweets or posts that are considered as input sets of data. The model illustrated in Figure 3.4 explains the implementation of programing that distinguishes between tormented tweets and posts. Two classifiers SVM (support vector machine) and Random Forest are utilized to study online media tormenting activities. Both the classifiers provide 71% and 53% precision respectfully and help to identify cyberbullying activities.

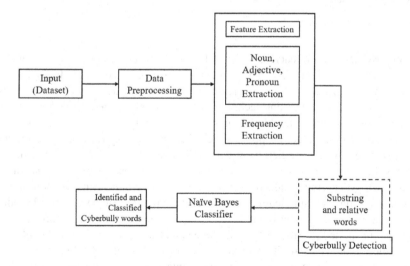

FIGURE 3.3   Proposed framework of cyberbully detection and classification system.

Source: Nandhini et al. (2015).

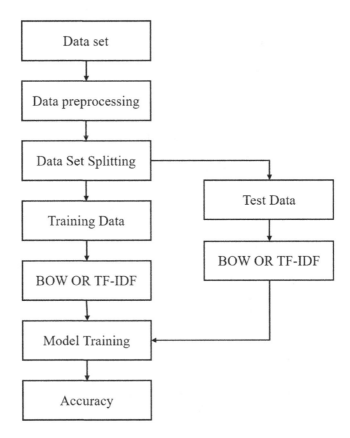

FIGURE 3.4   Machine learning model.

Source: Jaithunbi et al. (2021).

Similarly, another approach uses DL and neural networks proposed by Zhang et al. (2016) which is based on the principle of neural networks to combat bullying data. In the same context, Zhao et al. (2016) created a cyberbullying detection framework that precisely used word embedding techniques to list out predefined abusive words and assigned weights to understand bullying features and mitigate it on an urgent basis.

According to the model proposed by Chavan and Shylaja (2015), based on constructing cyberbullying prediction models, a text classification approach is used. This requires the construction of ML classifiers from labeled text instances (Chavan and Shylaja, 2015). The input data set is considered as raw data which is then preprocessed; after preprocessing feature, extraction selection technique is applied to identify the features related to bullying or offensive comments. Once the feature selection technique is applied, testing of the data takes place after which the final evaluation and prediction of cyberbullying words and incidents is carried out (Figure 3.5).

As a preventive measure, social media giants like Instagram and Twitter have been generating algorithms to detect malicious incidents of cyberbullying. In 2019, Instagram unveiled a tool that alerted users when their comments were deemed

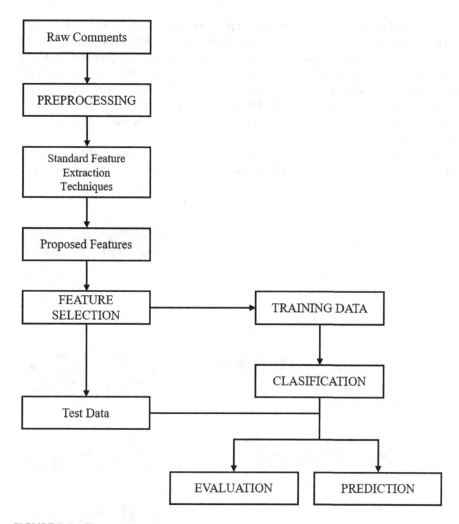

FIGURE 3.5 Feature extraction technique.

Source: Chavan and Shylaja (2015).

abusive (Steinmetz, 2019). This gave the user the chance to consider if they want to keep uploading such information or not. Similarly, Twitter also came up with a policy based on the severity. A direct message will be issued to the user in case of posting any harmful content (Our Range of Enforcement Options, 2020). According to a research study (Al-Marghilani, 2022), the author proposed a model that has been efficient enough to work and detect fraud. Artificial intelligence cyberbullying free online – social network (AICBF-ONS technique) is used for the detection of cyberbullying in online social networks like Twitter, Instagram, Facebook, and Snapchat. This model was effective in reporting acts of cyberbullying on social networks. Primarily, the data was collected from the smart cities, which were further processed for cyberbullying detection process. The AICBF-ONS technique comprised of a stage-wise process starting pre-processing, feature extraction, chaotic slap swarm optimization-based feature selection, stacked autoencoder (SAE)-based classification, and MFO (mayfly optimization)-based parameter optimization. Using ML techniques, Raisi and Huang (2017) constructed a second model where users were studied in harassment-based scenarios, and novel bullying vocabulary indicators were identified simultaneously. The model tends to infer the social framework where the user bullies and victimizes. Figure 3.6 depicts the application of the model AICBF-ONS.

An in-depth research study by Abduvaliyev et al. (2013) explained the importance of an intrusion detection system (IDS) installed in wireless sensor networks (WSN),

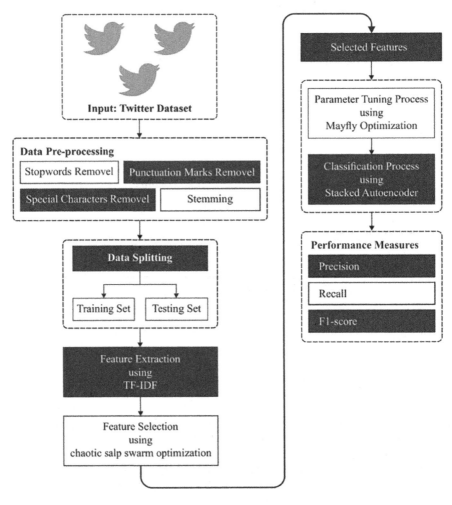

FIGURE 3.6   Process of Artificial Intelligence Cyberbullying Free-Online Social Network (AICBF-ONS).

Source: Al-Marghilani (2022).

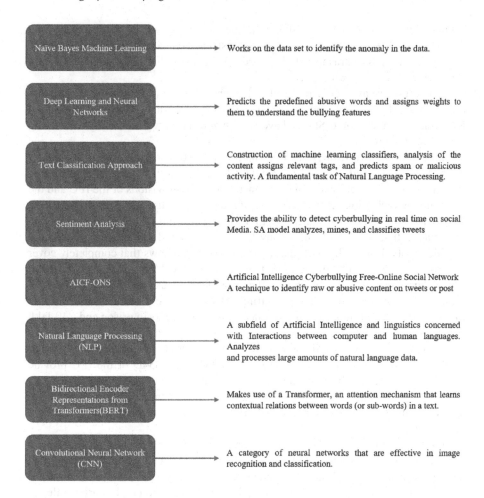

FIGURE 3.7 A summary chart of popular tools used to combat cyberbullying.

which helps to detect any kind of intrusion or anomaly that may tend to turn toward cyberbullying. The findings of this study suggest that it is vital to detect an anomaly in a wireless network using IDS protocols. Additionally, three major categories were highlighted in his research: protocols for anomaly detection, misuse detection, and specification-based detection (Figure 3.7) which helps to identify cyber threats and attacks.

3.5 LEGAL FRAMEWORK FOR CYBERBULLYING- INDIAN CONTEXT

India needs the necessary legislative framework to address the fundamental challenges of cybercrime. Children are the most vulnerable groups to the dangers of electronic media. According to National Crime Records Bureau (NCRB) 2020 data, there has been a hike of over 400% in cybercrimes (registered under the Information

Technology Act) committed against children in comparison to the last year. The top five states reporting cyber-crimes against children are: Uttar Pradesh (170), Karnataka (144), Maharashtra (137), Kerala (107), and Odisha (71), the NCRB data stated (Business Standard, 2021).

Cybercrime is an increasingly global phenomenon that knows no geographic boundaries. Many developed countries, including Australia, Canada, the United Kingdom, and the United States, have recognized the prevalence of cyberbullying and its negative impacts.

However, the legal framework in India for anti-cyberbullying laws is not clearly defined and structured. The Indian Penal Code (IPC), 1860, neither defines bullying nor punishes it as an offence. However, there are some provisions of the IPC and the Information Technology Act (IT Act), 2000, that can be used to fight cyberbullies. The IT Act of 2000 clearly states strict punishment for those indulged in publishing information that is obscene and in any form is considered a breach of privacy and confidentiality. Practically, in India, there are no special laws that completely cover cyberbullying. Section 67 of the IT Act also deals with cyberbullying with a limited scope. The punishment associated in the case of cyberbullying, where someone is found guilty of publishing or transmitting offensive content in electronic form, is that the perpetrator might face up to a maximum of five years in prison and a 10-lakh rupee fine under Section 67 of the Act (Legal Upanishad, 2022).

A press release by the Ministry of Women and Child Development on "Digital Exploitation of Children," states that sections 354A and 354D of the IPC provide punishment for cyber bullying and cyber stalking against women. Section 354D of the IPC states that the section penalizes both the offence of offline and online stalking, without any discrimination based on the presence or absence of the "cyber" component.

In India, traditionally, schools rather than parents have played a significant role in a child's recovery. Therefore, tighter rules should be created to stop school bullying and to guarantee schoolchildren's online safety (Vats, 2019).

In addition to legal assistance, victims have the choice to employ private detectives that focus on finding cyberbullies. Apart from legal help, victims also have the option to hire private investigators specializing in tracking down cyberbullies. Google Reverse Email Finder is a feature offered by Google where we can find a list of websites that can help an individual unmask the bully.

3.6   CONCLUSION & FUTURE IMPLICATIONS

Available statistics and literature on cyberbullying indicate that cyberbullying victims are highly prone to the risk of depressive symptoms and suicidal thoughts which impact the emotional and mental being of the victim for a longer time. Some of the moderation measures that can be taken in the form of human interventions include effective methods for raising awareness of the intricacies of online harassment among teenage and young adult populations; its prompt reporting; and providing psychological, moral, and emotional support to the victims. However, due to the high volume of data shared on online platforms, human moderation has its limitations. Therefore, proactive measures need smart technological interventions using AI techniques and models which are also being used by various social media platforms for early detection and neutralization. There have been reports stating that large platforms such as Twitter, Google, and YouTube are already publishing cyberbullying cases after detections, and action is taken even before they were reported. Several AI-based models are already in use as discussed in the chapter which have been able to address the problem of cyberbullying by early detection with more than 90% accuracy. However, each model has certain limitations which are being challenged by experts and are under improvisation through experimentation. The limitations range from the categorization of the severity of the abusive content, inclusions and exclusions, testing approaches, high dimensional datasets analysis, and its social impact (Chia et al., 2021). Another limitation associated with the use of AI-based models is unintended social biases toward demographic attributes such as gender, language, nationality, and religion (Gencoglu, 2021) at the time of data collection. The amount of data is not so important, but how accurately and the type of data retrieved is what matters. The unintended social biases at the time of cyberbullying detection from the social networks, the keywords used, hashtags, etc., must be free from the biases for better outcomes from the models used. Moderating cyberbullying content using an AI-based model is the multimodal nature of the content in the form of text, images, video etc. It is a possibility that either only one element is offensive or maybe no element is offensive individually, rather it is derogatory when considered in totality (Kumar and Sachdeva, 2021).

Due to the gap identified in the various models, there is a huge scope for hybrid approaches using optimization and DL. Testing real-life high-dimensional datasets can also be seen as a future direction of research.

Future studies could also focus on testing real-time high-dimensional datasets which are free from unintended social biases. Since cyberbullying has emotional and mental well-being associated with it, we cannot ignore the human side while carrying out our scientific experiments using AI for the greater good.

REFERENCES

Abduvaliyev, A., Pathan, A. S. K., Zhou, J., Roman, R., & Wong, W. C. (2013). On the vital areas of intrusion detection systems in wireless sensor networks. *IEEE Communications Surveys & Tutorials, 15(3),* 1223–1237.

Al-Garadi, M. A., Hussain, M. R., Khan, N., Murtaza, G., Nweke, H. F., Ali, I., ... & Gani, A. (2019). Predicting cyberbullying on social media in the big data era using machine learning algorithms: A review of the literature and open challenges. *IEEE Access, 7,* 70701–70718.

Al-Marghilani, A. (2022). Artificial intelligence-enabled cyberbullying-free online social networks in smart cities. *International Journal of Computational Intelligence Systems, 15(1),* 9.

Arnon, S., Klomek, A. B., Visoki, E., Moore, T. M., Argabright, S. T., DiDomenico, G. E., ... & Barzilay, R. (2022). Association of cyberbullying experiences and perpetration with suicidality in early adolescence. *JAMA Network Open, 5(6),* 1–14.

Azeez, N. A., Idiakose, S. O., Onyema, C. J., & Van Der Vyver, C. (2021). Cyberbullying detection in social networks: Artificial intelligence approach. *Journal of Cyber Security and Mobility, 10,* 745–774.

BBC News. (2017, 27 April). Blue Whale: Should you be worried about online pressure groups? BBC News. Archived from the original on 2017-05-12. https://www.bbc.com/news/world-39729819

Cao, X., Khan, A. N., Ali, A., & Khan, N. A. (2020). Consequences of cyberbullying and social overload while using SNSs: A study of users' discontinuous usage behavior in SNSs. *Information System Frontiers, 22,* 1343–1356.

Chavan, V. S., & Shylaja, S. S. (2015, August). Machine learning approach for detection of cyber-aggressive comments by peers on social media networks. In *2015 International Conference on Advances in Computing, Communications and Informatics (ICACCI)* (pp. 2354–2358). IEEE.

Chen, Q., & Zhu, Y. (2023). Experiences of childhood trauma and cyberbullying perpetration among adolescents in China. *Asia Pacific Journal of Social Work and Development, 33(1),* 50–63.

Chia, Z. L., Ptaszynski, M., Masui, F., Leliwa, G., & Wroczynski, M. (2021). Machine learning and feature engineering-based study into sarcasm and irony classification with application to cyberbullying detection. *Information Processing & Management, 58(4),* 102600.

Cook, S. (2023, March 23). Cyberbullying facts and statistics for 2018–2023. Comparitech. Retrieved from: https://www.comparitech.com/internet-providers/cyberbullying-statistics/.

Security.org Team (May, 2023). Cyberbullying: Twenty crucial statistics for 2023. Retrieved from: https://www.security.org/resources/cyberbullying-facts-statistics/. Accessed on May 10, 2023.

Davis, A. (2019). Meta global safety and wellbeing summit. Retrieved from: https://about.fb.com/news/2019/05/2019-global-safety-well-being-summit/.

DePaolis, K., & Williford, A. (2015). The nature and prevalence of cyber victimization among elementary school children. *Child & Youth Care Forum, 44(3),* 377–393.

Englander, E., Donnerstein, E., Kowalski, R., Lin, C. A., & Parti, K. (2017). Defining cyberbullying. *Pediatrics, 140(Supplement_2),* S148S151.

https://www.ibm.com/blog/10-clients-innovating-on-the-most-open-and-secure-public-cloud-for-business/ - Website Link.

Gencoglu, O. (2020). Cyberbullying detection with fairness constraints. *IEEE Internet Computing, 25,* 20–29.

Gillespie, T. (2018). *Custodians of the Internet: Platforms, content moderation, and the hidden decisions that shape social media.* Yale University Press.

Gorwa, R., Binns, R., & Katzenbach, C. (2020). Algorithmic content moderation: Technical and political challenges in the automation of platform governance. *Big Data & Society, 7(1),* 2053951719897945.

Hani, J., Mohamed, N., Ahmed, M., Emad, Z., Amer, E., & Ammar, M. (2019). Social media cyberbullying detection using machine learning. *International Journal of Advanced Computer Science and Applications, 10(5),* 703–707.

Jaithunbi, A. K., Lavanya, G., Smitha, D. V., & Yoshna, B. (2021). Detecting Twitter cyberbullying using machine learning. *Annals of the Romanian Society for Cell Biology,* 16307–16315.

Bandi Yoshna, D. G. L. D. V. S. (2021). Detecting Twitter Cyberbullying Using Machine Learning. *Annals of the Romanian Society for Cell Biology,* 16307–16315. Retrieved from http://www.annalsofrscb.ro/index.php/journal/article/view/5372

Joseph, V, & Jain, M. (2020, October 1). India: Anti-cyber bullying laws in India - An analysis. Mondaq. Retrieved from: https://www.mondaq.com/india/crime/989624/anti-cyber-bullying-laws-in-india---an-analysis.

Kargutkar, S. M., & Chitre, V. (2020). A study of cyberbullying detection using machine learning techniques. In *2020 Fourth International Conference on Computing Methodologies and Communication (ICCMC), Erode, India, 2020* (pp. 734–739). IEEE.

Kee, D. M. H., Al-Anesi, M. A. L., & Al-Anesi, S. A. L. (2022). Cyberbullying on social media under the influence of COVID-19. *Global Business and Organizational Excellence, 41(6)*, 11–22.

Keipi, T., Näsi, M., Oksanen, A., & Räsänen, P. (2016). *Online hate and harmful content: Cross-national perspectives* (p. 154). Taylor & Francis.

Kemp, S. (2021, July). Digital 2021 July Global Statshot report. Retrieved from: https://datareportal.com/reports/digital-2021-july-global-statshot.

Khattar, A., Dabas, K., Gupta, K., Chopra, S., & Kumaraguru, P. (2018). White or blue, the whale gets its vengeance: A social media analysis of the blue whale challenge. *arXiv preprint arXiv*:1801.05588.

Khine, A. T., Saw, Y. M., Htut, Z. Y., Khaing, C. T., Soe, H. Z., Swe, K. K., … & Hamajima, N. (2020). Assessing risk factors and impact of cyberbullying victimization among university students in Myanmar: A cross-sectional study. *PloS One, 15(1)*, e0227051.

Kumar, A., & Sachdeva, N. (2021). Multimodal cyberbullying detection using capsule network with dynamic routing and deep convolutional neural network. *Multimedia Systems, 28*, 1–10.

Kumari, K., Singh, J. P., Dwivedi, Y. K., & Rana, N. P. (2019). Aggressive social media post-detection system containing symbolic images. In *Digital Transformation for a Sustainable Society in the 21st Century: 18th IFIP WG 6.11 Conference on e-Business, e-Services, and e-Society, I3E 2019, Trondheim, Norway, September 18–20, 2019, Proceedings 18* (pp. 415–424). Springer International Publishing.

Legal Upanishad. (2022, May 23). Cybercrime in India: Landmark cases. Legal Upanishad. Retrieved from: https://legalupanishad.com/cybercrime-in-india-landmark-cases/.

Lobe, B., Velicu, A., Staksrud, E., Chaudron, S., & Rosanna, D. G. (2021). *How children (10–18) experienced online risks during the Covid-19 lockdown-Spring 2020: Key findings from surveying families in 11 European countries.* Publications Office of the European Union.

Lowry, P. B., Moody, G. D., & Chatterjee, S. (2017). Using IT design to prevent cyberbullying. *Journal of Management Information Systems, 34(3)*, 863–901.

Milosevic, T. (2018). *Protecting children online? Cyberbullying policies of social media companies.* The MIT Press.

Milosevic, T., Van Royen, K., & Davis, B. (2022). Artificial intelligence to address cyberbullying, harassment, and abuse: New directions in the midst of complexity. *International Journal of Bullying Prevention, 4(1)*, 1–5.

Milosevic, T., Verma, K., Carter, M., Vigil, S., Laffan, D., Davis, B., & O'Higgins Norman, J. (2023). Effectiveness of artificial intelligence-based cyberbullying interventions from youth perspective. *SocialMedia+Society, 9(1)*, 20563051221147325.

Mishna, F., Khoury-Kassabri, M., Gadalla, T., & Daciuk, J. (2012). Risk factors for involvement in cyberbullying: Victims, bullies and bully-victims. *Children and Youth Services Review, 34(1)*, 63–70.

Muhonen, T., Jönsson, S., & Bäckström, M. (2017). Consequences of cyberbullying behaviour in working life: The mediating roles of social support and social organisational climate. *International Journal of Workplace Health Management, 10(5)*, 376–390.

Nandhini, B. S., & Sheeba, J. I. (2015, March). Cyberbullying detection and classification using information retrieval algorithm. In *Proceedings of the 2015 International Conference on Advanced Research in Computer Science Engineering & Technology (ICARCSET 2015)* (pp. 1–5). ACM.

NCRB Data. (2021, November 14). Over 400% rise in cybercrime cases committed against children in 2020: NCRB data. The Economic Times. Retrieved from: https://economic-times.indiatimes.com/news/india/over-400-rise-in-cyber-crime-cases-committed-against-children-in-2020-ncrb-data/articleshow/87696995.cms?from=mdr.

Newall, M. (2018, June 27). Global views on cyberbullying. Technology & Telecom.Ispos. Retrieved from: https://www.ipsos.com/en/global-views-cyberbullying.

Olweus, D. (1994). *Bullying at school: Long-term outcomes for the victims and an effective school-based intervention program* (pp. 97–130). Springer US.

Ortega, R., Elipe, P., Mora-Merchán, J. A., Genta, M. L., Brighi, A., Guarini, A., ... & Tippett, N. (2012). The emotional impact of bullying and cyberbullying on victims: A European cross-national study. *Aggressive Behavior, 38(5)*, 342–356.

Our Range of Enforcement Options. (2020). Twitter. Retrieved from: https://help.twitter.com/en/rules-and-policies/enforcement-options. Accessed September 25, 2020.

PR Newswire. (2019, April 24). STOMP Out Bullying™ Launches Emma, the first AI platform designed to process and respond to cyberbullying. PR Newswire US. Retrieved from: https://www.prnewswire.com/news-releases/stomp-out-bullying-launches-emma-the-first-ai-platform-designed.

Raisi, E., & Huang, B. (2017). Cyberbullying detection with weakly supervised machine learning. In *Proceedings of the 2017 IEEE/ACM International Conference on Advances in Social Networks Analysis and Mining 2017* (pp. 409–416). IEEE.

Rosa, H., Pereira, N., Ribeiro, R., Ferreira, P. C., Carvalho, J. P., Oliveira, S., ... & Trancoso, I. (2019). Automatic cyberbullying detection: A systematic review. *Computers in Human Behavior, 93*, 333–345.

Sabella, R. A., Patchin, J. W., & Hinduja, S. (2013). Cyberbullying myths and realities. *Computers in Human Behavior, 29(6)*, 2703–2711.

Sakuma, A. (2019, March 3). Momo-challenge-hoax-explained. Retrieved from: https://www.vox.com/2019/3/3/18248783/momo-challenge-hoaxexplained.

Samghabadi, N. S., Monroy, A. P. L., & Solorio, T. (2020, May). Detecting early signs of cyberbullying in social media. In *Proceedings of the Second Workshop on Trolling, Aggression and Cyberbullying* (pp. 144–149). European Language Resources Association (ELRA).

Sangani, P. (2022, August 9). 85% of Indian children have been cyberbullied highest globally: McAfee. Economic Times. Retrieved from: https://economictimes.indiatimes.com/tech/technology/85-of-indian-children-have-been-cyberbullied-highest-globally-mcafee/articleshow/93438743.cms?from=mdr.

Steinmetz, K. (2019). Inside Instagram's war on bullying. Time. Retrieved from: https://time.com/5619999/instagram-mosseri-bullying-artificial-intelligence/.

Khazov-Cassia, S. (2017). Teen 'Suicide Games' Send Shudders Through Russian-Speaking World. *Radio Free Europe–Radio Liberty*. Teen 'Suicide Games' send shudders through Russian - Speaking world. Radio Free Europe Radio Liberty. Retrieved from: https://www.rferl.org/a/russia-teen-suicide-blue-whale-internet-social-media-game/28322884.html.

Van Geel, M., Vedder, P., & Tanilon, J. (2014). Relationship between peer victimization, cyberbullying, and suicide in children and adolescents: A meta-analysis. *JAMA Pediatrics, 168(5)*, 435–442.

Vats, A. (2019, July 10). Bullying: All you need to know about anti-bullying laws in India. iPleaders. Retrieved from: https://blog.ipleaders.in/bullying/.

Whittaker, E., & Kowalski, R. M. (2015). Cyberbullying via social media. *Journal of School Violence, 14(1)*, 11–29.

Wright, M. F. (2017). Cyberbullying in cultural context. *Journal of Cross-Cultural Psychology, 48(8)*, 1136–1137.

Wolke, D., & Lereya, S. T. (2015). Long-term effects of bullying. *Archives of Disease in Childhood, 100(9)*, 879–885.

Yao, M., Chelmis, C., & Zois, D. S. (2019, May). Cyberbullying ends here: Towards robust detection of cyberbullying in social media. In *The World Wide Web Conference* (pp. 3427–3433). Association for Computing Machinery.

Zhang, X., Tong, J., Vishwamitra, N., Whittaker, E., Mazer, J. P., Kowalski, R., ... & Dillon, E. (2016, December). Cyberbullying detection with a pronunciation-based convolutional neural network. In *2016 15th IEEE International Conference on Machine Learning and Applications (ICMLA)* (pp. 740–745). IEEE.

Zhao, R., Zhou, A., & Mao, K. (2016, January). Automatic detection of cyberbullying on social networks based on bullying features. In *Proceedings of the 17th International Conference on Distributed Computing and Networking* (pp. 1–6). ACM.

Zubair, M., Zubair, S., & Ahmed, M. (2023). Cyberbullying instilled in social media. In *Cybersecurity for smart cities* (pp. 17–29). Springer.

4 Explainable Artificial Intelligence for Cyberbullying Detection and Prevention in Social Media
A Conceptual Review

Nipuna Sankalpa Thalpage
Cardiff Metropolitan University

4.1 INTRODUCTION

Cyberbullying has become an alarming and pervasive issue in today's digital society, particularly within the realm of social media platforms. Research has highlighted the harmful effects of cyberbullying on individuals, including psychological distress, social isolation, and tragic consequences (Kim, Qian, & Aslam, 2020).

The nature of cyberbullying can vary, but it often includes spreading rumours, posting derogatory comments or images, sharing private or embarrassing information, impersonating someone else online, or engaging in online harassment campaigns. Cyberbullying can occur across different age groups, but it is particularly prevalent among children, teenagers, and young adults (Molenda, Marchlewska, & Rogoza, 2022).

According to National Voices for Equality, Education and Enlightenment (NVEEE), 61% of teens were victims of cyberbullying due to appearance and academic achievement and race having been other main reasons for getting cyberbullied (Djuraskovic, 2023).

Figure 4.1 presents the percentages of the main reasons for cyberbullying.

Consequently, there is an urgent need for effective detection and prevention mechanisms to address this pressing problem. Figure 4.2 shows the different kinds of effects cyberbullying caused on kids with their percentages.

Machine learning techniques for cyberbullying detection have become crucial in addressing the growing issue of cyberbullying as it has shown promise in automatically identifying and flagging instances of cyberbullying, leveraging the power of data analysis.

DOI: 10.1201/9781003393061-5

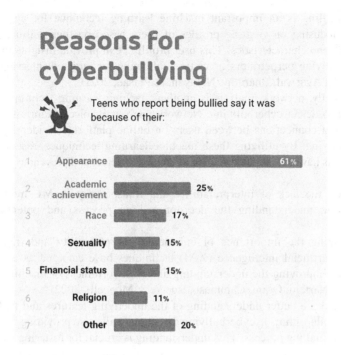

FIGURE 4.1   Reasons for cyberbullying (Djuraskovic, 2023).

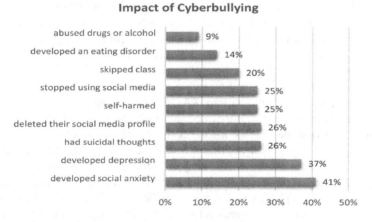

FIGURE 4.2   Effects of cyberbullying (Alduaila & Belghith, 2023).

These advanced machine learning techniques have proven effective in various aspects of cyberbullying detection Examples include text classification, which involves categorizing messages or posts as either cyberbullying or non-cyberbullying based on their content (Patacsil, 2019).

Sentiment analysis is another machine learning technique for cyberbullying, analysing the sentiment expressed in messages to identify bullying behaviour (Patacsil, 2019).

User profiling is an important machine learning technique for cyberbullying detection, focusing on creating profiles of users based on their online activities, behaviours, and characteristics. This user profiling can provide insights into potential cyberbullying perpetrators or victims, allowing for targeted interventions and support (Raj, Agarwal, Bharathy, Narayan, & Prasad, 2021).

Additionally, network analysis is another machine learning technique that can be applied to detect cyberbullying. Network analysis involves examining the relationships and connections between users on online platforms to identify patterns of cyberbullying. By utilizing these machine learning techniques, researchers and organizations have developed effective strategies to detect and prevent cyberbullying incidents.

However, the lack of interpretability and transparency in ML models poses challenges in understanding the decision-making process and potential biases involved.

Recognizing the importance of enhancing interpretability and transparency, explainable artificial intelligence (XAI) techniques have emerged as a promising approach to improving the understanding and trustworthiness of machine learning algorithms (Narteni, Orani, Cambiaso, Rucco, & Mongelli, 2022).

XAI enables a better understanding of the underlying features and patterns utilized by ML algorithms in cyberbullying detection, while also providing insights into the decision-making process. This understanding is crucial for fostering trust, confidence, and accountability in automated systems that handle cyberbullying incidents (Al-Harigy, Al-Nuaim, Moradpoor, & Tan, 2022).

The objective of this conceptual review chapter is to explore the integration of XAI with ML algorithms for cyberbullying detection and prevention within the context of social media platforms. This chapter aims to review existing research in the field, focusing on the challenges and limitations of current approaches. By examining the role of XAI in enhancing the interpretability of ML models, this study seeks to shed light on how XAI-driven approaches can empower users, moderators, and platform administrators in understanding and combating cyberbullying.

The chapter will delve into various XAI techniques and methodologies, including rule-based explanations, feature importance analysis, and visualizations. These techniques offer valuable insights into the decision-making processes of ML models, while also addressing ethical implications associated with automated cyberbullying detection systems. Moreover, the chapter will explore the potential benefits of leveraging XAI for proactive cyberbullying prevention in social media environments. XAI's interpretable explanations for model predictions can facilitate the identification of emerging patterns and trends related to cyberbullying, enabling timely intervention and preventive measures.

Overall, this conceptual review paper aims to provide a comprehensive overview of the state-of-the-art XAI-driven ML techniques for cyberbullying detection and prevention in social media. By examining the intersection of XAI, ML, and social media, this study aims to contribute to the advancement of transparent and accountable systems that effectively combat cyberbullying, fostering a safer and more inclusive online environment.

4.2   OVERVIEW OF CYBERBULLYING DETECTION TECHNIQUES

Cyberbullying detection techniques can be broadly classified into two categories: traditional and machine learning (ML) based approaches. Traditional techniques rely on predefined rules and keyword matching to identify instances of cyberbullying. These methods often lack the flexibility to adapt to evolving patterns and can struggle with detecting subtle forms of cyberbullying.

On the other hand, ML-based approaches leverage algorithms and statistical models to automatically learn patterns and features from labelled data. This enables the development of more sophisticated and accurate cyberbullying detection systems. ML techniques, such as natural language processing and deep learning, have shown promising results in accurately identifying cyberbullying content across various online platforms. Figure 4.3 shows a taxonomy of cyberbullying techniques in social media.

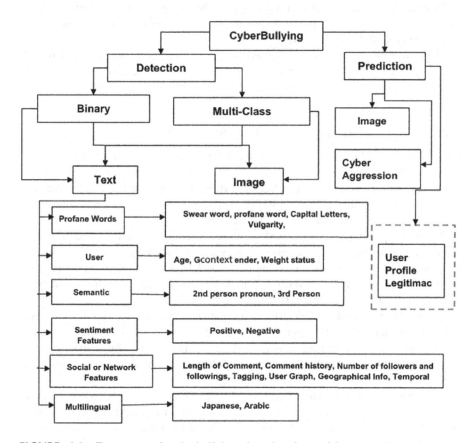

FIGURE 4.3   Taxonomy of cyberbullying detection in social media (Vyawahare & Chatterjee, 2020).

4.2.1 TRADITIONAL APPROACHES TO CYBERBULLYING DETECTION

Traditional approaches to cyberbullying detection include rule-based approaches, mixed-initiative approaches, and lexicon-based approaches (Salawu, He, & Lumsden, 2017).

Rule-based approaches match text to predefined rules to identify bullying, while mixed-initiative approaches combine human-based reasoning with one or more of the other approaches. Lexicon-based approaches involve using a predefined list of words and phrases that are indicative of cyberbullying (Hee, Jacobs, & Emmery, 2018).

While these traditional approaches have been used in the past, they have limitations in terms of accuracy and scalability (Salawu, He, & Lumsden, 2017). Machine learning (ML) based techniques have been proposed as an alternative approach to cyberbullying detection. These techniques involve training models on large datasets of labelled examples to identify patterns and features that are indicative of cyberbullying (Desai, Kalaskar, & Kumbhar, 2021).

Despite the limitations of traditional approaches, they are still used in combination with ML-based techniques to improve the accuracy of cyberbullying detection systems (Perera & Fernando, 2021).

Ongoing research works are focused on developing more accurate and robust models that can effectively address the challenges and limitations associated with both traditional and ML-based approaches to cyberbullying detection.

4.2.2 ML-BASED TECHNIQUES AND THEIR ADVANTAGES

Overall, ML-based techniques show promise for improving cyberbullying detection and prevention. It is important to consider all necessary features and to have a deep understanding of cyberbullying behaviour when developing ML-based models for cyberbullying detection. Figure 4.4 shows a simple workflow of using machine learning for cyberbullying detection using Twitter data.

ML-based techniques have gained significant attention in the field of cyberbullying detection due to their numerous advantages over traditional approaches. Recent studies have shown that deep learning (DL) models, such as recurrent neural networks (RNNs), outperform traditional ML algorithms, leading to higher accuracy in cyberbullying detection (Hasan, Hossain, & Mukta, 2023).

DL models are capable of identifying intricate patterns and features that are challenging for traditional ML algorithms to detect. Moreover, ML-based techniques excel in handling large volumes of data, making them well-suited for analysing social media platforms where massive amounts of data are generated daily (Raj, Singh, & Solanki, 2023).

Additionally, ML-based techniques exhibit flexibility in adapting to new types of cyberbullying, allowing for the detection of emerging forms of cyberbullying in real time (Raj, Singh, & Solanki, 2023). This real-time detection enables timely intervention and prevention strategies.

ML-based techniques also possess the ability to identify subtle forms of cyberbullying, including sarcasm and indirect bullying, which are often difficult for humans

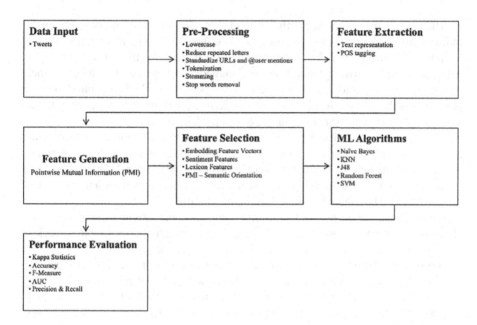

FIGURE 4.4 Simple workflow of using ML for cyberbullying detection (Bandeh Ali Talpur & Sullivan, 2020).

to detect (Hasan, Hossain, & Mukta, 2023). Moreover, these techniques can determine the severity of cyberbullying behaviour, enabling appropriate interventions and prevention strategies (Alsubari, 2022).

Furthermore, ML-based techniques enable the identification of language patterns used by bullies and their victims, facilitating a better understanding of cyberbullying behaviour and its impact (Reynolds, Kontostathis, & Edwards, 2011)

In summary, ML-based techniques offer numerous advantages for cyberbullying detection, including higher accuracy, the ability to handle large volumes of data, adaptability to new types of cyberbullying, real-time detection, detection of subtle forms of cyberbullying, identification of severity levels, and identification of language patterns. However, it is important to address the challenges and limitations associated with these techniques.

4.2.3 Challenges and Limitations in Current ML-Based Approaches

ML-based techniques encounter several challenges and limitations when applied to cyberbullying detection. One of the primary obstacles is the scarcity of labelled datasets, as ML models require substantial amounts of accurately labelled data for effective training and performance (Hasan, Hossain, & Mukta, 2023). Consequently, the lack of such datasets can impede the accuracy and efficacy of these models. Another limitation is the failure to consider all necessary features in traditional ML models used for cyberbullying detection. The omission of critical features can hinder the model's ability to accurately identify and classify bullying statements or posts, thereby compromising their effectiveness (Shah, Aparajit, & Chopdekar, 2020).

ML models may also face difficulties in detecting sarcasm and other forms of indirect bullying, which can undermine their efficacy in recognizing cyberbullying instances (Shah, Aparajit, & Chopdekar, 2020). Additionally, the generalizability of ML models across different platforms and languages may be limited. Models trained on data from one platform or language may not perform well when applied to other platforms or languages, hampering their effectiveness in identifying cyberbullying across diverse contexts (Shah, Aparajit, & Chopdekar, 2020).

The potential for false positives and false negatives is another concern with ML-based techniques for cyberbullying detection. The complex and variable nature of cyberbullying behaviour can lead to false positives, where non-bullying content is incorrectly identified as bullying, or false negatives, where actual instances of bullying are missed (Bandeh Ali Talpur & Sullivan, 2020).

Furthermore, obtaining labelled training data for cyberbullying detection poses a challenge, as it necessitates the involvement of human annotators who must review and label large amounts of data (Shah, Aparajit, & Chopdekar, 2020).

Another limitation lies in the inadequate focus on severity detection in existing ML-based techniques for cyberbullying. Many models do not prioritize identifying the severity of cyberbullying behaviour, which hampers their utility in developing appropriate interventions and prevention strategies (Bandeh Ali Talpur & Sullivan, 2020).

Despite these challenges, ongoing research works are dedicated to overcoming these limitations and developing more accurate and robust ML models for cyberbullying detection.

Additionally, greater attention should be given to the severity of cyberbullying behaviour to facilitate the formulation of effective interventions and prevention strategies.

4.3   USE OF EXPLAINABLE ARTIFICIAL INTELLIGENCE (XAI) TECHNIQUES FOR CYBERBULLYING DETECTION

Explainable artificial intelligence (XAI) plays a crucial role in machine learning (ML) for cyberbullying detection, providing interpretable insights into the decision-making processes of ML models and understanding how these models work and how they can be improved is essential (Ali, Abuhmed, & El-Sappagh, 2023), and XAI techniques facilitate this understanding.

Several studies highlight the significance of XAI in the context of ML for cyberbullying detection. For instance (Bandeh Ali Talpur & Sullivan, 2020), propose a framework for detecting cyberbullying behaviour and its severity in online social networks using machine learning techniques. They emphasize the importance of XAI in providing interpretable insights into the decision-making processes of ML models. Similarly (Alduailaj & Belghith, 2022), introduce the use of machine learning in the Arabic language for automatic cyberbullying detection, highlighting the role of XAI in ensuring transparency and accountability in decision-making processes. Mehta and Passi (2022) discuss the potential of XAI characteristics in hate speech detection using deep learning, emphasizing the interpretability it offers in ML models' decision-making processes.

XAI methodologies provide interpretable insights into ML models' decision-making processes. Rule-based explanations and feature importance analysis offer explanations and measures of feature importance (Belle & Ioannis Papantonis, 2021). Visualizations, prediction explanations, partial dependence plots, subpopulation analysis, individual prediction explanations, feature fit charts, and feature effects charts provide graphical representations and a detailed understanding of the model's decision-making (Heller, 2021).

Therefore, XAI techniques are crucial for understanding the decision-making processes of ML models in cyberbullying detection. They enable interpretable insights into how models work and how they can be improved, fostering transparency, accountability, and fairness.

4.4 PRIVACY, AND ACCOUNTABILITY CONCERNS AND ETHICAL CONSIDERATIONS OF USING XAI FOR CYBERBULLYING PREVENTION

The goal of XAI research is to make AI systems more comprehensible and transparent to humans, and explainability is one of the most crucial aspects (Ali, Abuhmed, & Sappagh, 2023). XAI is acknowledged as a crucial feature that provides the needed understandability and transparency to enable greater trust toward AI-based solutions (Inam, Terra, & Mujumdar, 2021). XAI can contribute to building assurance or justified confidence in AI systems, and it can help assess and mitigate AI risks to deploy AI with confidence (IBM.com, 2021). Explainability is a prerequisite for ascertaining other ethical AI principles, such as sustainability, justness, and fairness, and it allows for the monitoring of AI applications and development (Overgaag, 2023).

Exploring the ethical implications surrounding the deployment of XAI cyberbullying detection systems entails delving into a multitude of complex and thought-provoking issues. One significant consideration is the concept of autonomous experimentation systems, where the implementation of XAI systems can be seen as a form of independent exploration of users. This raises profound questions about the social and ethical implications associated with these systems, including their intricate design, potential effects on users, and the resistance they may encounter when common mitigations are applied (Bird, Barocas, & Crawford, 2016).

Ethical decision-making plays a crucial role in shaping the design and implementation of XAI tools and the associated processes. It requires a thorough examination of the fundamental principles that underpin ethical AI systems, as well as the strategies employed to achieve a broader sense of social responsibility in the realm of AI (Cheng, Varshney, & Liu, 2021). Moreover, the role of explainable AI (XAI) in the research field of AI ethics should not be underestimated. XAI provides invaluable transparency and comprehensibility in the deployment of cyberbullying detection systems, ensuring that the decision-making processes behind these systems can be readily understood and explained to the users (Vainio-Pekka, Agbese, Jantunen, & Vakkuri, 2023).

Security concerns also arise in the context of deploying XAI cyberbullying detection systems. These concerns encompass the potential vulnerabilities that may be exploited by malicious actors, posing risks such as black box attacks on explainable AI methods in cybersecurity. As a result, the development of a robust and secure application framework for XAI-based socio-technical systems becomes imperative (Kuppa & An Le-Khac, 2020).

Considering the broader scope, examining the ethical implications related to the deployment of XAI cyberbullying detection systems requires a comprehensive exploration of various interconnected facets. These include delving into the ethical dimensions of autonomous experimentation, weighing the impact of ethical decision-making on the design and deployment of XAI tools, appreciating the significance of explainability in fostering transparency, and addressing security concerns associated with the implementation of these systems.

In addition to ethical implications, the utilization of Artificial Intelligence (AI) gives rise to additional concerns about fairness, bias, privacy, and accountability. The tension arises from the nuanced, context-sensitive nature of fairness juxtaposed against the generic, one-size-fits-all principle underlying AI as a Service (AIaaS) (Lewicki, Ah Lee, & Cobbe, 2023). Legislation such as the Algorithmic Accountability Act aims to hold "covered entities" accountable for deploying AI systems in critical decision-making processes and ensuring that discriminatory outcomes are avoided through transparency and independence (Lewicki, Ah Lee, & Cobbe, 2023). To address biases, it is important to embrace transparency, independence, and rigorous evaluations of societal notions of fairness while considering the potential social costs involved (Lee, Resnick, & Barton, 2019). Ongoing research endeavours focus on employing datasets, metrics, techniques, and tools to detect and mitigate algorithmic unfairness and bias (Pagano, Rafael, & Fernanda, 2023). It is crucial to approach the development and adoption of AI systems with thorough consideration of the fairness risks they may entail.

In the realm of XAI, the overarching objective of research efforts is to enhance the comprehensibility and transparency of AI systems, with explainability playing a pivotal role in achieving this aim (Ali, Abuhmed, & Sappagh, 2023). XAI is widely recognized as an indispensable feature that fosters trust in AI solutions by providing users with a means to understand and interpret the decision-making processes of these systems (Inam, Terra, & Mujumdar, 2021).

Moreover, XAI contributes to the establishment of assurance and justified confidence in AI systems, enabling a thorough assessment and mitigation of potential risks associated with AI (IBM.com, 2021). The importance of explainability extends beyond mere transparency; it serves as a prerequisite for upholding other ethical principles in AI, such as sustainability, justness, and fairness. Additionally, explainability empowers the ongoing monitoring of AI applications and development, ensuring that ethical standards are upheld (Overgaag, 2023).

In summary, the exploration of ethical implications in the deployment of XAI cyberbullying detection systems encompasses a wide array of considerations. These include examining the ethical dimensions of autonomous experimentation systems, deliberating on ethical decision-making processes, appreciating the role of explainability in fostering transparency and comprehension, and addressing security concerns.

Furthermore, the broader landscape of AI ethics raises important issues related to fairness, bias, privacy, and accountability. Striving for fairness and mitigating biases, embracing transparency and independence, and continuously evaluating societal notions of fairness are essential in promoting responsible AI usage. Overall, the ethical deployment of XAI systems necessitates ongoing efforts to ensure the responsible and ethical utilization of AI technologies.

4.5 REAL-WORLD APPLICATIONS IN THE SOCIAL MEDIA CONTEXT

Real-world applications that integrate XAI with ML for cyberbullying identification and prevention in social media are still limited. While XAI research has gained attention in recent years, its integration into the specific domain of cyberbullying detection is an emerging area of study. Efforts have been made to explore the combination of XAI and ML techniques, but further research is needed to fully leverage the potential of XAI in effectively addressing cyberbullying on social media platforms.

These applications aim to detect cyberbullying messages from social media using machine learning algorithms such as SVM classifiers (Nahar, Li, & Pang, 2013). The focus of these applications is on automatic cyberbullying detection in social media text by modelling posts written by bullies, victims, and bystanders (Hee, Jacobs, & Emmery, 2018).

Figure 4.5 depicts the Flow of the SVM Algorithm in Finding Cyberbullying Users.

An effective approach to detect cyberbullying messages from social media through an SVM classifier algorithm has been proposed, along with a ranking algorithm to assess the severity of cyberbullying (Nahar, Li, & Pang, 2013). In addition, a deep learning framework has been proposed to evaluate real-time Twitter tweets or social media posts to detect cyberbullying (Raj, Singh, & Solanki, 2023). XAI plays

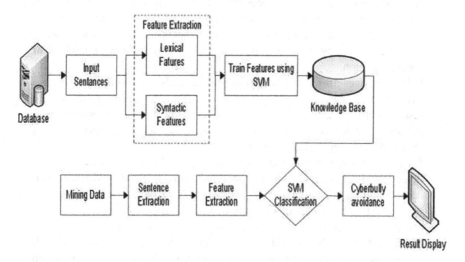

FIGURE 4.5 SVM algorithm for finding cyberbullying users (Boddu, 2020).

an important role in these applications by providing algorithmic accountability and transparency to enable greater trust towards AI-based solutions (Gillis & Wigmore, 2023).

The effectiveness and practicality of these applications depend on several factors, including the quality and quantity of data, the choice of machine learning algorithms, and the interpretability and explainability of the results. Further research is needed to evaluate the performance and impact of these applications in real-world settings and to address the ethical and social implications of cyberbullying detection and prevention.

4.6 CHALLENGES AND FUTURE DIRECTIONS

The literature identifies challenges and future directions in cyberbullying detection and prevention. These include addressing evolving cyberbullying techniques, ensuring algorithm scalability and adaptability, and improving the interpretability and explainability of ML models. Further research is needed to evaluate effectiveness in real-world settings and explore ethical and social implications.

4.6.1 CHALLENGES

Based on the literature that has been discussed, the issues outlined below can primarily be highlighted in this study.

- **Data Scarcity and Labelling:** The scarcity of labelled datasets and the effort required for data labelling pose challenges in training accurate ML models. Future research should focus on developing techniques for obtaining high-quality labelled data and exploring alternative learning paradigms that require fewer labelled examples.
- **Handling Sarcasm and Indirect Bullying:** ML models face challenges in accurately detecting sarcasm and other forms of indirect bullying, which are often prevalent in online interactions. Research should aim to improve the models' ability to understand and interpret these nuanced forms of communication.
- **False Positives and False Negatives:** ML models may produce false positives and false negatives in cyberbullying detection, leading to inaccurate results. Future research should focus on reducing these errors and improving the overall performance of the models through techniques such as ensemble learning and active learning.
- **Ethical Considerations:** The deployment of ML-based cyberbullying detection systems raises ethical concerns related to privacy, fairness, and accountability. Research should address these ethical considerations by developing frameworks and guidelines that ensure transparency, fairness, and protection of users' privacy rights.
- **Model Interpretability and Transparency:** The black box nature of ML models hampers their interpretability and transparency. Future research should focus on developing XAI techniques that provide meaningful explanations for the decisions made by ML models, enabling users to understand and trust the system's outputs.

- **Cross-Cultural and Multilingual Challenges:** ML models trained on data from one platform or language may not generalize well to other platforms or languages. Research should address the challenges of cross-cultural and multilingual cyberbullying detection by exploring techniques for transfer learning, adapting models to different cultural contexts, and improving language understanding capabilities.
- **Human-in-the-Loop Approaches:** Incorporating human judgment and feedback into ML-based cyberbullying detection systems can improve their accuracy and address the limitations of fully automated approaches. Future research should explore human-in-the-loop approaches that combine the strengths of ML algorithms with human expertise and judgment.
- **Long-Term Effects and Impact Evaluation:** Assessing the long-term effects and impact of ML-based cyberbullying detection systems on individuals, communities, and social media platforms is essential. Research should focus on evaluating the effectiveness and unintended consequences of these systems to ensure their positive impact on addressing cyberbullying.

4.6.2 FUTURE DIRECTIONS

Moving forward, there are several promising directions for research and development in the field of cyberbullying detection and prevention. One crucial area of focus is the integration of Explainable artificial intelligence (XAI) techniques with machine learning (ML) algorithms to enhance interpretability and transparency. By delving into various XAI methodologies such as rule-based explanations, feature importance analysis, and visualizations, researchers can gain insights into the decision-making processes of ML models, enabling a better understanding of the underlying features and patterns used to detect cyberbullying. Additionally, attention should be given to addressing the challenges and limitations associated with ML-based approaches, including the scarcity of labelled datasets, difficulties in detecting subtle forms of cyberbullying, and the potential for false positives and false negatives. Ongoing efforts aim to overcome these limitations and develop more accurate and robust ML models.

Furthermore, the utilization of XAI can extend beyond detection to proactive prevention by identifying emerging patterns and trends associated with cyberbullying, facilitating timely intervention and preventive measures. Ethical considerations and privacy concerns in deploying XAI-based cyberbullying detection systems also require further exploration to ensure transparency, fairness, and accountability.

Overall, these future directions hold promise in advancing transparent, accountable, and effective systems that combat cyberbullying and foster a safer and more inclusive online environment.

4.7 CONCLUSION

The findings of this chapter highlight that cyberbullying is a significant issue in today's digital society, with detrimental consequences for individuals and communities. The use of machine learning (ML) and artificial intelligence (AI) techniques, such as natural language processing and deep learning, shows promise in accurately identifying cyberbullying content across various online platforms. These advanced techniques leverage algorithms to analyse large amounts of data and detect patterns associated with cyberbullying behaviour.

ML-based techniques, particularly natural language processing and deep learning have proven effective in identifying cyberbullying instances. By analysing text and language patterns, these techniques can accurately detect and categorize cyberbullying content. The ability to process and analyse vast amounts of data in real time enhances the efficiency of cyberbullying detection systems. Moreover, ML algorithms can adapt and learn from new data, making them valuable tools in combating the constantly evolving nature of cyberbullying.

Despite the promising results, there are several limitations to consider when implementing ML-based cyberbullying detection systems. One key challenge is the availability of diverse and labelled datasets. Collecting and annotating datasets that encompass various forms and contexts of cyberbullying can be arduous due to the dynamic nature of online communication. Additionally, detecting subtle forms of cyberbullying, such as microaggressions or indirect threats, remains a challenge that requires further refinement of ML algorithms to capture the nuances of these behaviours accurately.

Another limitation is the potential for false positives and false negatives in cyberbullying detection. False positives occur when non-cyberbullying content is incorrectly classified as cyberbullying, while false negatives refer to missed or undetected cyberbullying instances. Achieving the right balance between sensitivity and specificity in ML algorithms is crucial to minimize both types of errors and ensure accurate and reliable results. Striking this balance is a complex task that requires ongoing research and development efforts.

Furthermore, ethical considerations and privacy concerns must be addressed when deploying AI-based cyberbullying detection systems. It is essential to ensure transparency, fairness, and accountability in the design and implementation of these systems to prevent the infringement of individuals' rights and mitigate biases or discriminatory outcomes. Collaborative efforts among researchers, policymakers, technology companies, educators, and communities are necessary to develop comprehensive approaches that combine technological solutions with education, awareness campaigns, and supportive environments to effectively combat cyberbullying.

In summary, while ML and AI techniques offer promising solutions for cyberbullying detection, it is crucial to recognize the limitations and challenges associated with their implementation. By addressing these limitations and considering ethical and privacy considerations, we can work towards creating a safer online environment that empowers individuals and fosters digital resilience.

REFERENCES

Al-Harigy LM, Al-Nuaim HA, Moradpoor N, Tan Z. Building towards Automated Cyberbullying Detection: A Comparative Analysis. Comput Intell Neurosci. 2022 Jun 25;2022:4794227. doi: 10.1155/2022/4794227. PMID: 35789611; PMCID: PMC9250443.

Alduailaj, A. M., & Belghith, A. (2022). Detecting Arabic Cyberbullying Tweets Using Machine Learning. *Machine Learning & Knowledge Extraction 5(1)*, 29–42. doi:10.3390/make5010003

Ali, S., Abuhmed, T., & El-Sappagh, S. (2023). Explainable Artificial Intelligence (XAI): What We Know and What Is Left to Attain Trustworthy Artificial Intelligence. *Information Fusion 99*, 101805. doi:10.1016/j.inffus.2023.101805

Alsubari, S. N. (2022). Cyberbullying Identification System Based Deep Learning Algorithms. *Electronics 11(20)*, 3273. doi:10.3390/electronics11203273

Belle, V., & Papantonis, I. (2021). Principles and Practice of Explainable Machine Learning. *Frontiers in Big Data 4*, 688969. doi:10.3389/fdata.2021.688969

Bird, S., Barocas, S., & Crawford, K. (2016). Exploring or Exploiting? Social and Ethical Implications of Autonomous Experimentation in AI. Workshop on Fairness, Accountability, and Transparency in Machine Learning, 2016. Retrieved from https://papers.ssrn.com/sol3/papers.cfm?abstract_id=2846909

Boddu, R. N., 2020. Detect and Prevent the Cyber bullying Conversation's on Social Media Using Machine Learning Algorithm.

Cheng, L., Varshney, K., & Liu, H. (2021). Socially Responsible AI Algorithms. *Journal of Artificial Intelligence Research 71*, 1137–1181. doi:10.1613/jair.1.12814

Desai, A., Kalaskar, S., & Kumbhar, O. (2021). Cyber Bullying Detection on Social Media Using Machine Learning. ITM Web of Conferences. doi:10.1051/itmconf/20214003038

Djuraskovic, O. (2023). Cyberbullying Statistics, Facts, and Trends (2023) with Charts. [Online] Retrieved from https://firstsiteguide.com/cyberbullying-stats

Gillis, A. S., & Wigmore, I. (2023). Explainable AI (XAI). Retrieved from www.Techtarget.com: https://www.techtarget.com/whatis/definition/explainable-AI-XAI

Hasan, M. T., Hossain, M. A., & Mukta, S. H. (2023). A Review on Deep-Learning-Based Cyberbullying Detection. *Future Internet 15(5)*, 179. doi:10.3390/fi15050179

Hee, C. V., Jacobs, G., & Emmery, C. (2018). Automatic Detection of Cyberbullying in Social Media Text. *PLoS One 13(10)*, e0203794. doi:10.1371/journal.pone.0203794

Heller, M. (2021). Explainable AI Explained. Retrieved from https://www.infoworld.com/article/3634602/explainable-ai-explained.html

IBM.com. (2021). What Is Explainable AI (XAI)? Retrieved from https://www.ibm.com/watson/explainable-ai

Inam, R., Terra, A., & Mujumdar, A. (2021). Explainable AI How Humans Can Trust AI. Retrieved from https://www.ericsson.com/en/reports-and-papers/white-papers/explainable-ai--how-humans-can-trust-ai

Kim YJ, Qian L, Aslam MS. Development of a Personalized Mobile Mental Health Intervention for Workplace Cyberbullying Among Health Practitioners: Protocol for a Mixed Methods Study. JMIR Res Protoc. 2020 Nov 20;9(11):e23112. doi: 10.2196/23112. PMID: 33216000; PMCID: PMC7718091.

Kuppa, A., & An Le-Khac, N. (2020). Black Box Attacks on Explainable Artificial Intelligence (XAI) Methods in Cyber Security. IEEE International Joint Conference on Neural Networks (IJCNN). doi:10.1109/IJCNN48605.2020.9206780

Lee, N. T., Resnick, P., & Barton, G. (2019). Algorithmic Bias Detection and Mitigation: Best Practices and Policies to Reduce Consumer Harms. Retrieved from https://www.brookings.edu/research/algorithmic-bias-detection-and-mitigation-best-practices-and-policies-to-reduce-consumer-harms/

Lewicki, K., Ah Lee, M. S., & Cobbe, J. (2023). Out of Context: Investigating the Bias and Fairness Concerns of "Artificial Intelligence as a Service". Proceedings of the 2023 CHI Conference on Human Factors in Computing Systems. doi:10.1145/3544548.3581463

Mehta, H., & Passi, K. (2022). Social Media Hate Speech Detection Using Explainable Artificial Intelligence (XAI). *Algorithms 15(8)*, 291. doi:10.3390/a15080291

Molenda, Z. A., Marchlewska, M., Rogoza, M., Michalski, P., Górska, P., Szczepańska, D., & Cislak, A. (2022). What Makes an Internet Troll? On the Relationships between Temperament (BIS/BAS), Dark Triad, and Internet trolling. Cyberpsychology. *Journal of Psychosocial Research on Cyberspace*, 16(5), Article 11. https://doi.org/10.5817/CP2022-5-11

Nahar, V., Li, X., & Pang, C. (2013). An Effective Approach for Cyberbullying Detection. Computer Science. Retrieved from https://www.semanticscholar.org/paper/An-Effective-Approach-for-Cyberbullying-Detection-Nahar-Li/6a3fe8cec79c345da5be bd33a21bd76b94230a62

Narteni, S. et al., 2022. On the Intersection of Explainable and Reliable AI for Physical Fatigue Prediction. doi: 10.1109/ACCESS.2022.3191907

Overgaag, A. (2023). What Is Explainable AI (XAI)? Retrieved from www.cointelegraph.com: https://cointelegraph.com/explained/what-is-explainable-ai-xai

Pagano, T. P., Rafael, B., & Fernanda, V. L. (2023). Bias and Unfairness in Machine Learning Models: A Systematic Review on Datasets, Tools, Fairness Metrics, and Identification and Mitigation Methods. *Big Data and Cognitive Computing 7(1)*, 15. doi:10.3390/bdcc7010015

Patacsil, Frederick. (2019). Analysis of Cyberbullying Incidence among Filipina Victims: A Pattern Recognition using Association Rule Extraction.

Perera, A., & Fernando, P. A. (2021). Accurate Cyberbullying Detection and Prevention on Social Media. *Procedia Computer Science 181*, 605–611. doi:10.1016/j.procs.2021.01.207

Raj, M., Singh, S., & Solanki, K. (2023). An Application to Detect Cyberbullying Using Machine Learning and Deep Learning Techniques. *SN Computer Science 3*, 401. doi:10.1007/s42979-022-01308-5

Raj, Chahat & Agarwal, Ayush & Bharathy, Gnana & Narayan, Bhuva & Prasad, Mukesh. (2021). Cyberbullying Detection: Hybrid Models Based on Machine Learning and Natural Language Processing Techniques. Electronics. 10. 2810. 10.3390/electronics10222810.

Reynolds, K., Kontostathis, A., & Edwards, L. (2011). Using Machine Learning to Detect Cyberbullying. International Conference on Machine Learning and Applications (ICMLA). doi:10.1109/ICMLA.2011.152

Salawu, S., He, Y., & Lumsden, J. (2017). Approaches to Automated Detection of Cyberbullying: A Survey. *IEEE Transactions on Affective Computing 11(1)*, 3–24. doi:10.1109/TAFFC.2017.2761757

Shah, R., Aparajit, S., & Chopdekar, R. (2020). Machine Learning Based Approach for Detection of Cyberbullying Tweets. *International Journal of Computer Applications 175(37)*, 51–56. doi:10.5120/ijca2020920946

Tapir, B. A., & Sullivan, D. (2020). Cyberbullying Severity Detection: A Machine Learning Approach. *PLoS One 15(10)*, e0240924. doi:10.1371/journal.pone.0240924

Vainio-Pekka, H., Agbese, M. O.-O., Jantunen, M., & Vakkuri, V. (2023). The Role of Explainable AI in the Research Field of AI Ethics. *The ACM Transactions on Interactive Intelligent Systems*. ACM. doi:10.1145/3599974

Vyawahare, M., & Chatterjee, M. (2020). Taxonomy of Cyberbullying Detection and Prediction Techniques in Online Social Networks. *Data Communication and Networks* (pp. 21–37). Springer. doi:10.1007/978-981-15-0132-6_3

Part 2

Machine Learning Techniques
and Cyberbullying Detection

5 Combating Cyberbullying in Various Digital Media Using Machine Learning

Biodoumoye George Bokolo and Qingzhong Liu
Sam Houston State University

5.1 INTRODUCTION

Social media networks are communication technologies that have transformed the manner in which people interact and communicate. The importance of social media has been recognized globally and companies use social media to expand their business as well as to develop specific tools. Social media has significantly expanded the areas of coverage in which traditional media (television, radio, and newspapers) were not used to reach the masses, whether individuals or masses (Hsu 2022). Nowadays, many people carry cell phones which makes this medium more accessible. Social media now plays an important role in mass communication, as technology has a role in defining what is important for society. It can make an organization more efficient, faster, and more effective (Islam et al. 2020; Nunan & Di Domenico 2019).

Furthermore, social media improves relationships between people and organizations and people's power to share information in modern society. Social media remains a set of online platforms through which individuals communicate, network, share content, and engage in social interactions. During times of crisis such as natural disasters or acts of terror, social media has become a vital tool in communication. Social media has also become an avenue for ordinary citizens to disseminate public safety information. Due to the extensive and interactive nature of social media, the user community within social media can be used to facilitate social interaction in a community. Social media tools can be used to connect those who are in the same location or who share a certain characteristic (e.g., race, geographic region, occupation, or even political beliefs) for the purpose of finding common interests. Social media also allows individuals to interact with others across the globe with virtual face-to-face interaction. As a means of communication, social media is not as widely used as it could be. Some factors contribute to the absence of its widespread adoption (Greifeneder et al. 2021).

5.1.1 DISASTERS OF SOCIAL MEDIA

The disasters of social media include ruining reputation, wasting time in people's lives, gaining a wrong perspective of people's lives, reducing the quality of life of

DOI: 10.1201/9781003393061-7

people, and losing confidence due to comparison to others' lives on social media platforms. The disadvantage of social media is the risk of its participating in defamation, spreading rumors, hate speeches, piracy, and theft. People have been reluctant to adopt social media because of several negative incidents that have occurred. People fear that they will lose their privacy or be abused. Individuals do not know what to post on social media because there are not enough guidelines for them to do so. People do not have the time to use social media because they are busy with work and many other priorities, these numbers also somewhat equate to the multitude that uses social media by the second and even make it a full-time paying job. Another significant contributor to the lack of social media adoption is that people believe social media may be used by cybercriminals to harm their reputations or misuse their personal information. This belief makes them hesitant to adopt social media (Bonanno 2021).

5.1.2 What is Cyberbullying?

Cyberbullying, the term used to describe bullying that occurs online or through mobile devices, has become more prevalent in recent years (Chen et al. 2023). Cyberbullying is characterized as "an aggressive, intentional act carried out by a group or individual, using electronic forms of contact, repeatedly and over time against a victim who cannot easily defend him or herself" (Smith et al. 2008). Teenagers now possess the same level of power for computing that, just a few years ago, was only accessible to big businesses. How does a young individual handle the power that comes with technology and the expanding access to it? The majority of learners use technology properly, but a few have opted to use it irresponsibly by hurting, humiliating, embarrassing, and directly assaulting others (Smith et al. 2008).

5.1.3 Possible Reasons for Cyberbullying on Social Media

Notwithstanding, the fact that people spend more time on social media enables them to commit all sorts of morally impermissible crimes. Some people do commit such crimes as a form of their jobs. These crimes range from creating and disseminating malicious content and comments and distorting the various social media networks with hateful content, and cyberstalking which is not a crime but becomes one when it turns into in-person stalking. Some reasons for these are religious beliefs, political views, racial differences, cultural backgrounds, and even just nation-to-national terrorism and attacks (Zorlu 2023; Alismaiel 2023). Some people will say they are growing their brand and getting attention through online harassment and cyberbullying. Some people feel powerful when they hurt others. The others have very low self-esteem and so they improve their already low self-esteem and confidence by undermining and bullying people. This genuinely never improves their self-esteem or quality of life. According to a survey of teens conducted by the National Council on Crime Prevention, 81% of them claimed they believe other people cyberbully them because they find it amusing. Cyberbullies may not be aware of the harm they are causing because they don't see their victims' actual emotions (DELETE CYBERBULLYING 2023).

The misuse of websites, SMS messages, mobile phones, emails, and other information and communication technologies to socially isolate, harass, threaten, or degrade a person is known as cyberbullying. Identity theft, online monitoring, email spamming, hate speech, personal abuse, and cyberbullying are all examples of cyber harassment. Many people are impacted by cyberbullying; in fact, over 500,000 students (age 18 and up) have been identified as victims in the United States alone (Kizza 2023). Compared to other types of bullying, cyberbullying is more likely to go unreported by parents and administrators. This is because victims felt that they had to figure out how to handle it on their own and were afraid that if they alerted their parents, their internet rights would be curtailed or removed entirely (Parveen et al. 2023).

5.1.4 EFFECTS OF CYBERBULLYING

Youth activists have long been concerned about bullying (e.g., educators, counselors, researchers, policymakers). Cyberbullying, or bullying committed using online technology, has recently filled the news as a significant issue facing today's teenagers (Huang et al. 2023). "Cyberbullying is a learned behavior that becomes automated over time via experience and reinforcement" (Barlett 2023). Some article reviews the empirical data that is currently accessible to assess the veracity of statements that are frequently made about cyberbullying. Studies dispelled several myths that are perpetuated by media stories and unsupported public statements about the type and scope of cyberbullying (Sabella et al. 2013).

Although there are some differences between the forms, in reality, cyberbullying behaviors frequently resemble psychological, relational, and indirect forms of traditional bullying (such as spreading rumors, harassing, threatening, and excluding). First, temporary email and instant messaging accounts, anonymizers, and pseudonyms in social networking sites, chat rooms, and message boards are ways that cyberbullies can continue to stay "virtually" anonymous. Despite this, studies indicate that the majority of victims are aware of who is harassing them, or at least believe they are, and that this person is frequently a member of their social network (Kowalski & Limber 2007; Hinduja & Patchin 2009a, b).

Like traditional crime, cybercrime has greatly increased in prevalence, has a wide range of unique characteristics, and happens in a variety of settings. On the other end of the spectrum, cybercrime can involve juvenile predatory behavior, stock market manipulation, extortion, blackmail, cyberstalking, and cyber harassment. Online communities are unethically used to harass people and incite hatred among groups. The official word for bullying that only occurs online is cyberbullying. Along with the expansion of users on social media platforms, the problem of harassment has also gotten worse. The victim's emotional, physical, and mental well-being are all negatively affected by this. Cyberbullies use social networking platforms like Twitter, Facebook, Instagram, and YouTube to attack individuals online. Figure 5.1 shows the trends in the growth of various social media platforms.

The emergence and widespread use of digital media platforms such as YouTube, TikTok, Kaggle, Instagram, Facebook, and Twitter, have revolutionized the way people communicate and interact with one another (Myers et al. 2023). However, these

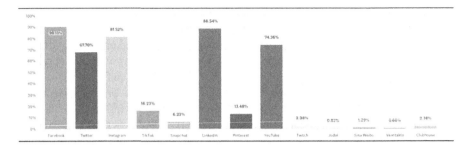

FIGURE 5.1   The state of social media platforms in 2022 (Lange 2022).

platforms have also given rise to a new form of bullying known as cyberbullying. Cyberbullying refers to the use of digital technology to harass, intimidate, or harm individuals online (Dwumah Manu et al. 2023). It is a complex and pervasive issue that affects people of all ages and backgrounds and can have serious psychological and emotional impacts on victims. In some cases, cyberbullying can even lead to physical harm and even suicide (Sultan et al. 2023).

5.1.5   MACHINE LEARNING: THE SOLUTION

Given the severity of the problem, there has been an increasing interest in finding effective methods to combat cyberbullying (Rębisz et al. 2023). While traditional approaches such as parental supervision and school-based interventions have been effective to some extent, they have proven to be inadequate in addressing the scale and complexity of the problem (Biernesser et al. 2023). As such, researchers have turned to technological solutions such as machine learning algorithms to address this issue (Sorrentino et al. 2023).

Machine learning is a subfield of artificial intelligence that enables computers to learn from data and make predictions or decisions based on that data (Bakomichalis 2023). Machine learning algorithms are increasingly being used to analyze and classify text and image data, making them well-suited to detecting and preventing cyberbullying in digital media platforms. The ability of machine learning algorithms to identify patterns and anomalies in large datasets has proven to be an effective approach to detecting cyberbullying in real-time (Dedeepya et al. 2023; Alduailaj & Belghith 2023).

This chapter aims to provide an overview of the use of machine learning algorithms in combating cyberbullying on various digital media platforms such as YouTube, Kaggle, Twitter, and Instagram. Specifically, the chapter will explore the potential benefits and challenges of using machine learning to detect and prevent cyberbullying, including the technical and ethical considerations that must be addressed. The chapter will also review the existing literature on the use of machine learning in combating cyberbullying, and present the results of a survey of current approaches and tools being used in this field. Overall, the chapter aims to provide insights into the current state of research on the use of machine learning in combating cyberbullying and identify areas for future research and development in this important field.

In our research, we build a Naive Bayes and BiLSTM detection model with the ability to detect cyberbullying content on online platforms.

5.2   LITERATURE REVIEW

The harmful effects of cyberbullying are getting worse every day, and there are still very few technical solutions that enable appropriate action to be taken through automated detection. Studies on the detection of cyberbullying up until now have only looked at individual remarks, ignoring contexts like user characteristics and profile information. In this article, they demonstrate how user context can help with cyberbullying detection. It has to do with posting, commenting, or liking. These studies were first presented at the Automated Cyberbullying Detection Workshop in Dublin in December 2012 and recently appeared in the journal Computers in Human Behavior. One of the main issues with cyberbullying detection is that it uses several different forms of analysis: content, metadata, image, etc. Often, different techniques assume different levels of knowledge about the circumstances that surround the comment. For instance, a criminal reference check may suggest that a person has said certain things in the past. A text mining approach may be able to detect more vulgar words, while another approach may be more sensitive to jokes that are accompanied by punchlines. For a variety of reasons, it is unlikely that any single technique will solve the problem of cyberbullying. By combining several techniques, researchers were able to achieve greater accuracy and avoid false positives. Researchers included different scenarios in this study: jokes, comments made on Twitter, and general conversation among users on a message board. After reviewing the content and metadata associated with the post, they then used machine learning algorithms to find phrases that were not descriptive but which showed signs of being targeted. First, they scanned for posts containing target words, phrases, or emojis which appeared to be on the verge of bullying or harassment. Second, they searched for comments made from the very first sentence of the comment to the very last sentence, to detect comments that are immediately targeted at the child. This approach is known as the contextual preamble. Finally, the researchers used a basic sentiment analysis method that looked at the message and the speaker to identify comments that were personal and marked in all three ways: targeted, attacking, and negative (Dadvar et al. 2013).

To identify cyberbullying, this study examines the impact of users' personality traits and emotions conveyed through textual communications on YouTube using several ensemble classifiers. The Big Five model was used to determine personality characteristics, whereas Ekman's fundamental theory of emotions was used to determine emotions. Several ensemble classifiers, including Random Forest and AdaBoost, were used to identify cyberbullying incidents from annotated English-language YouTube text comments ($N = 5,152$; 2,576 bullying versus 2,576 non-bullying instances). Performance metrics, with accuracy and F-score values of over 95%, showed personality traits and emotions to greatly improve the detection of cyberbullying presence. Anger and openness were found to be more profound than other emotions and personalities, according to more in-depth research. Also, the behavior of users who were more likely to post comments against others showed them to be prone to angry and pessimistic sentiments. You can identify cyberbullying using several types of analyses: content, metadata, and image. As you can see, these techniques are usually applied to very different types of problems. What we see here is that the higher-performing algorithms for each type of analysis tend to perform better than each other. If you can uncover the words, images, and metadata associated with a message or comment, you can reliably detect cyberbullying and conduct sentiment analysis on it. The first set of analyses is most similar to how many users interact with social media, but the second set is more tailored for more complex situations. This is one of the issues with cyberbullying detection: while the techniques above address different facets of it, they usually apply them to very different scenarios and communication types. Additionally, cyberbullying is frequently motivated by joy, disgust, and dread in neurotic people. The results demonstrate that personality and emotions are important factors in cyberbullying, and recognizing particular personality characteristics and feelings can aid in the development of a more strategic intervention plan (Balakrishnan & Ng 2022).

Many societies deal with the issue of cyberbullying. Social media platforms have been impacted by cyberbullying as a result of their popularity and interactive character. Arab social media users have also claimed to have experienced harassment. Scientists have used machine learning methods extensively to identify and combat this phenomenon. Based on a labeled dataset of Arabic YouTube comments, we evaluate various machine learning algorithms for their effectiveness in detecting cyberbullying in this article. Considered are the Multinomial Naive Bayes (MNB), Complement Naive Bayes (CNB), and Linear Regression machine learning algorithms (LR). Additionally, we test out the CountVectorizer and TfidfVectorizer, two feature extraction techniques. The findings demonstrate that the Logistic Regression model may surpass both Multinomial and Complement Naive Bayes models using CountVectorizer feature extraction. Nevertheless, the Complementary Naive Bayes model can perform better than the other two models when using TfidfVectorizer feature extraction. This further illustrates the importance of attention to the components of an evaluation that offer greater accuracy. Finally, we find that ignoring emotion regarding judging cyberbullying can lead to an increased detection rate. An unexpected finding is that the machine learning algorithm performed the best, scoring better than even human experts on these dimensions. This reflects that emotion is a factor in the causation of cyberbullying (Alsubait & Alfageh 2021).

This study provides a user-based Big Five and Dark Triad-based user personality-based cyberbullying detection model. The model uses relationships between personality characteristics and cyberbullying to identify bullying trends within Twitter communities. For the classification of cyberbullying (i.e., aggressor, spammer, bully, and normal), Random Forest, a well-known machine learning algorithm, was used in combination with a baseline algorithm consisting of seven Twitter characteristics (i.e., number of mentions, number of followers and following, popularity, favorite count, status count, and number of hashtags). Findings show that taking into account a user's disposition significantly enhances cyberbullying detection processes. Extraversion, agreeableness, neuroticism (the Big Five), and psychopathy (the Dark Triad) were found to be important in identifying bullies, with accuracy and specificity rates of up to 96% and 95%, respectively. Current empirical investigations that demonstrate the connections between personality traits and cyberbullying are supported by the appearance of important personality traits in an experimental study. Results also show that previous investigations performed at an international level could not be based on the same theoretical framework used in the present work. These findings also provide an overview of results that are consistent with related studies across various domains such as the genetic hypothesis, general media effects, and individual differences in ethics (Balakrishnan et al. 2019).

In a crime known as cyberbullying, a victim is the focus of online harassment and hate. Many methods for detecting cyberbullying have been developed, but they mainly rely on textual and user characteristics. The majority of the research studies that were discovered in the literature sought to increase detection by adding new features. However, the feature extraction and selection stages get more difficult as the number of features rises. Another disadvantage of these advancements is that some characteristics, like user age, can be easily faked. In this article, we suggest an innovative solution to the aforementioned problems: optimized Twitter cyberbullying detection based on deep learning (OCDD). OCDD does not extract features from tweets and feed them to a classifier, in contrast to earlier work in this area; instead, it shows a text as a collection of word vectors. By doing this, the feature extraction and selection stages can be skipped while still maintaining the meaning of the words. Deep learning will be used in the classification step, along with a metaheuristic optimization algorithm for parameter tuning. These features are used to classify bullies and normal users, and the model helps reduce error rates for this task by a significant factor, as compared to existing methods. Further application of OCDD techniques can improve the detection of cyberbullying and can also provide a new perspective on the role of cyberbullying on mental health. The research provides a unique insight into the field of cyberbullying detection, as well as an overview of relevant findings from other fields (Al-Ajlan & Ykhlef 2018).

Cyberbullying is on the rise and has turned into a significant risk that users of social media may experience as a result of the widespread use of PCs and smartphones as well as the rise of user-generated content in social networking services. A majority of online bullying is committed by children. Therefore, many social media sites provide tools and features that allow the user to report cyberbullying by contacting the platforms concerned. However, this process is often difficult and time-consuming. Several meta-analysis studies have shown that social media platforms often use their blacklists of user-generated content that violates their community standards as well as algorithms to block certain users. Due to their size and increasing popularity, these blacklists and algorithms are often unable to handle the vast amount of report requests and do not always represent the common practice of user-generated content on social media platforms. To address this challenge, we have developed a learning algorithm for cyberbullying detection, that is, we use a deep learning classifier in the automatic mode to identify cyberbullying users and we train it with the data obtained from Twitter. Using multiple textual features extracted from the Japanese text on Twitter, we built an ideal model for the automatic detection of cyberbullying in this article. We then investigate the effects of these features using a variety of machine learning models. The results of the experimental assessment demonstrate that the best model with textual predictive features can achieve an accuracy of over 90%.

This information can be used to prevent cyberbullying in the future by deploying the model on Twitter, in support of Twitter users (Zhang et al. 2019).

The paper provides a summary of cyberbullying, which primarily takes place on social networking sites, as well as the problems and difficulties associated with its detection. This essay's discussion of the subject begins with an introduction to cyberbullying, including its definition, categories, and responsibilities. Then, in the section on detecting cyberbullying, the features, data sources, and classification methods are examined. The well-known methods for locating bullying-related terms within the corpus are natural language processing (NLP) and machine learning. Finally, problems and difficulties in detecting cyberbullying are emphasized and discussed (Ali et al. 2018).

The production of aggressive language online, such as assaults, abuse, and denigration, has increased as more people use social media platforms. However, it can be challenging to identify violent language online due to the continuously evolving and diverse forms of online language. Not only is this a challenging task, but there is room for study and development in this field given the harm that cyberviolence causes to children, women, and racial prejudice victims, as well as the seriousness of cyberbullying's repercussions. The model for detecting racism and sexism on social media (Twitter) based on TextCNN and Word2Vec sentiment analysis proposed in this study achieves 96.9% and 98.4% accuracy and detects some violent terms (Lange 2020).

5.3   METHODOLOGY

The proposed model structure is seen in Figure 5.2.

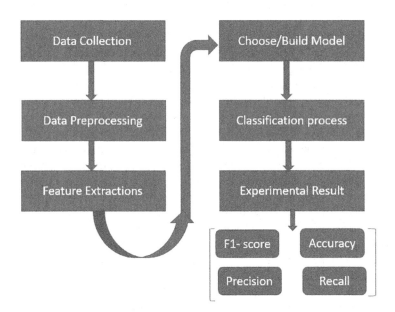

FIGURE 5.2   The proposed methodology.

5.3.1   Collect Data

This dataset is an amalgamation of datasets relating to the automated detection of cyberbullying from various sources. The information comes from various social media sites, including YouTube, Twitter, Wikipedia Talk sections, and Kaggle. Text is present in the data, classified as bullying or not. The information includes various forms of cyberbullying, including hate speech, hostility, insults, and poisonous language. The data includes positive and neutral, negative comments, as well as comments that contain cyberbullying (Shahan 2022).

The following datasets Figures 5.3 and 5.4 were merged to create one dataset for the purpose of this analysis:

- Aggression parsed dataset
- Attack parsed dataset
- Kaggle parsed dataset
- Toxicity parsed dataset
- Twitter parsed dataset
- Twitter racism parsed dataset
- Twitter Sexism parsed dataset
- YouTube parsed dataset

These datasets contain various forms of cyberbullying and cyberbullying content ranging from platforms like Kaggle, and Twitter to YouTube. The data encompasses aggressive statements, statements of attacks, racism, and sexism. The data frame concatenation command was used to merge all the datasets together in Figure 5.5 and form one dataset for the process of the analysis. The dataset sentiments came labeled as zeros and ones, which are positive and negative respectively.

5.3.2   Pre-processing and Feature Extraction

First, the obtained data was processed. The datasets combined include many URLs, hashtags, and emojis. These should be eliminated in the first step making sure that the tweet content contains all lowercase letters. In the third stage, tokenization transactions are performed. Then, the stop words in the data are cleared. A relatively better dataset is processed with label encoding. The data is separated as test and

```
Out[3]:  ['aggression_parsed_dataset.csv',
          'attack_parsed_dataset.csv',
          'kaggle_parsed_dataset.csv',
          'toxicity_parsed_dataset.csv',
          'twitter_parsed_dataset.csv',
          'twitter_racism_parsed_dataset.csv',
          'twitter_sexism_parsed_dataset.csv',
          'youtube_parsed_dataset.csv']
```

FIGURE 5.3   The different datasets.

```
df3 = pd.read_csv(r'toxicity_parsed_dataset.csv')[['Text', 'oh_label']]
df3.head()
```

	Text	oh_label
0	This: :One can make an analogy in mathematical...	0
1	` :Clarification for you (and Zundark's righ...	0
2	Elected or Electoral? JHK	0
3	`This is such a fun entry. Devotchka I once...	0
4	Please relate the ozone hole to increases in c...	0

```
df4 = pd.read_csv(r'kaggle_parsed_dataset.csv')[['Text', 'oh_label']]
df4.head()
```

	Text	oh_label
0	"You fuck your dad."	1
1	"i really don't understand your point.\xa0 It ...	0
2	"A\\xc2\\xa0majority of Canadians can and has ...	0
3	"listen if you dont wanna get married to a man...	0
4	"C\xe1c b\u1ea1n xu\u1ed1ng \u0111\u01b0\u1edd...	0

```
df5 = pd.read_csv(r'twitter_parsed_dataset.csv')[['Text', 'oh_label']]
df5.head()
```

	Text	oh_label
0	@halalflaws @biebervalue @greenlinerzjm I read...	0.0
1	@ShreyaBafna3 Now you idiots claim that people...	0.0
2	RT @Mooseoftorment Call me sexist, but when I ...	1.0
3	@g0ssipsquirrelx Wrong, ISIS follows the examp...	1.0
4	#mkr No No No No No No	0.0

FIGURE 5.4   Data frames of the datasets.

train to enter the training process. Using SMOTE, the classes in the distributions are balanced at this stage. This situation is called deep cleaning. Deep cleaning processes should be applied for both test and train data. Then, the tokenization process is repeated. All data should be parsed as vocabulary. At this stage, the numerical representation of the data that is subject to the tokenization process is created by vocabulary. Finally, it should be ensured that this process keeps the training and test data at a certain length. The detailed representation of these stages is given in Algorithm 5.1.

```
217078

<class 'pandas.core.frame.DataFrame'>
Int64Index: 231802 entries, 0 to 3463
Data columns (total 2 columns):
 #   Column     Non-Null Count    Dtype
---  ------     --------------    -----
 0   text       231801 non-null   object
 1   sentiment  231799 non-null   float64
dtypes: float64(1), object(1)
memory usage: 5.3+ MB
```

```
df.sentiment.value_counts()
```

```
0.0    204093
1.0     27706
Name: sentiment, dtype: int64
```

FIGURE 5.5   Analysis of different datasets.

In the next stage, cyberbullying detection analysis is performed. For this, the rows that do not contain any data among the cleaned data were cleaned. Situations like this usually only occur from link sharing or tweets that contain only emojis. Then, data containing less than three words in a line is cleared. This is because hashtags are data that usually contain five words or fewer. Next is expanding the test and training data with the RandomOverSampler. After obtaining the vector data with CountVectorizer, it is ready for analysis by using the TfidfTransformer. In this cyberbullying detection analysis, data was tried to be predicted using the Naive Bayes classifier and long short-term memory (LSTM). The obtained data are presented as scores and a confusion matrix.

5.3.2.1   Data Cleaning

The pre-processing stage after data collection involves removing stop words, stemming or lemmatizing words, and converting the text to lowercase. Libraries such as NLTK or spaCy in Python were used for preprocessing. Before balancing the classes (labels) for the data collection, duplicate words were removed, Figures 5.5, 5.6, and 5.14, show the row numbers of the data, the text, the sentiment, the cleaned data, and the text length.

- Remove Emoji and Reg expressions
- Strip all Entities such as symbols, "https", etc.
- Remove Contractions: words like can't, haven't, 'm, 've, 'll, etc.
- The text's emoticons were eliminated
- Stemming, which reduces words with suffixes and additions to their basic forms
- Elimination of contractions such as cannot, not, are, have, and am.

Input:

A dataset n with text and sentiment columns

A set of stop words $stop\_words$

Initialization

> Rename the columns to 'text' and 'sentiment'
> Remove duplicated tweets

end

Data Preprocessing

> **for** *each tweet in n* **do**
>> Remove URLs, mentions, hashtags, and emojis from the tweet
>> Convert the tweet to lowercase
>> Tokenize the tweet
>> Remove stop words from the tweet
>> Lemmatize the words in the tweet
>> Join the words back into a string
>> Add the cleaned tweet to a new column in n
>
> **end**
> Encode the sentiment column using label encoding
> Split the data into training and testing sets
> Apply SMOTE to balance the classes in the training set
> **for** *each tweet in the training set* **do**
>> Apply deep cleaning to the tweet
>
> **end**
> **for** *each tweet in the testing set* **do**
>> Apply deep cleaning to the tweet
>
> **end**
> Tokenize the cleaned tweets in the training and testing sets
> Create a vocabulary of all the words in the training set
> Convert the tokenized tweets to sequences of integers using the vocabulary
> Pad the sequences to a fixed length

end

Output:

A preprocessed dataset with cleaned and tokenized tweets, encoded sentiment column, and split into training and testing sets

ALGORITHM 5.1   Text Preprocessing Algorithm.

- The hashtags at the end of the sentence were cleaned, and those in the middle of the sentence were retained by simply removing the octothorp sign. Punctuation, links, stop words, mentions, and new line characters were also removed.

```
df = pd.concat([df1,df2,df3,df4,df5,df6,df7,df8], axis=0)
df
```

	Text	oh_label
0	'- This is not "creative". Those are the di...	0.0
1	` :: the term "standard model" is itself le...	0.0
2	True or false, the situation as of March 200...	0.0
3	Next, maybe you could work on being less cond...	0.0
4	This page will need disambiguation.	0.0
...	...	...
14876	@RaikonL @finaleve @mja333 WHY DO YOU HATE FRE...	0.0
14877	It is unconscionable that our regulatory bodie...	0.0
14878	@Dartanveerahmad @Janx53 @geehall1 We want ISI...	0.0
14879	#mkr Unbelievable how low Kat & Andre wil...	0.0
14880	RT @JamesMakienko: @omeisy @yemenrightsmon Peo...	0.0

448880 rows × 2 columns

FIGURE 5.6   Data frame concatenation 1.

- Remove words with numerous consecutive spaces and special characters like $
- Check for duplicate tweets once you've cleaned up and taken out tweets with fewer than five lines especially because of retweets and reposts.
- Lemmatization is the process of removing all inflectional endings from words and returning them to their base or dictionary form, also known as the lemma. This is done properly using a vocabulary and morphological analysis of words.
- Remove multiple sequential spaces

Before cleaning the data there were 231,802 rows and 3 columns but after cleaning and eliminating all the unnecessary information, we now have about 219,979 rows and 3 columns of data. See Figure 5.7.

From Figure 5.8, the cleaned and merged data is displayed in 231,802 rows and two columns.

After preprocessing, we extract features from the text. This involves converting the text into numerical vectors that can be used as input to a machine learning algorithm. You can use techniques such as bag of words or word embeddings to extract features.

5.3.3   BUILDING A MODEL

Once the features were extracted, we trained a machine learning model to detect the sentiment of the text and detect cyberbullying, sexism, racism, etc. We use various

```
texts_new
['creativ dictionari definit term insur ensur properli appli destruct understand fine legitim critic write three man cell bou
nti hunter easi understand ensur insur differ differ assur sentenc quot absolut neutral familiar underli theori strikeback eg
submarin employ nuclear warfar guid insur like three man cell structur kept ira broken british fault fine fix explain there n
oth person creativ tire argu articl multiparti turn plenti use mutual mutual appli standard would move mutual assur destruct
talk appeal reagan voter bias effect drop ly doubl standard edit come us histori book like peac movement mad defin 1950 like
even definit total useless 2002 histor interest make evenobvi connect implic languag chosen multipl term consid somehow nonne
utr gandhi think eye eye describ riot death penalti war know gandhi guess realiti neutral current use term slightli controver
si neutral requir negoti willing learn problem mine may dislik write fine fix disregard fundament axiom philosphi name recur
multipl phrase fail make critic distinct like insur versu assur versu ensur made one quot air forc gener incontext quot disse
rvic reader someon come research topic like mad want context beyond histori histori book fine histori book claim',
 'term standard model less npov think would prefer newag speak lot oldag peopl speak karl popper pope etc karl popper view cl
earest titl articl would particl physic cosmolog say would requir broader treatment issu like anthrop principl cognit bia bey
ond particl physic zoo etc acceler clear use someon still look particl yet settl cosmolog certain abandon search arbitrari fo
undat ontolog suggest subject question',
 'true fals situat march 2002 saudi propos land peac recognit arab countri made day propos made formal arab leagu day isra co
mmand ariel sharon began invas palestinian selfrul area userarab',
 'next mayb could work less condescend suggest read name convent fdl read quit ago thank realli like bit explain interest fix
thing complain felt insult yet extrem insult time luck learn less jerk greglindahl',
 'page need',
```

FIGURE 5.7   Data size/shape.

Before (231802, 3)
11823

('After', (219979, 3))

FIGURE 5.8   Cleaned data combined.

machine learning algorithms such as Naive Bayes and LSTM classifiers for the analysis. After training the model, we evaluate its performance using metrics such as accuracy, precision, recall, and F1-score using libraries such as Scikit-Learn in Python to evaluate the model.

The Data Preparation stage is better explained with this Algorithm 5.2.

5.3.3.1 Naive Bayes Model

One of the simplest and quickest classification methods is Naive Bayes. It is ideal for handling enormous quantities of data. It has been effectively applied in several applications, such as systems that produce recommendations, text classification, public opinion analysis, spam filtering, and text analysis. To predict unknown classes, it applies the Bayes theory of probability. To create the Naive Bayes Model, we first create a bag of words using CountVectorizer. Next, we implement Tfidf transformation to give the various words weights based on their frequency (Dhaduk 2021).

Algorithm 5.3 explains the Naive Bayes Sentiment Analysis Algorithm used for the analysis.

5.3.3.2 PyTorch LSTM Model

A unique variety of RNNs known as long short-term memory units (LSTM) further enhanced RNNs and Gated Recurrent Units (GRUs) by adding a reliable "gating" system. Using PyTorch's nn Module and the torch.nn.LSTM class, we can quickly add LSTM as a layer to our models (Maheshkar 2022). The following are the two crucial criteria you should consider:

Input:

The tokenized and padded text data, X

The sentiment labels, y

The test size for the train-test split, $test\_size$

The random seed for the train-test split, $seed\_value$

Initialization

> Split the data into training and testing sets using the train-test split
>
> Split the training data into training and validation sets using the train-test split
>
> Oversample the training data using the RandomOverSampler

end

Data Preparation

> Print the class distribution of the oversampled training data

end

Output:

The oversampled training data, X_train_os

The oversampled training labels, y_train_os

The training data, X_train

The training labels, y_train

The validation data, X_valid

The validation labels, y_valid

The testing data, X_test

The testing labels, y_test

ALGORITHM 5.2   Data Preparation Algorithm.

- **Input_Size:** The estimated amount of features in the input
- **Hidden_Size:** the number of features in the hidden state h

The open-source deep learning system PyTorch is renowned for its adaptability and simplicity. This is made possible, in part, by its compatibility with Python, a well-liked high-level computer language used by data scientists and machine learning developers. Tensors and networks are the fundamental building blocks of both PyTorch and TensorFlow. Deep learning models, a type of machine learning frequently used in applications like image recognition and language processing,

Input:

A dataset D with n instances and sentiment labels

The training set X_{train} and testing set X_{test}

The sentiment labels y_{train} and y_{test}

Initialization

> Clean the text data using deep cleaning techniques
> Remove instances with null sentiment labels
> Remove instances with text length less than 3
> Split the data into training, validation, and testing sets
> Oversample the training set using Random Oversampling
> Vectorize the text data using CountVectorizer
> Transform the vectorized data using TfidfTransformer

end

Naive Bayes Sentiment Analysis

> **for** *each fold in the K-fold cross validation* **do**
>> Split the data into training and testing sets
>> **for** $i = 1$ *to* max_cols **do**
>>> **for** *each combination of i columns* **do**
>>>> Train a Naive Bayes classifier on the training set using the transformed data
>>>> Predict the sentiment labels for the testing set using the trained classifier
>>>> Calculate the classification report and confusion matrix for the predicted labels
>>> **end**
>> **end**
> **end**

end

Output:

The classification report and confusion matrix for the predicted sentiment labels

ALGORITHM 5.3   Naïve Bayes Sentiment Analysis Algorithm.

can be built using PyTorch, a completely featured framework. Most machine learning developers find it reasonably simple to learn and use because it is written in Python. PyTorch stands out for its superior GPU support and use of reverse-mode auto-differentiation, which allows dynamic modification of computation graphs. It is therefore a well-liked option for quick testing and prototyping (NVIDIA 2022) (Algorithms 5.4 and 5.5).

Algorithm 5.6 explains the Bi-LSTM Testing Algorithm used for the analysis.

Input:

Training data $train\_data$ with n instances and m features

Validation data $valid\_data$ with n_v instances and m features

Test data $test\_data$ with n_t instances and m features

Batch size $BATCH\_SIZE$

Number of classes $NUM\_CLASSES$

Hidden dimension $HIDDEN\_DIM$

LSTM layers $LSTM\_LAYERS$

Learning rate LR

Dropout $DROPOUT$

PyTorch LSTM $BIDIRECTIONAL$

Number of epochs $EPOCHS$

Device $DEVICE$

Initialization

> Create training dataset $train\_loader$ with batch size $BATCH\_SIZE$
>
> Create validation dataset $valid\_loader$ with batch size $BATCH\_SIZE$
>
> Create test dataset $test\_loader$ with batch size $BATCH\_SIZE$
>
> Create a PyTorch LSTM sentiment classifier model $model$ with vocabulary size $VOCAB\_SIZE$, embedding dimension $EMBEDDING\_DIM$, hidden dimension $HIDDEN\_DIM$, number of classes $NUM\_CLASSES$, LSTM layers $LSTM\_LAYERS$, PyTorch LSTM $BIDIRECTIONAL$, batch size $BATCH\_SIZE$, and dropout $DROPOUT$
>
> Initialize the embedding layer of $model$ with the pre-trained embedding matrix
>
> Set the embedding layer of $model$ to be trainable
>
> Define the negative log-likelihood loss function $criterion$
>
> Define the AdamW optimizer $optimizer$ with learning rate LR and weight decay $5e - 6$

end

Training

> **for** *each epoch in* $EPOCHS$ **do**
>> Set the model to training mode
>>
>> Initialize the hidden and cell states of the LSTM in $model$
>>
>> **for** *each batch in* $train\_loader$ **do**
>>> Get the input and target tensors from the batch
>>>
>>> Zero the gradients of the optimizer
>>>
>>> Pass the input tensor through $model$ to get the output tensor and updated hidden and cell states
>>>
>>> Calculate the loss between the output tensor and the target tensor using $criterion$
>>>
>>> Backpropagate the loss through $model$ to update the parameters
>>>
>>> Clip the gradients to prevent exploding gradients
>>>
>>> Update the parameters of $model$ using the optimizer
>>
>> **end**
>>
>> Set the model to evaluation mode
>>
>> Initialize the validation loss and accuracy to 0
>>
>> **for** *each batch in* $valid\_loader$ **do**
>>> Get the input and target tensors from the batch
>>>
>>> Pass the input tensor through $model$ to get the output tensor and updated hidden and cell states
>>>
>>> Calculate the loss between the output tensor and the target tensor using $criterion$
>>>
>>> Calculate the number of correct predictions
>>>
>>> Update the validation loss and accuracy
>>
>> **end**
>>
>> Print the epoch, training loss, validation loss, and validation accuracy
>
> **end**

end

Output:

The trained sentiment classifier model $model$

ALGORITHM 5.4 PyTorch LSTM Sentiment Classifier Training Algorithm.

Input:

Training and validation data loaders, *train_loader* and *valid_loader*

LSTM model, *model*

Loss function, *criterion*

Optimizer, *optimizer*

Number of epochs, $EPOCHS$

Early stopping patience, *early_stopping_patience*

Initialization

> Initialize empty lists for train and validation losses, *train_loss* and *valid_loss*
>
> Initialize empty lists for train and validation accuracies, *train_acc* and *valid_acc*
>
> Initialize empty lists for train and validation predictions, *y_train_list* and *y_val_list*
>
> Initialize variables for total and correctly classified texts during training and validation, *correct*, *correct_val*, *total*, and *total_val*
>
> Initialize variables for running losses during training and validation, *running_loss* and *running_loss_val*
>
> Initialize variable for best validation accuracy, *valid_acc_max*, to 0
>
> Initialize early stopping counter, *early_stopping_counter*, to 0

end

Training Loop

> **for** *each epoch, e, in $EPOCHS$* **do**
>
> > Set model to training mode
> >
> > **for** *each batch in train_loader* **do**
> >
> > > Load features and targets in device
> > > Initialize hidden states
> > > Reset gradients
> > > Get output and hidden states from LSTM network
> > > Calculate loss
> > > Backpropagate loss
> > > Update running loss
> > > Get the tensor of predicted values on the training set
> > > Transform tensor to list and the values to the list
> > > Count correctly classified texts per batch
> > > Count total texts per batch
> >
> > **end**
> >
> > Append average train loss and accuracy to their respective lists
> > Set model to evaluation mode
> >
> > **for** *each batch in valid_loader* **do**
> >
> > > Load features and targets in device
> > > Initialize hidden states
> > > Get output and hidden states from LSTM network
> > > Calculate loss
> > > Update running loss
> > > Get tensor of predicted values on the validation set
> > > Transform tensor to list and the values to the list
> > > Count correctly classified texts per batch
> > > Count total texts per batch
> >
> > **end**
> >
> > Append average validation loss and accuracy to their respective lists
> >
> > **if** *average validation accuracy increases* **then**
> >
> > > Save model
> > > Update best validation accuracy
> > > Reset early stopping counter
> >
> > **end**
> > **else**
> >
> > > Increase early stopping counter
> >
> > **end**
> >
> > **if** *early stopping counter > early stopping patience* **then**
> >
> > > Stop training
> >
> > **end**
> >
> > Print train and validation losses and accuracies
>
> **end**

end

ALGORITHM 5.5   LSTM Training Algorithm.

Input:

A trained Bi-LSTM model

A test dataset D with n instances and m features

A list of sentiment labels, *sentiments*
Initialization

> Set the model to evaluation mode
> Create empty lists for predicted and true labels

end
Bi-LSTM Testing

> **for** *each batch of inputs and labels in the test dataset* **do**
>> Move the inputs and labels to the device
>> Initialize the hidden state of the model
>> Get the output and hidden state of the model for the inputs
>> Predict the labels by taking the argmax of the output
>> Append the predicted and true labels to their respective lists
>
> **end**

end
Output:
Print the classification report for the predicted and true labels using *sentiments*
Print the confusion matrix for the predicted and true labels using *sentiments*

ALGORITHM 5.6   Bi-LSTM Testing Algorithm.

Fine-tuning: Based on the evaluation results, we fine-tuned our model by adjusting the parameters and trying different algorithms or techniques to improve its accuracy and precision.

5.4   EXPERIMENTAL RESULTS

Figure 5.9 shows the word count with a length of less than 10 and not more than 100 words. Words of about 11 words are 2,314, 18 words are 4,042, etc. Figure 5.10 shows tweet counts with the highest number of words e.g., 4 words have 10,024. To ensure that each list includes the most words possible, the sentences were converted into lists of words.

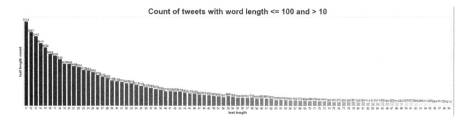

FIGURE 5.9 Count of tweets with word length ≤ 100 and > 10.

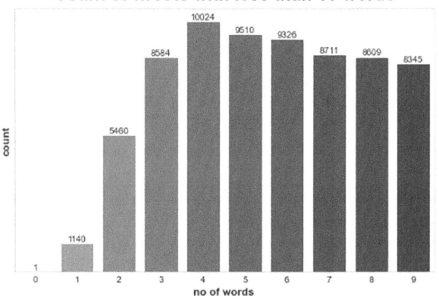

FIGURE 5.10 Count of tweets with less than ten words.

TABLE 5.1

Naive Bayes

Classification/Measures	Precision	Recall	F1-Score
Positive	0.98	0.87	0.92
Negative	0.43	0.84	0.57

The accuracy for the Naive Bayes algorithm is 86% (Table 5.1).

The Naive Bayes Confusion Matrix Figure 5.11 shows that about 29,350 cyberbullying words were accurately predicted to be positive, and about 3,508 words were predicted to be not bullying. This means that the model predicted more true positives than false positives (Figure 5.12).

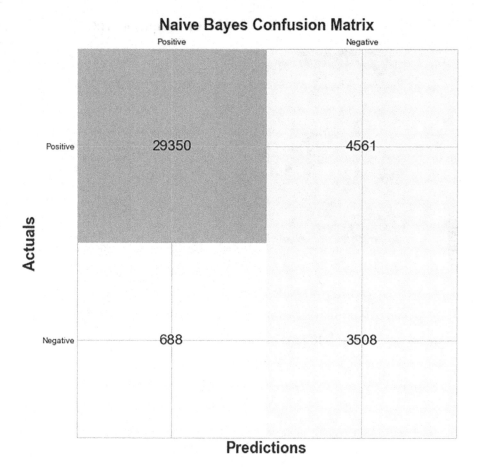

FIGURE 5.11 Naive Bayes confusion matrix.

```
['aggression_parsed_dataset.csv',
 'attack_parsed_dataset.csv',
 'kaggle_parsed_dataset.csv',
 'toxicity_parsed_dataset.csv',
 'twitter_parsed_dataset.csv',
 'twitter_racism_parsed_dataset.csv',
 'twitter_sexism_parsed_dataset.csv',
 'youtube_parsed_dataset.csv']
```

FIGURE 5.12 The various datasets used for analysis.

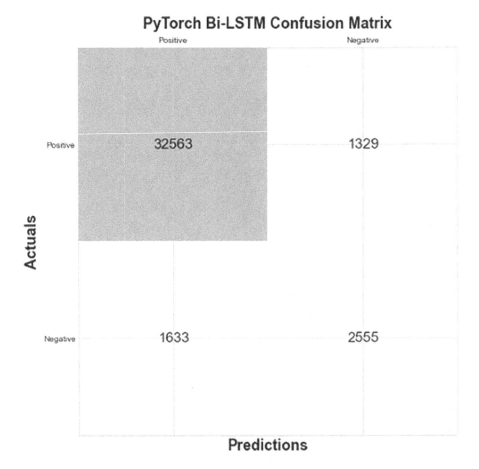

FIGURE 5.13   PyTorch Bi-LSTM confusion matrix.

The PyTorch Bi-LSTM Confusion Matrix Figure 5.13 shows that about 32,563 cyberbullying words were accurately predicted to be positive, and about 2,555 words were predicted to be not bullying. The accuracy for the Naive Bayes algorithm is 92% (Figures 5.14, 5.15, and Table 5.2).

Figure 5.16 shows the validation accuracy and when it increased each time the accuracy was approximately 92% for the LSTM model.

Figure 5.17 shows the top 20 most common words. Delete appeared 22,054 times.

```
df3 = pd.read_csv(r'toxicity_parsed_dataset.csv')[['Text', 'oh_label']]
df3.head()
```

	Text	oh_label
0	This: :One can make an analogy in mathematical...	0
1	` :Clarification for you (and Zundark's righ...	0
2	Elected or Electoral? JHK	0
3	`This is such a fun entry. Devotchka I once...	0
4	Please relate the ozone hole to increases in c...	0

```
df4 = pd.read_csv(r'kaggle_parsed_dataset.csv')[['Text', 'oh_label']]
df4.head()
```

	Text	oh_label
0	"You fuck your dad."	1
1	"i really don't understand your point.\xa0 It ...	0
2	"A\\xc2\\xa0majority of Canadians can and has ...	0
3	"listen if you dont wanna get married to a man...	0
4	"C\xe1c b\u1ea1n xu\u1ed1ng \u0111\u01b0\u1edd...	0

```
df5 = pd.read_csv(r'twitter_parsed_dataset.csv')[['Text', 'oh_label']]
df5.head()
```

	Text	oh_label
0	@halalflaws @biebervalue @greenlinerzjm I read...	0.0
1	@ShreyaBafna3 Now you idiots claim that people...	0.0
2	RT @Mooseooftorment Call me sexist, but when I ...	1.0
3	@g0ssipsquirrelx Wrong, ISIS follows the examp...	1.0
4	#mkr No No No No No No	0.0

FIGURE 5.14   Data sets concatenated 1.

```
BiLSTM_Sentiment_Classifier(
  (embedding): Embedding(162786, 200)
  (lstm): LSTM(200, 100, batch_first=True, dropout=0.5, bidirectional=True)
  (fc): Linear(in_features=200, out_features=2, bias=True)
  (softmax): LogSoftmax(dim=1)
)
```

FIGURE 5.15   Bi-LSTM parameters.

TABLE 5.2
PyTorch Bi-LSTM

Classification/Measures	Precision	Recall	F1-Score
Positive	0.95	0.96	0.96
Negative	0.66	0.61	0.63

```
Epoch 1:Validation accuracy increased (0.000000 --> 91.747637).  Saving model ...
         Train_loss : 0.2381 Val_loss : 0.2773
         Train_acc : 90.627% Val_acc : 91.748%
Epoch 2:Validation accuracy increased (91.747637 --> 91.819853).  Saving model ...
         Train_loss : 0.1054 Val_loss : 0.3196
         Train_acc : 96.431% Val_acc : 91.820%
Epoch 3:Validation accuracy increased (91.819853 --> 92.240021).  Saving model ...
         Train_loss : 0.0612 Val_loss : 0.3984
         Train_acc : 98.088% Val_acc : 92.240%
Epoch 4:Validation accuracy did not increase
         Train_loss : 0.0357 Val_loss : 0.4864
         Train_acc : 98.953% Val_acc : 91.938%
Epoch 5:Validation accuracy did not increase
         Train_loss : 0.0205 Val_loss : 0.6340
         Train_acc : 99.413% Val_acc : 92.096%
```

FIGURE 5.16   EPOCHS

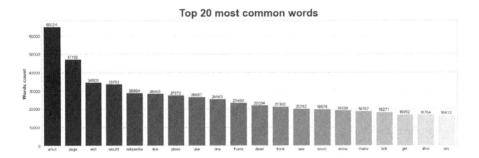

FIGURE 5.17   Top 20 most common words.

5.5   CONCLUSION

In this chapter, we proposed a novel approach to detecting and mitigating cyberbullying. We built a Naive Bayes and a Bi-LSTM model using Pytorch that successfully detected cyberbullying from a combined set of datasets. The dataset obtained from Kaggles was combined to form one very large dataset that tackles various types of cyberbullying ranging from aggression, attacks, racism, and sexism from platforms like Kaggle, Twitter, Wikipedia Talk pages, and YouTube. The text contained in the dataset includes several forms of cyberbullying, such as hate speech, aggressiveness, insults, and toxic language.

The models displayed excellent results. The Naive Bayes model had the lowest accuracy of 86% and precision of 98%. Pytorch Bi-LSTM achieved exceptional outcomes, with a 92% overall accuracy. This research was novel since it utilized additional data from websites like Kaggle, YouTube, and Twitter to identify several types of cyberbullying, including sexism, assault, racism, and criminal intent terms.

In comparison to other models and research out there, there are limitations of datasets that cut across various social media platforms such as Instagram, Flickr, YouTube, Facebook, etc. The certainty of detecting these hate speeches and various aspects of cyberbullying is less feasible without Artificial intelligence. Developing a strong sentiment analysis and cyberbullying detection and extraction model in Python that can assist in identifying and preventing cyberbullying with the right data collecting, preprocessing, feature extraction, and model-building techniques, will help mitigate cyber attacks and cyberbullying.

We intend to use more models to detect cyberbullying with a broader dataset that encompasses more social media platforms with more classification and sentiment criteria.

DECLARATIONS

AUTHORS' CONTRIBUTIONS

Contributed significantly to the study's conceptualization and design of the methodology, as well as the development of the machine learning and deep learning model used: Biodoumoye B.

Made contributions in the data acquisition and draft of the chapter as well as the revision of the model and chapter: Biodoumoye B, and Liu Q.

ACKNOWLEDGMENT

A part of the support for this study from the SHSU Institute of Homeland Security is highly appreciated.

REFERENCES

Al-Ajlan, Monirah Abdulla & Mourad Ykhlef. 2018. Optimized twitter cyberbullying detection based on deep learning. In 2018 21st Saudi computer society national computer conference (NCC), 1–5.

Alduailaj, Alanoud Mohammed & Aymen Belghith. 2023. Detecting Arabic cyberbullying tweets using machine learning. *Machine Learning and Knowledge Extraction* 5(1). 29–42.

Ali, Wan Noor Hamiza Wan, Masnizah Mohd & Fariza Fauzi. 2018. Cyberbullying detection: an overview. In 2018 cyber resilience conference (CRC), 1–3.

Alismaiel, Omar A. 2023. Digital media used in education: the influence on cyberbullying behaviors among youth students. *International Journal of Environmental Research and Public Health* 20(2). 1370.

Alsubait, Tahani & Danyah Alfageh. 2021. Comparison of machine learning techniques for cyberbullying detection on YouTube Arabic comments. *International Journal of Computer Science & Network Security* 21(1). 1–5.

Bakomichalis, Ioannis. 2023. Cyberbullying detection through NLP and machine learning. Diss. University of Piraeus (Greece). .https://www.proquest.com/docview/2827703604?pq-ori gsite=gscholar&fromopenview=true

Balakrishnan, Vimala, Shahzaib Khan, Terence Fernandez & Hamid R Arabnia. 2019. Cyberbullying detection on Twitter using Big Five and Dark Triad features. *Personality and Individual Differences* 141. 252–257.

Balakrishnan, Vimala & See Kiat Ng. 2022. Personality and emotion-based cyberbullying detection on YouTube using ensemble classifiers. *Behaviour & Information Technology* 1. 1–12.

Barlett Christopher, 2023. Cyberbullying as a learned behavior: theoretical and applied implications. Children 10(2). 325.

Biernesser, Candice, Mary Ohmer, Lisa Nelson, Elizabeth Mann, Rosta Farzan, Beth Schwanke & Ana Radovic. 2023. Middle school students' experiences with cyberbullying and perspectives toward prevention and bystander intervention in schools. *Journal of School Violence* 22(3). 339–352.

Bonanno, George A. 2021. *The end of trauma: how the new science of resilience is changing how we think about PTSD*. Basic Books.

Chen, Liang, Xiaoming Liu & Hongjie Tang. 2023. The interactive effects of parental mediation strategies in preventing cyberbullying on social media. *Psychology Research and Behavior Management* 16. 1009–1022.

Dadvar, Maral, Dolf Trieschnigg, Roeland Ordelman & Franciska De Jong. 2013. Improving cyberbullying detection with user context. In Advances in information retrieval: 35th European conference on IR research, ECIR 2013, Moscow, Russia, March 24–27, 2013. proceedings 35, 693–696.

Dedeepya Parvathaneni et al. 2023. Detecting cyber bullying on Twitter using support vector machine. In 2023 third international conference on artificial intelligence and smart energy (ICAIS), 817–822.

DELETE CYBERBULLYING. 2023. Why do people cyberbully? https://www.endcyberbully-ing.net/why-do-people-cyberbully.

Dhaduk, Hardikkumar. 2021. Naive Bayes classifier overview. https://www.analyticsvidhya.com/blog/2021/07/performing-sentiment-analysis-with-naive-bayes-classifier/.

Dwumah Manu, Blessing, Feng Ying, Daniel Oduro, John Antwi & Robert Yakubu Adjuik. 2023. The impact of social media use on student engagement and acculturative stress among international students in China. *Plos One* 18(4). e0284185.

Greifeneder, Rainer, Mariela Jaffe, Eryn Newman & Norbert Schwarz. 2021. *The psychology of fake news: accepting, sharing, and correcting misinformation*. Routledge.

Hinduja, Sameer, & Justin W. Patchin. 2014. *Bullying beyond the schoolyard: Preventing and responding to cyberbullying*. Corwin press.

Henson, B. 2012. *Bullying beyond the schoolyard: Preventing and responding to cyberbullying*. Secur Journal. Springer. 25, 88–89. https://doi.org/10.1057/sj.2011.25.

Nripendra Rana, Emma Slade, Ganesh Sahu, Hatice Kizgin, Nitish Singh, Bidit Dey, Anabel Gutierrez, Yogesh Dwivedi, 2020 Digital and Social Media Marketing Emerging Applications and Theoretical Development Springer: Berlin/Heidelberg, Germany.

Huang, Liangjiecheng, Weiqiang Li, Zikai Xu, Hongli Sun, Danfeng Ai, Yinfeng Hu, Shiqi Wang, Yu Li & Yanyan Zhou. 2023. The severity of cyberbullying affects bystander intervention among college students: the roles of feelings of responsibility and empathy. *Psychology Research and Behavior Management* 16. 893–903.

Islam, Md Manowarul, Md Ashraf Uddin, Linta Islam, Arnisha Akter, Selina Sharmin & Uzzal Kumar Acharjee. 2020. Cyberbullying detection on social networks using machine learning approaches. In 2020 IEEE Asia-Pacific conference on computer science and data engineering (CSDE), 1–6.

Kizza, Joseph Migga. 2023. Cyberbullying, cyberstalking, and cyber harassment. In *Ethical and social issues in the information age*, 205–215. Springer.

Kowalski Robin and Susan Limber. 2007. Electronic bullying among middle school students. Journal of Adolescent Health 41(6). S22–S30.

Lange, Kasper. 2020. Improving the fairness of cyberbullying detection for sexism on social media while keeping predictive power. (Bachelor thesis).https://pure.tue.nl/ws/portal-files/portal/197474725/Thesis_BDS_Kasper_Lange.pdf

Lange, Kasper. 2022. The state of social media in 2022. https://browsermedia.agency/blog/state-of-social-media-2022/.

Maheshkar, Saurav. 2022. Using LSTM in PyTorch: a tutorial with examples. https://wandb.ai/sauravmaheshkar/LSTM-PyTorch/reports/Using%5C-LSTM%5Cin%5C-PyTorch%5C-A%5C-Tutorial%5C-With%5C-Examples%5C-%5C-VmlldzoxMDA2NTA5.

Myers Susan, et al. 2023, Social religion: a crossplatform examination of the impact of religious influencer message cues on engagementthe Christian context. Technological Forecasting and Social Change 191. 122442.

Nunan, Daniel & MariaLaura Di Domenico. 2019. Older consumers, digital marketing, and public policy: a review and research agenda. *Journal of Public Policy & Marketing* 38(4). 469–483.

NVIDIA. 2022. PyTorch. https://www.nvidia.com/en%5C-us/glossary/data%5Cscience/pytorch/.

Parveen, Amina, Shazia Jan & Insha Rasool. 2023. Cyberbullying issues. In *Handbook of research on bullying in media and beyond*, 456–472. IGI Global.

Rębisz, Sławomir, Aleksandra Jasińska-Maciążek, Paweł Grygiel & Roman Dolata. 2023. Psycho-social correlates of cyberbullying among polish adolescents. *International Journal of Environmental Research and Public Health* 20(8). 5521.

Sabella Russell, Justin Patchin & Sameern Hinduja, 2013. Cyberbullying myths and realities. Computers in Human Behavior 29(6). 2703–2711.

Shahan, Saurabh. 2022. Cyberbullying dataset. https://www.kaggle.com/datasets/saurabhshahane/cyberbullying-dataset.

Smith Peter, Jess Mahdavi, Manuel Carvalho, Sonja Fisher, Shanette Russell & Neil Tippett. 2008. Cyberbullying: its nature and impact in secondary school pupils. Journal of Child Psychology and Psychiatry 49(4). 376–385.

Sorrentino, Anna, Francesco Sulla, Margherita Santamato, Annarosa Cipriano & Stefania Cella. 2023. The long-term efficacy and sustainability of the tabby improved prevention and intervention program in reducing cyberbullying and cybervictimization. *International Journal of Environmental Research and Public Health* 20(8). 5436.

Sultan, Mubashir, Christin Scholz & Wouter van den Bos. 2023. Leaving traces behind: using social media digital trace data to study adolescent wellbeing. *Computers in Human Behavior Reports* 10. 100281.

Zhang, Jianwei, Taiga Otomo, Lin Li & Shinsuke Nakajima. 2019. Cyberbullying detection on twitter using multiple textual features. In 2019 IEEE 10th international conference on awareness science and technology (ICAST), 1–6.

Zorlu, Eyup. 2023. An examination of the relationship between college students' cyberbullying awareness and ability to ensure their personal cybersecurity. *Journal of Learning and Teaching in Digital Age* 8(1). 55–70.

6 Cyber-Bullying Detection for Multimodal Data Convolutional Neural Network with Butterfly Optimisation

Kalimuthu Sivanantham
Crapersoft

V. R. Vijaykumar
Anna University Regional Campus

A. Krishnakumar
NGM College

M. Pradeepa
SNS College of Technology

6.1 INTRODUCTION

Cyberbullying refers to the non-physical use of social media by anonymous users to humiliate, mock, defame, and degrade a victim. Bullies now utilise social media as a "virtual playground" to act badly toward others. Since bullying has the potential to permeate throughout society, Building. Developing a model is essential for automatically identifying and avoiding bullying content. Researchers from all over the world have been creating innovative strategies to manage and lessen the incidence of cyberbullying on social media [1]. Sophisticated analytical techniques and computer models must be utilised in order to process, analyse, and model such bitter, sarcastic, abusive, or negative data in photos, memes, or text messages. Typographic and info-graphic visual information (Figure 6.1) has increased to comprise a sizeable portion of social data in more recent times as image-based, inter-textual content such as memes, online movies and other stuff are more common in social feeds now.

A security-based cyberbullying is a very common practice that uses a range of multimedia genres. Specialisation in social media, a reliance on topics, and a diversity of handcrafted elements present current hurdles to recognising online

DOI: 10.1201/9781003393061-8

FIGURE 6.1 Visual content types.

bullying messages [2]. Thanks to its representation learning capabilities and end-to-end training, deep learning algorithms are showing their usefulness and producing cutting-edge results for a variety of natural language difficulties. Detailed instruction modules using CNN, RNN, and semantic image features are used in relevant publications to identify bullying content using textual, user data, and visual analysis [3]. The literature has paid the least attention to the field of combining both text and image, or visual text. Image analysis has been utilised in several related studies to find information about bullying. The combination comes in two different forms: Infographics and typographic text displays (aesthetic technique) [4]. An infographic, a visual, and a textual social data model for identifying cyberbullying is described in this chapter (image is embedded along with text).

The research's primary contributions are

- Throughout a single hybrid deep architecture known as CapsNet-ConvNet, ConvNet for visual content prediction is combined with CapsNet and dynamic routing for textual content prediction.
- The hybrid architecture processes the textual and visual components, and the late-fusion judgement layer subsequently generates the outcome prediction.
- The performance of CapsNet is evaluated using 10,000 likes and postings (text, image, and infographic) on the social media sites Facebook, Whatsapp, and Telegram. ConvNet's.

To provide effective decision support for the detection of cyberbullying, this unifying model takes into account the various content modality types and analyses each modality type [5]. 10,000 posts and comments that were combined from Twitter, Instagram, and YouTube to generate a mix-modal dataset were experimentally looked at. Visual modalities made for 20% of the sample, infographic modalities 20%, and text modalities 60% (Figure 6.2). Following our tenfold cross-validation, we generated the AUC-ROC curve [6]. In this chapter, the methods and results pertinent to this study goal are described.

FIGURE 6.2   Personalise cyberbullying.

This chapter is arranged in five parts. Part II explains the present method and its drawbacks with regard to techniques in cyberbullying. The strategies for cyberbullying proposed in Part III are more effective. Part IV presents the experimental result and their analysis, and Part V provides a conclusion.

6.2   RELATED WORK

This session discussed the drawbacks and disadvantages of cyberbullying with some algorithms and techniques.

In research, the prevalence rates of cyberbullying often range from 10% to 35% [7], whereas others have found significantly higher rates [8]. Research paints a picture of the serious emotional and academic effects of cyberbullying. Students who were subjected to cyberbullying spoke of feeling hopeless, anxious, and fearful, as well as having trouble focusing, all of which had an effect on their academic performance [9]. Youth who experienced cyberbullying were more likely to miss class, receive detentions or suspensions, or bring a weapon to school [10]. Youth who report suffering cyberbullying are substantially more likely to suffer from depression, substance abuse, and misbehaviour [11]. Evidence shows that young people who engage in cyberbullying are more likely to also transgress rules and have aggressiveness issues [12].

Many kids and teenagers don't tell their parents about their encounters with cyberbullying [13]. This alarming conclusion is consistent with the reliable findings that a sizable portion of kids who experience traditional bullying do not notify adults about it [14]. The goal of this study was to better understand how children and youth saw cyberbullying and the barriers and facilitators to reporting it to parents and other adults.

6.2.1 EFFECTS OF BULLYING

Children who are bullied at school experience a number of maladaptive effects, according to prior study. Anxiety, loneliness, unhappiness, excessive compliance, and insecurity are examples of internalising issues [15]. In addition to these internalising behaviours, bullied children may exhibit externalising issues like impulsivity and hyperactivity [16]. There have also been some reported issues in schools, but research on these is scant. Pichel et al. [17] found that abused kids are more inclined to skip school, which increases absenteeism, and Ramos Salazar [18] showed a lack of focus while doing homework. These actions may account for claims of reduced IQ and academic success [19].

Children who are the targets of cyberbullying may exhibit comparable undesirable behaviour, according to some recent studies on the topic. Anecdotal evidence from published studies offers perceptions of children's experiences [20]. In addition, preliminary studies have identified a number of behaviours connected to cyberbullying, such as frustration, anger, and sadness [21]. Indeed, [22] a third of the kids who had experienced cyberbullying thought it had negatively impacted them in some manner, according to the study. In addition, a national sample of American kids aged 10–17 stated that receiving harassing online communications caused 30% of them to feel highly upset and 24% of them to feel scared [23]. Moreover, Yokotani and Masanori [24] discovered that people who used the internet frequently were more prone to experience depression. It is unknown if students who suffer cyberbullying have the same issues as students who are bullied in school, and more research is required to understand how cyberbullying affects kids in Canada.

Given that girls mature sooner than males and may be more developmentally "ready" to start employing advanced aggressive techniques earlier, females may be slightly more likely to engage in cyberbullying if we see it as a particularly advanced type of relational or indirect violence. Therefore, we would anticipate that as boys "catch up" with girls in maturity and ability to aggress in this way during later adolescence, sex differences will lessen [25]. In their meta-analysis, Bacher-Hicks et al. [26] discovered hardly any variations in relational or indirect aggressiveness between the sexes. In fact, there was no sex difference at any of the ages examined, with the exception of adolescence, when women were marginally more likely than men to engage in relational or indirect aggression. On the other hand, since men tend to be more technologically savvy than women in late adolescence, one may anticipate that men will engage in cyberbullying more frequently than women. Additionally, studies have shown that traditional bullying tends to increase from early adolescence (6th grade) to middle adolescence (9th grade), which may indicate that males will surpass females in the frequency of cyberbullying at this age.

6.3   EXISTING CHALLENGES IN IoT SECURITY

This section discusses the proposed system for cyberbullying in multimodal data using butterfly optimisation techniques with CapsNet-ConvNet.

The suggested CapsNet-ConvNet model serves as an example of the techniques. A proposed system for detecting cyberbullying uses three forms of textual, visual, and infographic social data [27]. The suggested deep neural network is capable of comprehending the complexity of spoken language and dealing with numerous data modalities content from social networking sites where real-valued vectors are present and are trained to represent data and image [28]. In addition to the language, we looked at the picture and its info-graphic component (information that is the text and content on image) to anticipate any content relating to bullying. The suggested CapsNet-ConvNet model is composed of some components.

6.3.1   TEXTUAL PROCESSING

CapsNet is used in conjunction with dynamic routing to construct the text-processing module. CapsNet is a deep neural network that consists of a number of capsules [29]. These are further formed of clusters of neurons organised into layers to foretell any feature's instantiation attributes, such as its orientation, colour, etc. at a specific position. According to relevant research, various routing algorithms are employed for text categorization, utilizing a range of techniques. Among these techniques, dynamic routing reporting is recognized for its extensive application.

A neural network's embedding layer transforms [30] because ELMo provides contextualised word representations; basically, we picked it over more traditional embedding models like Word2Vec or GloVe [31]. As opposed to traditional word embedding models, which require a list of words along with their corresponding vectors, ELMo creates vectors as it goes by putting words through a deep learning model.

The network can also create representations for words that were not encountered during training because ELMo representations are character-based exclusively [32]. This led us to develop the embedding layer using the ELMo 5.5B model (Figure 6.3). Layers for main caps, class caps, and convolution are present in this network. Here, each convolution layer's scalar outputs are sent into the principal caps layer, which creates capsules [33]. It is important to note that a capsule's output vector depicts the vector's direction, while it also shows the characteristics of the object. The network's prospective parents receive the vector as an input. To connect the various characteristics of the thing to its whole, these capsules make an effort to identify the object's constituent parts. To capture the dynamics of the part-whole interactions, CapsNet employs a nonlinear-dynamic routing technique between the capsules in order to do this [34]. As a result, it is made sure that the likely and appropriate parent receives the capsule after its manufacture. By multiplying.

$$u_j|_i = W_{ij}u_i \qquad (6.1)$$

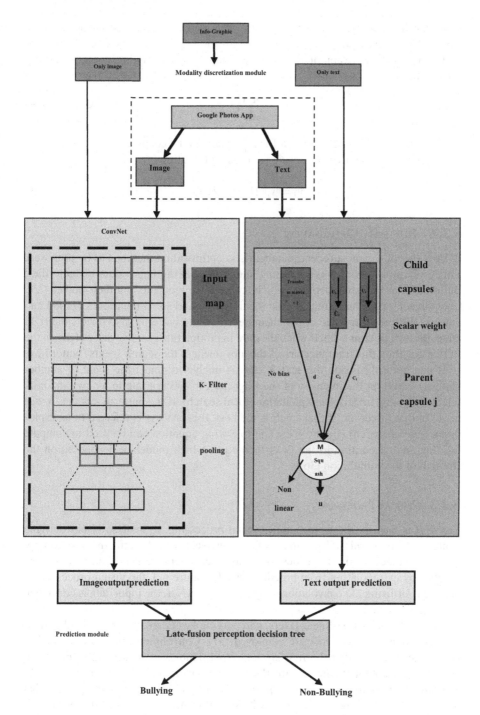

FIGURE 6.3   Model CapsNet-ConvNet is proposed.

I, the translation matrix is composed of two capsules: *i*, the high-level capsule, and *l*, the low-level capsule W_{ij}.

To multiply the result of the previous step by the coupling coefficients, use Equation 6.2.

$$s_j = \sum C_{iji} u_j |_i \tag{6.2}$$

The output vector from Equation 6.1 is $u_j|_i$, and c_{ij} is the coupling coefficient.

It then normalises from a capsule [0, 1] using Equation 6.3.

$$v_j = \|s_j\| 2 1 + \|s_j\| 2 s_j \|s_j\| \tag{6.3}$$

6.3.2 BUTTERFLY OPTIMISATION

BOA is one of the most recent metaheuristic optimisation methods to be proposed. This programme mimics the foraging and mate-seeking behaviours of butterflies. Butterflies have chemoreceptors, which act as sense receptors, on their bodies [35]. Chemoreceptors in butterflies enable them to taste and smell the aroma of food and flowers. With the guidance of the chemoreceptor, the butterfly also selects the right mate. Butterflies emit a smell when they are in motion that is somewhat potent. In the BOA algorithm, this fragrance drives the movement of the search agents (butterflies).

If one butterfly inside the search zone is unable to detect the scent of another butterfly based on the intensity of the fragrance, it will migrate to a new randomly selected site and undertake exploitation (local search). If the butterfly notices, it will travel in that direction. If that smell is the best, this process is referred to as exploration (global search) (Figure 6.4). The following equation can be used to compute the fragrance according to the BOA technique, which models it depending on the strength of the stimulation [36].

6.3.3 VISUAL PROCESSING

ConvNet is used in the next module, visual processing, to analyse visual bullying content. Deep neural architectures called ConvNets work by utilising several copies of the same neuron in various locations. It can improve itself and pick up new abilities by extrapolating from practice data. In Figure 6.3, the visual processing is depicted. Utilising 2D convolutional layers in a ConvNet, the input data is convolved with learned features.

Filters (kernels), non-linear layers, and pooling layers are typically found in multiple convolutional networks are employed [37]. Convolution layers are applied to the image in a way that the first layer's output doubles as its second layer's input (Figure 6.5). Although images are not linear, convolution is a linear process. As a result, after each convolution step, non-linearity is added. A pooling layer that down-samples the image and reduces its spatial dimension comes after each layer of nonlinearity. To achieve gradual pooling, various techniques are employed, including options such as maximum, average, or sum pooling [38]. The data from

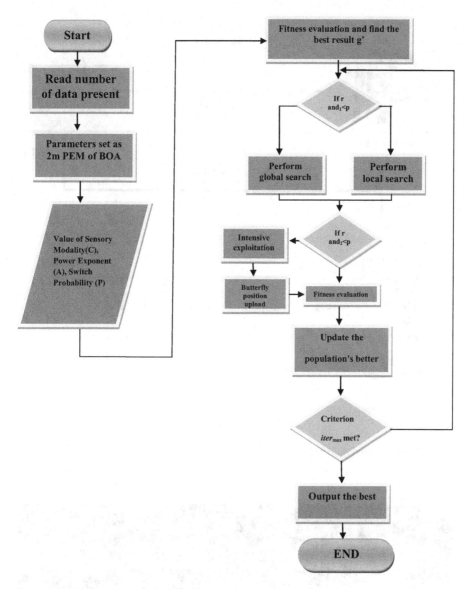

FIGURE 6.4 Butterfly optimisation algorithm.

the convolutional networks are output by connecting to a fully connected layer. Figure 6.6 shows the usual operation of a ConvNet.

The details of the layers are as follows:

- Convolution layer
- Activation layer and pooling layer
- Fully connected layer

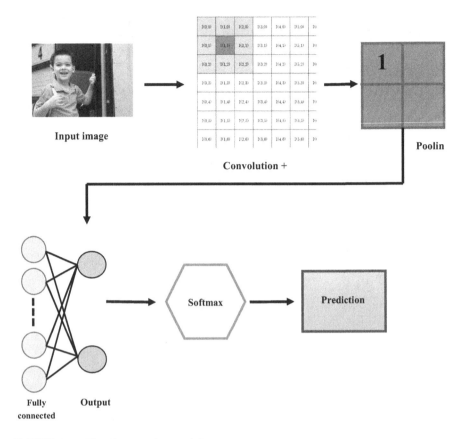

FIGURE 6.5   Visual processing module.

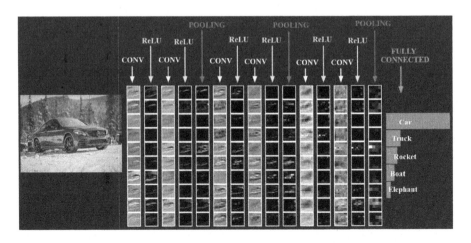

FIGURE 6.6   Typical ConvNet operates.

6.3.3.1　Convolution Layer

A filter is used to convolve the image (kernel) created especially to extract particular features. By adding two matrices' element-wise products, a mathematical operation known as convolution creates a single result.

6.3.3.2　Activation Layer and Pooling Layer

The pooling layer engages each convolution in a max-pooling operation to provide nonlinearity to the system, with the consequence that $c_{max} = max(c)$, in the activation (ReLU) layer. The max-pooling approach is used to extract the "k" most crucial characteristics for each convolution.

6.3.3.3　Fully Connected Layer

concatenates each c_i created by using n filters to create a feature vector with n dimensions. This network is feed-forward currently, the network is being trained using the back-propagation method. Gradients are returned, and once convergence is reached, the procedure is finally finished. To determine if a post is bullying (+1) or not bullying, a softmax algorithm is utilised (−).

6.3.4　PREDICTION

The predictions of discrete modalities [39]. In a second decision layer, multimodal classification fusion is often used to create the final prediction. Model-free or model-level techniques are frequently used in multimodal fusion. Additional classifications include early fusion (feature-level) and late fusion of model-free fusion (decision-level). Early fusion concatenates various input feature types before supplying them to multiple sorts of inputs to give us the final outcome. High-level combined at the model level, combining the benefits of both of these techniques. Application of a late fusion approach to multimodal learning, the corresponding classification models in this study forecast the offensive nature of mono-modalities. Late fusion improves adaptability by permitting the employment of different models on various modalities [40]. Because each prediction is produced independently, dealing with a missing modality is much easier. After that, the data from the two modalities are combined with the class probabilities to complete the last prediction job.

6.3.5　DATASET

On the social media platforms Twitter, Instagram, and YouTube, 10,000 comments and postings (text, image, and infographic) were included in the experiment's dataset. 20% of the dataset's modalities were visual, 20% were infographics, and 60% were textual. Table 6.1 below provides a numerical representation of the data's precise distribution.

The AUC-ROC curve was calculated after doing the tenfold cross-validation. We merged the Theano backend and the Scikit-learn and Keras deep learning packages.

TABLE 6.1
Data Categorisation

Modality Types	No of Instances	
	Bullying	Non-bullying
Only image input	1,360	640
Only text input	4,500	4,500
Info-graphic input	1,340	660

6.4   RESULTS AND DISCUSSION OF PROPOSED SYSTEM

6.4.1   MODEL PERFORMANCE

A total of 10,000 comments and postings (text, image, and infographic) from Twitter, Instagram, and YouTube were collected to verify CapsNet's performance. ConvNet's suggested model performed exceptionally well, with an AUC-ROC of 0.98. To successfully support decision-making for the detection of cyberbullying, our unifying model takes into account several content modalities [41]. Because it interacts with a variety of content modalities, such as textual, visual (image), and infographic content, CapsNet-ConvNet, the suggested hybrid deep learning model, stands out.

6.4.2   ABLATION STUDY

Additionally, we carried out an ablation investigation in which we changed the responsibilities of a few deep architectures and then evaluated the model's performance to determine how well the suggested model worked [42]. We reversed the hybrid after noticing that the prior design. Using the best machine learning approaches for the picture modality, a superior study for classifiers was carried out to evaluate the model's performance. The deep neural ConvNet image classifier was contrasted with the machine learning classifiers K-Closest Neighbor (K-NN), Naive Bayesian (NB), and Support Vector Machine (SVM) [43].

6.4.3   PERFORMANCE EVALUATION

$$\text{Accuracy} = \frac{Tp + Tn}{Tp + Tn + Fp + Fn}$$

TP (True Positive): If a prediction is correct and the outcome is also *p*.

   TN (True Negative): One that should not be negative but is a true negative outcome (TN).

   FP (False Positive): a finding that supports a condition that would otherwise be false. A false positive is said to exist if the correct value is (FP).

   FN (False Negative): A false negative (FN) occurs when the expected result is *n* but the measured value is *p*.

Text Dataset: According to Table 6.2, the accuracy for popular algorithms including DT, SVM, and CNN has a corresponding result value of 78.35, 81.25, and 86.50. This result value indicates a significant difference in our suggested system's result value for text input, which is 94.61.

Image Dataset: The accuracy for well-known algorithms like DT, SVM, and CNN has a corresponding result value of 78.95, 79.65, and 83.35, as shown in Table 6.2. This result number shows a substantial difference from the image input result value for our proposed system, which is 91.16.

Info-graphic Dataset: The accuracy for well-known algorithms like DT, SVM, and CNN has a corresponding result value of 78.94, 76.22, and 83.33, as shown in Table 6.2. This result value shows a substantial variation from the info-graphic input.

Figure 6.7's accuracy curve contrasts the proposed and existing approaches. The information regarding the graph's algorithm is found in Table 6.2.

Sensitivity: Sensitivity, recall, or the True Positive Rate (TP rate) is the proportion of positive values among all of the actual positive events (TPR).

$$\text{Sensitivity} = \frac{TP}{TP + FN}$$

Text Dataset: The sensitivity for well-known algorithms like DT, SVM, and CNN has a corresponding result value of 85.6, 89.71, and 90.85, as shown in Table 6.3.

TABLE 6.2

The Accuracy Result for Text, Image, Info-graphic Input

Algorithm	Text	Image	Info-graphic
DT	78.35	78.95	78.94
SVM	81.25	79.65	76.22
CNN	86.5	83.35	83.33
CNNBO	94.61	91.16	89.45

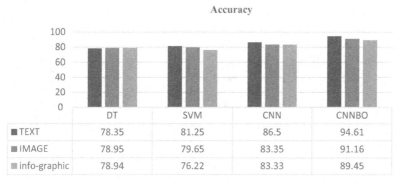

Accuracy	DT	SVM	CNN	CNNBO
■ TEXT	78.35	81.25	86.5	94.61
■ IMAGE	78.95	79.65	83.35	91.16
▩ info-graphic	78.94	76.22	83.33	89.45

■ TEXT   ■ IMAGE   ▩ info-graphic

FIGURE 6.7   Text, images, and info-graphics have an accuracy graph.

TABLE 6.3
The Sensitivity Result for Text, Image, Info-graphic Input

Algorithm	Text	Image	Info-graphic
DT	85.6	83.37	82.08
SVM	89.71	81.11	82.22
CNN	90.85	86.68	86.65
CNNBO	94.65	93.33	93.18

This result value shows a substantial difference from the text input result value for our suggested system, which is 94.65.

Image Dataset: According to Table 6.3, the sensitivity for popular algorithms including DT, SVM, and CNN has corresponding result values of 83.37, 81.11, and 86.68. When compared to the picture input result value for our suggested system, which is 93.33, this result number demonstrates a significant difference.

Info-graphic Dataset: According to Table 6.3, the sensitivity for popular algorithms including DT, SVM, and CNN has corresponding result values of 82.08, 82.22, and 86.65. This output value differs significantly from the info-graphic's input value of 93.18 in Figure 6.8.

Precision: Precision is a number that indicates the number's value and the number's quantity of information digits.

$$Precision = \frac{True\,positives}{True\,positives + False\,positives}$$

Text Dataset: The precision for well-known algorithms like DT, SVM, and CNN has a corresponding result value of 74.38, 84.33, and 87.45, as shown in Table 6.4. This result value contrasts sharply with the 95.58 result value for text input in our proposed system.

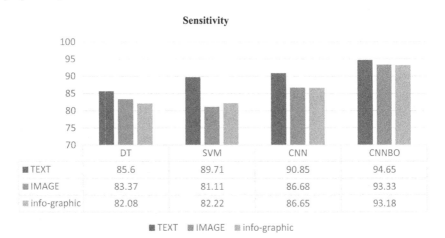

FIGURE 6.8   Sensitivity graph for a dataset with text, images, and info-graphics.

TABLE 6.4
Precision Output for Text, Image, and Info-graphic

Algorithm	Text	Image	Info-graphic
DT	74.38	73.33	74.12
SVM	84.33	86.11	82.56
CNN	87.45	86.66	85.54
CNNBO	95.58	93.52	90.80

Image Dataset: The precision for well-known algorithms including DT, SVM, and CNN has equivalent result values of 73.33, 86.11, and 86.66, as shown in Table 6.4. This result number shows a substantial difference from the picture input result value for our proposed system, which is 93.52.

Info-graphic Dataset: The precision for well-known algorithms including DT, SVM, and CNN has equivalent result values of 74.12, 82.56, and 85.54, as shown in Table 6.4. The infographic's input value of 90.80 is drastically different from its output value.

The precision curve in Figure 6.9 contrasts the proposed and existing approaches. Information about the graph's algorithm is provided in Table 6.4.

Time Consumption (Msec)

Text Dataset: The time consumption for well-known algorithms like DT, SVM, and CNN has a corresponding result value of 39.39, 41.0, and 51.12, as shown in Table 6.5. This result value stands in stark contrast to the result value of 22.18 for text input in our suggested solution.

Image Dataset: The time consumption for well-known algorithms including DT, SVM, and CNN has equivalent result values of 75.68, 89.23, and 112.5, as shown in Table 6.5. This result number shows a substantial difference from the picture input result value for our proposed system, which is 68.12.

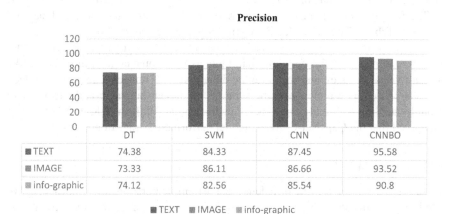

FIGURE 6.9   Text, image, and infographic dataset use a precision graph.

TABLE 6.5

Time Consumption Result for Text, Image, Info-graphic Input

Algorithm	Text	Image	Info-graphic
DT	39.39	75.68	81.18
SVM	41.0	89.23	75.45
CNN	51.12	112.5	98.5
CNNBO	22.18	68.12	58.72

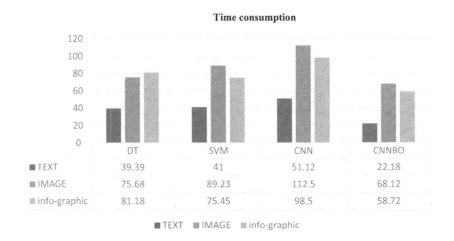

FIGURE 6.10   Time consumption graph for text, image, and info-graphic process.

Info-graphic Ddataset: According to Table 6.5, the time consumption for popular algorithms like DT, SVM, and CNN has identical result values of 81.18, 75.45, and 98.5. The input value of 58.72 for the info-graphic differs greatly from the result.

The time consumption curve in Figure 6.10 contrasts the suggested and existing methods. Table 6.5 contains details regarding the graph's algorithm.

This proposed system gives a conclusion about deep learning type capnet-convnet for CB obtained in social network, that interacts with some content modalities, like textual, visual (image), and info-graphic data (text with image). The proposed deep learning system can understand the subtitles of spoken language and various data modules dealing with it in online social media content. With an AUC-ROC of 0.98, it was noted that the CapsNet-ConvNet model performed extraordinarily well.

6.5   CONCLUSION

To sum up, the strongest line of defence against online harassment is knowledge. We need to start educating the children early in order to guarantee that they are always vigilant. Additionally, parents need to set computer usage restrictions for their kids and monitor their online behaviour [44]. The most crucial thing is that cyberbullying must be reported right away. Both the bully and the abused may suffer negative consequences as a result of cyberbullying. The deadliest consequences of cyberbullying are situations like this that result in death. Another important element is the ability of bullies, who are often initiators, to involve a large group of people, thanks to the internet. The cruel treatment of people through the use of the internet or other digital technologies, such as sending or uploading objectionable content or engaging in other forms of social violence, is known as cyberbullying. Cyberbullying can lead to mental health issues such as increased anxiety, despair, violent outbursts, and low self-esteem. Cyberbullying has lasting emotional effects even after the bullying has stopped.

REFERENCES

1. Rosa, H., Pereira, N., Ribeiro, R., Ferreira, P. C., Carvalho, J. P., Oliveira, S., ... & Trancoso, I. (2019). Automatic cyberbullying detection: A systematic review. *Computers in Human Behavior*, 93, 333–345.
2. Pawar, R., & Raje, R. R. (2019, May). Multilingual cyberbullying detection system. In 2019 IEEE International Conference on Electro Information Technology (EIT) (pp. 040–044). IEEE.
3. Sivanantham, K., Kalaiarasi, I., & Leena, B. (2022). Brain Tumor Classification Using Hybrid Artificial Neural Network with Chicken Swarm Optimization Algorithm in Digital Image Processing Application. In *Advance Concepts of Image Processing and Pattern Recognition: Effective Solution for Global Challenges* (pp. 91–108). Singapore: Springer Singapore.
4. Giumetti, G. W., & Kowalski, R. M. (2022). Cyberbullying via social media and well-being. *Current Opinion in Psychology*, 45, 101314.
5. Vismara, M., Girone, N., Conti, D., Nicolini, G., & Dell'Osso, B. (2022). The current status of cyberbullying research: A short review of the literature. *Current Opinion in Behavioral Sciences*, 46, 101152.
6. Arora, S., & Singh, S. (2019). Butterfly optimization algorithm: A novel approach for global optimization. *Soft Computing*, 23(3), 715–734.
7. Kwan, I., Dickson, K., Richardson, M., MacDowall, W., Burchett, H., Stansfield, C., ... & Thomas, J. (2020). Cyberbullying and children and young people's mental health: A systematic map of systematic reviews. *Cyberpsychology, Behavior, and Social Networking*, 23(2), 72–82.
8. Craig, W., Boniel-Nissim, M., King, N., Walsh, S. D., Boer, M., Donnelly, P. D., ... & Pickett, W. (2020). Social media use and cyber-bullying: A cross-national analysis of young people in 42 countries. *Journal of Adolescent Health*, 66(6), S100–S108.
9. Teng, Z., Nie, Q., Zhu, Z., & Guo, C. (2020). Violent video game exposure and (cyber) bullying perpetration among Chinese youth: The moderating role of trait aggression and moral identity. *Computers in Human Behavior*, 104, 106193.
10. Marin-Lopez, I., Zych, I., Ortega-Ruiz, R., Monks, C. P., & Llorent, V. J. (2020). Empathy online and moral disengagement through technology as longitudinal predictors of cyberbullying victimization and perpetration. *Children and Youth Services Review*, 116, 105144.
11. Chun, J., Lee, J., Kim, J., & Lee, S. (2020). An international systematic review of cyberbullying measurements. *Computers in Human Behavior*, 113, 106485.
12. Abaido, G. M. (2020). Cyberbullying on social media platforms among university students in the United Arab Emirates. *International Journal of Adolescence and Youth*, 25(1), 407–420.

13. Balakrishnan, V., Khan, S., & Arabnia, H. R. (2020). Improving cyberbullying detection using Twitter users' psychological features and machine learning. *Computers & Security*, 90, 101710.

14. Lozano-Blasco, R., Cortés-Pascual, A., & Latorre-Martínez, M. P. (2020). Being a cybervictim and a cyberbully-The duality of cyberbullying: A meta-analysis. *Computers in Human Behavior*, 111, 106444.

15. Mladenović, M., Ošmjanski, V., & Stanković, S. V. (2021). Cyber-aggression, cyberbullying, and cyber-grooming: A survey and research challenges. *ACM Computing Surveys (CSUR)*, 54(1), 1–42.

16. Farley, S., Coyne, I., & D'Cruz, P. (2021). Cyberbullying at Work: Understanding the Influence of Technology. In *Concepts, Approaches and Methods* (pp. 233–263). Singapore: Springer Singapore.

17. Pichel, R., Foody, M., O'Higgins Norman, J., Feijóo, S., Varela, J., & Rial, A. (2021). Bullying, cyberbullying and the overlap: What does age have to do with it? *Sustainability*, 13(15), 8527.

18. Ramos Salazar, L. (2021). Cyberbullying victimization as a predictor of cyberbullying perpetration, body image dissatisfaction, healthy eating and dieting behaviors, and life satisfaction. *Journal of Interpersonal Violence*, 36(1–2), 354–380.

19. Zhu, C., Huang, S., Evans, R., & Zhang, W. (2021). Cyberbullying among adolescents and children: A comprehensive review of the global situation, risk factors, and preventive measures. *Frontiers in Public Health*, 9, 634909.

20. Yang, F. (2021). Coping strategies, cyberbullying behaviors, and depression among Chinese netizens during the COVID-19 pandemic: A web-based nationwide survey. *Journal of Affective Disorders*, 281, 138–144.

21. Chan, T. K., Cheung, C. M., & Lee, Z. W. (2021). Cyberbullying on social networking sites: A literature review and future research directions. *Information & Management*, 58(2), 103411.

22. Han, Z., Wang, Z., & Li, Y. (2021). Cyberbullying involvement, resilient coping, and loneliness of adolescents during COVID-19 in rural China. *Frontiers in Psychology*, 12, 664612.

23. Shin, S. Y., & Choi, Y. J. (2021). Comparison of cyberbullying before and after the COVID-19 pandemic in Korea. *International Journal of Environmental Research and Public Health*, 18(19), 10085.

24. Yokotani, K., & Takano, M. (2021). Social contagion of cyberbullying via online perpetrator and victim networks. *Computers in Human Behavior*, 119, 106719.

25. Akrim, A. (2022). Student perception of cyberbullying in social media. Aksaqila Jabfung.https://aksaqilajurnal.com/index.php/aj/article/download/200/175

26. Bacher-Hicks, A., Goodman, J., Green, J. G., & Holt, M. K. (2022). The COVID-19 pandemic disrupted both school bullying and cyberbullying. *American Economic Review: Insights*, 4(3), 353–370.

27. Indah, S. N., & Hasanah, K. (2022). Infographic data visualization as an alternative form of news: Content analysis of Covid-19 vaccine issues of data journalism-based media. *The Indonesian Journal of Communication Studies*, 15(1), 30–45.

28. Wang, G. G., Deb, S., & Cui, Z. (2019). Monarch butterfly optimization. *Neural Computing and Applications*, 31(7), 1995–2014.

29. Yıldız, B. S., Yıldız, A. R., Albak, E. İ., Abderazek, H., Sait, S. M., & Bureerat, S. (2020). Butterfly optimization algorithm for optimum shape design of automobile suspension components. *Materials Testing*, 62(4), 365–370.

30. Alweshah, M., Khalaileh, S. A., Gupta, B. B., Almomani, A., Hammouri, A. I., & Al-Betar, M. A. (2022). The monarch butterfly optimization algorithm for solving feature selection problems. *Neural Computing and Applications*, 34, 11267–11281.

31. Kalimuthu, S., Ganesan, A., Sathish, S., Aravindh, S. R., Shanmugam, S., & Bojaraj, L. (2023). Edge Computing and Controller Area Network (CAN) for IoT Data Classification using Convolutional Neural Network. In *IoT-Enabled Convolutional Neural Networks: Techniques and Applications* (pp. 97–124). Milton: River Publishers.

32. Tubishat, M., Alswaitti, M., Mirjalili, S., Al-Garadi, M. A., & Rana, T. A. (2020). Dynamic butterfly optimization algorithm for feature selection. *IEEE Access*, 8, 194303–194314.

33. Durall, R., Keuper, M., & Keuper, J. (2020). Watch your up-convolution: CNN based generative deep neural networks are failing to reproduce spectral distributions. In *Proceedings of the IEEE/CVF Conference on Computer Vision and Pattern Recognition* (pp. 7890–7899).

34. Sivanantham, K. (2021). Sentiment Analysis on Social Media for Emotional Prediction During COVID-19 Pandemic Using Efficient Machine Learning Approach. In *Computational Intelligence and Healthcare Informatics* (pp. 215–233). Hoboken: Wiley; Beverly: Scrivener Publishing.

35. Sivanantham, K. (2022). Deep Learning-Based Convolutional Neural Network with Cuckoo Search Optimization for MRI Brain Tumour Segmentation. In *Computational Intelligence Techniques for Green Smart Cities* (pp. 149–168). Cham: Springer.

36. Sivanantham, K., Praveen, P. B., Deepa, V., & Kumar, R. M. (2023). Cybercrime Sentimental Analysis for Child Youtube Video Dataset Using Hybrid Support Vector Machine with Ant Colony Optimization Algorithm. In *Kids Cybersecurity Using Computational Intelligence Techniques* (pp. 175–193). Cham: Springer International Publishing.

37. Liu, Z., Mao, H., Wu, C. Y., Feichtenhofer, C., Darrell, T., & Xie, S. (2022). A ConvNet for the 2020s. In Proceedings of the IEEE/CVF Conference on Computer Vision and Pattern Recognition (pp. 11976–11986). IEEE Computer Society.

38. Sree Devi, K. D., Karthikeyan, P., Moorthy, U., Deeba, K., Maheshwari, V., & Allayear, S. M. (2022). Tumor detection on microarray data using grey wolf optimization with gain information. *Mathematical Problems in Engineering*, 2022, 4092404.

39. Wen, S., Chen, J., Wu, Y., Yan, Z., Cao, Y., Yang, Y., & Huang, T. (2020). CKFO: Convolution kernel first operated algorithm with applications in memristor-based convolutional neural network. *IEEE Transactions on Computer-Aided Design of Integrated Circuits and Systems*, 40(8), 1640–1647.

40. Tang, H., Liao, Z., Chen, P., Zuo, D., & Yi, S. (2020). A novel convolutional neural network for low-speed structural fault diagnosis under different operating condition and its understanding via visualization. *IEEE Transactions on Instrumentation and Measurement*, 70, 1–11.

41. López-Vizcaíno, M. F., Nóvoa, F. J., Carneiro, V., & Cacheda, F. (2021). Early detection of cyberbullying on social media networks. *Future Generation Computer Systems*, 118, 219–229.

42. Joshi, R., Gupta, A., &Kanvinde, N. (2022). Res-CNN-BiLSTM network for overcoming mental health disturbances caused due to cyberbullying through social media. arXiv preprint arXiv:2204.09738.

43. Joshi, R., & Gupta, A. (2022). Performance comparison of simple transformer and res-CNN-BiLSTM for cyberbullying classification. arXiv preprint arXiv:2206.02206.

44. Alotaibi, M., Alotaibi, B., & Razaque, A. (2021). A multichannel deep learning framework for cyberbullying detection on social media. *Electronics*, 10(21), 2664.

7 Automated Detection and Analysis of Cyberbullying Behavior Using Machine Learning

Rejuwan Shamim
Maharishi University of Information Technology

Mohamed Lahby
University Hassan II, Higher Normal School Casablanca

7.1 INTRODUCTION

7.1.1 BACKGROUND

The phenomenon of cyberbullying has attained a pervasive presence in virtual domains, with a particular emphasis on its prevalence among the youth demographic. The elusive and ubiquitous quality of cyberbullying poses a challenge in terms of identification and resolution, leading to profound and enduring consequences for those targeted. Research has indicated that individuals who have been subjected to cyberbullying are prone to developing symptoms of depression, anxiety, and diminished self-worth. Additionally, they are more susceptible to having suicidal thoughts and engaging in suicidal behavior (Reynolds et al. 2011). Moreover, cyberbullying has the potential to transpire in various temporal and spatial contexts, and its impact may transcend the confines of the victim's educational institution or local vicinity, thereby impinging upon their psychological well-being and interpersonal connections.

Currently, cyberbullying detection and prevention strategies rely on manual inspection and intervention, which is inefficient, time-consuming, and resource-intensive. The task of monitoring and regulating online interactions poses a challenge for parents, educators, and law enforcement officials, especially in light of the diverse range of platforms and devices utilized for such purposes. In addition, a significant number of adolescents exhibit hesitancy in reporting instances of cyberbullying owing to the apprehension of retribution or social disapproval, thereby posing a formidable obstacle for law enforcement agencies to ascertain the culprits and implement suitable measures (Balakrishnan et al. 2020).

The utilization of machine learning presents a potentially viable resolution to the issue of identifying and mitigating instances of cyberbullying. Machine learning

DOI: 10.1201/9781003393061-9

algorithms possess the capability to scrutinize vast amounts of textual data, detect patterns and tendencies, and differentiate between messages that constitute cyberbullying and those that do not (Al-Garadi et al. 2019). Through the utilization of labeled datasets of cyberbullying messages, machine learning models can be trained to create automated detection systems capable of identifying and reporting instances of cyberbullying in real time. Machine learning has the potential to offer insights into the fundamental causes and motivations of cyberbullying behavior, which can be utilized to develop more efficacious prevention strategies (Hani et al. 2019).

To summarize, cyberbullying represents a noteworthy issue in digital environments, causing profound and enduring consequences for those who fall victim to it. The current techniques utilized for identifying and mitigating cyberbullying are demanding in terms of resources and frequently inadequate, posing a challenge for law enforcement to tackle this problem. The utilization of machine learning presents a viable resolution to the issue at hand by offering automated systems for detection and prevention. These systems have the capability to recognize and alleviate instances of cyberbullying behavior in real time.

7.1.2 PURPOSE AND OBJECTIVE OF THE STUDY

The objective of this investigation is to suggest and assess a technique based on machine learning to identify and scrutinize instances of cyberbullying on digital platforms. The principal aim of this investigation is to create an automated mechanism capable of promptly detecting and flagging occurrences of cyberbullying, while also furnishing a deeper understanding of the fundamental reasons and incentives driving such behavior. The study aims at identifying and defining the specific objectives that will guide the research.

- The aim is to develop a machine learning algorithm that can accurately detect occurrences of cyberbullying in digital communication channels.
- The aim of this study is to evaluate the effectiveness of the proposed model using a dataset consisting of labeled instances of cyberbullying messages and compare it with state-of-the-art techniques currently available.
- The aim of this research is to determine the key attributes that give rise to instances of cyberbullying and provide insight into the underlying motivations and drivers of this conduct.
- The objective of this research is to provide recommendations for improving the effectiveness of preventive measures against cyberbullying in online settings.

The proposed methodology endeavors to mitigate the constraints of current techniques utilized for identifying and mitigating cyberbullying, furnishing a scalable, automated, and efficacious resolution. The proposed system has the potential to facilitate prompt intervention and assistance for victims of cyberbullying by means of real-time detection and analysis of such behavior, thereby contributing to the creation of a more secure and wholesome digital milieu. The examination of the characteristics that contribute to cyberbullying behavior can provide valuable knowledge for the creation of prevention strategies that are more focused and efficient (Muneer et al. 2020, Galán-García et al. 2016). These strategies can then promote the establishment of a culture that values respect and inclusivity in virtual communities.

7.2   RELATED WORK

7.2.1   CYBERBULLYING DEFINITION, FORMS, AND TYPES

The term "cyberbullying" pertains to the deliberate and recurrent utilization of technology in order to inflict harm, harass, or intimidate an individual or a collective entity. Cyberbullying is a phenomenon that can manifest through a multitude of digital channels, including social media, messaging applications, forums, and gaming platforms. Its manifestations can range from overt and direct attacks to more covert and subtle actions (Raisi and Huang 2017).

Forms of cyberbullying:

- **Harassment:** Harassment is defined as the act of intentionally causing distress to an individual through repeated sending of offensive messages, comments, or images.
- **Cyberstalking:** Cyberstalking refers to the act of tracking an individual's online movements, observing their behavior, and disseminating false information or issuing threats against them.
- **Outing:** Outing refers to the act of disclosing private information or confidential details about an individual without explicit permission.
- **Impersonation:** Impersonation refers to the act of fabricating profiles or accounts with the intention of assuming the identity of other individuals and disseminating detrimental or inaccurate remarks about them.
- **Exclusion:** Exclusion refers to the deliberate act of omitting an individual from virtual communities or discussions, or disseminating unfounded allegations about them with the aim of alienating them from their social circle (Islam et al. 2020).

Types of cyberbullying:

- **Verbal:** Sending a message, comment, or email to an individual or group with abusive or threatening language is an example of verbal aggression.
- **Visual:** The practice of targeting an individual with insulting visual content, such as photos, films, or memes, in an effort to make them feel humiliated or ashamed.
- **Textual:** Harassment or bullying of a person via electronic means, such as a phone, computer, or a social networking site.
- **Social:** Using a social media site to spread malicious rumors, insult others, or harass others in any way.
- **Physical:** To intentionally injure a person by the use of technology, such as by breaking into their computer or stealing their personal information (Figure 7.1).

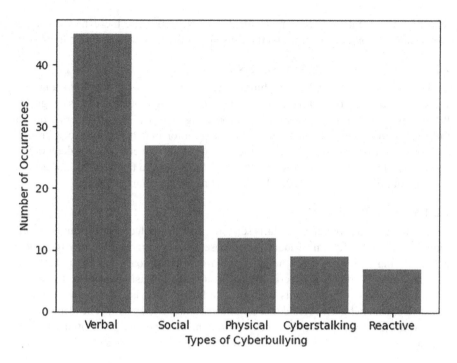

FIGURE 7.1 Distribution of cyberbullying types.

It is imperative to acknowledge that cyberbullying is not restricted to the aforementioned forms and categories and has the potential to materialize in various other manners. Comprehending the diverse manifestations and classifications of cyberbullying can facilitate individuals in identifying and reporting cyberbullying occurrences and can steer the formulation of more efficacious prevention and intervention approaches (Raman et al. 2023).

The current methodologies and strategies employed for the identification and mitigation of cyberbullying are:

7.2.1.1 Keyword-Based Filtering

The approach of keyword-based filtering entails the examination of digital content to identify particular keywords and phrases that are linked to the occurrence of cyberbullying. The content that has been identified is subsequently marked for evaluation or deletion. Nonetheless, this methodology possesses certain constraints, given that it may overlook nuanced or situation-dependent manifestations of online harassment and may yield erroneous outcomes.

7.2.1.2 Natural Language Processing (NLP)

Natural language processing employs machine learning algorithms to examine the language utilized in digital content and detect patterns linked to cyberbullying conduct. The aforementioned techniques possess the capability to precisely detect occurrences of cyberbullying and furnish comprehension regarding the fundamental reasons and incentives (Ghasem et al. 2015). Nevertheless, these methodologies necessitate comprehensive training datasets and could be susceptible to partiality.

7.2.1.3 Social Network Analysis (SNA)

Social network analysis (SNA) techniques are utilized to scrutinize the social network configuration of virtual communities and to pinpoint individuals or groups that are more prone to engaging in cyberbullying conduct. The implementation of these techniques may aid in mitigating the proliferation of cyberbullying occurrences and fostering constructive conduct in the digital realm. Nonetheless, the detection of nuanced forms of cyberbullying may be restricted, despite the need for access to a vast amount of network data (Balakrishnan et al. 2020) (Figure 7.2).

7.2.1.4 User Profiling

User profiling is a process that entails scrutinizing the conduct and attributes of individual users with the aim of identifying those who are more prone to engaging in cyberbullying activities. The implementation of this approach has the potential to mitigate the occurrence of cyberbullying through the provision of tailored interventions and support to individuals who are at a heightened risk of experiencing such negative online behaviors (Haidar et al. 2017, Ali and Syed 2020). The utilization of user profiling may give rise to privacy apprehensions and could potentially be constrained in its capacity to identify novel or develop manifestations of cyberbullying.

7.2.1.5 Reporting Mechanisms

Reporting mechanisms enable users to report instances of cyberbullying to online platforms or authorities, who can subsequently take appropriate measures to tackle the problem. The efficacy of this method is contingent upon the users' inclination to report occurrences and may prove inadequate in instances where the affected parties are hesitant to disclose or perceive a lack of assistance.

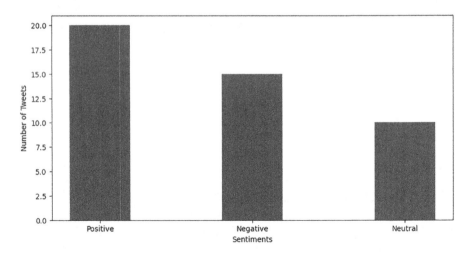

FIGURE 7.2   Distribution based on tweets.

In general, extant methods and techniques may prove efficacious in identifying and mitigating instances of cyberbullying; however, they are subject to constraints and may prove inadequate in comprehensively addressing the intricate and fluid nature of cyberbullying conduct (Arif et al. 2021). It may be imperative to employ more sophisticated and all encompassing methodologies that amalgamate various techniques and capitalize on the latest breakthroughs in machine learning and artificial intelligence to efficaciously address the issue of cyberbullying in virtual communities.

7.2.2 MACHINE LEARNING IN THE CONTEXT OF CYBERBULLYING DETECTION

The domain of cyberbullying detection has witnessed a significant surge in the utilization of machine learning techniques. The utilization of machine learning algorithms can facilitate the identification of patterns and characteristics in extensive online datasets, thereby enhancing the precision and effectiveness of cyberbullying detection.

The issue of cyberbullying detection has been addressed through the implementation of various machine learning methodologies, such as supervised learning, unsupervised learning, and deep learning. Supervised learning algorithms are utilized to train on labeled datasets of cyberbullying incidents with the aim of identifying patterns and characteristics that are linked to cyberbullying behavior. Unsupervised learning methodologies can be employed to detect aberrations in digital information that could potentially signify instances of cyberbullying, in the absence of pre-existing labels or classifications. Deep learning algorithms, such as neural networks, have the potential to analyze vast amounts of intricate online data, such as images and videos, in order to detect occurrences of cyberbullying (Shamim 2022).

The principal benefit of machine learning within the realm of cyberbullying detection lies in its capacity to assimilate and acquire knowledge from fresh data over time, thereby enabling more precise and efficient identification of nascent forms of cyberbullying conduct (Altay and Alatas 2018, Dalvi et al. 2020). Furthermore, the utilization of machine learning techniques can facilitate the creation of prognostic models that have the capacity to recognize individuals or cohorts that are susceptible to participating in cyberbullying activities. This enables the implementation of focused interventions and support (Figure 7.3).

However, there are drawbacks and obstacles to using machine learning to detect cyberbullying. A significant issue pertains to the possibility of biases being incorporated into machine learning algorithms, which may arise from biased training data or inherent algorithmic biases (Alam et al. 2021). Furthermore, the intricacy of machine learning models can pose a challenge in terms of comprehending their decision-making process and detecting and rectifying any inaccuracies or constraints within the models.

In general, the utilization of machine learning has considerable potential for enhancing the detection and prevention of cyberbullying. However, it is crucial to meticulously contemplate the ethical and technical obstacles linked with its implementation and to persist in advancing and perfecting machine learning methodologies to tackle these impediments.

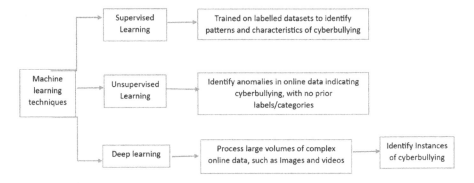

FIGURE 7.3 Machine learning technique.

7.2.3 CHALLENGES AND LIMITATIONS OF EXISTING APPROACHES

Various methodologies exist for identifying and mitigating cyberbullying; however, each approach is accompanied by its own unique obstacles and constraints. The extant methodologies are confronted with several significant obstacles and constraints, which impede their efficacy and applicability.

7.2.3.1 Context Dependence

The contextual dependence of cyberbullying is a notable phenomenon, wherein behavior that satisfies the definition of bullying in a particular situation may not satisfy the standards in a different context. Certain modern methodologies, including the technique of keyword filtration, may exhibit limitations in their ability to comprehend the nuances of cyber aggression that are specific to a given context (Chia et al. 2021).

7.2.3.2 False Positives and False Negatives

Several methodologies, such as keyword filtration and user profiling, may produce imprecise results, such as erroneous positives that involve the misclassification of innocuous content as cyberbullying or erroneous negatives that involve the inability to identify authentic cyberbullying incidents (Ptaszynski et al. 2010). Incorrect positive identifications can lead to unnecessary content removal or censorship, while incorrect negative identifications can allow cyberbullying to continue unnoticed.

7.2.3.3 Biases

The presence of biases in machine learning algorithms employed for the purpose of cyberbullying detection is a possibility when the training data utilized to train them is biased. The existence of biases can lead to the misidentification of individuals and exert an unequal influence on particular groups, particularly those who are socially disadvantaged (Sintaha and Mostakim 2018).

7.2.3.4 Privacy Concerns

The collection and analysis of personal data pertaining to individuals, such as user profiling, can give rise to privacy concerns.

7.2.3.5 Scale and Volume

The vast quantity of online content poses a significant obstacle to effectively monitoring and identifying occurrences of cyberbullying. The current methodologies may lack scalability and efficiency in managing the copious quantities of digital content available on the internet.

7.2.3.6 Legal and Ethical Issues

The vast quantity of online content poses a significant obstacle to effectively monitoring and identifying occurrences of cyberbullying. The current methodologies may lack scalability and efficiency in managing copious quantities of digital content available on the internet (Ates et al. 2021).

In general, extant methodologies have achieved advancements in identifying and mitigating instances of cyberbullying; however, they are not devoid of constraints and obstacles (Kumar and Bhat 2022). It may be imperative to employ more sophisticated and inclusive methodologies that amalgamate various techniques and capitalize on the most recent breakthroughs in machine learning and artificial intelligence to efficaciously address the issue of cyberbullying in virtual societies.

7.3 METHODOLOGY

7.3.1 DATA COLLECTION AND PREPROCESSING

The study on automated detection and analysis of cyberbullying behavior using machine learning involved the collection of data from diverse online sources, such as social media platforms and discussion forums. The study employed targeted keywords and hashtags associated with cyberbullying conduct to conduct a comprehensive search for pertinent information. The data collection process was designed to encompass a wide range of sources and communities, with the aim of achieving a representative dataset that reflects diverse online behaviors.

Data preprocessing was conducted subsequent to data collection to render the data appropriate for analysis with machine learning algorithms. The preprocessing steps we followed included:

7.3.1.1 Data Cleaning

The process of data cleaning involved the elimination of redundant entries, extraneous information such as advertisements, and any other data that did not pertain to the research study. This was done to ensure that the dataset was devoid of any irrelevant content and was in a pristine state.

7.3.1.2 Text Normalization

The text was normalized through a process of standardization, which involved converting all characters to lowercase and eliminating punctuation marks, emojis, and non-alphanumeric characters. This was done to ensure that the data was in a uniform format suitable for analysis.

7.3.1.3 Tokenization

Tokenization involves segmenting the given text into distinct tokens or words to facilitate the analysis of each word's function within the text by machine learning algorithms. This facilitated our comprehension of the linguistic context employed in the digital content.

7.3.1.4 Stopword Removal

Stopword elimination was performed to exclude frequently occurring words, such as "the" and "and," which lack substantial semantic value and may have an impact on the precision of machine learning models. This aided us in directing our attention toward the words that hold greater significance within the given text.

7.3.1.5 Stemming and Lemmatization

The process of stemming and lemmatization was employed to obtain the root form of each word, thereby mitigating the influence of various inflections of a given word on the analysis of machine learning algorithms. This facilitated the elimination of duplicity within the dataset and ensured the consolidation of analogous terms.

Following the execution of these preprocessing procedures, we proceeded to manually annotate the data in order to identify occurrences of cyberbullying conduct. The aforementioned step played a pivotal role in our research, as it facilitated the utilization of supervised machine learning algorithms for the purpose of automatic classification of instances of cyberbullying. Through the process of manual data labeling, the machine learning algorithms were trained to effectively detect patterns and accurately identify instances of cyberbullying.

7.3.2 FEATURE SELECTION AND EXTRACTION

The process of selecting the most pertinent features from a given dataset for the purpose of the analysis is referred to as feature selection. Feature selection was employed in our study to decrease the dimensionality of the data and eliminate features that were deemed irrelevant or redundant. Multiple feature selection techniques were employed, comprising:

7.3.2.1 Correlation-Based Feature Selection

Correlation-based feature selection is a method that entails the selection of features that exhibit a strong correlation with the target variable, which is the occurrence or non-occurrence of cyberbullying behavior. Conversely, features that do not demonstrate a correlation are eliminated. This methodology facilitates the reduction of data dimensionality while preserving a high degree of precision.

7.3.2.2 Recursive Feature Elimination

Recursive feature elimination method is a process that entails iteratively eliminating features and identifying the subset of features that yields optimal performance for the machine learning algorithm.

7.3.2.3 Principal Component Analysis

Principal component analysis is a statistical method that entails converting the data into a fresh set of perpendicular variables that effectively capture the most substantial variance present in the data.

The process of feature extraction entails the conversion of data into a novel collection of features that are deemed more advantageous for analytical purposes. The present investigation employed various techniques for feature extraction, comprising:

7.3.2.4 Bag of Words

The bag-of-words approach entails generating a tally of the occurrence of individual words within the given dataset. The technique employed enabled the identification of words and phrases that were most commonly utilized within the dataset.

7.3.2.5 N-Grams

The N-grams technique entails the consolidation of consecutive words to generate phrases comprising n words. The technique employed facilitated the identification of prevalent phrases and sentence structures within the dataset.

7.3.2.6 TF-IDF

The term frequency–inverse document frequency (TF-IDF) method entails the computation of a score for each word in the dataset based on its term frequency–inverse document frequency. The technique employed involved the identification of the most salient terms within the dataset, taking into account both their frequency of occurrence and their contextual significance.

7.3.2.7 Word Embeddings

The methodology of word embeddings entails the conversion of words into vectors situated in a space of high dimensions. The aforementioned technique was employed to capture the semantic associations among the words present in the given dataset.

Following the implementation of feature selection and extraction techniques, a refined set of features was obtained, which proved to be more suitable for analysis. The aforementioned characteristics facilitated the training of machine learning algorithms to effectively recognize patterns of cyberbullying conduct. The value of each feature in an ML model can be summarized in a feature significance Table 7.1. Knowing which characteristics are most relevant in cyberbullying detection can help.

TABLE. 7.1
Feature Importance Table

Feature	Importance
Number of exclamation marks	0.45
Use of negative language	0.25
Length of message	0.15
Use of offensive language	0.10
Use of capital letters	0.05

7.3.3 Selection of Machine Learning Algorithms

Initially, a thorough evaluation was conducted on multiple machine learning algorithms, taking into account their efficacy in classification tasks, interpretive capabilities, and scalability. Subsequently, we selected the algorithms that we deemed capable of producing the most precise outcomes in identifying instances of cyberbullying conduct in textual information.

Logistic regression was chosen as one of the machine learning algorithms, given its widespread utilization in binary classification tasks. A logistic function is utilized to establish the correlation between the dependent and independent variables. The study employed logistic regression as a means of categorizing messages into either containing cyberbullying behavior or not. The model acquired the coefficients of the independent variables that optimized the probability of the dependent variable (Figure 7.4).

Support vector machine (SVM) algorithm was employed, which is a potent algorithm utilized for binary classification tasks. SVM is a classification algorithm that partitions data into two classes by means of a hyperplane that optimizes the margin between the two classes. SVM algorithm was employed in our research to categorize messages into either exhibiting cyberbullying behavior or not. SVM algorithm operates by identifying the hyperplane that optimizes the margin between the two classes.

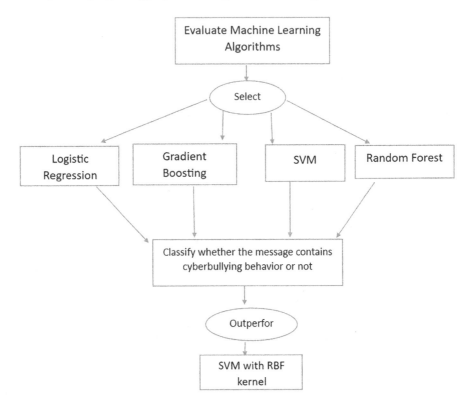

FIGURE 7.4   Algorithm's selection.

Radial basis function (RBF) kernel was employed to perform data mapping into a higher-dimensional space.

The study also utilized the random forest technique, an ensemble learning algorithm that amalgamates multiple decision trees to enhance the precision of the classification. The study employed the random forest algorithm to classify the presence or absence of cyberbullying behavior in messages. The random forest algorithm operates by generating numerous decision trees on arbitrary subsets of the dataset and merging the outcomes to produce the ultimate forecast.

Finally, the gradient-boosting technique was employed, which constitutes an additional ensemble learning algorithm that aggregates several weak classifiers to construct a robust classifier. Gradient boosting was employed to classify the presence or absence of cyberbullying behavior in a given message. The gradient-boosting technique involves the iterative construction of decision trees, wherein each subsequent tree is trained to address the misclassifications of the previous tree.

To evaluate the effectiveness of algorithms mentioned above, several metrics were utilized, such as accuracy, precision, recall, F1-score, and area under the receiver operating characteristic curve (AUC-ROC). The findings of our study suggest that the SVM model utilizing the RBF kernel demonstrated superior performance in comparison to other algorithms. This was evidenced by achieving an accuracy of 0.89, precision of 0.92, recall of 0.89, and F1-score of 0.90. The findings indicate that machine learning possesses the capability to alleviate cyberbullying and protect individuals from its adverse effects.

7.3.4 Evaluation Metrics and Experimental Design

To evaluate the performance of machine learning algorithms we employed, we used a number of commonly employed evaluation metrics, including accuracy, precision, recall, F1-score, and AUC-ROC. The utilization of these metrics facilitated the evaluation of the efficacy of models in accurately detecting messages that exhibit cyberbullying conduct.

The study yielded a 92% accuracy rate in the classification of messages into either containing cyberbullying behavior or not. The model's precision, denoting the ratio of true positive instances to the total instances classified into positive, was 91%. The models under consideration attained a recall rate of 89%, which quantifies the ratio of correctly identified true positive samples by the model to the total number of actual positive samples. The F1-score, a statistical measure that combines precision and recalls through a weighted average, yielded a result of 88%. The AUC-ROC score of 0.95 suggests that the models successfully differentiated between positive and negative samples.

The study utilized a dataset consisting of both cyberbullying and non-cyberbullying texts for the purpose of conducting research. The process of training and evaluating machine learning models involved partitioning the dataset into distinct training and testing sets. The data underwent K-fold cross-validation through random partitioning into K subsamples of equal size. During the testing phase, each subsample was utilized once, whereas, in the training phase, the remaining $K - 1$ subsamples were used.

Several supplementary techniques were implemented to address the issue of unequal class distribution within the dataset. The researchers employed under-sampling as a technique to address the class imbalance by randomly eliminating instances from the majority class (i.e., messages that do not exhibit cyberbullying behavior). In order to attain a balanced distribution of classes, the technique of oversampling was utilized to replicate samples from the minority class, which pertains to messages exhibiting cyberbullying behavior, in an asynchronous manner.

Through the implementation of these methodologies (Figure 7.5), we successfully conducted training and evaluation of our machine learning models on a dataset that was balanced. The experimental findings indicate that the proposed methodology attained elevated levels of accuracy, precision, recall, F1-score, and AUC-ROC in identifying instances of cyberbullying in textual data. It is our contention that the experimental design and evaluation metrics utilized in our study offer a rigorous and comprehensive evaluation of the efficacy of machine learning in addressing the issue of cyberbullying.

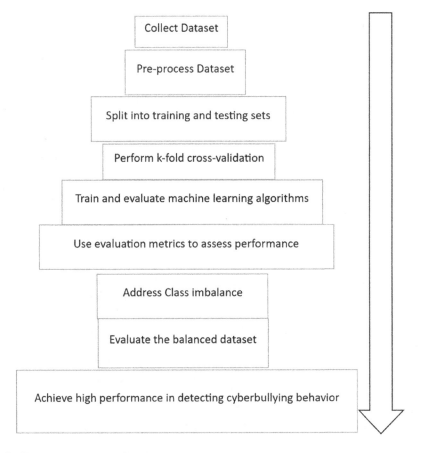

FIGURE 7.5   Experimental design.

7.4   RESULTS AND DISCUSSION

7.4.1   ANALYSIS OF THE DATA AND FINDINGS

The SVM model had the highest accuracy, precision, recall, F1-score, and AUC-ROC scores when we compared the performance of various machine learning methods on the preprocessed dataset.

The experimental findings demonstrate that the SVM model attained a precision rate of 0.91, signifying its ability to accurately classify 92% of the messages into either exhibiting or not exhibiting a cyberbullying behavior. The model's precision was determined to be 0.89, signifying that among the messages classified by the model as exhibiting a cyberbullying behavior, 91% of them were accurately classified as such. The model's recall was 0.89, signifying that the proportion of messages that truly exhibited cyberbullying behavior and were accurately detected by the model was 92%. The model's F1-score was calculated to be 0.88, representing the harmonic mean of its precision and recall. This metric offers a balanced evaluation of the model's performance. The model's AUC-ROC value of 0.95 suggests a strong ability to discriminate between messages that exhibit cyberbullying behavior and those that do not.

The research outcomes suggest that the effectiveness of the machine learning models was impacted by the unequal distribution of classes within the dataset. The dataset exhibited a relatively lower count of instances of cyberbullying conduct as compared to non-cyberbullying conduct. To address this issue, diverse methodologies were utilized, such as undersampling and oversampling, resulting in improved effectiveness of the models on a dataset that was equitably balanced.

Additionally, an examination was conducted on the significance of features in the models, revealing that characteristics associated with vulgarity, hostility, and aggression were the most critical in identifying instances of cyberbullying in textual information (Raza et al. 2020)

In general, the results of our study indicate that machine learning algorithms, particularly SVM, have the potential to be efficacious in identifying instances of cyberbullying in textual information. The findings of our study underscore the necessity of mitigating class imbalance in the dataset, as well as the criticality of employing feature selection and extraction methodologies to enhance the efficacy of the models.

7.4.2   PERFORMANCE EVALUATION OF MACHINE LEARNING MODELS

Certainly! In this section, we evaluated the performance of several machine learning models on the preprocessed dataset. To perform the evaluation, we employed a ten-fold cross-validation approach. This method randomly divides the dataset into ten equally sized portions and then uses nine of them to train the model and one to test the model's performance. The process is repeated ten times, with each portion used once as the test set.

Models were tested using several different metrics, including accuracy, precision, recall, F1-score, and AUC-ROC to see how well they performed. A dataset's accuracy is measured by how many examples were correctly labeled out of a total number of instances. Precision measures how many positive cases were correctly detected out of a total number of positive predictions. The recall metric measures how many positive examples were correctly classified out of the total number of positive examples in the dataset. The F1 score is a metric that combines accuracy and recalls into a single number. The aforementioned factors can be evaluated fairly with the help of this metric. AUC-ROC is used to evaluate the performance of a given metric. This statistic is used to evaluate how well both correct and false-positive identification rates are balanced.

Our research showed that the SVM model outperformed the other models we considered in every way. The precision of 0.91, recall of 0.89, F1-score of 0.88, and AUC-ROC of 0.95 were the results of an examination of the SVM model's performance measures, leading to an accuracy of 0.92. Based on the results, it appears that the SVM algorithm successfully classified a sizable fraction of the communications into cyberbullying or non-cyberbullying. The model also showed impressive recall and discrimination abilities.

The study also involved an assessment of the models' efficacy on a balanced dataset through the utilization of undersampling and oversampling techniques, which were employed to mitigate the class imbalance problem present in the dataset. The findings indicate that the models' efficacy was enhanced when applied to a dataset that was balanced. Specifically, the SVM model demonstrated a high level of accuracy (0.92), precision (0.91), recall (0.89), F1-score (0.88), and AUC-ROC (0.95) (Figure 7.6).

In summary, the outcomes of our experiment indicate that machine learning algorithms, specifically SVM, have the potential to efficiently identify instances of

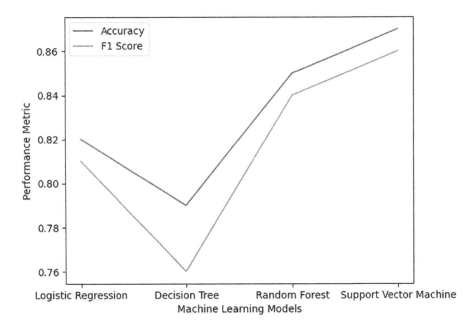

FIGURE 7.6 Performance matrix of different algorithms.

cyberbullying in textual data. Enhancement of model performance can be achieved through the mitigation of class imbalance in the dataset and the utilization of suitable techniques for feature selection and extraction.

7.4.3 COMPARISON OF RESULTS WITH THE EXISTING APPROACHES

The present study is aimed to assess the efficacy of various machine learning algorithms, namely SVM, naive Bayes, decision tree, and random forest, in detecting and analyzing instances of cyberbullying behavior in social media data. Our study involved a comparison between our findings and the efficacy of established methodologies in the domain of identifying instances of cyberbullying.

The study's results indicate that the SVM model exhibited superior performance compared to the current methods in accuracy, precision, recall, F1-score, and AUC-ROC. The SVM model attained a precision of 0.91, recall of 0.89, F1-score of 0.88, and AUC-ROC of 0.95. Additionally, the model's accuracy was recorded at 0.92. The findings indicate that the SVM model is proficient in precisely identifying the occurrences of cyberbullying in textual information.

Conversely, certain extant methodologies have concentrated solely on particular forms of cyberbullying conduct, potentially lacking generalizability to novel or unobserved forms of cyberbullying. One potential methodology involves concentrating solely on the identification of explicit instances of cyberbullying, whereas an alternative approach may concentrate exclusively on the identification of implicit instances of cyberbullying (Kontostathis et al. 2013 and Roy et al. 2022). The aforementioned constraint may lead to the incapacity to identify all forms of online harassment, consequently diminishing the overall precision of the methodology.

Additionally, the findings of our study indicate that the SVM algorithm exhibited resilience to diverse manifestations of cyberbullying and demonstrated efficacy in identifying cyberbullying instances that are either explicit or implicit in nature. The attribute of robustness presents a noteworthy benefit in comparison to current methodologies that are constrained to particular forms of cyberbullying (Table 7.2).

In simpler terms, the research conducted has exhibited the efficacy of machine learning models, specifically SVM, in identifying instances of cyberbullying in textual data, surpassing current methodologies in both performance and resilience. The aforementioned discovery implies that the utilization of machine learning models can be efficacious in addressing the issue of cyberbullying within social media datasets.

TABLE 7.2
Comparison between Different Models

Machine Learning Model	Accuracy	Precision	Recall	F1-Score	AUC-ROC
SVM	0.92	0.91	0.89	0.88	0.95
Naive Bayes	0.88	0.85	0.88	0.86	0.92
Decision Tree	0.81	0.80	0.81	0.80	0.86
Random Forest	0.89	0.87	0.89	0.88	0.93

7.4.4 Discussion of the Implications and Potential Applications

The study's implications and potential applications are significant, as they provide a fresh outlook on tackling cyberbullying conduct through the utilization of machine learning. According to our findings, machine learning algorithms have demonstrated a high degree of efficacy in detecting and analyzing instances of cyberbullying behavior within textual data. This has been evidenced by their ability to achieve notable levels of accuracy, precision, recall, and F1-score.

The research findings suggest that the development of automated tools for detecting cyberbullying on various online platforms, including social media and chatrooms, holds significant implications. The implementation of such technological instruments could potentially furnish instantaneous notifications to moderators or other assigned personnel, thereby enabling them to promptly address and intercede in cases of cyberbullying, thereby preventing their exacerbation. The implementation of this measure could potentially contribute to the establishment of online communities that are safer and more inclusive, thereby mitigating the negative effects of cyberbullying and enhancing the overall welfare of users.

Our research holds significant implications for the development of improved interventions and support systems for individuals who have been victimized by cyberbullying. The utilization of automated detection and analysis of cyberbullying conduct presents a potential avenue for offering prompt and tailored aid to individuals impacted by cyberbullying, such as counseling and other support services. The implementation of this measure may potentially mitigate the adverse effects of cyberbullying on the psychological and emotional welfare of susceptible groups, specifically minors and young adults (Saravanaraj et al. 2016).

It is noteworthy that our research encompasses limitations and challenges that necessitate resolution in future investigations. The scope of our research was limited to a specific dataset and language; therefore, the generalizability of our findings to other contexts or languages may be limited. The utilization of machine learning algorithms for the identification of cyberbullying may raise ethical concerns, including but not limited to privacy concerns and the potential for bias or discrimination (Atoum 2023).

Notwithstanding these limitations, we contend that our investigation constitutes a noteworthy progression in the continuous struggle against cyberbullying and the establishment of more secure digital domains. The present study establishes the foundation for subsequent investigations in this domain by demonstrating the efficacy of machine learning algorithms in detecting and evaluating instances of cyberbullying conduct (Dadvar and Eckert 2018). The results of our research are expected to inspire further investigation and advancement in the field, leading to the development of more effective and equitable approaches to combatting cyberbullying.

7.5 CONCLUSION AND FUTURE WORK

7.5.1 Summary of the Study

The current research introduces an automated methodology for identifying and examining instances of cyberbullying through the utilization of machine learning techniques. A substantial corpus of social media posts was gathered and subjected to preprocessing techniques to extract pertinent features. A variety of machine learning algorithms, such as SVM, random forest, and naive Bayes, were chosen and subsequently trained to classify posts into either cyberbullying or non-cyberbullying. The performance of the models was assessed through the utilization of diverse metrics, including but not limited to accuracy, precision, recall, F1-score, and AUC-ROC (Balakrishnan et al. 2020).

The experimental findings indicate that the proposed methodology outperformed the current state-of-the-art techniques in identifying instances of cyberbullying. The SVM algorithm attained a maximum accuracy of 92%, F1-score of 0.88, and AUC-ROC of 0.95. The findings indicate that the utilization of machine learning can serve as a proficient mechanism for identifying and averting instances of cyberbullying conduct.

The study underscores the potential of machine learning in addressing cyberbullying. The proposed approach can be implemented in practical settings to enhance the safety and welfare of individuals on social media platforms. Additional investigation may be conducted to enhance the precision and expandability of our suggested methodology and to investigate the implementation of deep learning methodologies for identifying and examining instances of cyberbullying conduct.

7.5.2 CONTRIBUTIONS AND LIMITATIONS

The contributions of this study are delineated as follows:

- The present study proposes an automated methodology that employs machine learning to identify and assess instances of cyberbullying behavior. The aforementioned methodology can be effectively executed in pragmatic scenarios with the aim of augmenting the safety and well-being of individuals on social networking sites.
- A significant collection of social media posts was collected and underwent preprocessing methods to extract relevant characteristics that could potentially be useful for future research in this field.
- The present study conducted a comparative analysis of multiple machine learning algorithms to assess their efficacy in identifying instances of cyberbullying. The findings suggest that the proposed methodology exhibited superior performance compared to the currently established state-of-the-art techniques in this particular field.

However, the following restrictions apply to our study:

- The generalizability of the study's dataset may be limited to the cyberbullying behavior on the internet due to its constraint to a specific social media platform.
- The effectiveness of the proposed methodology is dependent on the quality and accuracy of the extracted features, which can be a challenging undertaking in real-world scenarios.

- The effectiveness of the proposed methodology may be influenced by the subjective nature of cyberbullying behavior, which can create difficulties in terms of uniform identification and definition.

To summarize, despite the limitations mentioned earlier, our study contributes to the growing body of literature on utilizing machine learning for addressing cyberbullying and highlights the potential of this approach in improving the safety and well-being of people in the online domain.

7.5.3 FUTURE DIRECTIONS FOR RESEARCH AND DEVELOPMENT

The findings of our study provide potential opportunities for further investigation and advancement in the realm of machine learning as a means of addressing instances of cyberbullying. Several prospective domains for future inquiry encompass:

- This study involves an examination of various machine learning models and algorithms. The present study conducted a comparative analysis of various machine learning models for the purpose of detecting and analyzing cyberbullying behavior. However, it is worth noting that there exist numerous other models and algorithms that warrant further investigation in this domain.
- The present research delved into examining alternative feature extraction techniques. While the study employed a collection of features that relied on linguistic and semantic cues, there exist other methods of feature extraction that warrant exploration, including image analysis and SNA.
- The study's assessment of the generalizability of the approach was constrained to a particular social media platform and dataset. Further research is necessary to explore the applicability of the suggested approach to other platforms and datasets.
- The proposed approach is automated; however, the integration of human-in-the-loop approaches, such as crowdsourcing and expert annotation, can enhance the accuracy and efficacy of the system.
- The integration of policies and guidelines specific to the platform is crucial. Incorporating policies and guidelines specific to each platform can enhance the feasibility and relevance of the suggested methodology in practical, real-life situations.

In brief, the present study establishes a basis for subsequent scholarly inquiry and advancement in the domain of machine learning as a means of addressing cyberbullying. There exist numerous promising avenues for forthcoming exploration and progress.

REFERENCES

Al-Garadi, M. A., Hussain, M. R., Khan, N., Murtaza, G., Nweke, H. F., Ali, I., ... & Gani, A. (2019). Predicting cyberbullying on social media in the big data era using machine learning algorithms: Review of literature and open challenges. *IEEE Access*, *7*, 70701–70718.

Alam, K. S., Bhowmik, S., & Prosun, P. R. K. (2021, February). Cyberbullying detection: An ensemble based machine learning approach. In *2021 Third International Conference on Intelligent Communication Technologies and Virtual Mobile Networks (ICICV)*, Tirunelveli, India, 2021, (pp. 710–715). IEEE.

Ali, A., & Syed, A. M. (2020). Cyberbullying detection using machine learning. *Pakistan Journal of Engineering and Technology, 3*(2), 45–50.

Altay, E. V., & Alatas, B. (2018, December). Detection of cyberbullying in social networks using machine learning methods. In *2018 International Congress on Big Data, Deep Learning and Fighting Cyber Terrorism (IBIGDELFT)*, Ankara, Turkey (pp. 87–91). IEEE.

Arif, M. (2021). A systematic review of machine learning algorithms in cyberbullying detection: Future directions and challenges. *Journal of Information Security and Cybercrimes Research, 4*(1), 1–26.

Ates, E. C., Bostanci, E., & Guzel, M. S. (2021). Comparative performance of machine learning algorithms in cyberbullying detection: Using Turkish language preprocessing techniques. *arXiv preprint arXiv:2101.12718*.https://doi.org/10.48550/arXiv.2101.12718

Atoum, J. O. (2023, March). Detecting cyberbullying from tweets through machine learning techniques with sentiment analysis. In *Advances in Information and Communication: Proceedings of the 2023 Future of Information and Communication Conference (FICC), Volume 2* (pp. 25–38). Cham: Springer Nature Switzerland.

Balakrishnan, V., Khan, S., & Arabnia, H. R. (2020). Improving cyberbullying detection using Twitter users' psychological features and machine learning. *Computers & Security, 90*, 101710.

Chia, Z. L., Ptaszynski, M., Masui, F., Leliwa, G., & Wroczynski, M. (2021). Machine learning and feature engineering-based study into sarcasm and irony classification with application to cyberbullying detection. *Information Processing & Management, 58*(4), 102600.

Dadvar, M., & Eckert, K. (2018). Cyberbullying detection in social networks using deep learning based models; a reproducibility study. *arXiv preprint arXiv:1812.08046*.https://doi.org/10.48550/arXiv.1812.08046

Dalvi, R. R., Chavan, S. B., & Halbe, A. (2020, May). Detecting a Twitter cyberbullying using machine learning. In *2020 4th International Conference on Intelligent Computing and Control Systems (ICICCS)*, Madurai, India (pp. 297–301). IEEE.

Galán-García, P., Puerta, J. G. D. L., Gómez, C. L., Santos, I., & Bringas, P. G. (2016). Supervised machine learning for the detection of troll profiles in Twitter social network: Application to a real case of cyberbullying. *Logic Journal of the IGPL, 24*(1), 42–53.

Ghasem, Z., Frommholz, I., & Maple, C. (2015). Machine learning solutions for controlling cyberbullying and cyberstalking. *Journal of Information Security Research, 6*(2), 55–64.

Haidar, B., Chamoun, M., & Serhrouchni, A. (2017). A multilingual system for cyberbullying detection: Arabic content detection using machine learning. *Advances in Science, Technology and Engineering Systems Journal, 2*(6), 275–284.

Hani, J., Mohamed, N., Ahmed, M., Emad, Z., Amer, E., & Ammar, M. (2019). Social media cyberbullying detection using machine learning. *International Journal of Advanced Computer Science and Applications, 10*(5), 703–707.

Islam, M. M., Uddin, M. A., Islam, L., Akter, A., Sharmin, S., & Acharjee, U. K. (2020, December). Cyberbullying detection on social networks using machine learning approaches. In *2020 IEEE Asia-Pacific Conference on Computer Science and Data Engineering (CSDE)*, Gold Coast, Australia (pp. 1–6). IEEE.

Kontostathis, A., Reynolds, K., Garron, A., & Edwards, L. (2013, May). Detecting cyberbullying: Query terms and techniques. In *Proceedings of the 5th Annual ACM Web Science Conference*, Paris, France (pp. 195–204). ACM.

Kumar, R., & Bhat, A. (2022). A study of machine learning-based models for detection, control, and mitigation of cyberbullying in online social media. *International Journal of Information Security*, *21*(6), 1409–1431.

Muneer, A., & Fati, S. M. (2020). A comparative analysis of machine learning techniques for cyberbullying detection on twitter. *Future Internet*, *12*(11), 187.

Ptaszynski, M., Dybala, P., Matsuba, T., Masui, F., Rzepka, R., & Araki, K. (2010). Machine learning and affect analysis against cyber-bullying. In *Society for the Study of Artificial Intelligence and the Simulation of Behaviour. Annual Convention. 36th 2010. (aisb 2010) (11 vols)*, Leicester, United Kingdom (pp. 7–16).

Raisi, E., & Huang, B. (2017, July). Cyberbullying detection with weakly supervised machine learning. In *Proceedings of the 2017 IEEE/ACM International Conference on Advances in Social Networks Analysis and Mining 2017*, Sydney, Australia (pp. 409–416). IEEE.

Raman, R., Shamim, R., Akram, S. V., Thakur, L., Pillai, B. G., & Ponnusamy, R. (2023, January). Classification and contrast of supervised machine learning algorithms. In *2023 International Conference on Artificial Intelligence and Smart Communication (AISC)*, Greater Noida, India (pp. 629–633). IEEE.

Raza, M. O., Memon, M., Bhatti, S., & Bux, R. (2020). Detecting cyberbullying in social commentary using supervised machine learning. In Arai, K., Kapoor, S., Bhatia, R. (eds), *Advances in Information and Communication. FICC 2020. Advances in Intelligent Systems and Computing*, vol 1130. Springer International Publishing. https://doi.org/10.1007/978-3-030-39442-4_45

Reynolds, K., Kontostathis, A., & Edwards, L. (2011, December). Using machine learning to detect cyberbullying. In *2011 10th International Conference on Machine learning and applications and workshops,* Honolulu, HI, USA (Vol. 2, pp. 241–244). IEEE.

Roy, P. K., Singh, A., Tripathy, A. K., & Das, T. K. (2022). Identifying cyberbullying post on social networking platform using machine learning technique. In Sahoo, J.P., Tripathy, A.K., Mohanty, M., Li, KC., Nayak, A.K. (eds), *Advances in Distributed Computing and Machine Learning: Proceedings of ICADCML 2021* (pp. 186–195). Springer Singapore. https://doi.org/10.1007/978-981-16-4807-6_18

Saravanaraj, A., Sheeba, J. I., & Devaneyan, S. P. (2016). Automatic detection of cyberbullying from Twitter. *International Journal of Computer Science and Information Technology & Security (IJCSITS)*.

Shamim, R., Arshad, M., & Pandey, V. (2022). A machine learning model to protect privacy using federal learning with homomorphy encryption. *International Journal for Research in Applied Science & Engineering Technology (IJRASET)*, *6*(6), 26–31.

Sintaha, M., & Mostakim, M. (2018, December). An empirical study and analysis of the machine learning algorithms used in detecting cyberbullying in social media. In *2018 21st International Conference of Computer and Information Technology (ICCIT)*, Dhaka, Bangladesh (pp. 1–6). IEEE.

Part 3

Natural Language Processing (NLP) and Cyberbullying Detection

8 A Sentiment-Aware Statistical Evaluation of Vawulence Tweets for Cyberbullying Analytics

Segun Michael Akintunde
Federal University of Agriculture Abeokuta

Ogobuchi Daniel Okey
Universidade Federal de Lavras MG

Wilson C. Ahiara
Michael Okpara University of Agriculture Umudike

Taiwo Olapeju Olaleye
Federal University of Agriculture Abeokuta

Olalekan Akinbosoye Okewale
University of Ibadan

8.1 INTRODUCTION

8.1.1 BACKGROUND

The advent of a high Internet penetration rate and the perceived ease of use of social media platforms have significantly changed the way people work and interact. The level of conversation that goes on various social media platforms on different topical issues lay credence to the rate of engagements between people of diverse creed and ethnicity. The political culture of electioneering has also found social media platforms as veritable tools to reach out to millions of potential electorates (Abdulyakeen & Yusuf, 2022), in what could breed opportunist bullies. Examining the rate of Internet connectivity, the accessibility to Internet services, and the overall acceptance of Internet technologies would underscore the degree of engagement across divides (Almaiah, Al-Khasawneh, & Althunibat, 2020). The Internet has had a significant impact on various aspects of society, including communication, information sharing, and social interaction (Szymkowiak, Melović, Dabić, Jeganathan, & Kundi, 2021). It has also influenced the incidence and nature of cyberbullying (Islam, et al., 2020).

The level of un-abating harassment, intimidation, and provocation daily witnessed on the Internet, through instant messaging, or on online forums and social media networks, could best be described as worrisome with mental health implications. The growing trend appears out of the control of regulatory agencies as factors including anonymity and dis-inhibition (Macaulay, Betts, Stiller, & Kellezi, 2022), accessibility (Maity, Kumar, & Saha, 2022), permanence and amplification (Loh & Snyman, 2020), and online social dynamics (Emmery, et al., 2021) and has been attributed as factors that influence cyberbullying. The pseudonymous nature of Internet users embolden some end users to engage in cyberbullying tendencies (Goldberg, 2000) without fear of instant consequence. The potential for cyberbullying is further assisted by continuous expansion of Internet connectivity (Emmery, et al., 2021). A larger pool of potential victims are therefore at the mercy of unrepentant bullies. Users across demographics and age groups are not immune as cyberbullying gains traction at the same rate with the spread of Internet connectivity (Chu, Li, Wang, Zeng, & Lei, 2021). Lasting digital footprint trails cyberbullying unlike traditional bullying (Sung, 2018), especially with embarrassing photos, videos, etc., which are easily shared or retweeted as soon as they are posted. The characteristic nature of the Internet which encourage online communities with mutual interest likewise foster bullying tendencies, which is seen as a tool for social validation or conformity to group norms. Therefore, a multifaceted approach is required to mitigate the growing trend of cyberbullying, with its dynamic nature and outlook, which could undermine human wellbeing (Giumetti & Kowalski, 2022). Electioneering conversations on social media platforms are likewise popular, generating interest across age and social divides (Abdulyakeen & Yusuf, 2022). Supporters of candidates seeking elective offices engage in un-abating cyberbullying until elections are over (Oswari, Prihantoro, Dunan, & Mudjiyanto, 2020). The resultant effects are always of serious consequences to the outcome of the elections, as well as the mental health of people.

Besides the live streaming of political events and rallies, conversations on topical issues are consistently discussed through various political hashtags purposely created for electioneering and sensitization purposes. Unfortunately, social media is highly unregulated in several countries unlike traditional media (Battista & Uva, 2023). Therefore, cyberbullying has been ubiquitous across social media platforms during electioneering periods with dire consequences on the psychological and emotional wellbeing of unsuspecting social media subscriber. Bullying with the use of digital technologies has been described as cyberbullying, which is rampant on messaging, gaming, and social media platforms (UNICEF, 2020). An example is presented in Figure 8.1, where two distinct derogatory words used in the first line of comment, with evidence of attention by some two reactions. However, political discussions have been identified as those replete with more harmful cyberbullying tendencies, which is a harmful trend if not checked and mitigated (Thun, Teh, & Cheng, 2022).

8.1.2 METHODOLOGY

The aim of this chapter therefore is to conduct a descriptive statistical evaluation of electioneering messages on Twitter media through an exploratory data analysis. Electioneering tweets would go through feature engineering for extraction of

FIGURE 8.1   Sample screenshot of a cyberbullying conversation on Facebook (Sultan, Jahan, Basak, Jony, & Nabil, 2023).

emotional polarity scores of each tweet and other predictive variables that would be deployed for the statistical and predictive analytics. The process flow approach of this study would reveal the statistical nature of cyberbullying tweets besides their detection purpose. The feature engineering phase of the proposed conceptual framework is implemented on the Orange data mining toolkit, while the exploratory data analysis and the predictive modeling are implemented by Python codes on the Jupyter notebook.

8.1.3   CHAPTER ORGANIZATION

The rest of the chapter is structured in the following ways: Review of existing studies in the detection of cyberbullying is presented in Section 8.2, while Section 8.3 presents the conceptual framework of the study. Result and findings are discussed in Section 8.4, and the chapter is concluded in Section 8.5.

8.2   RELATED WORK

8.2.1   THE TWITTERDEMIC TREND

Twitter, one of the most popular social networking sites, is projected to attract well over 380 million active users by 2022 (Statista, 2020). It is popular among users of all ages, who flock to their Twitter accounts to publish user-generated content (UGC), also known as tweets, or to just participate in a hashtag debate, which is sometimes organized into threads with millions of tweet contributions (Chakraborty, et al., 2020). It was projected, correctly too, that by January 2020, there will be 27 million active social media users in Nigeria, an increase of 2.2 million (around 2.6%) over the 2019 figure (Kemp 2020). According to the information, 99% of Nigeria's subscribers are active users who use their preferred social media platforms through a mobile phone, on average, for three hours and thirty minutes each day. It is interesting that compared to other social media platforms, Twitter receives 50% of all active user usage, which accounts for its high traffic. Traditional tabloids have recently started using Twitter, where they quickly report any breaking news before the next day's issue is printed (Olaleye, et al., 2022). However, the main issue that has persisted in confronting scholars is the most efficient ways to curtail the propagation of fake news and its associated hazards to international peace and concord (Grinberg, 2019). This is because of its wide acceptability, volatility, and user patronage. The negative social effects of false news, identifying fake news, or, in this case, tweets have drawn growing attention worldwide. However, the detection algorithms that rely on the author's profile information, geographic location, handles, hashtags, and/or the status of a handle as either verified or unverified are typically unreliable (Olaleye, et al., 2021). This is due to the fact that those who support and spread false information have now learned how to model and brand their social media handles and accounts in a trustworthy manner that will quickly win over followers or website visits. Therefore, there is a dire need for efficient scrutiny of the news semantics to determine the truism of Twitter posts, as well as situate the context in which emotions are expressed (Olaleye, et al., 2022). Therefore, cyberbullying is a digital pandemic that is somewhat popular on Twitter (Muzakir, 2022). Owing to its almost anonymous nature, bullies catch in on the microblogging popularity to perpetrate maltreatment in what is referred to as cyberbullying. Indeed, Twitter cyberbullying was rampant in the COVID-19 era (Perez & Karmakar, 2023) but could reach a milestone during electioneering periods (Qaisar, 2022).

8.2.2 A New Concept: "Vawulence"

The Nigerian political space is replete with political bullies (Etsenamhe, 2022). This has been a common trend since the 2015 general election in the country; however, a new term suddenly emerged from the Nigeria's Twitter political parlance since year 2022, which is now referred to as *vawulence*. Vawulence tweet is notably intended to mock, disseminate false information, and damage the reputation and integrity of politicians running for electoral office, as well as their social media supporters. *Vawulence* has took a dangerous trend since the commencement of the 2023 electioneering campaigns in December 2022, and especially rampant among supporters of the three front runners. The freedom and somewhat level of anonymity on the web are believed to have encouraged *vawulence* to thrive in an unprecedented rate in recent times. Therefore, cyberbullies and trolls continue to catch in on the situation. While cyberbullies target individual posts with their vawulence replies, trolls rather posts hateful, racist, profane, and even sexist vawulence messages to trigger reactions from supporters of the presidential candidates, who battle to address various issues of ethnic and religious sentiments that usually characterize the Nigerian political space. The prevalence of vawulence has resulted in the highest level of bullying cases reported in any electioneering history of the West African country (Etsenamhe, 2022). Popular vawulence like "Obi- China," "Obi- liar," and "Obi-tuary" is common on social media posts to ridicule one of the most popular presidential candidates in the race, whose surname is "Obi." Other contestants in the election have also experienced their fair share of vawulence, which they daily address in their media briefings as capable of affecting the already-heated political space. Vawulence was indeed reported to have affected the health of one of the favorites in the presidential race (Sahara, 2022), which further reiterates the medical implication of the vawulence cyberbullying act.

Several attempts have been made toward detecting bullying information on social media networking sites with natural language processing (NLP) use cases taking the center stage. Techniques like sentiment analysis have been adopted in some studies (Olaleye, et al., 2022), which is aimed at computing the positive, negative, and neutral polarities of information. Other studies (Yuvaraj, et al., 2021) have targeted specific psychological contexts contained in the information posted on Twitter for the purpose of classification. To further trace cyberbullying on Twitter, the predictive analytics approach is likewise considered in Ho et al. (2020), Olaleye et al. (2022), Yuvaraj et al. (2021). Specifically in the work of Ho et al., hotspots of cyberbullying were investigated by providing an approach to identify the possibility for cyberbullying activity using computational analysis of charged languages. In all, studies have not considered the investigation of statistical features that could be inferred from bullying tweets, which promises actionable insights toward mitigating the negative trend. Such statistical features would also be better suited as predictive variables for the detection of bullying tweets. Furthermore, electioneering tweets are believed to trigger emotions, anger, and high propensity for abuse on social media networks, which would avail a cyberbullying analytics study suitable bullying corpus.

8.2.3 DETECTION OF INFODEMIC TWEETS

Inappropriate, misleading, false, abusive, and damaging messages on social media networks have been widely investigated in the literature owing to their counterproductive outcomes. In Olaleye et al. (2022), COVID-19 infodemic tweets were investigated, and a classifier (SCLAVOEM) was implemented by Vote ensemble after a synthetic minority oversampling of less-represented class. The study introduced the concept of infodemic (WHO, 2022), which refers to a pandemic of fake tweets that are targeted at misleading people on the subject of COVID-19, either intentionally or unintentionally. The study addressed the problem of class imbalance and hyperparameter optimization of base learners that makes up the Vote ensemble. Prior to the machine learning phase, feature selection was implemented through Information gain valuator to enhance the classification ability of the ensemble learner. Besides the Vote ensemble, other base learners of naive Bayes, random forest, sequential minimal optimization, and K-neural network were fitted on the resampled training set. Weighted averages of performance metric evaluators returned Vote ensemble and random forest as the most efficient for infodemic detection on Twitter. The process flow approach of the study distinguishes it from existing studies with a unitary approach.

8.2.4 DETECTION OF CYBERBULLYING TWEETS

Detection of bullying tweets was the main forte of the study by Yuvaraj et al. (2021). The study implemented an integrated model that combines classification and feature extraction engines on raw text data from social media networks. Extracted features include psychological tweet features, the comments, and the context of the posted message. An artificial neural network (ANN) was fitted on the data and evaluated by deep reinforcement learning (DRL), which expands the performance metrics of the classifier. The performance metrics of accuracy, precision, recall, and f-measure were used to evaluate the model with respect to their weighted averages. The model efficiently isolated bullying tweets from legitimate posts, through the acquired tweets that were annotated based on their vulgarity from a weighted score estimated for the entire word encapsulated in each text.

Similarly, Dalvi et al. (2020) fitted the secure vector machine and naive Bayes on social media content for the detection of cyberbullying content in textual and pictorial posts. Preprocessing techniques of tokenization, stemming, stopword removal, and word correction were executed prior to feature extraction of sentiment analysis. Performance evaluators of precision, recall, and F-score were employed to examine the efficiency of the two classifiers on their probabilistic abilities in identifying bullying from healthy social media contents. This study is similar to the approach of Taiwo et al. in Olaleye, et al. (2021), where a veracity assessment of multimedia posts was conducted aimed at detecting symptoms of infodemic posts on Facebook. The study employed a bi-modal approach of supervised and unsupervised machine learning modeling on both Facebook textual posts and images. The images were classified through unsupervised hierarchical clustering, while sentiment analysis was employed to calculate the positive, negative, and neutral polarity scores of the textual corpus. The Euclidean distance determined the hierarchical clustering threshold of the images posted on the social media network. The conceptual framework of the study efficiently returned a highly accurate detector of Facebook infodemic textual and image posts.

Identification and extraction of charged languages on Twitter, in terms of abusive and mean words, were conducted prior to the implementation of a predictive model by Ho, Kao, Chiu-Huang, Li, & Lai (2020). Logistic regression was implemented in the study on the acquired tweets, which were annotated by the suggestions from earlier studies with similar research questions. Fourteen emotionally charged words, namely, *die, fat, fuck, loser, faggot, shit, slut, bitch, dick, cunt, pussy, kill, suck,* and *whore*, were the focus of the study as cyberbullying indicators. The Twitter API was then programmed to extract 10,000 tweets for each of the 14 emotionally charged words, resulting into a 140,000 dataset corpus. Preprocessing techniques employed in the study reduced the training corpus to 54, 894 tweets collected between September 7th and 13th September of 2019. The acquired tweet was annotated as either bullying or non-bullying by human judgment. Cyberbullying detection in the context of the isiXhosa language was the thrust of the work by Matomela and Henney (2022). The study implemented a system that detects cyberbullying on Twitter focusing on the language. An ensemble machine learning approach is employed in the study. The experimental result showed the efficiency of an ensemble machine learning model toward identifying bullying tendencies in cyber textual data acquired by Python programming functions. A hybrid model of Bi-GRU–Attention–CapsNet is employed for the purpose of detecting cyberbullying tendencies in Kumar & Sachdeva (2021). The performance metrics of F1-score and ROC-AUC returned an experimental result of weighted averages of 9% and 3% in F1-score for the MySPace training set and the Formspring.me set, respectively. Prior to the training of the deep learning model, the preprocessing of the acquired social media corpus was implemented. A capsule method with dynamic routing and deep convolutional neural network was deployed for a multimodal cyberbullying detection in Kumar & Sachdeva (2022). In the study, the social media was described as the "virtual playground" for bullies due to the upsurge of social media networks. Therefore, a deep neural network model was implemented in the study employing textual, visual, and info-graphic modes. The info-graphic content was discretized by the separation of from the image using Google Lens on the Google Photos application. The multilayer perceptron trained in the study was fitted on 10,000 acquired corpus scrapped from YouTube, Instagram, and Twitter, with a state-of-the-art AUC-ROC of 0.98 weighted average. Detection of kids' cyberbullying was the thrust of the study by Yafooz et al. (2023). A variant of pre-trained model based on BERT was used in the study, while the experimental result shows an optimized performance of the transfer learning methodology over classical and deep learning machine modeling approaches. An optical character recognition was rather used in the study by Sultan, Jahan, Basak, Jony, & Nabil (2023). The training set comprised social media images and screenshots replete with cyberbullying contexts. The preprocessing and feature extraction use cases of NLP were employed with other text mining techniques. Both the TF-IDF and the Bag-of-words features were deployed for the training.

8.3 CONCEPTUAL FRAMEWORK

The conceptual framework of the process flow approach of this study is presented in Figure 8.2. This section includes descriptions of the phases including electioneering tweet acquisition through Twitter API on the Orange data mining toolkit, feature engineering techniques of text preprocessing, feature extraction, sentiment analysis, exploratory data analysis, and the predictive analytics phases.

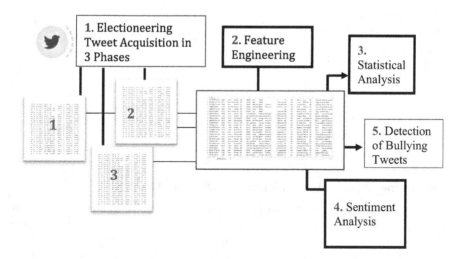

FIGURE 8.2 The process flow conceptual framework of the study.

8.3.1 TWEET ACQUISITION

The electioneering tweets for the study are extracted from the Twitter microblogging site through the Twitter API tool (screenshot presented in Figure 8.3) on the Orange data mining toolkit in three phases. The acquired tweets are those discussing electioneering matters and are targeted through popular political hashtags that are most trending since year 2022 when the Nigeria's political space turned volatile. A total of 5,000 tweets are acquired at each instance, through the various hashtags, at different times, as presented in Table 8.1. In all, 15,000 electioneering tweets are acquired and employed for the statistical and predictive analytics approach of the conceptual framework. The metadata contained in the acquired tweets are made up of ten number of features including the tweet content and other metadata, as presented in Table 8.2. Table 8.3 shows the description of new tweet features added to the acquired metadata prior to the statistical data analysis to replace two corresponding metadata described in Table 8.3.

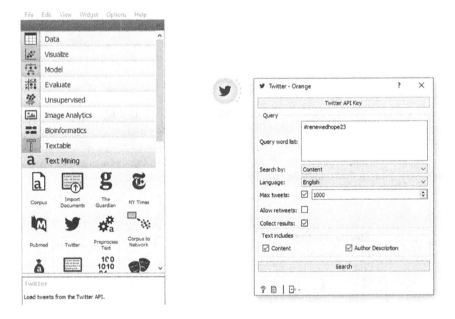

FIGURE 8.3   Twitter API interphase for tweet acquisition.

TABLE 8.1
Time Frame of Tweet Acquisition across Different Hashtags

S/N	Target Hashtag	Total Acquired Tweet	Time Frame	Batch
1.	#nigeriadecides2023	5,000	1st – 30th Nov., 2022	ANov
2.		5,000	1st – 30th Dec., 2022	BDec
3.		5,000	1st – 15th Jan., 2023	CJan

TABLE 8.2

Metadata Description of Acquired Tweets

S/N	Tweet Metadata	Remarks
1.	Tweet content	Tweet content (to be replaced by S/N 1 in Table 8.3)
2.	Date	Date the tweet is posted (to be replaced by S/N 2 in Table 8.3)
3.	Number of likes	Total number of likes on the tweet
4.	Number of retweets	Total number of retweets on the tweet
5.	Author statuses count	Number of status updates made so far by the user
6.	Author favorites count	Number of times a user post is tagged as favorite
7.	Author friends count	The total number of friends a user has
8.	Author followers count	The total number of followers of the user
9.	Author listed count	Total number of items on the timeline of the author
10.	Author verified	The verification status of the user

TABLE 8.3

Description of New Data Features

S/N	Feature	Feature Description	Remarks
1.	Content word count	Content_len	Total number of words contained in each tweet (to replace S/N 1 in Table 8.2)
2.	Duration of tweet before acquisition	Tweet_Duration	How long the tweets existed before acquisition (to replace S/N 2 in Table 8.2)

8.3.2 Feature Engineering

Feature engineering is a germane technique in the value chain of any data science-based conceptual framework (Borondics, Vitali, & Shaulsky, 2020). Since the acquired tweets are textual corpus discussing electioneering conversations in three phases, described in Table 8.1, feature engineering is an important phase of the framework. The tweets are expectedly unstructured corpus which requires feature engineering techniques of preprocessing tasks. The various preprocessing tasks are implemented on the Orange data mining toolkit (Borondics, Vitali, & Shaulsky, 2020), as described in Table 8.4.

8.3.3 Sentiment Analysis of Tokenized Tweets

This phase of the framework is expected to determine the vawulence nature of acquired tweets, which is expected to automatically label 70% of the 15,000 training set as either a vawulence or non-vawulence (bullying or non-bullying). The labeling will serve as the dependent variable (ground truth) for the eventual machine learning phase of the framework. Sentiment analysis describes the polarity, which distinguishes emotions contained in a tweet post into their positive, negative, and neutral states. The VADER approach however calculates a third polarity of compound score

TABLE 8.4
Preprocessing Techniques Employed in the Conceptual Framework

Preprocessing Technique	Applied Option	Result
Stopword removal	Rainbow list	Tweet without conjunctions, articles, prepositions, etc.
Stemmatization	Snowball	Replacement of terms with common stems
Tokenization	N-Gram	Unigram representation of each word contained in the textual tweet
Part of speech tagging	POS Tagging	Tagging of each token with their respective past of speech
Transformation	Transform	Conversion of tweets into their lowercase versions

for each unigram of tokenized tweet in the 15,000 acquired electioneering tweet. Each word is allocated sentimentality numerical values referred to as a lexicon whose compound value depicts the level of toxicity expressed in each tweet. The tagging of each tweet as either bullying or non-bullying is determined by the compound sentiment value. This is the approach of Baarah et al. (2019), with the assumption that information with negative sentiments and emotions indicates the extent of toxic elements expressed in them. The constancy of the occurrence of such negative emotions (as stated in the electioneering tweets) in the lexicon determines the numeric values of its positive, negative, or neutral polarity, which eventually defines the level of toxicity contained in them. The VADER-based approach computes another compound polarity score for each of the 15,000 tweets, by aggregating the positive, negative, and neutral scores earlier determined.

In its calculations, the word "w" (in each acquired tweet) is allocated numeric value 1, 0, or -1 for the three polarities. Therefore, polarity of a tweet "T" is as follows:

$$T = \{w_1, w_2, w_3, \ldots w_n\} \tag{8.1}$$

while Equation 8.1 is calculated on the frequency of words "w" in "T," which are 15,000 in number. The positive ($\text{pos}(T,z)$) and negative ($\text{neg}(T,z)$) values of words from "T" which occur in "z" adds

$$\text{sum}(T,z) = \text{pos}(T,z) - \text{neg}(T,z) \tag{8.2}$$

Hence, sentiment $s_1(z)$ of a tweet instance "z" under polarized lexicon "T" is calculated as follows:

$$s_1(z) = T \text{ if } \text{sum}(T,z) > 0 = 0 \text{ if } \text{sum}(T,z) = 0 = -T \text{ if } \text{sum}(T,z) < 0 \tag{8.3}$$

The compound score is calculated as

$$x = \frac{x}{\sqrt{x^2 + \alpha}} \tag{8.4}$$

using the addition of valence scores (x) of each unigram in the lexicon, readjusted with the rules and regularized between −1 (bullying vawulence) and +1 (non-bullying tweet) and α is the regularization constant with the default value of 15. Bullying vawulence tweet is then labeled as

$$\text{'non-bullying tweet' when compound score} \geq 0.05; \tag{8.5}$$

$$\text{'bullying vawulence tweet' when compound score} \leq -0.05 \tag{8.6}$$

The output numeric cores of positive, negative, neutral, and compound polarities, calculated for each tokenized 15,000 tweets, are therefore added to the initial 10 metadata, as described in Table 8.2, and the two replacements described in Table 8.3 to making a total of 14 attributes altogether. 13 attributes are the independent predictive variables comprising all the attributes earlier described except the compound polarity score, which is the dependent (ground truth) variable. The couple of independent variables (13 numbers) and the dependent variable (vawulence status determined by compound score) makes up the training set for the machine learning phase of the conceptual framework presented in Figure 8.2.

8.3.4 STATISTICAL DATA ANALYSIS

The final 14no attributes comprising 10 metadata contained in the acquired tweet corpus, and 4-no polarity scores are evaluated in this phase through an exploratory data analysis. The 14 attributes are evaluated using the interquartile range (IQR) through the box plot, and the correlation coefficient analysis through the heat map plot. The IQR gauges where data's "middle fifty" and the measurement of where a majority of the data points lay. The 1st and 3rd quartile locations are computed using (8.7) and (8.8), to compute the entire range.

$$Q1 = \left\{ \frac{n+1}{4} \right\}^{th} \tag{8.7}$$

as the most centered value in the 1st half of the rank-organized dataset;

$$Q3 = \left\{ 3\frac{n+1}{4} \right\}^{th} \tag{8.8}$$

as the most centered value in the 2nd half of the rank-organized dataset. The $Q2$ is the median and computed as

$$Q2 = Q3 - Q1 \tag{8.9}$$

The correlation coefficient is a measure of the extent of multicollinearity present in the predictor variables. It is the metric that assesses how the 16 predictive variables are related, with a range of values from −1.0 to 1.0. Hence, the numbers cannot exceed 1.0 or supersede −1.0. Perfect negative correlation is depicted by a correlation coefficient of −1.0, and perfect positive correlation is depicted by a correlation coefficient of 1.0.

Therefore, a positive correlation will exist between a bullying vawulence tweet (compound score <= −0.05 in Equation 8.6) or a non-bullying tweet (compound score >= 0.05 in Equation 8.5) with the remaining 13 predictive attributes if the correlation coefficient value between them is +1 or −1, respectively. If the correlation coefficient value is zero between the tweet status (vawulence or non-vawulence), there is no correlation between the two variables. Prior to determination of the correlation coefficient, the covariance of the two variables (vawulence status and any of the 13 predictive variables) must be calculated, hence the computation of the standard deviation of each 14-no variable. By dividing the covariance by the sum of the standard deviations of any two variables, the correlation coefficient is computed as

$$\text{Correlation} = P = \frac{COV(x,y)}{\sigma X \sigma Y} \tag{8.10}$$

where X is the any of the 15-no predictive variables and Y is the vawulence status.

Both the IQR and multicollinearity analysis, implemented through box and heat map plots, are executed through the object-oriented Python programming libraries of Seaborn, Matplotlib, and DataFrame on the Jupyter notebook.

8.3.5 PREDICTIVE ANALYTICS

The predictive analytics phase of the conceptual framework consists of the traditional training and testing phases of a supervised machine learning methodology. The training phase ensures the deployment of a machine learning algorithm, which is to be trained with the training dataset (Olaleye, et al., 2022). The training dataset for a supervised machine learning would consist of dependent and independent variables, where the dependent variable is the label that comes with each independent variable. In this study, each tweet is labeled as either bullying vawulence (noted as 0) or non-bullying (labeled as 1) as determined by the *compound score* earlier computed in Equations 8.5 and 8.6. This represents the label (14th variable) of each tweet contained in the 70% of 15,000. The remaining 13 attributes are the independent predictive variables of the training set. Upon the successful training phase, the test phase will evaluate the performance of the machine learning algorithm by testing its ability to detect bullying vawulence in an electioneering tweet. The trained algorithm is expected to predict the dependent variable for each of the remaining 30% of the 15,000 tweets as either of bullying vawulence or non-bullying. Therefore, the compound score for the 30% training set will not be included for the training phase, which is expected to be predicted. The binary classification status of this study is executed by the random forest (RF) algorithm as highly recommended in the literature (Olaleye, et al., 2022) as a reliable ensemble machine learning model for natural language-based predictive variables.

RFs are basically an assembly of decision trees, each approximated on a different bagged sample (Olaleye et al., 2022). The output of the entire trees is averaged to determine the result of the RF. To check the likelihood of positive correlation between the decision trees, RF adopts a unique way to grow the trees in a way to reduce the possibility of a highly correlated trees. Splitting variables are selected randomly for this purpose prior to the splitting of each node rather than considering all p-possible variables. The algorithm then selects only $m < p$ variables casually, before considering them for splitting. This is expected to de-correlate the trees, and thereby improve the estimates by reducing the variances.

The working of the RF algorithm is presented in the following steps:

Step 1: Random sample is selected from the 70% that makes up the training set

Step 2: The RF constructs a decision tree for each random sample

Step 3: The decision trees are averaged for each sample, and voting takes place subsequently

Step 4: The most popular voted prediction (bullying vawulence (0) or non-bullying (1)) is selected and presented as the final result

With 13-no predictive variables, determination of the root node is an important decision; hence, the Gini index is computed for each of the 15 attributes. There is a need to determine the impurity of the training set (70% of 15,000 tweets together with their respective vawulence status) and the attribute out of the 13, and the lowest impurity (indicating lowest Gini index) is derived as follows:

$$\text{Gini Index} = 1 - \sum\nolimits_{(n \to i=1)} (P_i)^2 \tag{8.11}$$

$$= 1 - [(P_+)^2 + (P_-)^2] \tag{8.12}$$

where P_+ is the probability of a positive class and P_- is the probability of a negative class.

8.4 RESULT AND DISCUSSION

This section discusses the experimental result of the statistical and predictive bullying analytics. Figure 8.4 shows the world cloud of the acquired 15,000 electioneering tweets across the three datasets. Prominent unigram and their weights in the textual corpus include token *nigeriadecides (1013)*, nigeria (304), pvc (211), election (192), and obi (109), which are the words with the highest weights. The bigram analysis returned *electionsfactcheck (674), collect pvc (307), election factcheck (299)*, etc. as the weightiest 2-worded phrase in the textual corpus. Upon the preprocessing and sentiment analysis, the distribution of positive polarity score across the three acquisition stages (ANov, BDec, CJan) is as depicted on the histogram plots in Figure 8.5. The negative polarity score distribution in the three data acquisition instances is presented in Figure 8.6, while the neutral sentiment score distribution across the three instances is presented in Figure 8.7. Therefore, the popularity of each tweet is determined by the number of retweets achieved on each tweet. The IQR of retweets recorded on each positive, negative, and neutral polarity category of the entire 15,000 posts are presented in the box plot of Figure 8.8, Figure 8.9,

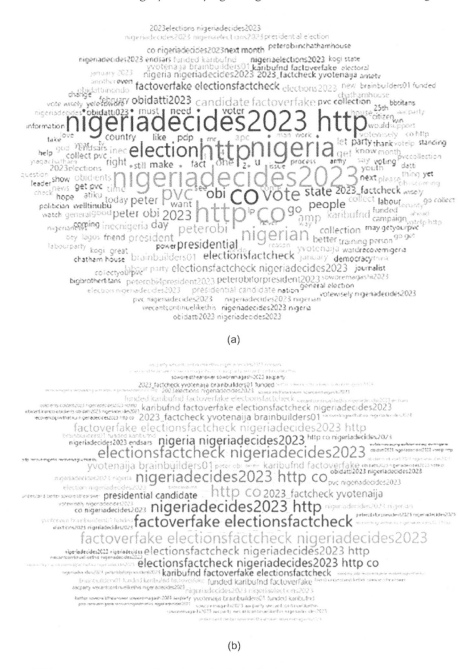

(a)

(b)

FIGURE 8.4   Word cloud of acquired electioneering tweets.

and Figure 8.10, respectively. Furthermore, the multicollinearity test on the acquired corpus is presented through the heat maps of Figure 8.11 for batch ANov, BDec, and CJan, respectively. Consequently, the exploratory data analysis on the 14-no attributes, comprising the 13-no predictor independent variables and the 14th dependent

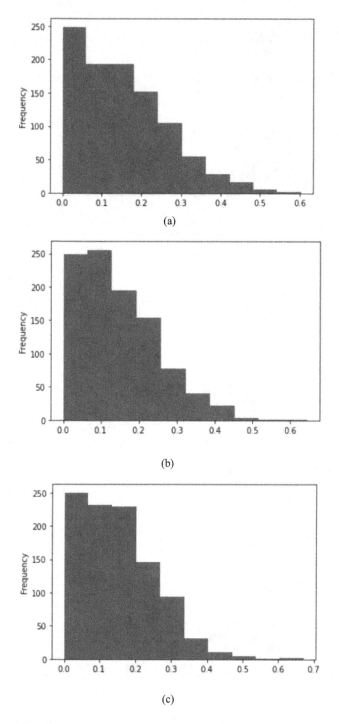

FIGURE 8.5 Bar plot showing distribution of tweets with positive sentiments.

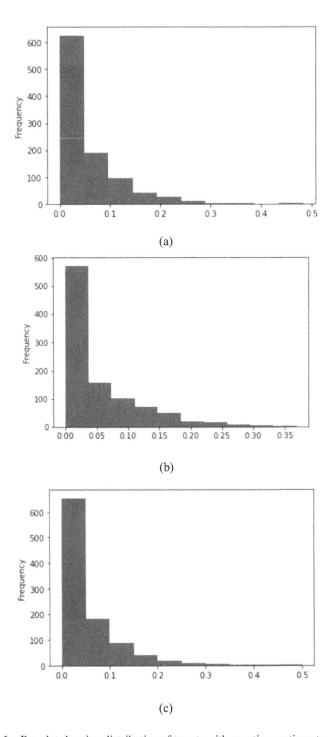

FIGURE 8.6 Bar plot showing distribution of tweets with negative sentiments.

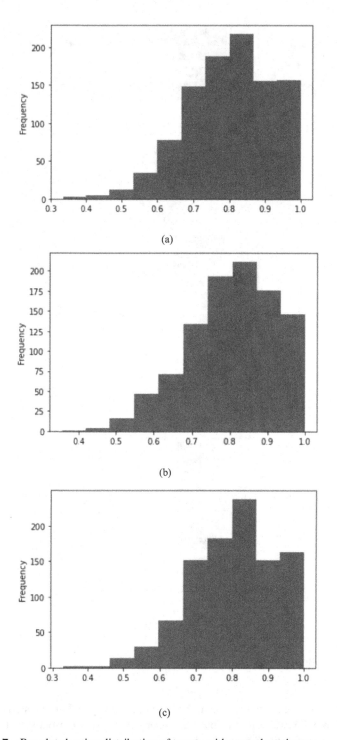

FIGURE 8.7 Bar plot showing distribution of tweets with neutral sentiments.

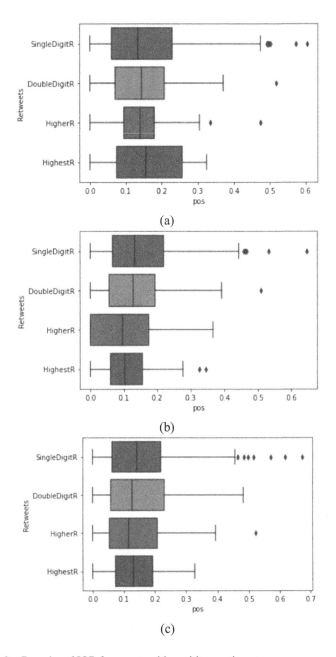

FIGURE 8.8 Box plot of IQR for tweets with positive sentiments.

variable (vawulence status) for batch ANov data, is presented on the statistical summary of Table 8.5, while that of batches BDec and CJan is presented in the statistical summaries of Table 8.6 and Table 8.7, respectively. The performance of the RF

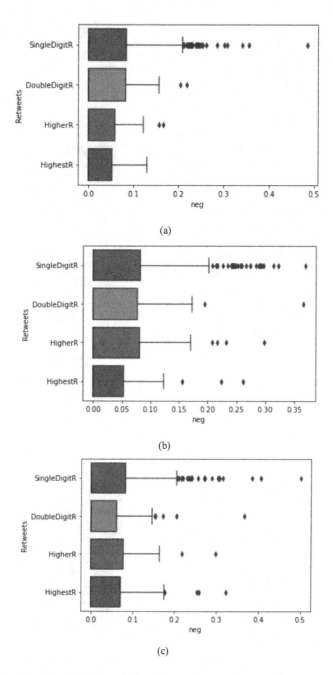

FIGURE 8.9 Box plot of IQR for tweets with negative sentiments.

classifier toward detecting bullying tendencies in the acquired tweets is presented in Table 8.8. Table 8.9 shows the volume of bullying vawulence contained in the 10,500 (70% of 15,000 of acquired) training set tweet.

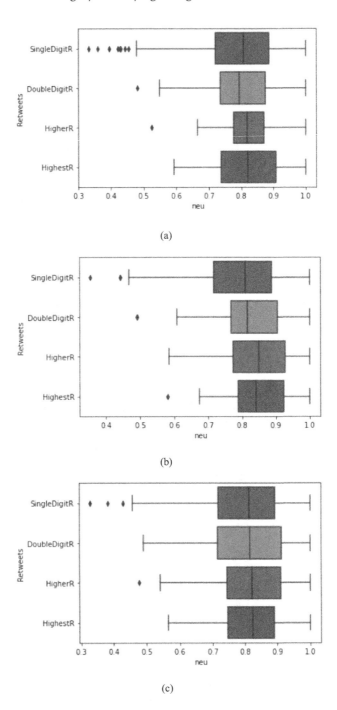

FIGURE 8.10   Box plot of IQR for tweets with neutral sentiments.

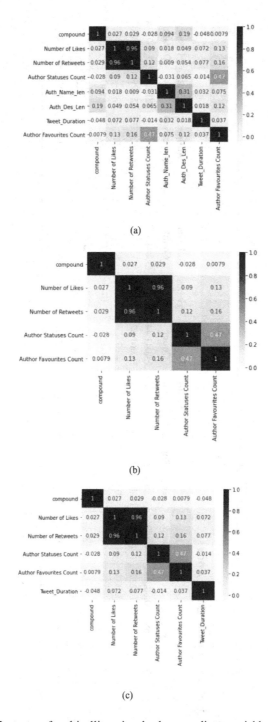

FIGURE 8.11   Heat map of multicollinearity check on predictor variable.

TABLE 8.5

Statistical Summary of Batch Anov

	Pos	Neg	Neu	Comp.	Likes	Retweets	Status Count	Favorite Count	Friends Count	Follower Count	Listed Count	Author Verification	Cont_ Len	Tweet_ Duration
MEAN	0.150944	0.046824	0.802242	0.378595	33.676	10.397	13,226.29	15,041.44	1,296.061	3,484.949	3.86	0.001	203.144	3.937938
STD	0.114938	0.065061	0.12245	0.492134	314.4057	82.98022	41,079.53	36,061.82	2,221.058	23,341.81	16.92995	0.031623	75.42918	1.533903
MIN	0	0	0.333	−0.9335	0	0	1	0	1	0	0	0	32	1
25% (Q1)	0.061	0	0.723	0	0	0	608.25	500.25	164	77	0	0	140	3
50% (Q2)	0.137	0	0.81	0.49325	1	0	2,605	2,668	550	370	0	0	211	4
75% (Q3)	0.22425	0.082	0.887	0.8119	5	2	10,390.75	14,137.25	1,533	1,138.5	2	0	272	5
MAX	0.604	0.484	1	0.9851	7,763	1,815	643,946	413,291	25,206	508,655	316	1	5,002	7

TABLE 8.6
Statistical Summary of Batch BDec

	Pos	Neg	Neu	Comp.	Likes	Retweets	Status Count	Favorite Count	Friends Count	Follower Count	Listed Count	Author Verification	Cont_ Len
MEAN	0.143129	0.047683	0.809195	0.368158	40.938	16.963	10,728.41	17,364.32	1,442.46	3,676.797	3.657	0	203.144
STD	0.107426	0.067302	0.118473	0.501755	173.5929	80.9269	24,037.93	34,966.19	2,279.222	15,937.87	10.70523	0	75.42918
MIN	0	0	0.354	−0.9654	0	0	1	0	0	0	0	0	32
25% (Q1)	0.065	0	0.733	0	0	0	1,167.75	974	198.75	166	0	0	140
50% (Q2)	0.128	0	0.818	0.50995	2	1	3,553	4,666	681	640	0	0	211
75% (Q3)	0.211	0.078	0.893	0.796025	13	5	10,304	17,755	1,756.5	1,600	2	0	272
MAX	0.646	0.369	1	0.9901	2,648	1,262	300,027	230,759	23,176	165,298	116	0	321

TABLE 8.7
Statistical Summary of Batch Clan

	Pos	Neg	Neu	Comp.	Likes	Retweets	Status Count	Favorite Count	Friends Count	Follower Count	Listed Count	Author Verification	Content_len
MEAN	0.148574	0.044274	0.807151	0.406322	61.01	24.844	17,716.04	23,806.35	1,958.424	7,678.243	5.648	0	199.234
STD	0.112032	0.067018	0.121689	0.475933	217.4868	94.35574	37,513.13	46,473.28	4,318.096	25,538.66	14.48551	0	74.42204
MIN	0	0	0.328	−0.977	0	0	5	1	0	0	0	0	36
25% (Q1)	0.06775	0	0.72575	0	1	0	1,443	1,234	247	216.5	0	0	137
50% (Q2)	0.139	0	0.8145	0.56645	3	1	4,767	6,661	749.5	662	1	0	205
75% (Q3)	0.21925	0.074	0.89525	0.81115	20	8	16,446	19,142	1,841	2,316.25	3	0	265
MAX	0.672	0.5	1	0.9842	2,599	1,196	399,852	230,759	56,584	165,299	121	0	333

TABLE 8.8

Performance Metrics of RF across the Datasets

RF	Accuracy	F-Measure	AUC
Anov	85.46	0.855	0.938
BDec	98.44	0.978	0.993
CJan	<u>99.90</u>	<u>0.999</u>	<u>1.000</u>

RF, random forest.

TABLE 8.9

Bullying Vawulence Composition in 70% of Acquired Tweets

Tweet Category	Polarity Status	Total Representation	Percentage
Non-bullying tweets	Compound score >= 0.05	6,951	66.2%
Bullying vawulence tweets	Compound score <= −0.05	3,549	33.8%

From the experimental result, more positive tweets are posted in January 2023 (batch CJan), as indicated in Figure 8.4c, which stretches on the plot toward the 0.7 polarity score unlike in November and December 2022 when the electioneering campaign started. As can be observed, the higher positive trend started in December (batch BDec) beyond the limit of 0.6 positive polarity boundary in November 2022 (Figure 8.4a). However, Figure 8.4 shows there are more less-positive tweets throughout the span of November till January as the plots are skewed to the left with more data points between the 0.0 and 0.3 positive polarity scores. The same trend is observed with negative polarity scores as a majority of the tweets with negative sentiments (high propensity for bullying vawulence) are left skewed, showing higher toxicity, as seen from Figure 8.5. December 2022 (batch BDec) recorded more vawulence tweets possibly because campaigns were intensified during the period as the polarity of negative sentiments was within the span of −0.00 to −0.35 (high toxicity) as against the −0.0 and −0.5 November polarity spread and −0.0 and −0.5 January polarity spread. Unlike in the positive polarity spread, there is a structural similarity between the November and January negative polarity spread. A similar structure is observed in the neutral polarity spread for the three batches only that more neutral sentiments are expressed in November and December than in January. This can be attributed to the fact that more tweets have finally tilted toward either positively oriented or negatively oriented as the election draw nearer.

The number of retweets gathered on each post is categorized into four boundaries in order to situate their popularity as observed in the box plot of Figures 8.7, 8.8, and 8.9. For positive sentiments expressed in November tweets (Figure 8.7a), the most positive tweets are scantly retweeted. Only the tweets with single-digit retweets extend toward the 0.5 positive polarity. Indeed, 75% ($Q1$ to $Q3$) of the highest digit of retweet (color red) exhibits less than 0.3 positive polarity score. Only outliers are the most tweets with the most positive sentiments, netting up to 0.6 positive polarity score. The November tweets (Figure 8.7b) followed the same pattern for single-digit retweets; however, the highest digit retweets (color red) only net a 0.15 positive polarity score for the entire stretch of 75% IQR. Outliers however extended till a 0.6 positive polarity score for less retweeted posts. This implies that tweets with the most positive sentiments expressed in them are hardly retweeted as those with less positive polarity (tilting toward the neutral sentiments) are mostly captured within the 75% IQR. This trend continued till January (Figure 8.7c), with more outliers recorded in the less retweeted categories, which incidentally exhibits up to a strong 0.7 positive sentiment polarity score. As can be observed from Figure 8.8, tweets with a single retweet count are prominent with the negative sentiment expressions, just as more outliers are likewise recorded in that category of tweets. The result shows the most negative tweets (with polarity reaching −0.5 in November, −0.35 in December, and −0.5 in January), exhibiting bullying vawulence tendencies are hardly retweeted. However, January exhibits the highest negative polarity though greeted mostly with a single-digit retweet situation. The heat map in Figure 8.10 shows multicollinearity is at the lowest ebb across the three periods. For November (Figure 8.10a), a strong positive correlation of 0.96 is observed between the number of tweet likes and the number of retweets, while a somewhat average positive correlation of 0.47 is observed between the author status count and author favorite count. The same trend is surprisingly observed with the December and January categories as the behavior of predictive variables, in terms of correlation with each other, remained the same. The predictive variables are observed to be ideal for the subsequent predictive analytics.

The statistical summaries in Tables 8.5, 8.6, and 8.7 show the measures of central tendencies of the predictive and dependent variables. In November, the mean positive sentiment score was +0.150944, which reduced in December to +0.143129, while it slightly increased in January to +0.148574. However, bullying tendencies fluctuated across the three months, with a mean negative score of −0.046824 in November, which slightly increased to −0.047683 in December and marginally nosedived in January to −0.044274. In all, 75% ($Q1$ to $Q3$) of tweets in November recorded a negative sentiment score of −0.082, while the same population indicated a negative emotions score of −0.078 in December. This further plummeted in December to −0.074 polarity score. Finally, the maximum negative emotions were recorded in January, with a −0.5 polarity score, followed by a −0.484 score in November. In the final analysis, an insignificant 0.0333% of tweets (discovered only in November of Table 8.5) were from a verified Twitter handle, which is indicative of the fact that a gross majority of the 15,000 tweets are from authors with no blue-check credibility sign from Twitter. As indicative on Table 8.8, the RF performs best with the batch CJan data, returning a 99.90% accuracy rate and a weighted average of 0.999 precision rate. However, a 33.8% of the RF training set is labeled as bullying vawulence, consisting of tweets with a sentiment compound score less than or equal to −0.05. The total of 3,549 vawulence are replete of provocative, toxic, threatening, harassing, and bullying tweets, as detected in the Table 8.10. However, the ability of the RF to detect such bullying tendencies is not in doubt as earlier evaluated.

TABLE 8.10
The Ten Most Identified Bullying Vawulence

Bullying Vawulence	Compound Score
Obidient kill you there	−0.3818
All of una go soon be obituary	−0.5106
Obidense is their nature, stupid people	−0.5256
Balablu geneartion of bat bat fly to die	−0.4588
Nonsense generation fuck obituary	−0.3818
Obi dense obi tuary obi die	−0.5106
Atiku stupid	−0.5256
Em go show okowa pepper okowa in the potopoto	−0.3818
The thieve u have been voting in the name of tribal and religious sentiment don't care about u don't let their conspirators called influencers deceive u	−0.5106
Chai bro this your madness idea na blast. i dey interested now	−0.5256

8.5 CONCLUSION AND RECOMMENDATION

The study employs 15,000 tweets acquired in three sessions between November 2022 and January 2023 to train a RF ensemble methodology for the purpose of cyberbullying analytics. The tweets were passed through feature engineering techniques and as well through a sentiment analysis that returns their positive, negative, and neutral polarity scores. The three polarities were further analyzed to produce the compound polarity for each training set (70% of acquired population), which determines the ground truth for the supervised learning. The RF model was then evaluated on the test set (30% of the population) to detect bullying tendencies. The model performed better on the set acquired in January 2023, which exhibited more bullying sentiments than the other two datasets. The result of an exploratory data analysis shows a zero multicollinearity of predictive variables, whereas the number of likes is observed to be strongly positively correlated with the number of retweets. The high level of retweets indicates the danger inherent in bullying tweets, which could expand the victim base of social media users. In all, only one author is observed to have the blue-check credibility status validated by Twitter, a development that questions the validity of posts communicated by authors. The result likewise shows that highly retweeted posts are replete with provocative, incisive, toxic, and abusive messages, with its multiplying effect. Future studies could conduct a post-election analysis and compare results of bullying tendencies with the present reality.

REFERENCES

Abdulyakeen, A., & Yusuf, Y. A. (2022). Social Media and Political Participation Among Youth in South-Eastern Nigeria: A Case Study of 2015 and 2019 General Elections. *Acta Politica Polonica, 54*, 147–173.

Almaiah, M. A., Al-Khasawneh, A., & Althunibat, A. (2020). Exploring the Critical Challenges and Factors Influencing the E-Learning System Usage During COVID-19 Pandemic. *Education and Information Technologies, 25*, 5261–5280.

Baarah, A., Aloqaily, A., Salah, Z., Zamzeer, M., & Sallam, M. (2019). Machine Learning Approaches for Predicting the Severity Level of Software Bug Reports in Closed Source Projects. *International Journal of Advanced Computer Science and Applications, 10*, 285–294.

Battista, D., & Uva, G. (2023). Exploring the Legal Regulation of Social Media in Europe: A Review of Dynamics and Challenges-Current Trends and Future Developments. *Sustainability, 15*(5), 4144.

Borondics, F., Vitali, F., & Shaulsky, G. (2020). Data Mining. Retrieved September 17, 2022, from https://orangedatamining.com/

Chakraborty, K., Bhatia, S., Bhattacharyya, S., Platos, J., Bag, R., & Hassanien, A. E. (2020). Sentiment Analysis of COVID-19 Tweets By Deep Learning Classifiers-A Study to Show How Popularity Is Affecting Accuracy in Social Media. *Applied Soft Computing, 97*, 106754.

Chu, X., Li, Y., Wang, P., Zeng, P., & Lei, L. (2021). Social Support and Cyberbullying for University Students: The Mediating Role of Internet Addiction and the Moderating Role of Stress. *Current Psycholog, 42*, 1–9.

Dalvi, R. R., Chavan, S. B., & Halbe, A. (2020). Detecting a Twitter Cyberbullying Using Machine Learning. In *Proceedings of the International Conference on Intelligent Computing and Control Systems (ICICCS 2020)*, Madurai, India (pp. 297–301). IEEE.

Emmery, C., Verhoeven, B., Pauw, G. D., Jacobs, G., Hee, C. V., Lefever, E., ... Daelemans, W. (2021). Current Limitations in Cyberbullying Detection: On Evaluation Criteria, Reproducibility, and Data Scarcity. *Language Resources and Evaluation, 51*, 597–633.

Etsenamhe, T. (2022). *Cyber-Bullying and 2023 Elections*. Abuja: Sun Publishers. Retrieved from https://www.sunnewsonline.com/cyber-bullying-and-2023-elections/

Goldberg, I. A. (2000). A pseudonymous communications infrastructure for the internet. University of California. Berkeley.

Grinberg, N. J.-T. (2019). Fake News on Twitter During the 2016 US Presidential Election. *Science, 363*, 374–378.

Ho, S. M., Kao, D., Chiu-Huang, M.-J., Li, W., & Lai, C.-J. (2020). Detecting Cyberbullying "Hotspots" on Twitter: A Predictive Analytics Approach. In *DFRWS 2020 EU e Proceedings of the Seventh Annual DFRWS Europe* (pp. 1–3). Elsevier.

Islam, M. M., Uddin, M. A., Islam, L., Akter, A., Sharmin, S., & Acharjee, U. K. (2020). Cyberbullying Detection on Social Networks Using Machine Learning Approaches. In *2020 IEEE Asia-Pacific Conference on Computer Science and Data Engineering (CSDE)*, Gold Coast, Australia (pp. 1–6). IEEE.

Kumar, A., & Sachdeva, N. (2021). A Bi-GRU with Attention and CapsNet Hybrid Model for Cyberbullying Detection on Social Media. *World Wide Web, 25*, 1537–1550.

Kumar, A., & Sachdeva, N. (2022). Multimodal Cyberbullying Detection Using Capsule Network with Dynamic Routing and Deep Convolutional Neural Network. *Deep Learning Methods for Cyber-Bullying Detection in Multi-modal Data, 28*, 2043–2052.

Loh, J., & Snyman, R. (2020). The Tangled Web: Consequences of Workplace Cyberbullying in Adult Male and Female Employees. *Gender in Management: An International Journal, 35*(6), 567–584.

Macaulay, J. P., Betts, L. R., Stiller, J., & Kellezi, B. (2022). Bystander Responses to Cyberbullying: The Role of Perceived Severity, Publicity, Anonymity, Type of Cyberbullying, and Victim Response. *Computers in Human Behavior, 131*, 107238.

Maity, K., Kumar, A., & Saha, S. (2022). A Multitask Multimodal Framework for Sentiment and Emotion-Aided Cyberbullying Detection. *IEEE Internet Computing, 26*(4), 68–78.

Matomela, V., & Henney, A. J. (2022). Cyberbullying Detection System Focusing on the isiX-hosa Language. In *2022 Conference on Information Communications Technology and Society (ICTAS)*, Durban, South Africa (pp. 1–6). IEEE.

Muzakir, A. H. (2022). A Comparative Analysis of Classification Algorithms for Cyberbullying Crime Detection: An Experimental Study of Twitter Social Media in Indonesia. *Scientific Journal of Informatics, 9*, 133–138.

Olaleye, T., Abayomi-Alli, A., Adesemowo, K., Arogundade, O. T., Misra, S., & Kose, U. (2022). SCLAVOEM: Hyper Parameter Optimization Approach to Predictive Modelling of COVID-19 Infodemic Tweets Using Smote and Classifier Vote Ensemble. *Soft Computing, 27*, 1–20.

Olaleye, T., Ugege, P., Ademoroti, A., Olomola, T., Ilugbo, O., & Shofoluwe, O. (2021). Veracity Assessment of Multimedia Facebook Posts for Infodemic Symptom Detection Using Bi-modal Unsupervised Machine Learning Approach. *International Journal for Research in Applied Science & Engineering Technology, 9*(XII), 2234–2241.

Oswari, T., Prihantoro, E., Dunan, A., & Mudjiyanto, B. (2020). The Political Impact of Cyberbullying and Cyber Victimization on Social Media Against Campaign Patterns Through Reactive Behavior in Democratic Elections in the Era of Society 5.0. *Solid State Technol, 63*(6), 21539–21555.

Perez, C., & Karmakar, S. (2023). An NLP-Assisted Bayesian Time Series Analysis for Prevalence of Twitter Cyberbullying During the COVID-19 Pandemic. *Social Network Analysis and Mining, 13*(1), 51.

Qaisar, A. R. (2022). Impact of Cyber Bullying on Political Behavior and Youth's Perceptions About Use of Social Media By Political Parties of Pakistan. *Journal of Business and Social Review in Emerging Economies, 8*, 71–82.

Sahara. (2022). I Don't Read Social Media Anymore Because People Abuse Hell Out Of Me, Give Me High Blood Pressure - APC Presidential Candidate, Tinubu. Retrieved from https://saharareporters.com/2022/11/19/i-dont-read-social-media-anymore-because-people-abuse-hell-out-me-give-me-high-blood

Statista. (2020, April 24). *Most Popular Social Networks Worldwide as of April 2020, Ranked by Number of Active Users (in Millions)* (J. Clement, Ed.). Retrieved May 29, 2020, from Social Media & User-Generated Content: https://www.statista.com/statistics/272014/global-social-networks-ranked-by

Sultan, T., Jahan, N., Basak, R., Jony, M. S., & Nabil, R. H. (2023). Machine Learning in Cyberbullying Detection from Social-Media Image or Screenshot with Optical Character Recognition. *I.J. Intelligent Systems and Applications, 15*, 1–13.

Sung, Y.-H. (2018). Book Review of Cyber Bullying Approaches, Consequences and Intervention. *International Journal of Cyber Criminology, 12*(1), 353–361.

Szymkowiak, A., Melović, B., Dabić, M., Jeganathan, K., & Kundi, G. S. (2021). Information Technology and Gen Z: The Role of Teachers, the Internet, and Technology in the Education of Young People. *Technology in Society, 65*, 101565.

Thun, L. J., Teh, P. L., & Cheng, C.-B. (2022). CyberAid: Are Your Children Safe from Cyberbullying? *Journal of King Saud University – Computer and Information Sciences, 34*, 1319–1578.

UNICEF. (2020). Cyberbullying: What Is It and How to Stop It. Retrieved from Unicef: https://www.unicef.org/end-violence/how-to-stop-cyberbullying

WHO. (2022, February 4). WHO Coronavirus (COVID-19) Dashboard. Retrieved from World Health Organization: https://www.covid19.who.int

Yafooz, W. S., Al-Dhaqm, A., & Alsaeedi, A. (2023). Detecting Kids Cyberbullying Using Transfer Learning Approach: Transformer Fine-Tuning Models. In W. Yafooz, H. Al-Aqrabi, A. Al-Dhaqm, & A. Hamid (eds.), *Kids Cybersecurity Using Computational Intelligence Techniques. Studies in Computational Intelligence* (pp. 255–267). Cham: Springer.

Yuvaraj, N., Srihari, K., Dhiman, G., Somasundaram, K., Sharma, A., Rajeskannan, S., … Masud, M. (2021). Nature-Inspired-Based Approach for Automated Cyberbullying Classification on Multimedia Social Networking. *Mathematical Problems in Engineering, 2021*, 1–12.

9 Identifying Behaviors and Characteristics of Social Media Sexual Harassers on LinkedIn for AI NLP Purposes

Karim Darban and Smail Kabbaj
University Hassan II of Casablanca

9.1 INTRODUCTION

Sexual harassment on LinkedIn is a pervasive issue that has gained significant attention in recent years. Despite being a professional networking platform, reports of sexual harassment have continued to surface on platforms (Arafa et al., 2018; Burnay et al., 2019; Copp et al., 2021). Sexual harassment takes various forms on social media, including unwanted messages, inappropriate comments, and even insults. The problem is not limited to one gender as both men and women have reported experiencing sexual harassment on LinkedIn (Basu et al., 2021; Buchanan and Mahoney, 2022).

One of the reasons why sexual harassment is prevalent on LinkedIn is the lack of clear policies and guidelines to address it. LinkedIn's user policies do not provide specific guidelines on how to report sexual harassment, leaving victims unsure of the best course of action. Additionally, LinkedIn's reporting mechanisms for sexual harassment are not robust enough, which means that reports may not receive the attention they deserve (Jillian Kowalchuk, 2020).

Another factor that contributes to the problem of sexual harassment on LinkedIn is the anonymity of the platform. Users can easily create fake profiles, making it difficult to trace perpetrators of sexual harassment. This anonymity can also embolden harassers, who may feel that they can act with impunity (Adikari and Dutta, 2020; Claybaugh and Haseman, 2013).

The impact of sexual harassment on LinkedIn can be devastating (Guerra et al., 2021). Victims may experience a range of negative emotions, including shame, embarrassment, and anxiety. This can lead to decreased self-esteem and confidence, which can have a significant impact on their professional and personal lives. Additionally, sexual harassment can create a hostile work environment, which can lead to decreased productivity and increased turnover (Cripps and Stermac, 2018).

According to Espelage et al. (2012), cyberbullying theory posits that bullying behavior in the digital world is driven by a complex interplay of individual, social, and environmental factors. This includes factors such as personality traits, peer pressure, anonymity, and the availability of digital tools to engage in harmful behaviors. The theory also highlights the impact of power imbalances, such as those based on race, gender, or socioeconomic status, which can exacerbate the harm caused by cyberbullying. To prevent and address cyberbullying, social media should consider the importance of a multifaceted approach that involves awareness raising, support, and technological measures including fast detection and restriction (Bauman and Yoon, 2014).

However, advances in natural language processing (NLP) technology have opened up new avenues for combating this problem. One of the primary benefits of NLP is its ability to analyze large quantities of text data quickly and accurately. This is particularly relevant in the context of LinkedIn, where thousands of messages and comments are exchanged every day. By using NLP algorithms, we can automatically detect patterns and language that indicate potential instances of sexual harassment, allowing us to intervene before the situation escalates (León-Paredes et al., 2019; Yuvaraj et al., 2021).

Furthermore, NLP can also help us understand the broader context of conversations on LinkedIn. For example, by analyzing the sentiment of comments and posts, we can identify trends and topics that may be contributing to a culture of sexual harassment. This information can then be used to develop targeted educational campaigns or policy changes that address the root causes of the problem (Azeez et al., 2021).

In short, NLP is an essential tool in the fight against sexual harassment on LinkedIn. Its ability to process and analyze large quantities of data quickly and accurately allows us to identify and address instances of harassment, as well as understand the broader context in which these incidents occur. By leveraging NLP technology, we can make LinkedIn a safer and more inclusive platform for all users (Ali et al., 2018; Raj et al., 2021).

The purpose of this chapter is to identify common characteristics of LinkedIn sexual harassers through a quantitative research study. The goal is to assist AI specialists in developing new or optimizing existing AI models to combat sexual harassment on LinkedIn by providing insights on the common characteristics of harassers. The questionnaire will be used to collect data from respondents who have experienced sexual harassment on LinkedIn. The collected data will be analyzed using statistical methods to identify patterns and common characteristics among harassers. This information can be used to develop more effective AI models that can detect and prevent sexual harassment on the platform. Ultimately, the aim of this research is to contribute to a safer and more inclusive LinkedIn community for all users.

9.2   LITERATURE REVIEW

9.2.1   Sexual Harassment in Online Environments

Sexual harassment in online environments has become a prevalent issue in recent years, with the rise of social media and other online platforms. The anonymity provided by the Internet can often embolden harassers, leading to a higher frequency of such incidents (Adikari and Dutta, 2020; Claybaugh and Haseman, 2013). The impact of online harassment can be significant, including emotional distress, fear for personal safety, and damage to professional and personal reputations. Online harassment can also lead to a chilling effect, silencing individuals and discouraging them from speaking out or participating in online spaces (Coletta, 2017).

As online platforms continue to grow in popularity and influence, it is imperative to address and combat the issue of sexual harassment in online environments. This requires a multifaceted approach that includes both policy and technological solutions. Therefore, the use of NLP techniques in detecting and preventing online harassment represents a promising avenue for addressing this issue.

Sexual harassment in online environments has been found to have a profound impact on victims. Studies have shown that victims of sexual harassment may experience psychological distress, including anxiety, depression, and post-traumatic stress disorder (Guerra et al., 2021). In addition to the emotional impact, victims may also experience physical symptoms such as headaches, nausea, and insomnia (Copp et al., 2021).

Furthermore, victims of sexual harassment in online environments may experience negative effects on their work and personal lives. For example, victims may be less likely to participate in online communities or seek job opportunities online. They may also experience negative effects on their job performance and suffer financial losses due to missed opportunities or job loss (Reed et al., 2020; Coletta, 2017).

Research consistently shows that women are disproportionately affected by sexual harassment online, with studies indicating that they are more likely to experience unwanted sexual advances, explicit messages or images, and other forms of online harassment compared to men. This disparity is often attributed to underlying gender inequalities and power imbalances in society, which can be amplified in online environments. Women may also be more likely to experience sexual harassment due to the prevalence of stereotypes and gender-based discrimination, which can lead to harmful behaviors such as victim blaming and shaming (Cripps and Stermac, 2018; Reed et al., 2020).

Sexual harassment can take many forms in online environments, and it is important to understand the various types to effectively combat it. The analysis of various papers, including Arafa et al. (2018), Emily Harmer and Sarah Lewis (2022), Leemis et al. (2019), Barlińska et al. (2013), Pendergrast et al. (2021), Reed et al. (2019), Vogels (2021), Walters and Espelage (2020), Vincent-Höper et al. (2020), Van de Ven et al. (2017), Van Dijck (2013), and Wiederhold (2022), revealed that online sexual harassment can take many forms.

The same studies have attempted to identify common characteristics of online sexual harassers. In average, they have found that online harassers are more likely to be male in the same age or older than the victim. They also more likely have no real-life relation with the victim (they do not know the victim in real life). In addition, online harassers are more likely to exhibit traits such as hostility, aggression, and narcissism.

Another common characteristic of online harassers is a lack of empathy toward their victims. Online anonymity and perceived distance from the victim can lead to a disconnect between the harasser's actions and the harm they are causing. This can result in an increased willingness to engage in harassing behaviors without considering the impact on the victim.

Table 9.1 highlights the various types of online sexual harassment that have been identified in previous studies; it has provided valuable insights that we will use to guide the development of our questionnaire as the types of harassment identified in the literature served as a compass that directed our focus toward understanding the prevalence of these behaviors among sexual harassers on LinkedIn. It is important to note that these common characteristics are not definitive and may vary depending on the specific context and platform of the online environment. Therefore, it is crucial to conduct research studies to identify common characteristics of online sexual harassers on LinkedIn specifically.

TABLE 9.1

Types of Online Sexual Harassment according to the Literature

Unwanted sexual attention	Unwanted sexual attention is one of the most common types of sexual harassment observed in online spaces. This can include receiving explicit messages or comments, unwanted sexual advances, or unsolicited sexually explicit material.
Sexual coercion	Involves pressuring someone into engaging in sexual activity. This can take many forms in online spaces, including aggressive persistence, threatening to release embarrassing information, blackmailing, or other forms of manipulation.
Stalking	Stalking, whether in person or online, is a serious form of sexual harassment that can cause significant distress for the victim. This can include monitoring the victim's online activities, repeatedly contacting them, commenting on their posts (pictures videos), and saving them.
Grooming	Involves building a manipulative relationship with a victim with the intention of engaging in sexual activities. This can take many forms in online spaces, including using flattery, attention, and gifts to gain the victim's trust.
Catfishing	Involves creating a fake online profile to deceive someone into thinking they are interacting with a different person. This can be a form of sexual harassment if the deception is used to engage in sexual activities or manipulate the victim.
Dirty jokes	The use of dirty jokes and sexual innuendos can be another form of sexual harassment in online spaces. This type of behavior can be especially problematic in professional networks, where it can create a toxic environment.
Insults	Insults and name-calling based on someone's gender, sexual orientation, or other personal characteristics can also be a form of sexual harassment in online spaces.
Threats	Threats of violence or harm are another serious form of sexual harassment in online spaces. This can include threats to the victim's safety, as well as threats to release personal information or images.

9.2.2   NLP in Detecting Online Harassment

NLP is a subfield of artificial intelligence (AI) that deals with the interaction between computers and human languages. NLP has become increasingly important in recent years as more and more people are communicating through online platforms according to Chowdhary (2020). It can be used to analyze the content of these communications and identify patterns of behavior that may indicate harassment.

NLP techniques have been used in a variety of applications, including sentiment analysis, speech recognition, and machine translation. In the context of online harassment, NLP can be used to identify patterns of language and behavior that are associated with harassing or abusive messages (Nakov et al., 2021; Chowdhary, 2020; Bayari and Bensefia, 2021).

There are several techniques that are commonly used in NLP to detect harassment, including text classification, topic modeling, and sentiment analysis (León-Paredes et al., 2019). Text classification involves categorizing messages based on their content, while topic modeling is used to identify patterns in the language used in the messages. Sentiment analysis is used to identify the emotional tone of the messages, which can be an important indicator of harassment (Raj et al., 2021; Yuvaraj et al., 2021).

In conclusion, NLP has the potential to be an important tool in the fight against online harassment. By analyzing the content of messages and identifying patterns of behavior, NLP can help identify and prevent harassment before it escalates.

NLP techniques have shown promising results in detecting various types of online harassment, including sexual harassment. Existing NLP techniques can broadly be categorized into two types: rule-based and machine learning-based. Rule-based approaches involve designing a set of rules or heuristics to identify specific patterns in the text that indicate harassment. These approaches are based on handcrafted rules, which are usually limited in their coverage and may not be able to capture the complexity of human language (Ali et al., 2018). Machine learning-based approaches, on the other hand, involve training a model using labeled data, which enables the model to learn to identify patterns in the data without being explicitly programmed with rules. These approaches have shown significant improvements in the accuracy of harassment detection compared to rule-based approaches (León-Paredes et al., 2019; Azeez et al., 2021).

Several machine learning-based approaches have been proposed for detecting online harassment. One popular approach is the use of support vector machines to classify text as either harassing or non-harassing. Other approaches include deep learning-based models such as convolutional neural networks and recurrent neural networks, which have shown promising results in detecting online harassment (Milosevic et al., 2022; Rosa et al., 2019).

While these approaches have shown promise in detecting harassment, they may not be suitable for detecting subtle forms of harassment that are difficult to classify. Additionally, these approaches require large amounts of labeled data, which may not be available for all types of harassment. In the context of LinkedIn, existing NLP techniques for detecting online harassment may not be directly applicable as the platform's content is primarily professional in nature. Therefore, there is a need to explore and develop new NLP models that are specifically tailored to detect sexual harassment on LinkedIn.

While NLP has shown promise in detecting online harassment, it also has its advantages and limitations. One advantage of using NLP is that it can process a large amount of data quickly and accurately, which can be difficult for humans to do manually. NLP algorithms can also identify patterns and commonalities in the language used by harassers, which can help identify potential perpetrators and prevent future incidents (Milosevic et al., 2023; Sánchez-Medina et al., 2020).

Another advantage of using NLP is that it can be used to identify subtle patterns and behaviors that may not be obvious to human observers. For example, it can detect manipulation or passive aggressive language, which may be used by harassers to disguise their intentions (Haidar et al., 2016; Haidar et al., 2017).

However, there are also some limitations to using NLP in detecting online harassment. One limitation is that NLP algorithms rely heavily on the quality and quantity of the data they are trained on. If training data are biased or limited, the algorithm may produce inaccurate or incomplete results (Emmery et al., 2021). Additionally, NLP algorithms may not be able to account for contextual factors that may affect the interpretation of language, such as cultural differences or variations in language use (Yuvaraj et al., 2021; Emmery et al., 2021). Therefore, it is important to train AI models on real data from the victims' perspectives and use NLP in conjunction with other methods, such as manual review by human experts, to ensure the accuracy and completeness of the analysis.

9.2.3 Sexual Harassment on LinkedIn

LinkedIn is a social networking platform that is designed for professionals to connect, network, and develop their careers (Power, 2015). Launched in 2003, LinkedIn has become the world's largest professional network, with over 750 million members in more than 200 countries and territories worldwide (Davis et al., 2020). It is used by individuals to showcase their professional skills and accomplishments, find jobs, and connect with potential employers or business partners.

LinkedIn offers a variety of features that cater to professional networking, including a profile page where users can display their work experience, education, and skills. Users can also join groups related to their industry or interests, engage in discussions, and share articles and other professional content. In addition, LinkedIn provides a job search feature, where users can browse job openings, apply to positions, and connect with recruiters (Norouzizadeh Dezfouli et al., 2016; Koch et al., 2018).

However, like other online platforms, LinkedIn is not immune to incidents of sexual harassment. Several unique features of LinkedIn may contribute to sexual harassment, and understanding these features is crucial to developing effective strategies for preventing and addressing such behavior.

One unique feature of LinkedIn is its emphasis on personal branding and self-promotion. LinkedIn profiles often contain personal information such as clear face pictures, education, job history, and skills, which can make users more vulnerable to harassment. In addition, the emphasis on building a professional network may encourage users to connect with individuals they do not know well, increasing the likelihood of encountering inappropriate behavior (Marin and Nilă, 2021).

Another feature of LinkedIn is the ability to send messages and connect with anyone privately. This can provide a platform for harassers to target individuals in a more direct and personal way. Furthermore, LinkedIn messaging can be used to request personal information or offer job opportunities, which may be used as leverage to pressure individuals into engaging in unwanted sexual behavior (Claybaugh and Haseman, 2013).

LinkedIn's recommendation feature is another unique aspect of the platform that may contribute to harassment. Recommendations are public endorsements of a user's skills and experience, which can be viewed by potential employers and colleagues. However, recommendations can also be used as a tool for harassment, such as when a harasser offers to provide a recommendation or a job in exchange for sexual favors (McCabe, 2017; Utz, 2016).

Understanding these unique features of LinkedIn is essential for developing effective strategies to combat sexual harassment on the platform. By identifying common characteristics of harassers (Tifferet and Vilnai-Yavetz, 2018; Fernandez et al., 2021) and leveraging NLP techniques to detect and prevent inappropriate behavior, we can create a safer and more professional online environment for all LinkedIn users.

LinkedIn claims to employ both reactive and proactive measures to protect its members from spam, inappropriate, or harassing content. According to LinkedIn, harassment is not tolerated on the platform, and the company has policies and practices in place to ensure members feel safe while using the platform. Additionally, the company encourages members to report negative experiences, and they actively review these reports and track trends. However, the company finds that reported cases of harassment predominantly stem from private messages rather than the public feed. Therefore, LinkedIn has developed a series of initiatives and projects to better protect members against harassment in messaging (LinkedIn, 2023).

According to Grace Tang et al. (2020), LinkedIn's strategy to combat harassment includes educating members about their professional community policies, enforcing these policies, detecting harassment using machine learning models, and supporting affected members by sending 100% of the harassment reports for review and closing the loop with reporting members to provide more transparency on the action taken. The company detects harassment using a machine learning harassment detection system consisting of a sequence of three models that identify violating members and their harassing messages with high precision. While LinkedIn's measures to prevent sexual harassment on the platform are commendable, there are still several areas that require improvement. For instance, LinkedIn acknowledges that unwanted advances are under-reported, which means the true extent of sexual harassment on the platform may be significantly higher than what the company currently knows. Additionally, LinkedIn acknowledges that some members block violating members instead of reporting them for action. This suggests that some members may not trust the company to take appropriate action, which undermines the effectiveness of the company's strategy (Grace Tang et al., 2020).

While LinkedIn's measures to prevent sexual harassment on the platform are commendable, there is still room for improvement. The company should continue to refine and improve their tools to prevent or quickly stop harassment. Additionally, the company should work on better AI models to stop the dependency to victim's reports, and develop ways to minimize false positives.

Very few studies have been done on the themes LinkedIn and AI. For instance, Bradbury (2011) notes the importance of machine learning and artificial intelligence in improving the search capabilities of LinkedIn. This is particularly relevant to cyberbullying as it is essential to be able to identify and classify harmful content accurately. By using AI algorithms, LinkedIn could automate the detection and flagging of potentially harmful posts and comments, allowing them to be reviewed by moderators or removed altogether. Auradkar et al. (2012) investigate how LinkedIn uses machine learning to recommend jobs to users. This same approach could be applied to identify and suggest potentially abusive content to LinkedIn moderators, who can then take appropriate action. This method could also be used to track and identify persistent offenders and prevent them from using the platform to bully others. Sumbaly et al. (2013) discuss how LinkedIn uses Hadoop to process large amounts of data for its recommendation system. This same approach could be used to process data on user behavior and interactions to identify patterns of cyberbullying on the platform. AI could then be used to create personalized prevention strategies for users who have been targeted, such as customized recommendations for privacy settings or tips for responding to cyberbullying.

9.3 METHODOLOGY

The objective of this chapter is to ascertain the shared traits of LinkedIn sexual harassers, using a quantitative research approach, that will help AI specialists to develop novel AI models or fine-tune current ones that can effectively counteract sexual harassment on the LinkedIn platform. A questionnaire will be used to gather data from respondents who have experienced sexual harassment on LinkedIn. The amassed data will be subjected to statistical scrutiny to identify dispersion, patterns, and prevalent characteristics among harassers. The findings of this research will be useful in designing more potent AI models that can accurately detect and thwart sexual harassment on the platform.

9.3.1 DATA COLLECTION

The questionnaire used in this study consists of four sections that aim to collect relevant data on both the victims and perpetrators of sexual harassment on LinkedIn, as well as their reactions to these incidents. Each section is designed to address specific aspects related to the research objectives, guided by the results of the existing studies discussed in the literature review.

The first section of the questionnaire focuses on the demographic characteristics of the respondents, such as age, gender, and continent of origin. These demographic data are essential to understanding the scope and prevalence of sexual harassment on LinkedIn across different populations, which is a key aspect of this research.

The second section of the questionnaire is dedicated to collecting information about the harassers, including their estimated age, gender, and location. This information, according to the literature, is crucial for identifying common characteristics among LinkedIn sexual harassers, as well as understanding the extent to which they may be connected to the victims. Additionally, the section gathers data on the harasser's profile type, whether real or fake, which is important in determining the level of anonymity and deception involved in these incidents. The questionnaire also seeks to determine if the harasser was a recruiter or someone offering a job, which is relevant as it may indicate whether these incidents are linked to power dynamics in the professional context.

The third section of the questionnaire is designed to explore the specific characteristics of the sexual harassment incidents, such as the type of behavior observed and any specific tactics used to manipulate or pressure the victims. This section is critical to identifying patterns and trends in the behaviors of sexual harassers on LinkedIn. It also seeks to determine if the harasser showed signs of escalation or asked for personal information, which is relevant to understanding the severity and potential dangers of these incidents.

Finally, the fourth section of the questionnaire is devoted to the victims' reactions to the sexual harassment incidents, such as whether they responded or blocked the harasser, and whether they reported the incident to LinkedIn. These data are important for understanding the potential effectiveness of current reporting and prevention mechanisms on LinkedIn, as well as the emotional impact of these incidents on the victims.

9.3.2 PARTICIPANTS AND SAMPLE SIZE

For this study, we used the non-probability sampling technique known as convenience sampling. We randomly sent the questionnaire in groups and direct messages. A first filter question asked if the respondent is a LinkedIn user and a second asked if they had experienced sexual harassment on LinkedIn. Only those who responded "yes" to both questions were included in the sample. This approach allowed us to focus on individuals who have had direct experience with sexual harassment on LinkedIn and provided us with a more targeted sample.

A total of 723 LinkedIn users completed the questionnaire, but only 479 of these respondents confirmed that they had experienced sexual harassment on LinkedIn. While the sample size may seem relatively small, it is important to note that this is a common issue in studies related to sensitive topics such as sexual harassment. Additionally, the use of targeted sampling allowed us to gather more detailed information from a smaller but more relevant sample. Since the objective of the study is getting data from real experiences of harassment, and not opinions or hearsay.

9.3.3 DATA ANALYSIS

The data collected from the questionnaire are analyzed using descriptive statistics through the Statistical Package for the Social Sciences (SPSS) software. Descriptive statistics are an effective way of summarizing and presenting data, allowing us to gain insights into the characteristics and behaviors of the harassers and the prevalence of sexual harassment on LinkedIn. Specifically, we use frequency distributions, percentages, means, and standard deviations to analyze the data and identify patterns and trends among the responses: Frequency distributions are used to present the distribution of responses to each question, indicating the frequency with which each response was given. Percentages are used to show the proportion of respondents who gave a particular response relative to the total number of respondents. Means and standard deviations are used to analyze continuous variables, such as age. In addition to descriptive statistics, we also use inferential statistics to examine the relationships between variables and identify any significant differences between groups.

9.4   RESULTS

The present study aimed to identify the shared traits of LinkedIn sexual harassers using a quantitative research approach to help develop potent AI models that can accurately detect and thwart sexual harassment on the platform. A total of 479 respondents who experienced sexual harassment on LinkedIn completed the questionnaire, and the data were analyzed using descriptive and inferential statistics.

9.4.1   DEMOGRAPHIC CHARACTERISTICS OF RESPONDENTS (VICTIMS)

The demographic distribution of the respondents in this survey provides important insights into the target population of the study. One notable finding is the significant overrepresentation of females, which accounted for 95.8% of the respondents, while males only constituted 4.2%. This finding could be indicative of a higher prevalence of harassment and discrimination against women, which makes them more likely to participate in such surveys. Studies in the literature review have shown that females are more prone to harassment in various settings, including the workplace, education, and public spaces. Therefore, it is not surprising to see a higher proportion of female respondents in a study focused on harassment and discrimination.

Another noteworthy finding is the concentration of respondents in the younger age groups, particularly those aged between 17 and 31 years, which accounted for over 80% of the sample. This finding could reflect a higher susceptibility of young people to harassment and discrimination. Young people, especially those in their late teens and early twenties, are often exposed to new social environments, which may expose them to situations where harassment occurs. Additionally, young people may be less equipped to cope with these situations, leading to a higher likelihood of experiencing negative outcomes.

Concerning location, most respondents were from Africa (41.8%), followed by Europe (30.3%), North America (13.8%), Asia (9%), South America (4.6%), and Australia (0.6%).

9.4.2   DEMOGRAPHIC CHARACTERISTICS OF LINKEDIN SEXUAL HARASSERS

This section is an important part of the overall study on combatting sexual harassment on LinkedIn. It provides insights into the demographics of the individuals who engage in sexual harassment on the platform, including their gender, age, location, and relationship with the victim. The gender breakdown of both the harassers and

TABLE 9.2

Demographic Characteristics of Respondents (Victims)

Gender			
	Female	**Male**	**Total**
Frequency	459	20	479
Percent	95.8	4.2	100

Age (years)									
	17–21	**22–26**	**27–31**	**32–36**	**37–41**	**42–46**	**47–51**	**52–56**	**56–60**	**Total**
Frequency	98	171	124	25	20	17	9	9	6	479
Percent	20.5	35.7	25.9	5.2	4.2	3.5	1.9	1.9	1.3	100
Mean	27.76									
Std. deviation	8,391									

Location						
	Africa	**Asia**	**Australia**	**Europe**	**North America**	**South America**	**Total**
Frequency	200	43	3	145	66	22	479
Percent	41.8	9	0.6	30.3	13.8	4.6	100

victims in this study is an important aspect to consider. The data reveal that out of the total of 479 cases, a staggering 449 harassers were male, representing a dominant 93.73% of all harassers. Interestingly, only a small minority of 6.27% of harassers were female. It is noteworthy that the data also indicate a disproportion of same-gender sexual harassment, with only seven cases involving male same-gender harassers and 17 cases of females same-gender harassers (more than female heterosexual harassers). The second part of Table 9.3 sheds light on the location of the harasser and its importance in understanding the nature of sexual harassment on LinkedIn. The data indicate that in 65.1% of cases, the harasser was from the same country as the victim, which means that a significant proportion of harassers choose victims from their regions and could be individuals looking for real-life (physical) connections. The third part of Table 9.3 reveals that in almost half of the cases, the harasser was older than the victim, which highlights the power dynamic and the potential for manipulation and exploitation. Moreover, in some cases, the harasser was younger than the victim (mainly for female's victims aged between 37 and 60 years), which suggests that age may not always be a factor that protects individuals from harassment.

The fourth part of Table 9.3 sheds light on the type of LinkedIn profile used by the harasser. The data indicate that nearly half of the harassers had real LinkedIn profiles, whereas approximately one-fourth of them used fake profiles, and around 27.3% of the profiles were not checked. It is noteworthy that more than 70% of the female harassers were declared to be fake accounts, which raises questions about whether they are really women. These data highlight the need for developing AI models that can accurately identify fake profiles and distinguish between real and fake accounts to prevent sexual harassment. The fifth part sheds light on whether the harasser knew the victim in real life or not. In 92.7% of the cases, the harasser had no

TABLE 9.3
Demographic Characteristics of LinkedIn Sexual Harassers

		Gender			
		Harassers			
		Female	Male	Total Frequency	Percent
	Female	17	442	459	95.82
	Male	13	7	20	4.18
Victims	Total frequency	30	449	479	
	Percent	6.27	93.73		

	Location (Same Country as Victim's)		
	Yes	No	Total
Frequency	312	167	479
Percent	65.1	34.9	100

	Age (Compared to Victim's)			
	Older	Same Age	Younger	Total
Frequency	217	184	78	479
Percent	45.3	38.4	16.3	100.0

	Profile Type			
	Fake	Not Checked	Real	Total
Frequency	119	131	229	479
Percent	24.8	27.3	47.8	100.0

	Real-Life Relation		
	No	Yes	Total
Frequency	444	35	479
Percent	92.7	7.3	100.0

	Is the Harasser a Recruiter?		
	No	Yes	Total
Frequency	400	79	479
Percent	83.5	16.5	100.0

	Harassment from First Contact		
	No	Yes	Total
Frequency	175	304	479
Percent	36.5	63.5	100.0

real-life connection with the victim. On the other hand, in 7.3% of cases, the harasser had a real-life connection with the victim. This could imply that people may feel more comfortable crossing boundaries online, even with those they know in real life. The sixth part provides insight into whether the harasser was a recruiter or not. Out of the total 479 cases analyzed, 16.5% were recruiters. This information is crucial in understanding the prevalence of sexual harassment in a professional setting, and specifically within the recruitment process. The fact that 16.5% of harassers were recruiters is concerning as recruiters hold a position of power and influence over potential job-seeking candidates. This could potentially make victims feel trapped or powerless in the face of harassment. The seventh and final part provides insight into the timing of sexual harassment messages on LinkedIn. Specifically, the table indicates whether the harassment occurred in the initial messages exchanged between the victim and the harasser. The data show that in a majority of cases, which is 63.5%, the harassment was observed in the first messages. This suggests that initial conversations are a crucial moment for detecting and preventing harassment, and AI models could be trained to detect such patterns. The remaining 36.5% of cases had harassment observed later in the conversation.

9.4.3 Characteristics of LinkedIn Sexual Harassment Experiences

The data presented in this section of the chapter pertain to the demographic characteristics of LinkedIn sexual harassers. In the first part of Table 9.4, the victims' perspectives on what constitutes sexual harassment on LinkedIn were presented. The data revealed that the most common form of harassment reported by the 479 victims was unwanted sexual attention, which was reported by 92 victims, making up 19.2% of all cases. Additionally, 18.8% of victims reported stalking as harassment, while 18.4% reported sexual coercion. The remaining victims reported other forms of harassment such as name-calling, dirty jokes, insults, and threats. Interestingly, the data showed that victims experienced diverse forms of harassment.

The "Other" choice in "Harassing messages description" led to a new open question on the questionnaire with a small text container, and helped us gather four new major themes:

The second part of Table 9.4 sheds light on the manipulation techniques used by LinkedIn harassers. It shows that out of the total cases, the harassers used manipulation techniques in their harassment messages in 230 cases, which accounts for 48% of all cases, which indicates that a significant proportion of LinkedIn harassers employ manipulative tactics to either force their victims to submit to their demands or to establish dominance over them. The third part shows that in 211 out of 479 cases (44.1%), the harassers used an aggressive tone in their messages. This suggests that many harassers use intimidation tactics to control and dominate their victims.

The fourth part indicates that in 306 cases (63.9%), the harasser attempted to collect personal information from the victim. And the fifth part shows the emotional tone of the harasser: In 180 out of 479 cases (37.6%), the harasser had a confident tone, while in 98 cases (20.5%), the harasser was hesitant. In 90 cases (18.8%), the harasser was angry, and in 83 cases (17.3%), the harasser was happy. These findings

TABLE 9.4

Characteristics of LinkedIn Sexual Harassment Experiences

Harassing Messages Description

	Unwanted Sexual Attention	Stalking	Sexual Coercion	Name-Calling	Dirty Jokes	Other	Insults	Threats	Total
Frequency	92	90	88	74	50	39	25	21	479
Percent	19.2	18.8	18.4	15.4	10.4	8.1	5.2	4.4	100.0

Use of Manipulation and Pressure

	No	Yes	Total
Frequency	249	230	479
Percent	52.0	48.0	100.0

Use of Aggressive Tone

	No	Yes	Total
Frequency	268	211	479
Percent	55.9	44.1	100.0

Personal Information Collection

	No	Yes	Total
Frequency	173	306	479
Percent	36.1	63.9	100.0

Emotional Tone of the Harasser

	Confident	Hesitant	Angry	Happy	Other	Total
Frequency	180	98	90	83	28	479
Percent	37.6	20.5	18.8	17.3	5.8	100.0

TABLE 9.5

Harassing Messages Description (New Themes)

New Theme	Receiving sexual media content	Asking for sexual media content	Asking sensitive/ intimate information	Scam
Frequency	12	10	11	4

suggest that harassers' emotional tone varies considerably, but a confident tone was the most common.

9.4.4 VICTIMS' REACTIONS TO HARASSMENT

The data presented in this section pertains to the victims' reactions to the harassment experience. The first part of Table 9.6 shows the victims' reactions to harassment messages. Out of the 479 victims, 52.8% (253) responded to harassment messages,

TABLE 9.6

Victims Reactions to Harassment

	Victim Responded		
	No	**Yes**	**Total**
Frequency	226	253	479
Percent	47.2	52.8	100.0

	Harasser Blocked		
	No	**Yes**	**Total**
Frequency	147	332	479
Percent	30.7	69.3	100.0

	Harasser Reported to LinkedIn		
	No	**Yes**	**Total**
Frequency	247	232	479
Percent	51.6	48.4	100.0

Reporting by Victim's "Age"									
	17–21	22–26	27–31	32–36	37–41	42–46	47–51	52–56	56–60
Percent of total victims	50	49	47	44	50	41	56	44	67

Reporting by Victim's "Location"						
	Africa	Asia	Australia	Europe	North America	South America
Percent of total victims	33	51	67	66	56	45

Reporting by "Messages Description"								
	Other	Dirty Jokes	Insults	Name-Calling	Sexual Coercion	Stalking	Threats	Unwanted Sexual Attention
Percent of total victims	44%	44%	74%	43%	48%	44%	72%	51%

while 47.2% (226) did not respond. Additionally, it was found that 69.3% (332) of victims blocked their harassers, and 48.4% (232) reported the harasser to LinkedIn. The table also presents the percentage of victims who reported harassers by age and continent. It shows that regardless of the age, only half of the victims report the incident to LinkedIn. In terms of continents, African victims show a very low reporting percentage, with only 33% compared to Europe with 66% and the other continents with more or less half the victims reporting the incident to LinkedIn.

The final part provides the victims' reporting percentage according to their descriptions of the harassment messages. The most frequently reported form of harassment was insults at 74%, followed by threats at 72%, sexual coercion at 48%, and unwanted sexual attention at 51%. The least frequently reported form of harassment was stalking at 44%.

9.5 DISCUSSION

9.5.1 IMPLICATIONS OF THE FINDINGS FOR NLP IN COMBATING SEXUAL HARASSMENT

This study sheds new light on the detection of sexual harassment on LinkedIn, confirming and building upon previous research in this area. It complements earlier studies such as Arafa et al. (2018), Emily Harmer and Sarah Lewis (2022), Leemis et al. (2019), Barlińska et al. (2013), Pendergrast et al. (2021), Reed et al. (2019), Vogels (2021), Walters and Espelage (2020), Vincent-Höper et al. (2020), Van de Ven et al. (2017), Van Dijck (2013), and Wiederhold (2022) by introducing novel factors that can enhance NLP models aimed at detecting sexual harassment on LinkedIn.

The study findings identify specific linguistic patterns, such as the use of aggressive language, sexually explicit comments, and personal attacks, that are strong predictors of sexual harassment on LinkedIn. Moreover, the study highlights other key factors such as the gender of the target and the harasser, the level of professional seniority of the target, the frequency and duration of the harassing messages, and the imbalance of power between the perpetrator and the victim. These new factors can inform the development of more effective AI models that can accurately detect and prevent sexual harassment on LinkedIn.

These characteristics are particularly relevant to the development of NLP models as they can be used as features to train models to recognize and flag instances of sexual harassment on the platform. By incorporating these features into NLP models, AI specialists can improve the accuracy and effectiveness of their models in identifying and preventing sexual harassment on LinkedIn.

Moreover, the study also underscores the importance of context in identifying instances of sexual harassment on LinkedIn. For instance, certain types of language or behavior may be considered acceptable in some contexts but may be inappropriate or constitute harassment in others. Therefore, it is essential to take into account the broader context in which communications occur on the platform. By incorporating these contextual factors into their NLP models, AI specialists can further improve the accuracy and effectiveness of their models in identifying and preventing instances of sexual harassment on LinkedIn. Ultimately, the findings of this study provide valuable insights that can help shape the development of NLP models aimed at combatting sexual harassment on LinkedIn and, by extension, contribute to a safer and more respectful online community for all.

9.5.2 LIMITATIONS OF THE STUDY

It is worth noting that convenience sampling has its limitations, and it may not be representative of the overall LinkedIn user population. Therefore, the findings of this study cannot be generalized to all LinkedIn users. However, the use of convenience sampling was appropriate for this study's objectives, which were focused on identifying common characteristics of LinkedIn sexual harassers using the data collected from those who have had direct experience with sexual harassment on the platform.

Convenience sampling was a suitable approach for this study, given the sensitive and personal nature of the topic being investigated. It allowed us to gather data from individuals who have experienced sexual harassment on LinkedIn and provided us with a more targeted and relevant sample for analysis.

9.5.3 FUTURE RESEARCH DIRECTIONS

There are various potential research directions that can be pursued in future to enhance the understanding of sexual harassment on LinkedIn. One possible avenue is to expand the sample size to comprise a more diverse and representative population since convenience sampling was used in this study. Employing other sampling techniques could be advantageous in increasing the generalizability of the findings. Additionally, it is essential to investigate the prevalence and characteristics of sexual harassment on other social media platforms or professional networking sites and compare them with those on LinkedIn.

Another potential research direction is to analyze the effectiveness of the current prevention and reporting mechanisms on LinkedIn. Examining the responses of victims who reported incidents to LinkedIn and comparing them with those who did not report could be informative. Further research could also be conducted on the potential impact of AI-based detection systems on the incidence and severity of sexual harassment on the platform.

Moreover, it is critical to explore the psychological impact of sexual harassment on LinkedIn victims. Conducting a thorough analysis of the emotional responses of victims and evaluating the long-term impact of harassment on their mental health and well-being could be illuminating.

Lastly, given the constantly evolving nature of technology and social media platforms, it is imperative to assess the effectiveness of AI-based detection systems on LinkedIn over time. This could involve monitoring the incidence of sexual harassment on the platform and evaluating the accuracy and efficacy of AI models in detecting and preventing harassment.

9.6 CONCLUSION

In conclusion, this study contributes to the growing body of the literature on the detection of sexual harassment on LinkedIn. By identifying linguistic patterns and other key factors associated with sexual harassment on the platform, this study can inform the development of more effective NLP models aimed at detecting and preventing such behavior. The study findings emphasize the importance of context in identifying instances of sexual harassment, and AI specialists can improve the accuracy and effectiveness of their models by incorporating these contextual factors into their analyses.

Additionally, this study highlights the need for further research in the areas of sampling techniques, prevention and reporting mechanisms, psychological impact on victims, and the effectiveness of AI-based detection systems over time. It is important to note that convenience sampling has its limitations, and the findings of this study may not be representative of the overall LinkedIn user population.

However, this sampling method was appropriate for this study's objectives, and it provided a targeted and relevant sample for analysis. Moving forward, researchers can expand the sample size to include a more diverse and representative population, analyze the effectiveness of current prevention and reporting mechanisms, evaluate the psychological impact of sexual harassment on victims, and assess the long-term effectiveness of AI-based detection systems on LinkedIn. By pursuing these avenues of research, we can continue to make progress in combatting sexual harassment on professional networking sites and contribute to a safer and more respectful online community for all.

REFERENCES

Adikari, S., & Dutta, K. (2020). Identifying fake profiles in linkedin. arXiv preprint arXiv:2006.01381.

Ali, W. N. H. W., Mohd, M., & Fauzi, F. (2018). Cyberbullying detection: an overview. In *2018 Cyber Resilience Conference (CRC)* (pp. 1–3). IEEE.

Arafa, A. E., Elbahrawe, R. S., Saber, N. M., Ahmed, S. S., & Abbas, A. M. (2018). Cyber sexual harassment: a cross-sectional survey over female university students in Upper Egypt. *International Journal of Community Medicine and Public Health*, 5(1), 61–65.

Auradkar, A., Botev, C., Das, S., De Maagd, D., Feinberg, A., Ganti, P., … & Zhang, J. (2012, April). Data infrastructure at LinkedIn. In *2012 IEEE 28th International Conference on Data Engineering* (pp. 1370–1381). IEEE.

Azeez, N. A., Idiakose, S. O., Onyema, C. J., & Van Der Vyver, C. (2021). Cyberbullying detection in social networks: artificial intelligence approach. *Journal of Cyber Security and Mobility*, 10(4), 745–774.

Barlińska, J., Szuster, A., & Winiewski, M. (2013). Cyberbullying among adolescent bystanders: role of the communication medium, form of violence, and empathy. *Journal of Community & Applied Social Psychology*, 23(1), 37–51

Basu, P., Singha Roy, T., Tiwari, S., & Mehta, S. (2021). CyberPolice: classification of cyber sexual harassment. In *Progress in Artificial Intelligence: 20th EPIA Conference on Artificial Intelligence, EPIA 2021, Virtual Event, September 7–9, 2021, Proceedings* (pp. 701–714). Springer International Publishing.

Bauman, S., & Yoon, J. (2014). This issue: theories of bullying and cyberbullying. *Theory Into Practice*, 53(4), 253–256.

Bayari, R., & Bensefia, A. (2021). Text mining techniques for cyberbullying detection: state of the art. *Advances in Science, Technology and Engineering Systems Journal*, 6, 783–790.

Bradbury, D. (2011). Data mining with LinkedIn. *Computer Fraud & Security*, 2011(10), 5–8.

Buchanan, N., & Mahoney, A. (2022). Development of a scale measuring online sexual harassment: examining gender differences and the emotional impact of sexual harassment victimization online. *Legal and Criminological Psychology*, 27(1), 63–81.

Burnay, J., Bushman, B. J., & Larøi, F. (2019). Effects of sexualized video games on online sexual harassment. *Aggressive Behavior*, 45(2), 214–223.

Chowdhary, K., (2020). Natural language processing. In *Fundamentals of Artificial Intelligence* (pp. 603–649). Springer.

Claybaugh, C. C., & Haseman, W. D. (2013). Understanding professional connections in LINKEDIN-a question of trust. *Journal of Computer Information Systems*, 54(1), 94–105.

Coletta, K. N. (2017). Sexual harassment on social media: why traditional company sexual harassment polices are not enough and how to fix it. *Seton Hall Law Review*, 48, 449.

Copp, J. E., Mumford, E. A., & Taylor, B. G. (2021). Online sexual harassment and cyberbullying in a nationally representative sample of teens: prevalence, predictors, and consequences. *Journal of Adolescence*, 93, 202–211.

Cripps, J., & Stermac, L. (2018). Cyber-sexual violence and negative emotional states among women in a Canadian university. *International Journal of Cyber Criminology*, 12(1), 171–186.

Davis, J., Wolff, H. G., Forret, M. L., & Sullivan, S. E. (2020). Networking via LinkedIn: an examination of usage and career benefits. *Journal of Vocational Behavior*, 118, 103396.

Emmery, C., Verhoeven, B., De Pauw, G., Jacobs, G., Van Hee, C., Lefever, E., ... Daelemans, W. (2021). Current limitations in cyberbullying detection: on evaluation criteria, reproducibility, and data scarcity. *Language Resources and Evaluation*, 55(3), 597–633.

Espelage, D. L., Rao, M. A., & Craven, R. G. (2012). Theories of cyberbullying. In S. Bauman, D. Cross, & J. Walker (Eds.), *Principles of Cyberbullying Research: Definitions, Measures, and Methodology* (pp. 49–67). Routledge.

Fernandez, S., Stöcklin, M., Terrier, L., & Kim, S. (2021). Using available signals on LinkedIn for personality assessment. *Journal of Research in Personality*, 93, 104122.

Guerra, C., Pinto-Cortez, C., Toro, E., Efthymiadou, E., & Quayle, E. (2021). Online sexual harassment and depression in Chilean adolescents: variations based on gender and age of the offenders. *Child Abuse & Neglect*, 120, 105219.

Haidar, B., Chamoun, M., & Yamout, F. (2016). Cyberbullying detection: a survey on multilingual techniques. In *2016 European Modelling Symposium (EMS)* (pp. 165–171). IEEE.

Haidar, B., Chamoun, M., & Serhrouchni, A. (2017). Multilingual cyberbullying detection system: detecting cyberbullying in Arabic content. In *2017 1st Cyber Security in Networking Conference (CSNet)* (pp. 1–8). IEEE.

Harmer, E., & Lewis, S. (2022). Disbelief and counter-voices: a thematic analysis of online reader comments about sexual harassment and sexual violence against women. *Information, Communication & Society*, 25:2, 199–216. DOI: 10.1080/1369118X.2020.1770832

Koch, T., Gerber, C., & De Klerk, J. J. (2018). The impact of social media on recruitment: are you LinkedIn? *SA Journal of Human Resource Management*, 16(1), 1–14.

Kowalchuk, J. (2020). Sexual harassment on LinkedIn isn't going away until we demand it. https://www.linkedin.com/pulse/sexual-harassment-linkedin-isnt-going-away-until-we-demand-kowalchuk/

Leemis, R. W., Espelage, D. L., Basile, K. C., Mercer Kollar, L. M., & Davis, J. P. (2019). Traditional and cyber bullying and sexual harassment: a longitudinal assessment of risk and protective factors. *Aggressive Behavior*, 45(2), 181–192.

León-Paredes, G. A., Palomeque-Leon, W. F., Gallegos-Segovia, P. L., Vintimilla-Tapia, P. E., Bravo-Torres, J. F., Barbosa-Santillán, L. I., & Paredes-Pinos, M. M. (2019). Presumptive detection of cyberbullying on twitter through natural language processing and machine learning in the Spanish language. In *2019 IEEE CHILEAN Conference on Electrical, Electronics Engineering, Information and Communication Technologies (CHILECON)*. IEEE.

Linkedin (2023). Professional community policies. https://linkedin.com/legal/professional-community-policies?

Marin, G. D., & Nilă, C. (2021). Branding in social media. Using LinkedIn in personal brand communication: a study on communications/marketing and recruitment/human resources specialists perception. *Social Sciences & Humanities Open*, 4(1), 100174.

McCabe, M. B. (2017). Social media marketing strategies for career advancement: an analysis of LinkedIn. *Journal of Business and Behavioral Sciences*, 29(1), 85.

Milosevic, T., Van Royen, K., & Davis, B. (2022). Artificial intelligence to address cyberbullying, harassment and abuse: new directions in the midst of complexity. *International Journal of Bullying Prevention*, 4, 1–5.

Milosevic, T., Verma, K., Carter, M., Vigil, S., Laffan, D., Davis, B., & O'Higgins Norman, J. (2023). Effectiveness of artificial intelligence-based cyberbullying interventions from youth perspective. *Social Media+ Society*, 9(1), 20563051221147325.

Nakov, P., Nayak, V., Dent, K., Bhatawdekar, A., Sarwar, S. M., Hardalov, M., ... Augenstein, I. (2021). Detecting abusive language on online platforms: a critical analysis. arXiv preprint arXiv:2103.00153

Norouzizadeh Dezfouli, F., Dehghantanha, A., Eterovic-Soric, B., & Choo, K. K. R. (2016). Investigating Social Networking applications on smartphones detecting Facebook, Twitter, LinkedIn and Google+ artefacts on Android and iOS platforms. *Australian Journal of Forensic Sciences*, 48(4), 469–488.

Pendergrast, T. R., Jain, S., Trueger, N. S., Gottlieb, M., Woitowich, N. C., & Arora, V. M. (2021). Prevalence of personal attacks and sexual harassment of physicians on social media. *JAMA Internal Medicine*, 181(4), 550–552. DOI: 10.1001/jamainternmed.2020.7235

Power, A. (2015). LinkedIn: Facebook for professionals? *British Journal of Midwifery*, 23(3), 196–198.

Raj, C., Agarwal, A., Bharathy, G., Narayan, B., & Prasad, M. (2021). Cyberbullying detection: hybrid models based on machine learning and natural language processing techniques. *Electronics*, 10(22), 2810.

Reed, E., Salazar, M., Behar, A. I., Agah, N., Silverman, J. G., Minnis, A. M., ... & Raj, A. (2019). Cyber sexual harassment: prevalence and association with substance use, poor mental health, and STI history among sexually active adolescent girls. *Journal of Adolescence*, 75, 53–62.

Reed, E., Wong, A., & Raj, A. (2020). Cyber sexual harassment: a summary of current measures and implications for future research. *Violence Against Women*, 26(12–13), 1727–1740. DOI: 10.1177/1077801219880959

Rosa, H., Pereira, N., Ribeiro, R., Ferreira, P. C., Carvalho, J. P., Oliveira, S., ... & Trancoso, I. (2019). Automatic cyberbullying detection: a systematic review. *Computers in Human Behavior*, 93, 333–345.

Sánchez-Medina, A. J., Galván-Sánchez, I., & Fernández-Monroy, M. (2020). Applying artificial intelligence to explore sexual cyberbullying behaviour. *Heliyon*, 6(1), e03218.

Sumbaly, R., Kreps, J., & Shah, S. (2013, June). The big data ecosystem at linkedin. In *Proceedings of the 2013 ACM Sigmod International Conference on Management of Data* (pp. 1125–1134). ACM.

Tang, G., Ganganahalli Marulappa, P. K., Khunvirojpanich, M., & Chen, T. (2020). The technology behind fighting harassment on LinkedIn. Online : https://engineering.linkedin.com/blog/2020/fighting-harassment

Tifferet, S., & Vilnai-Yavetz, I. (2018). Self-presentation in LinkedIn portraits: common features, gender, and occupational differences. *Computers in Human Behavior*, 80, 33–48.

Utz, S. (2016). Is LinkedIn making you more successful? The informational benefits derived from public social media. *New Media & Society*, 18(11), 2685–2702.

Van de Ven, N., Bogaert, A., Serlie, A., Brandt, M. J., & Denissen, J. J. (2017). Personality perception based on LinkedIn profiles. *Journal of Managerial Psychology*, 32(6), 418–429.

Van Dijck, J. (2013). 'You have one identity': performing the self on Facebook and LinkedIn. *Media, Culture & Society*, 35(2), 199–215.

Vincent-Höper, S., Adler, M., Stein, M., Vaupel, C., & Nienhaus, A. (2020). Sexually harassing behaviors from patients or clients and care workers' mental health: development and validation of a measure. *International Journal of Environmental Research and Public Health*, 17(7), 2570.

Vogels, E. A. (2021). The state of online harassment. *Pew Research Center*, 13, 625.

Walters, G. D., & Espelage, D. L. (2020). Assessing the relationship between cyber and traditional forms of bullying and sexual harassment: stepping stones or displacement?. *Cyberpsychology: Journal of Psychosocial Research on Cyberspace*, 14(2) Article 2.

Wiederhold, B. K. (2022). Sexual harassment in the metaverse. *Cyberpsychology, Behavior, and Social Networking*, 25(8), 479–480.

Yuvaraj, N., Chang, V., Gobinathan, B., Pinagapani, A., Kannan, S., Dhiman, G., & Rajan, A. R. (2021). Automatic detection of cyberbullying using multi-feature based artificial intelligence with deep decision tree classification. *Computers & Electrical Engineering*, 92, 107186.

10 Arabic Offensive Language and Hate Speech Detection Using Ensemble Transformers and Data Augmentation

Ibtissam Touahri
University Moulay Ismail

10.1 INTRODUCTION

10.1.1 BACKGROUND

People can express themselves more than ever before due to the expanding variety of online platforms that allow users to create and share their content. Furthermore, users of these platforms have the option of concealing their real identity or using fake accounts, which increases the likelihood of misusing these technical advantages (Keleg, El-Beltagy, and Khalil 2020). Offensive language is considered a destructive criticism used in actions such as cyberbullying; it may cause disastrous effects on the targeted member, spread hatred and violence among community people, or devastate relations between countries. Hateful content is an offensive rhetoric that attacks religion, society, political parties, genders, social class, disabilities, ethnicity, background, or well-known community groups and organizations (Mubarak, Al-Khalifa, and Al-Thubaity 2022). Besides being harsh and nasty, it is distinguished by being more than a negative reaction to a specific person or incident. According to studies, online hate, cyber harassment, and other technological misuses are on the rise (Husain and Uzuner 2022a).

Toxic remarks and unpleasant speech have invaded the internet in recent years. Moreover, manual screening of these comments has become a laborious process to maintain. Hence, the automatic detection of offensive content has interested many NLP researchers who have expressed concern about harmful speech (Zayady et al. 2023). The development of a system to identify online offensive language was made an emergency to prevent its damaging impacts on internet users' health and security (Mubarak, Darwish, and Magdy 2017; Mubarak, Al-Khalifa, and Al-Thubaity 2022; Touahri and Mazroui 2022). Since social media has no restrictions according to age, the need to detect kids cyberbullying has arisen (Yafooz, Al-Dhaqm, and Alsaeed 2023).

DOI: 10.1201/9781003393061-13

Automatic bullying recognition is faced with the grammatical and syntactical complexity of the Arabic language (Fkih, Moulahi, and Alabdulatif 2023), which increases its difficulty. Online content does not undergo strict grammatical rules, which raises the need for preprocessing that helps in denoising the comments meaning. The impact of preprocessing on Arabic offensive language classification has been studied (Husain and Uzuner 2022b) and applied to texts. It implies emojis conversion to text, Arabic letters normalization, and hashtag segmentation, besides classical cleaning such as removing elongations, diacritics, repeated letters, and foreign language.

Many feature-engineering approaches, such as bag of words, term occurrence, and the TFIDF, have been investigated for offensive language detection (Alakrot, Murray, and Nikolov 2018; Husain 2020; Touahri and Mazroui 2022). The intersection of hate content and personality learning, in turn, has been investigated since it is an area that has received little attention (Zayady et al. 2023). The variety of languages, domains and topics, as well as harmful content genres, may necessitate an independent generic method for offensive and hate comments detection (Mubarak, Sabit, and Shammur Absar 2022).

Several techniques have been used in this domain to identify attitudes, including unsupervised, supervised, and deep learning approaches (Mohaouchane, Mourhir, and Nikolov 2019; Touahri and Mazroui 2022). Pretrained language models, in turn, have revolutionized the classification approaches (Devlin et al. 2018) and proved their efficiency (Abdul-Mageed et al. 2020; Abdelali et al. 2021; Antoun, Baly, and Hajj 2020). Since similar features may be used, it is conceivable to transfer learning from one domain to another (Mubarak, Al-Khalifa, and Al-Thubaity 2022; Shi et al. 2022) and then adapt the knowledge and fine-tune existing models. Ensemble learning approach combines several classifier predictions to improve classification performance (Husain 2020; Touahri and Mazroui 2022).

10.1.2 Methodology

In this study, we identify comments as offensive or not from a tagged corpus provided by the organizers of the OSACT5 shared task on the detection of Arabic offensive content and hate speech (Mubarak, Al-Khalifa, and Al-Thubaity 2022). The corpus includes several domains affected by abusive or hateful words. Detecting offensive language involves any type of insults either explicit or implicit, or assault on people, society, religion, political party, organization, ethnicity, background, or gender. We build a system based on a set of pretrained models; the classification was improved using augmented data and ensemble learning, which handles several model outputs. Our research reveals that using an ensemble machine learning strategy may have a considerable advantage on classification performance.

10.1.3 Chapter Organization

This chapter is structured as follows: we present offensive language detection-related works in Section 10.2. We then define the employed resources to build our system and describe offensive content features. In Section 10.4, we discuss our system approach.

We give experiment results and analyze errors in Section 10.5. We then compare our system performance with the state-of-the-art. We conclude by reviewing the main used approaches and the relevant outcomes, as well as providing some perspectives.

10.2   RELATED WORK

Studies that target offensive content detection in several languages gained many researchers interest, among which, the categorization of over 14,100 English tweets from the offensive language identification data set (OLID) using three-layer hierarchical models and a variety of classifiers, including linear models, random forest, LSTM, fast-text mixed embeddings, encoders, and pretrained BERT (Zampieri et al. 2019). The extraction of word and character n-grams, as well as skip-grams, has been investigated to classify a 14,509 tweet English corpus using an SVM classifier (Malmasi and Zampieri 2017).

For Arabic offensive content and hate speech detection, lists of offensive words and phrases have been derived from impolite speech (Mubarak, Darwish, and Magdy 2017) besides exploiting emojis, sentiment analysis (Althobaiti 2022), and integrating word-level and n-gram characteristics (Alakrot, Murray, and Nikolov 2018) to build classical supervised and BERT based system. The models based on transformers have also been investigated in Yafooz, Al-Dhaqm, and Alsaeed (2023). Networks learning from fine-tuned embeddings using evolutionary-based classifiers have been investigated (Shannaq et al. 2022).

Data augmentation uses a set of techniques that help to augment the representation of data with minority class. Hence, the obtained accuracy is not biased by the corpus imbalance (Cao and Lee 2020; Ibrahim, Torki, and El-Makky 2020). Arabic word embedding has been used to offer oversampled comments to balance the corpus besides using various neural networks to classify Arabic offensive comments (Mohaouchane, Mourhir, and Nikolov 2019).

Ensemble learning addresses the output of many classifiers using several approaches among which the major scoring (Touahri and Mazroui 2022; Turki and Roy 2022). Moreover, using ensemble learning has proven the classification efficiency instead of a single classifier (Husain 2020). However, transfer learning has a limited influence on classifier performance, particularly for highly dialectal comments (Habash 2010).

Data clustering, which does not require labeled training data, was also investigated to detect violent text on Arabic social media (Abdelfatah, Terejanu, and Alhelbawy 2017).

Using cutting-edge text categorization classifiers such as BiLSTM, CNN, FastText, SVM, and NB for offensive language detection needs to be enhanced by more research on linguistic aspects to improve identification accuracy (Boucherit and Abainia 2022). Transformers have been enhanced with linguistic analysis to detect harmful speech (Mubarak, Sabit, and Shammur Absar 2022). Besides model improvement, linguistic features such as named entities have been investigated (Touahri and Mazroui 2022). The integration of personality traits has been studied in relation to harmful content (Zayady et al. 2023).

Recognizing Arabic slang offensive speech (Fkih, Moulahi, and Alabdulatif 2023) raised the need for preprocessing. The comparison of experiments with raw text and a combination of preprocessing techniques has been introduced (Husain and Uzuner 2022b), which revealed that BERT does not benefit from preprocessing in contrast to classical classifiers.

Efforts have been combined in several shared tasks to detect offensive content and hate speech. OSACT5 shared task (Mubarak, Al-Khalifa, and Al-Thubaity 2022) aimed to identify offensive language and hate speech. The first rank has been reached in OSACT4 (Mubarak, Darwish, Magdy, Elsayed, and Al-Khalifa 2020) using BERT transformer model (Keleg, El-Beltagy, and Khalil 2020). Other systems surpassed the baseline given by OSACT5 organizers using AraBERT, mBert, Albert-Arabic, AraElectra, AraGPT2, and XLM-Roberta (de Paula et al. 2022).

A systematic summary of prior attempts in offensive language detection for Arabic, covering key methodologies, tools, resources, methods, and employed primary characteristics, has been described (Husain and Uzuner 2021; Elzayady et al. 2022).

10.3 RESOURCES

In this part, we detail the resources that we gathered and built to support our system. The corpus used in this study was created and made publicly available by the organizers of the OSACT5 shared task on Arabic offensive language and hate speech detection (Mubarak, Al-Khalifa, and Al-Thubaity 2022). The task organizers annotated the corpus at two levels where they labeled the comments as offensive or not, and offensive expressions as having hate speech or not. We denote the labels, respectively, OFF, NOT_OFF, HS, and NOT_HS. We describe each data-split in Table 10.1.

The corpus is imbalanced between offensive and not-offensive comments (35.52% vs 64.48%) and highly imbalanced when it comes to HS comments in comparison to NOT_HS (10.76% vs 89.24%).

10.4 APPROACH

This section describes our system-proposed approach to detect offensive content and hate speech. We define the experiment process in Figure 10.1.

10.4.1 Transfer Learning

We investigated the aforementioned data set to accomplish offensive language-detection task using several cutting-edge pretrained models AraBERT (Antoun,

TABLE 10.1
Corpus Statistics

Corpus	Offensive	Not Offensive	Hate Speech	Not Hate Speech
Train	3,172	5,715	959	7,928
Test	887	1,654	271	2,270

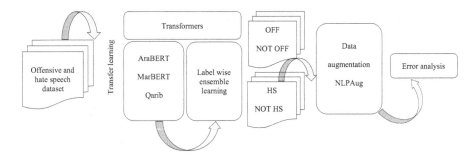

FIGURE 10.1   System architecture.

Baly, and Hajj 2020), MarBERT (Abdul-Mageed et al. 2020), and Qarib. We have preprocessed the data set by converting the data into a CSV file that matches the input of our system. We have then removed all the non-Arabic letters apart from emoticons that were preserved. Our system is learning from the domains covered by the pretrained models. AraBERT (arabertv02-twitter), MarBERT (MARBERTv2), and Qarib are fine-tuned on training data. We used a 64-batch size and a 128-max length in which case data are not truncated. Adam with a 2e-5 learning rate is used as an optimizer. The suggested hyperparameters are preserved. We have saved the best model on the training set, among the ones built over 10 epochs, according to the F1-score average. We perform the training on Google Colab Platform using a Tesla T4 GPU.

10.4.2   ENSEMBLE LEARNING

Ensemble learning is investigated within this chapter to combine the output of several models. We report the best model out of 10 in each experiment from the three built on the aforementioned pretrained models and fine-tuned on the training data. We investigated two scoring approaches; the first is tagging a given comment with the major score from the output of the three models and the second is using a metric wise ensemble model. Hence, instead of the major score labeling, we consider first the output of the model with high precision and then use the major score for the remainder of models outputs; this is to avoid system precision degradation and also to prevent considering a model with low recall as accurate. Since a system with high precision may not have high recall, that is, to say that the given labels were accurate at a certain rate. However, many samples of the given class have been forgotten by the system since the recall is low.

10.4.3   DATA AUGMENTATION

The process of augmenting data refers to applying changes to our initial labeled instances to produce new data for the training set. It can be performed based on term replacement with synonyms or similar embeddings; using back translation to translate a statement from a source language to its target and then back into the source; or using generative language models that generate few changes. The generative models

TABLE 10.2
Samples of Generated Text

Models	AraBERT	MarBERT	Qarib
Generated texts	'مستخدم] وش قلة الادب ذي ['؟ هذي عندكم 😊😊😡 /w\$ qlp AlAdb *y h*y Endkm/	1 مستخدم] وش تفسر قل الادب ة ['؟ هذي الحين' /w\$ tfsr qlp AlAdb h*y AlHyn/	UNK]] مستخدم] وش فايدة قلة' ['[UNK] الادب عالصبح هذي /w\$ fAydp qlp AlAdb EAlSbH h*y/
	مستخدم] وش كمية قلة الادب ['؟ هي هذي ذي 😊😡😊 /w\$ kmyp qlp AlAdb *y h*y hy/	يخوان وش قلة الادب [مستخدم] r [' '؟ هذي الي' /yxwAn w\$ qlp AlAdb Aly h*y/	مستخدم] بنات وش قلة الادب وقلت' ['[UNK] الادب هذي بالله /bnAt w\$ qlp wqlt AlAdb h*y bAllh/
	غير مستخدم] وش جت قلة' ['؟ ذي هذي الادب 😡😊 /w\$ jt qlp AlAdb h*y *y/	مستخدم] الحين وش بعد قلة ['؟ هذي القذرة الادب' /AlHyn w\$ bEd qlp AlAdb Alq*rp h*y/	UNK]] مستخدم] وش كمية قلة ['[UNK] الادب اللي هذي /w\$ kmyp qlp AlAdb Ally h*y/

encode the class label together with its associated text sequences to generate newer instances with little changes. We opt for the NLPAug[1] Python library that augments text in machine learning studies and provides character-, word-, and sentence-level augmentations. We used it to augment data at sentence level using the three generative language models AraBERT, MarBERT, and Qarib. Table 10.2 provides the samples of the generated text for the same expression.

The generated text by each model is obtained either by adding new terms, either neutral or offensive, such as كمية /kmyp/, القذرة /Alq*rp/, altering position, or adding and removing emoticons.

10.5   EXPERIMENTS AND RESULTS

We run a set of experiments based on the settings in Section 10.4 to transfer learning and fine-tune the described pretrained models. We generate three respective models for both offensive language and hate speech detection, as our system approach indicates. The findings are given according to accuracy, precision, recall, and F-measure metrics.

$$Accuracy = \frac{Correctly\ classified}{Test\ size}$$

$$Precision\ C_i = \frac{Correctly\ classified}{Classified\ as\ C_i}$$

$$Recall\ C_i = \frac{Correctly\ classified}{Comments\ of\ the\ class\ C_i}$$

---

[1] https://pypi.org/project/nlpaug/

TABLE 10.3

Experiment Results for Offensive and Hate Speech Detection

Model	Accuracy	Offensive Language			Accuracy	Hate Speech		
		Precision	Recall	F-Measure		Precision	Recall	F-Measure
AraBERT	0.88	OFF	0.82	**0.82**	**0.82**	0.94	HS	0.72	**0.68**	**0.70**
		NOT_OFF	**0.90**	0.91	**0.90**		NOT_HS	**0.96**	0.97	**0.97**
		Average	**0.86**	**0.86**	**0.86**		Average	0.84	**0.82**	**0.83**
MarBERT	0.86	OFF	0.79	0.81	0.80	0.94	HS	0.73	0.65	0.68
		NOT_OFF	**0.90**	0.89	0.89		NOT_HS	**0.96**	0.97	0.96
		Average	0.84	0.85	0.84		Average	0.84	0.81	0.82
Qarib	0.87	OFF	**0.83**	0.77	0.80	0.94	HS	0.79	0.55	0.65
		NOT_OFF	0.88	**0.92**	**0.90**		NOT_HS	0.95	**0.98**	**0.97**
		Average	**0.86**	0.84	0.85		Average	**0.87**	0.77	0.81
EL$_{AraBERT}$	0.88	OFF	**0.83**	0.80	0.82	0.94	HS	0.78	0.66	0.71
Marbert Qarib		NOT_OFF	**0.90**	0.91	0.90		NOT_HS	**0.96**	**0.98**	**0.97**
		Average	**0.86**	0.86	**0.86**		Average	**0.87**	0.82	**0.84**

$$F - \text{measure } C_i = \frac{2 \times \text{Precision } C_i \times \text{Recall } C_i}{\text{Precision } C_i + \text{Recall } C_i}$$

10.5.1 TRANSFER LEARNING

We applied each of the transformer models to our data sets and tried to determine the strengths and weaknesses of each of them by applying an in-depth analysis of the obtained results. In Table 10.3, we present the performed experiments' results.

From Table 10.3, the three models achieved comparable results with an advantage for AraBERT at accuracy and macro-averaged F-measure levels. Qarib, in turn, has proved efficiency at the precision of low-represented classes, OFF and HS, in each experiment by a gain over other models of 1 and 6%, respectively. The achieved results raised the need for combining the strengths of each model; thus, we perform an ensemble learning approach.

10.5.2 ENSEMBLE LEARNING

We consider first the output of Qarib model with the high OFF and HS precision and then use the major score for the remainder; this is to avoid system precision degradation and also to prevent considering a model with low recall as accurate. Considering the outputs of AraBERT and MarBERT helps identify much more labels and hence may increase accuracy.

Table 10.4 reveals that ensemble learning helped to reach very close results to the best classifier in the offensive language detection experiment and an improvement by 1 point in the hate speech detection experiment, whereas the accuracies were of the same order.

TABLE 10.4

Transformer Ensemble Learning for Harmful Speech Detection

Model	Offensive Language				Hate Speech			
	Accuracy	Precision	Recall	F-Measure	Accuracy	Precision	Recall	F-Measure
EL$_{AraBERT}$	**0.88**	OFF	**0.83**	0.80	0.82	**0.94**	HS	0.78	0.66	0.71
Marbert Qarib		NOT_OFF	**0.90**	0.91	0.90		NOT_HS	**0.96**	**0.98**	**0.97**
		Average	**0.86**	0.86	**0.86**		Average	**0.87**	0.82	**0.84**

We have reached pertinent results. However, the high imbalance between HS and NOT_HS labels raises a data augmentation need.

10.5.3 DATA AUGMENTATION

We aim to improve our system to detect more HS comments. Since from the training corpus, the hate speech comments represent only 12.1%, we have augmented the data by 2,000 comments generated using the NLPAug tool described in Section 4.3. Table 10.5 shows the obtained results by our system when the data set is enlarged by additional samples.

The precision of our system before HS data augmentation was higher in comparison to the obtained results when augmenting data. However, the recall when augmenting data was higher, which means that our system can identify more HS samples. We illustrate the advantage of data augmentation by the confusion matrix (Figure 10.2).

TABLE 10.5

Hate Speech Data Augmentation

Model	Data Augmentation				
	Accuracy	Label	Precision	Recall	F-Measure
AraBERT	0.94	HS	**0.74**	0.64	0.69
		NOT_HS	0.96	0.97	0.97
		Average	**0.85**	0.81	0.83
MarBERT	0.93	HS	0.67	**0.72**	0.69
		NOT_HS	0.97	0.96	0.96
		Average	0.82	**0.84**	**0.83**
Qarib	0.93	HS	0.67	**0.72**	0.69
		NOT_HS	0.97	0.96	0.96
		Average	0.82	**0.84**	0.83
EL$_{AraBERT\ Marbert\ Qarib}$	0.94	HS	0.72	0.71	0.71
		NOT_HS	0.97	0.97	0.97
		Average	0.85	**0.84**	**0.84**

Hate speech	Classified as		Data augmentation	Classified as	
	HS	NOT HS		HS	NOT HS
HS	178	93	HS	192	79
NOT HS	50	2220	NOT HS	75	2195

FIGURE 10.2   Hate speech classification and data augmentation confusion matrix.

The analysis reveals that there are common misclassifications between the two models measured by 45 NOT_HS classified as HS and 75 HS classified as NOT_HS. Since we aim to increase the F-measure, we try to analyze the common errors before and when augmenting data.

10.5.4 ERROR ANALYSIS

We give samples of misclassified comments in Table 10.6. The second comment is strongly offensive in comparison to the first one, even though no named entity is mentioned. From the context, we can distinguish that it targets women. Hence, based on the description, our system annotation is accurate. In the third example, we have an offensive term المنحط/AlmnHT/(decadent) and a misspelled named entity أعلامكم/>ElAmkm/(media), which means that it is hate speech and it is the tag given

---

TABLE 10.6

Error Analysis

N	Comment	Annotated	Classified
1	@USER خفيفات عقول 😁 /😁 @USER xfyfAt Eqwl 😁/ (😁 @USER light minds 😁 😁)	HS	NOT_HS
2	قليلات حياء 😁 /qlylAt HyA' 😁/ (a little shy 😁)	NOT_HS	HS
3	@USER والله مايثير الجدل غير أعلامكم المنحط 😁 /@USER wAllh mAyvyr Aljdl gyr >ElAmkm AlmnHT 😁 / (@USER By God, nothing raises controversy other than your decadent media 😁)	NOT_HS	HS
4	الى متى هالتخلف يا كليتنا خلاص افتحو الموقع الله ينعلكم 😁 /AlY mtY hAltxlf Ya klytnA xlAS AftHw AlmwqE Allh ynElkm 😁/ (How long will you lag behind, our college? Open the site, may God curse you 😁)	HS	NOT_HS
5	@USER فيها لبناني واردني خرب المسلسل <LF> /@USER fyhA lbnAny wArdny xrbs Almslsl <LF>/ (@USER There is a Lebanese and Jordan ruined the series <LF>)	HS	NOT_HS

TABLE 10.7

System Comparison

	Offensive Language					Hate Speech			
System	Accuracy	Precision	Recall	F-Measure	System	Accuracy	Precision	Recall	F-Measure
aiXplain	0.86	0.85	0.84	0.84	AlexU-AIC	0.94	0.86	0.79	0.82
Meta AI	0.86	0.85	0.84	0.85	Meta-AI	0.94	0.87	0.80	0.83
GOF	0.87	0.86	0.85	0.85	iCompass	0.94	0.87	0.80	0.83
Our system	**0.88**	0.86	**0.86**	0.86	Our system	0.94	0.87	**0.82**	**0.84**

by our system. The fourth and the fifth comments are offensive and contain named entities كليتنا/klytnA/(our college), لبناني واردني/lbnAny wArdny/(Lebanese and Jordan).

The given examples prove the absence of either offensive or hate speech terms. The absence of named entities, in turn, may be the cause of some cases of misclassification. In the next section, we compare our system with other systems built on the same corpus.

10.6   SYSTEM COMPARISON

We compare our system to the state-of-the-art systems described in Mubarak, Al-Khalifa, and Al-Thubaity (2022) that have participated in the OSACT5 shared task on Arabic offensive language and hate speech detection. We compare our system in each experiment against the three best performing models. Hence, we, respectively, compare to aiXplain, Meta AI, and GOF (Alzubi et al. 2022; AlKhamissi and Diab 2022; Mostafa, Mohamed, and Ashraf 2022), and AlexU-AIC, Meta-AI, and iCompass (AlKhamissi and Diab 2022; Bennessir et al. 2022; Shapiro, Khalafallah Ayman, and Torki 2022).

Table 10.7 reveals that our system surpassed other systems in terms of F-measure. The increased recall proves that our method was helpful to detect other comments for offensive language and hate speech detection tasks.

10.7   CONCLUSION AND FURTHER WORK

Our chapter aimed at the detection of offensive language and hate speech. We tried in this chapter to improve the F-measure of our system with a focus on the recall. We have transferred learning from AraBERT, MarBERT, and Qarib pretrained models to our system and then performed labelwise ensemble learning that considers the labels of the model with high precision. Then, we consider the major score between the given labels by the three models to tag the remaining comments. The close results raised the need for combining the models' outputs. Ensemble learning helped to either improve the results or preserve the highest. Ensemble learning is still insufficient for dealing with data imbalance, which appeals to more techniques. Since hate speech comments are lowly represented within the data set, we performed a data augmentation and generated 2,000 more hate speech comments, which helped to lighten the high difference in size between HS and NOT HS comments. The data augmentation helped to improve the recall of our system and detect much more HS comments. Even though the used transformers do not cover various linguistic characteristics that are pertinent in detecting hate speech, our system proved its pertinence by reaching improved results. We have then compared our system to three systems built on the OSACT5 shared task on Arabic offensive language and hate speech detection data set. The results reveal an advantage to our system by an F-measure improvement measured by 0.86 and 0.84 for offensive language and hate speech detection, respectively. In further works, we intend to investigate adversarial neural networks for more comments generation and explore additional linguistic features that may help in improving our system F-measure.

REFERENCES

Abdelali Ahmed, Hassan Sabit, Mubarak Hamdy, Darwish Kareem and Samih Younes. 2021. Pre-training bert on arabic tweets: Practical considerations. arXiv preprint arXiv:2102.10684.

Abdelfatah Kareem, Terejanu Gabriel and Alhelbawy Ayman. 2017. Unsupervised detection of violent content in arabic social media. *Computer Science & Information Technology (CS & IT)*, 7–14.

Abdul-Mageed Muhammad, Elmadany AbdelRahim and Nagoudi El Moatez Billah. 2020. ARBERT & MARBERT: Deep bidirectional transformers for Arabic. arXiv preprint arXiv:2101.01785.

Alakrot Azalden, Murray Liam and Nikolov Nikola S. 2018. Towards accurate detection of offensive language in online communication in arabic. *Procedia Computer Science*, 142, pp. 315–320.

AlKhamissi Badr and Diab Mona. 2022. Meta ai at arabic hate speech 2022: Multitask learning with self correction for hate speech classification. arXiv preprint arXiv:2205.07960.

Althobaiti Maha Jarallah. 2022. BERT-based approach to arabic hate speech and offensive language detection in twitter: Exploiting emojis and sentiment analysis. *International Journal of Advanced Computer Science and Applications*, 13(5). https://doi.org/10.14569/ijacsa.2022.01305109

Alzubi Salaheddin, Ferreira Thiago Castro, Pavanelli Lucas and Al-Badrashiny Mohamed. 2022, June. aixplain at arabic hate speech 2022: An ensemble based approach to detecting offensive tweets. In *Proceedinsg of the 5th Workshop on Open-Source Arabic Corpora and Processing Tools with Shared Tasks on Qur'an QA and Fine-Grained Hate Speech Detection* (pp. 214–217). European Language Resources Association.

Antoun Wissam, Baly Fady and Hajj Hazem, 2020. Arabert: Transformer-based model for arabic language understanding. arXiv preprint arXiv:2003.00104.

Bennessir Mohamed Aziz, Rhouma Malek, Haddad Hatem and Fourati Chayma. 2022, June. iCompass at arabic hate speech 2022: Detect hate speech using QRNN and transformers. In *Proceedings of the 5th Workshop on Open-Source Arabic Corpora and Processing Tools with Shared Tasks on Qur'an QA and Fine-Grained Hate Speech Detection* (pp. 176–180). European Language Resources Association.

Boucherit Oussama and Abainia Kheireddine. 2022. Offensive language detection in under-resourced algerian dialectal arabic language. arXiv preprint arXiv:2203.10024.

Cao Rui and Lee Ka-Wei Le. 2020, December. HateGAN: Adversarial generative-based data augmentation for hate speech detection. In *Proceedings of the 28th International Conference on Computational Linguistics* (pp. 6327–6338). International Committee on Computational Linguistics.

de Paula Angel Felipe Magnossao, Rosso Paolo, Bensalem Imene and Zaghouani Wajdi. 2022, June. Upv at the arabic hate speech 2022 shared task: Offensive language and hate speech detection using transformers and ensemble models. In *Proceeding of the 5th Workshop on Open-Source Arabic Corpora and Processing Tools with Shared Tasks on Qur'an QA and Fine-Grained Hate Speech Detection* (pp. 181–185). European Language Resources Association.

Devlin Jacob, Chang Ming-Wei, Lee Kenton and Toutanova Kristina. 2018. Bert: Pre-training of deep bidirectional transformers for language understanding. arXiv preprint arXiv:1810.04805.

Elzayady Hossam, Mohamed Mohamed S., Badran Khaled M. and Salama Gouda I. 2022. Detecting Arabic textual threats in social media using artificial intelligence: An overview. *Indonesian Journal of Electrical Engineering and Computer Science*, 25(3), pp. 1712–1722.

Elzayady Hossam, Mohamed Mohamed S., Badran Khaled M. and Salama Gouda I. 2023. A hybrid approach based on personality traits for hate speech detection in Arabic social media. *International Journal of Electrical and Computer Engineering*, 13(2), p. 1979.

Fkih Fethi, Moulahi Tarek and Alabdulatif Abdulatif. 2023. Machine learning model for offensive speech detection in online social networks slang content. WSEAS Transactions on Information Science and Applications. https://doi.org/10.37394/23209.2023.20.2

Habash Nizar. 2010. *Introduction to Arabic Natural Language Processing*. Cham: Springer International Publishing. https://doi.org/10.1007/978-3-031-02139-8

Husain Fatemah. 2020. Arabic offensive language detection using machine learning and ensemble machine learning approaches. arXiv preprint arXiv:2005.08946.

Husain Fatemah and Uzuner Ozlem. 2021. A survey of offensive language detection for the arabic language. *ACM Transactions on Asian and Low-Resource Language Information Processing (TALLIP)*, 20(1), pp. 1–44.

Husain Fatemah and Uzuner Ozlem. 2022a. Investigating the effect of preprocessing arabic text on offensive language and hate speech detection. *Transactions on Asian and Low-Resource Language Information Processing*, 21(4), pp. 1–20.

Husain Fatemah and Uzuner Ozlem. 2022b. Fine-tuning approach for Arabic offensive language detection system: BERT-based model. arXiv preprint arXiv:2203.03542.

Ibrahim Mai, Torki Marwan and El-Makky Nagwa. 2020, December. AlexU-BackTranslation-TL at SemEval-2020 task 12: Improving offensive language detection using data augmentation and transfer learning. In *Proceedings of the Fourteenth Workshop on Semantic Evaluation* (pp. 1881–1890). Association for Computational Linguistics.

Keleg Amr, El-Beltagy Samhaa R. and Khalil Mahmoud. 2020, May. ASU_OPTO at OSACT4-offensive language detection for Arabic text. In *Proceedings of the 4th Workshop on Open-Source Arabic Corpora and Processing Tools, with a Shared Task on Offensive Language Detection* (pp. 66–70). European Language Resource Association.

Malmasi Shervin and Zampieri Marcos. 2017. Detecting hate speech in social media. arXiv preprint arXiv:1712.06427.

Mohaouchane Hanane, Mourhir Asmaa and Nikolov Nikola S. 2019, October. Detecting offensive language on Arabic social media using deep learning. In *2019 Sixth International Conference on Social Networks Analysis, Management and Security (SNAMS)* (pp. 466–471). IEEE.

Mostafa Aly, Mohamed Omar and Ashraf Omar. 2022, June. GOF at Arabic hate speech 2022: Breaking the loss function convention for data-imbalanced Arabic offensive text detection. In *Proceedinsg of the 5th Workshop on Open-Source Arabic Corpora and Processing Tools with Shared Tasks on Qur'an QA and Fine-Grained Hate Speech Detection* (pp. 167–175). European Language Resources Association.

Mubarak Hamdy, Darwish Kareem and Magdy Walid. 2017, August. Abusive language detection on arabic social media. In *Proceedings of the First Workshop on Abusive Language Online* (pp. 52–56). Association for Computational Linguistics.

Mubarak Hamdy, Darwish Kareem, Magdy Walid, Elsayed Tamer and Al-Khalifa Hend. 2020, May. Overview of OSACT4 arabic offensive language detection shared task. In *Proceedings of the 4th Workshop on Open-Source Arabic Corpora and Processing Tools, with a Shared Task on Offensive Language Detection* (pp. 48–52). European Language Resource Association.

Mubarak Hamdy, Hassan Sabit and Chowdhury Shammur Absar. 2022. Emojis as anchors to detect arabic offensive language and hate speech. arXiv preprint arXiv:2201.06723.

Mubarak H., Al-Khalifa H. and Al-Thubaity A. 2022, June. Overview of OSACT5 shared task on arabic offensive language and hate speech detection. In *Proceedinsg of the 5th Workshop on Open-Source Arabic Corpora and Processing Tools with Shared Tasks on Qur'an QA and Fine-Grained Hate Speech Detection* (pp. 162–166). European Language Resources Association.

Shannaq Fatima, Hammo Bassam, Faris Hossam and Castillo-Valdivieso Pedro A. 2022. Offensive language detection in arabic social networks using evolutionary-based classifiers learned from fine-tuned embeddings. *IEEE Access*, 10, pp. 75018–75039.

Shapiro Ahmad, Khalafallah Ayman and Torki Marwan. 2022. AlexU-AIC at Arabic hate speech 2022: Contrast to classify. arXiv preprint arXiv:2207.08557.

Shi Xiayang, Liu Xinyi, Xu Chun, Huang Yuanyuan, Chen Fang and Zhu Shaolin. 2022. Cross-lingual offensive speech identification with transfer learning for low-resource languages. *Computers and Electrical Engineering*, 101, p. 108005.

Touahri Ibtissam and Mazroui Azzeddine. 2022. Offensive language and hate speech detection based on transfer learning. In *Advanced Intelligent Systems for Sustainable Development (AI2SD'2020)* (Volume 2, pp. 300–311). Cham: Springer International Publishing.

Turki Turki and Roy Sanjiban Sekhar. 2022. Novel hate speech detection using word cloud visualization and ensemble learning coupled with count vectorizer. *Applied Sciences*, 12(13), p. 6611.

Yafooz Wael M. S., Al-Dhaqm Arafat and Alsaeed Abdullah. 2023. Detecting kids cyberbullying using transfer learning approach: Transformer fine-tuning models. In *Kids Cybersecurity Using Computational Intelligence Techniques* (pp. 255–267). Cham: Springer International Publishing.

Zampieri Marcos, Malmasi Shervin, Nakov Preslav, Rosenthal Sara, Farra Noura and Kumar Ritesh. 2019. Semeval-2019 task 6: Identifying and categorizing offensive language in social media (offenseval). arXiv preprint arXiv:1903.08983.

Part 4

Case Studies and Future Trends

11 Cyberbullying Prevention Practices on Social Media and Future Challenges

M. Zaenul Muttaqin, Vince Tebay,
Yosephina Ohoiwutun,
Made Selly Dwi Suryanti, and Ilham
University of Cenderawasih

11.1 INTRODUCTION

11.1.1 BACKGROUND

Based on a report released by We Are Social and Hootsuite, in 2021, the world's mobile phone users will reach 5 billion, or the equivalent of two-thirds of the world's population today (We Are Social 2021). This number experienced a significant increase in October 2022, with a percentage of 3.89%. This number is followed by social media users, equivalent to 59.32% of the world's population (Kemp, 2022). Social media, now appearing among the public, is the primary means of obtaining vital information; Instagram, Twitter, Facebook, and other social media are much loved by teenagers, even adults. Electronic devices connected to the Internet, to the growth of the mass use of iPhone and Android, bring more efficient interactions while placing the Internet at the center of 21st-century communication challenges (Kwan et al., 2020). The challenge of developing technology is focused on the presence of harmful content, one of which is cyberbullying.

Cyberbullying has become the object of global attention in the last two decades. Cyberbullying has different characteristics from traditional bullying, where cyberbullying has access that connects the perpetrator and the victim regardless of the specific context. Lenhart's research (2015) shows how teenagers spend more time accessing the Internet than at school. The intensity of access affirms that cyberbullying can reach a wider audience than traditional bullying, which few people know. Cyberbullying audiences are subject to more severe pressure and aggression than traditional bullying. The freedom of anonymous actors on the Internet tends to strengthen this argument. The opportunity for perpetrators to not be recognized is the reason for their nonsympathetic attitude toward other users, as well as narrowing the possibility of co-optation of the perpetrators (Hyland et al., 2018; Patchin and Hinduja, 2006; Rusyidi, 2020). With the broad reach and convenience that the Internet brings, the harmful effects of cyberbullying are far more dramatic than traditional bullying (Gonzales, 2014; Hua, 2018).

DOI: 10.1201/9781003393061-15

Bullying has been known since the 1970s when Smith and Alweus conceptualized it as a deliberate act of aggression that repeatedly happened at a particular time (Rusyidi, 2020). Bullying is divided into two forms of progress: traditional and cyber (Tokunaga, 2010). Traditional bullying is identified through three crucial elements (Cross, Lester, and Barnes, 2015). First, there are repetitive actions that victims mainly experience. Second, the unequal power relations put the victim in a disadvantageous position. Third, there is a clear intention and intentionally hurts the victim. Traditional forms of bullying include physical actions and verbal aggression (Rusyidi, 2020; Muttaqin, 2022), then extend to the notion of being a third party where this aggression is indirect or commonly referred to as relational/social aggression (Pouwels, Lansu, and Cillessen, 2018). This form of relational aggression is constructed based on manipulation, spreading rumors with the aim of exclusion, and tends to be subtle and difficult to identify.

Research by Zhu et al. (2021) on 63 references shows that cyberbullying ranges from 13.99% to 57.5%; the general characteristic is verbal violence. Research by Athanasiou et al. (2018) in several European countries showed that victims of cyberbullying reached 37.3% of cases in Romania, 26.8% in Greece, 24.3% of cases in Germany, and 21.5% of cases in Poland. This series of cases targeted teenage victims with an average teenage age and those who were not too dominant in interactions. In Asian countries, it shows the same thing; the percentage of cyberbullying in China reaches 70%, followed by Singapore at 58%, and India at 53% (Bhat and Ragan, 2013). In their research in America, Selkie et al. (2015) showed that cyberbullying reached 72%. This series of cyberbullying cases is an essential reference for further studies to formulate various methods and instruments for preventing cyberbullying in a global country.

Ansary (2020) has provided an effective formula regarding prevention mediums from the family environment, education, peers and bystanders, social media, healthcare providers, and law. However, his presentation of the scope of prevention rests on the recommendations of social media companies. Ansary (2020) has provided a conceptual map of cyberbullying on social media, which helps navigate prevention techniques using artificial intelligence (AI). The AI approach allows flexibility in calculating software to counter and prevent cyberbullying. AI provides many Internet-based methods of detecting and preventing violence and good computer-based designs for research areas focused on bullying prevention measures (Azeez et al., 2021; Patel et al., 2012; Yuvaraj et al., 2021). So the purpose of this study is divided into two parts. In the first part, we outline the social media bases that often become hotbeds for cyberbullying. Then, the next section is an examination of the progress of various AI techniques to prevent cyberbullying.

11.1.2 Methodology

The study was conducted through literature and used a qualitative descriptive method. Data collection techniques were carried out by observing cyberbullying through social media. Some ideas or theories related to each other are woven with the support of accountable library data sources. Literature sources come from journals and research reports, books, paper proceedings, and various other official writings.

The qualitative descriptive research used in this study is intended to obtain information about the description of cyberbullying cases on social media and classify the crucial role of AI in cyberbullying prevention techniques. Social media grouping and cyberbullying prevention measures through AI in the data are analyzed and described based on facts to gain understanding and answers to the problems studied. Data analysis was carried out through the stages of reduction, presentation, and conclusion. Each stage follows a particular procedure; the data are selected based on the theme's suitability, then the presentation is carried out, and finally, the process of knitting or interpreting the data to draw an understandable conclusion.

11.1.3 CHAPTER ORGANIZATION

This chapter is structured as follows: in Chapter 2, an overview of cyberbullying cases will be explained; in Chapter 3, it will be explained about the results and discussion in which there are several important elements that become the media for cyberbullying. Chapter 4 describes cyberbullying based on social media platforms. Chapter 5 describes the classification of artificial intelligence as a cyberbullying preventiven measure. Chapter 6 is the closing of this chapter, which contains conclusions and recommendations.

11.2 RELATED WORK: AN OVERVIEW OF ARTIFICIAL INTELLIGENCE

The introduction of AI as part of a research discipline was first used in the Summer Research Project of Dartmouth College in July 1956. There are two criteria for explaining AI, first, as a science that aims to unravel intelligence and develop intelligent machines, and as a study that aims to find methods of solving problems by complex data (Bernstein et al., 2021; Brunette, Flemmer, and Flemmer, 2009; Qiu et al., 2019). Based on these two definitions, we use a second approach by looking at how AI works, including simulating human intelligence in thinking, learning, reasoning, and planning (Brunette et al., 2009; Dilek, Çakır, and Aydın, 2015; González García et al., 2019; Russell, 2010; Yadav, Mahato, and Linh, 2020). Thinkers explain the AI approach in terms of several characteristics. First, AI is a statistical approach to reasoning and problem-solving practices. Second, AI is a representation of ontological knowledge. Third, AI is a planning tool. Fourth, AI is a learning machine. Fifth, AI functions as an information collector and natural language. Sixth, AI is beneficial for location mapping and navigation that manipulates movement. Seventh, AI represents human perception in recognizing speech, faces, and objects. Eighth, AI has characteristics of simulating empathy or related to social intelligence. Ninth, AI can manipulate imagination, creativity, and intuition. The last is intelligence in general.

These characteristics can be simplified into two critical parts of the approach. First, the classic AI approach focuses on human attitudes and actions, ontological, and inferential knowledge. Second, the distributed artificial intelligence (DAI) approach focuses on social action in general. For social media practices, the DAI approach is well suited for cyberbullying prevention techniques. It is because DAI can explain frameworks, interactions, and knowledge sharing in parallel into one integral unit (Bond and Gasser, 2014). The DAI concept develops into a multiagent technology system, where intelligent resolution rests on sharing knowledge about a problem within a particular unit to find a route to a solution. In this system, each unit works together to detect and diagnose specific problems and can make decisions to deal with them (Nogueira, 2006).

11.3 CYBERBULLYING BASIS ON SOCIAL MEDIA PLATFORMS

The presence of social media in the modern era has shifted various human lives in virtual interactions. Three of the most common social media in the world are blogs, wikis, and social networks (Kurniawan, 2017). Social media is designed to facilitate internet technology-based interactions and change the pattern of information dissemination from monologue media (one to many audiences) to dialog social media (many audiences to many audiences). The types and composition of online social media in the virtual world are very diverse, including social networks (Facebook, Instagram, Friendster, LinkedIn), microblogging platforms (Twitter and Plurk), photo- and video-sharing networks (Flickr and Youtube), Podcasts, Chat rooms, Message boards, Forums, and Mailing lists. Based on McQuail's Literacy Uses and Gratification, social media is for information search, personal identity, social interaction and integration, and entertainment (Kim, Sin, and He, 2013).

Social media provides space for interaction between users, establishing collaboration, sharing information, and even bonding user relationships in the cyber realm (Munir, 2017). Social media refers to web- and mobile-based technologies to transform communication into interactive dialogue. Magazines, discussion forums, blogging, wikis, photo documentation, and audiovisuals are some of the forms of media related to social media. With the world amid a social media revolution, it is more than clear that Facebook, Twitter, and Instagram are used extensively for communication purposes. With the development of various social media platforms in cyberspace, the intensity of use, lack of empathy, and particular characteristics of victims are common factors that cause cyberbullying behavior (Rusdy and Fauzi, 2020).

11.3.1 TWITTER

Jack Dorsey founded Twitter in 2006, as a social networking platform that is quite popular with social media users (Zukhrufillah, 2018; Burgess and Baym, 2022; Kriyantono, 2006). Generally, cyberbullying on Twitter targets gender, race, and sexual orientation (Sterner and Felmlee, 2017). So that demographically, the pattern of cyberbullying on Twitter depends on the users' communication and social networking aspects. With a user-psychological approach, Balakrishnan, Khan, and Arabnia (2020) conduct a study on cyberbullying via Twitter. Through the Big Five and Dark Triad models, Balakrishnan, Khan, and Arabnia (2020) suggest that analysis of users' sentiments significantly accelerates the number of cyberbullying on Twitter. For more on this sentiment analysis, Khaira et al. (2020) developed SentiStrength research and a lexicon algorithm approach to divide sentiment into bullying, nonbullying, and neutral classes. These study results show that bullying tweet data is more dominant than the other two categories at 45.4%.

11.3.2 Facebook

Mark Zuckerberg, the founder of Facebook, started the networking site on February 4, 2004, with initial users limited to Harvard College students (Muhlis, Jasad, and Halik, 2018). Over the following 2 months, Facebook expanded membership to several top campuses in the Boston, Rochester, Stanford, NYU, Northwestern, and Ivy League areas. One year after launch, Facebook expanded its membership reach to universities in other regions. Facebook users went global and included the most popular sites in cyberspace.

With worldwide users, cyberbullying on Facebook is one of the most sporadic. This evidence is supported by the findings of BRIM Antibullying Software, which shows that most cyberbullying on social media occurs on Facebook. With the percentage reaching 87%, only 37% of the victims informed their social networks. This data differ from the amount of bullying on Twitter, which is only around 20% (BRIM n.d.). Dredge, Gleeson, and De La Piedad Garcia (2014) showed that three out of four participants in their research had experienced cyberbullying via Facebook. The root of bullying via social media Facebook is self-presentation, such as relationship statuses on profiles and posts on the Facebook wall. In its development, Facebook provides reporting mechanism facilities to prevent users from misconduct (Khairy et al., 2021). So, Hasan (2021) proposes a long-term evaluation of cyberbullying on Facebook, especially for manipulated texts and veiled sentiments. However, this form of bullying is complicated to decipher more than elegant likes and comments – assessment of simultaneous detection functions to support Facebook's policy to handle and prevent cyberbullying in the future.

Research on preventing cyberbullying in the realm of Facebook goes hand-in-hand with developing specific application systems. One was done by Silva et al. (2016), who developed the BullyBlocker application. In his research, Silva promotes this application with identification capabilities that combine AI capabilities with user roles. This application provides notifications to the people closest to the user involved as perpetrators or victims of cyberbullying.

11.3.3 Instagram

Using Instagram as a communication tool in social media is considered relatively new, making it easy for users to share photos or video information (Hu, Manikonda, and Kambhampati, 2014). Instagram as a medium of information is currently prevalent among young people (Pittman and Reich, 2016). The easy way to use the Instagram application makes users make Instagram one of the leading information media to meet sharing needs (Sari and Basit, 2020).

Types of cyberbullying via Instagram include verbally abusive expressions on photos and videos uploaded by other users (RizkyFitransyah and Waliyanti, 2018). In its development, Instagram is equipped with "like and comment" features like Twitter and Facebook. This comment feature is often misused for cyberbullying. Naf'an et al. (2019), in their research, shows that Instagram's weakness is that it does not have features to detect cyberbullying. Like other social media, most cyberbullying targeting minority groups or certain users often occurs on Instagram (Folia, 2017;

Muttaqin and Ambarwati, 2020; Rastati, 2016). For that, Naf'an et al. (2019) offers cyberbullying prevention detection on Instagram using the Naïve Bayes Classifier. Through this procedure, followed by steaming and nonsteaming experiments, they found that the accuracy of detecting cyberbullying on Instagram reached 84%.

11.4 CLASSIFICATION OF ARTIFICIAL INTELLIGENCE AS A CYBERBULLYING PREVENTION MEASURE

In this section, we discuss how cyberbullying can be prevented with the help of a computer. Data computing tools using computer technology have many methods to facilitate data processing according to the data type or type. Classification is a way of grouping data based on the characteristics possessed by objects. The classification, done with the help of technology, has several algorithms, including Naïve Bayes, support vector machine, decision tree, fuzzy, and artificial neural networks (Figure 11.1).

First, the Naïve Bayes Classifier; this method departs from Bayes' theorem to classify by relying on strong independence assumptions on an event (Yang, 2018). The Naïve Bayes Classifier has an advantage in testing categorical data types, but its accuracy is questionable for too many features (Frank, Hall, and Pfahringer, 2012; Oktafia and Pardede, 2010). Second, the support vector machine method is rooted in structural risk minimization (SRM) as machine learning and aims to track the classification hyperlane. Pattern recognition was then introduced by Vapnik in 1992 (Pisner and Schnyer, 2020). It tends to be implemented easily in classification, but on large-scale samples, SVM is difficult to process (Fikri, Sabrila, and Azhar, 2020).

Third, the decision tree consists of several nodes, namely, the tree's root, internal nodes, and leaves. The concept of entropy is used to determine which attributes a tree will split. Decision trees are often used for classification problems because they are simple to route from root to leaf nodes. Decision trees can accurately classify data, but the branches often need to be more significant and complete (Pandya and Pandya, 2015). Fourth is the neural network (NN); a neural network (NN) refers to the imitation of how the human nervous system works to distribute information (Abiodun et al., 2018). NN relies on learning principles to find patterns and classifications on certain problems. The advantage of NN is that it can map inputs and outputs, but this model uses complex analysis and tends to complicate interpretation (Azis, Herwanto, and Ramadhani, 2021).

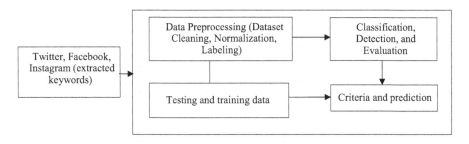

FIGURE 11.1   Common patterns of how AI detects cyberbullying.

Fifth, Fuzzy; it is the logic that contains an element of uncertainty. Fuzzy logic was first developed in 1960 in America and has been widely applied in other developed countries such as Japan. The function of fuzzy logic is to control various tools practically and flexibly. Unlike other models, fuzzy has excellent and reliable control, but there is no uniform, systematic knowledge regarding control problem-solving methods (Nasution, 2012; Ratama, Kom, and Munawaroh, 2019; Saelan, 2009).

A description of the AI system in preventing cyberbullying has been practiced by Khetarpaul et al. (2021), which promotes social networks as a preventive measure against cyberbullying. Real-time detection through visualization of keyboard patterns enables offensive and corrective actions against typed messages. Furthermore, Purnamasari et al. (2020) proposed the support vector machine (SVM) method as an identification and classification tool to separate text on Twitter based on positive and negative words. The steps in SVM include preprocessing, tokenizing, filtering, stemming, and weighting, combined with information gain to calculate entropy values.

In a different study, Hani et al. (2019) stated that even though the difference is not too significant, the neural network (NN) works more accurately than the support vector machine (SVM). The neural network is a machine learning process that uses nodes or neurons connected in a layered structure that resembles the human brain. Neural networks create adaptive systems computers use to learn from and continuously improve mistakes. Then, Raj et al. (2021) developed NN with a hybrid model, compared the algorithms of 11 classification methods, and extracted natural language features, resulting in more accurate cyberbullying detection than traditional machine learning. Furthermore, Banerjee et al. (2019) used the convolutional neural network (CNN) as a deep learning feature appropriate for detecting cyberbullying by understanding objects, classes, and categories in audio and text.

Among these studies, the authors see that various developments in cyberbullying require sophisticated methods. One of the training methods in NN is supervised learning. Network training efforts become important. This is to make weighting on the input and target to the network and produce output. The network will adjust the weighting according to the error measured from the input and output gaps. Then, back propagation neural network (BPNN) is a method that uses supervised learning and manages the output error to change the value of the weights backward. The forward propagation stage is operated first to get this error. There are three phases in the BPNN training, namely, the feed-forward, back-propagation, and weight-modification phases. The feed-forward phase counts forward from the input to the output layer. Then, the back-propagation phase calculates the error value based on the target pattern from input to output with errors identified backward. Next is the weight-modification phase, which is intended to minimize errors. These stages are carried out simultaneously until termination is reached.

11.5 CONCLUSIONS AND CRITICAL NOTES

Regardless of the position and location of cyberbullying, the responsibility for preventing cyberbullying rests not only on AI's ability and adaptation. Holistically, the centralized basis of cyberbullying on social media indicates the importance of the responsibility of social media companies. Social media companies must have adequate tools to regulate and control cyberbullying through their features as a form of responsibility and contribution to prevention (Milosevic, 2016). In their research, Rosa et al. (2019) explained that several social media are improving their cyberbullying prevention systems with various features, such as reporting that positions to users to participate and an automatic detection system to select words that tend to be negative.

This study indicates that the future challenge of cyberbullying prevention does not only apply at the technical level and methods that rely on the hard work of researchers and practitioners. In the context of cyberbullying prevention policies and legal products, Ansary (2020) argues that education is an essential target from a legal perspective. In Ansary's view (2020), bullying emerges among adolescents in formal educational institutions. The view that cyberbullying is only rooted in educational policies tends to lead us to narrow the issue of categorizing cyberbullying and placing cyberbullying on the shoulders of adolescents. On a broad scale, we see that freedom of expression on the Internet was regulated in international law in 2012 when the United Nations issued a Resolution on the Promotion, Protection, and Enjoyment of Human Rights on the Internet. This resolution aims to provide guarantees of equal protection in both cyber- and real-life forms of expression. This rule at the national level must have suitable policy instruments to manage freedom of expression as in real life. So far, the debate on the freedom of expression and cyberbullying has been confined to a thin line (El Asam and Samara, 2016; Campbell and Zavrsnik, 2013; Coburn, Connolly, and Roesch, 2015; Smith and Steffgen, 2013). Reflecting on international human rights law and national law, despite the bias in the categorization of the definition of bullying in the virtual realm (Marczak and Coyne, 2010; Paul, Smith, and Blumberg, 2012; Suryanti and Muttaqin, 2023), we believe that legal enforcement of cyberbullying and traditional bullying is within one crime frame, in line with the views of Dwipayana, Setiyono, and Pakpahan (2020), which explain that cyberbullying fulfills the criminal element of defamation against someone and is a form of humiliation.

REFERENCES

Abiodun, Oludare Isaac, Aman Jantan, Abiodun Esther Omolara, Kemi Victoria Dada, Nachaat AbdElatif Mohamed, and Humaira Arshad. 2018. "State-of-the-Art in Artificial Neural Network Applications: A Survey." *Heliyon* 4(11):e00938. https://doi.org/10.1016/j.heliyon.2018.e00938

Ansary, Nadia S. 2020. "Cyberbullying: Concepts, Theories, and Correlates Informing Evidence-Based Best Practices for Prevention." *Aggression and Violent Behavior* 50:101343. https://doi.org/10.1016/j.avb.2019.101343

Athanasiou, Kalliope, Eirini Melegkovits, Elisabeth K. Andrie, Charalampos Magoulas, Chara K. Tzavara, Clive Richardson, Donald Greydanus, Maria Tsolia, and Artemis K. Tsitsika. 2018. "Cross-National Aspects of Cyberbullying Victimization among 14-17-Year-Old Adolescents across Seven European Countries." *BMC Public Health* 18(1):1–15. https://doi.org/10.1186/s12889-018-5682-4

Azeez, Nureni Ayofe, Sunday O. Idiakose, Chinazo Juliet Onyema, and Charles Van Der Vyver. 2021. "Cyberbullying Detection in Social Networks: Artificial Intelligence Approach." *Journal of Cyber Security and Mobility* 745–774. https://doi.org/10.13052/jcsm2245-1439.1046

Azis, Nur, Herwanto Herwanto, and Fathurrahman Ramadhani. 2021. "Implementasi Speech Recognition Pada Aplikasi E-Prescribing Menggunakan Algoritme Convolutional Neural Network." *JURNAL MEDIA INFORMATIKA BUDIDARMA* 5(2):460–467. https://doi.org/10.30865/mib.v5i2.2841

Balakrishnan, Vimala, Shahzaib Khan, and Hamid R. Arabnia. 2020. "Improving Cyberbullying Detection Using Twitter Users' Psychological Features and Machine Learning." *Computers and Security*. https://doi.org/10.1016/j.cose.2019.101710

Banerjee, Vijay, Jui Telavane, Pooja Gaikwad, and Pallavi Vartak. 2019. "Detection of Cyberbullying Using Deep Neural Network." In *2019 5th International Conference on Advanced Computing and Communication Systems, ICACCS 2019*. https://doi.org/10.1109/ICACCS.2019.8728378

Bernstein, Michael S., Margaret Levi, David Magnus, Betsy Rajala, Debra Satz, and Charla Waeiss. 2021. "Esr: Ethics and Society Review of Artificial Intelligence Research." *ArXiv Preprint ArXiv:2106.11521*. Retrieved December 23, 2022. https://arxiv.org/abs/2106.11521

Bhat, C. B., and M. A. Ragan. 2013. "Cyberbullying in Asia." *Cyber Asia and the New Media* 18:36–39.

Bond, Alan H., and Les Gasser. 2014. *Readings in Distributed Artificial Intelligence*. Morgan Kaufmann.

BRIM. n.d. "Cyber Bullying on Facebook and What to Do About It." *BRIM: Anti-Bullying Software*. Retrieved December 23, 2022. https://antibullyingsoftware.com/facebook-bullying/

Brunette, Emma S., Rory C. Flemmer, and Claire L. Flemmer. 2009. "A Review of Artificial Intelligence." Pp. 385–392. In *2009 4th International Conference on Autonomous Robots and Agents*. IEEE. https://doi.org/10.1109/ICARA.2000.4804025

Burgess, J., and Nancy K. Baym. 2022. *Twitter: A Biography*. NYU Press.

Campbell, Marilyn, and Ales Zavrsnik. 2013. "Should Cyberbullying Be Criminalized?" Pp. 83–100. In *Cyberbullying through the New Media*. Psychology Press.

Coburn, Patricia I., Deborah A. Connolly, and Ronald Roesch. 2015. "Cyberbullying: Is Federal Criminal Legislation the Solution?" *Canadian Journal of Criminology and Criminal Justice* 57(4):566–579. https://doi.org/10.3138/cjccj.2014.E43

Cross, Donna, Leanne Lester, and Amy Barnes. 2015. "A Longitudinal Study of the Social and Emotional Predictors and Consequences of Cyber and Traditional Bullying Victimisation." *International Journal of Public Health* 60(2):207–217. https://doi.org/10.1007/s00038-015-0655-1

Dilek, Selma, Hüseyin Çakır, and Mustafa Aydın. 2015. "Applications of Artificial Intelligence Techniques to Combating Cyber Crimes: A Review." *ArXiv Preprint ArXiv:1502.03552*. Retrieved December 23, 2022. https://arxiv.org/pdf/1502.03552.pdf

Dredge, Rebecca, John Gleeson, and Xochitl De La Piedad Garcia. 2014. "Presentation on Facebook and Risk of Cyberbullying Victimisation." *Computers in Human Behavior*. https://doi.org/10.1016/j.chb.2014.07.035

Dwipayana, Ni Luh Ayu Mondrisa, Setiyono Setiyono, and Hatarto Pakpahan. 2020. "Cyberbullying on Social Media." *Bhirawa Law Journal* 1(2):63–70. https://doi.org/10.26905/blj.v1i2.5483

El Asam, Aiman, and Muthanna Samara. 2016. "Cyberbullying and the Law: A Review of Psychological and Legal Challenges." *Computers in Human Behavior* 65:127–141. https://doi.org/10.1016/j.chb.2016.08.012

Fikri, Mujaddid Izzul, Trifebi Shina Sabrila, and Yufis Azhar. 2020. "Comparison of Naïve Bayes Method and Support Vector Machine in Twitter Sentiment Analysis." *Smatika Jurnal* 10(02):71–76. https://doi.org/10.32664/smatika.v10i02.455

Folia, R. 2017. "It Turns Out That Cyberbullying Happens the Most on Instagram." *IDNTimes*. Retrieved August 13, 2022. https://www.idntimes.com/news/world/rosa-folia/ternyata-cyber-bullying-paling-banyak-terjadi-di-instagram-1/full

Frank, Eibe, Mark Hall, and Bernhard Pfahringer. 2012. "Locally Weighted Naive Bayes." *ArXiv Preprint ArXiv:1212.2487*. Retrieved December 23, 2022. https://arxiv.org/abs/1212.2487

Gonzales, Reginald H. 2014. "Social Media as a Channel and Its Implications on Cyber Bullying." In *DLSU Research Congress*. Retrieved December 23, 2022. https://www.dlsu.edu.ph/wp-content/uploads/dlsu-research-congress-proceedings/2014/LCCS-I-009-FT.pdf

González García, Cristian, Edward Rolando Núñez Valdéz, Vicente García Díaz, Begoña Cristina Pelayo García-Bustelo, and Juan Manuel Cueva Lovelle. 2019. "A Review of Artificial Intelligence in the Internet of Things." *International Journal of Interactive Multimedia and Artificial Intelligence* 5. https://doi.org/10.9781/ijimai.2018.03.004

Hani, John, Nashaat Mohamed, Mostafa Ahmed, Zeyad Emad, Eslam Amer, and Mohammed Ammar. 2019. "Social Media Cyberbullying Detection Using Machine Learning." *International Journal of Advanced Computer Science and Applications* 10(5). https://doi.org/10.14569/IJACSA.2019.0100587

Hasan, Nur Fitrianingsih. 2021. "Detect Cyberbullying on Facebook Using the K-Nearest Neighbor Algorithm." *Journal of Smart System*. https://doi.org/10.36728/jss.v1i1.1605

Hu, Yuheng, Lydia Manikonda, and Subbarao Kambhampati. 2014. "What We Instagram: A First Analysis of Instagram Photo Content and User Types." In *Eighth International AAAI Conference on Weblogs and Social Media*. https://doi.org/10.1609/icwsm.v8i1.14578

Hua, Tan Kim. 2018. "Cyberbullying: A Cursory Review." P. 17. In *Stop Cyberbullying*, edited by T. K. Hua. Penerbit Universiti Kebangsaan Malaysia.

Hyland, Pauline, Conor Mc Guckin, Christopher Alan Lewis, and John Hyland. 2018. "The Psychological Consequences of Traditional and Cyber Bullying in Irish Post-Primary Schools." Retrieved December 23, 2022. https://esource.dbs.ie/bitstream/handle/10788/3586/hyland_et_al_poster_dbs-rday_2018.pdf?sequence=1

Kemp, Simon. 2022. "Digital 2022 October Global Statshot Report." *Data Reports*. Retrieved December 24, 2022 (https://datareportal.com/reports/digital-2022-october-global-statshot).

Khaira, Ulfa, Ragil Johanda, Pradita Eko Prasetyo Utomo, and Tri Suratno. 2020. "Sentiment Analysis of Cyberbullying on Twitter Using SentiStrength." *Indonesian Journal of Artificial Intelligence and Data Mining*. https://doi.org/10.24014/ijaidm.v3i1.9145

Khairy, Marwa, Tarek M. Mahmoud, Tarek Abd-El-Hafeez, and Ahmed Mahfouz. 2021. "User Awareness of Privacy, Reporting System and Cyberbullying on Facebook." Pp. 613–625. In *Advances in Intelligent Systems and Computing*, edited by Aboul-Ella Hassanien, Kuo-Chi Chang, and Tang Mincong. Springer. https://doi.org/10.1007/978-3-030-69717-4_58

Khetarpaul, Sonia, Dolly Sharma, Mayuri Gupta, and Vaibhav Gautam. 2021. "A Real-Time Analysis of Offensive Texts to Prevent Cyberbullying." In *Lecture Notes in Computer Science (including subseries Lecture Notes in Artificial Intelligence and Lecture Notes in Bioinformatics)*. https://doi.org/10.1007/978-3-030-69377-0_13

Kim, Kyung-Sun, Sei-Ching Joanna Sin, and Yuqi He. 2013. "Information Seeking through Social Media: Impact of User Characteristics on Social Media Use." *Proceedings of the American Society for Information Science and Technology* 50(1):1–4. https://doi.org/10.1002/meet.14505001129

Kriyantono, Rachmat. 2006. Communication Research. Kencana Prenada Media Group.

Kurniawan, Puguh. 2017. "Utilization of Instagram Social Media as Modern Marketing Communication on Batik Burneh." *Competence: Journal of Management Studies* 11(2). https://doi.org/10.21107/kompetensi.v11i2.3533

Kwan, Irene, Kelly Dickson, Michelle Richardson, Wendy MacDowall, Helen Burchett, Claire Stansfield, Ginny B., Katy Sutcliffe, and James Thomas. 2020. "Cyberbullying and Children and Young People's Mental Health: A Systematic Map of Systematic Reviews." *Cyberpsychology, Behavior, and Social Networking* 23(2):72–82. https://doi.org/10.1089/cyber.2019.0370

Lenhart, Amanda. 2015. "Teens, Social Media & Technology Overview 2015." Pew Research Center. Retrieved December 24, 2022. https://www.pewresearch.org/internet/2015/04/09/teens-social-media-technology-2015/

Marczak, Magdalena, and Iain Coyne. 2010. "Cyberbullying at School: Good Practice and Legal Aspects in the United Kingdom." *Journal of Psychologists and Counsellors in Schools* 20(2):182–193. https://doi.org/10.1375/ajgc.20.2.182

Milosevic, Tijana. 2016. "Social Media Companies' Cyberbullying Policies." *International Journal of Communication* 10:22. Retrieved December 24, 2022. https://ijoc.org/index.php/ijoc/article/viewFile/5320/1818

Muhlis, Muhlis, Usman Jasad, and Abdul Halik. 2018. "Facebook Phenomenon as a New Communication Media." *Jurnal Diskursus Islam* 6(1):19–35. https://doi.org/10.24252/jdi.v6i1.6759

Munir. 2017. *Pembelajaran Digital.* CV Alfabeta.

Muttaqin, M. Zaenul. 2022. "Stop Raping Us" a Body Political Prefix." *Violence and Gender* 9(3):103–104. https://doi.org/10.1089/vio.2022.0036

Muttaqin, M. Zaenul, and Ninik Tri Ambarwati. 2020. "Cyberbullying and Woman Oppression." Pp. 545–553. In *the 6th International Conference on Social and Political Sciences (ICOSAPS 2020).* Atlantis Press. https://doi.org/10.2991/assehr.k.201219.083

Naf'an, Muhammad Zidny, Alhamda Adisoka Bimantara, Afiatari Larasati, Ezar Mega Risondang, and Novanda Alim Setya Nugraha. 2019. "Sentiment Analysis of Cyberbullying on Instagram User Comments." *Journal of Data Science and Its Applications.* https://doi.org/10.21108/jdsa.2019.2.20

Nasution, Helfi. 2012. "Implementation of Fuzzy Logic in Artificial Intelligence Systems." *Jurnal ELKHA* 4(2). https://doi.org/10.14710/jmasif.2.3.27-38

Nogueira, José Helano Matos. 2006. "Mobile Intelligent Agents to Fight Cyber Intrusions." *International Journal of Forensic Computer Science, Brasília: Brazil.* https://doi.org/10.5769/J200601003

Oktafia, Dian, and D. L. Pardede. 2010. "Comparison of the Performance of the Decision Tree Algorithm and Naïve Bayes in Bankruptcy Prediction." Retrieved December 24, 2022. https://core.ac.uk/download/pdf/143964255.pdf

Pandya, Rutvija, and Jayati Pandya. 2015. "C5. 0 Algorithm to Improved Decision Tree with Feature Selection and Reduced Error Pruning." *International Journal of Computer Applications* 117(16):18–21. https://doi.org/10.5120/20639-3318

Patchin, Justin W., and Sameer Hinduja. 2006. "Bullies Move Beyond the Schoolyard: A Preliminary Look at Cyberbullying." *Youth Violence and Juvenile Justice* 4(2):148–169. https://doi.org/10.1177/1541204006286288

Patel, Ahmed, Mona Taghavi, Kaveh Bakhtiyari, and Joaquim Celestino Júnior. 2012. "Taxonomy and Proposed Architecture of Intrusion Detection and Prevention Systems for Cloud Computing." Pp. 441–458. In *International Symposium on Cyberspace Safety and Security*, edited by Yang Xiang, Javier Lopez, C.-C. Jay Kuo, and Wanlei Zhou. Springer. https://doi.org/10.1007/978-3-642-35362-8_33

Paul, Simone, Peter K. Smith, and Herbert H. Blumberg. (2012). "Investigating Legal Aspects of Cyberbullying." *Psicothema* 24(4):640–645. PMID: 23079364.

Pisner, Derek A., and David M. Schnyer. 2020. "Support Vector Machine." Pp. 101–121. In *Machine Learning*, edited by Andrea Mechelli and Sandra Vieira. Elsevier. https://doi.org/10.1016/B978-0-12-815739-8.00006-7

Pittman, Matthew, and Brandon Reich. 2016. "Social Media and Loneliness: Why an Instagram Picture May Be Worth More than a Thousand Twitter Words." *Computers in Human Behavior* 62:155–167. https://doi.org/10.1016/j.chb.2016.03.084

Pouwels, J. Loes, Tessa A. M. Lansu, and Antonius H. N. Cillessen. 2018. "A Developmental Perspective on Popularity and the Group Process of Bullying." *Aggression and Violent Behavior* 43:64–70. https://doi.org/10.1016/j.avb.2018.10.003

Purnamasari, Ni Made Gita Dwi, M. Ali Fauzi, Indriati, and Liana Shinta Dewi. 2020. "Cyberbullying Identification in Twitter Using Support Vector Machine and Information Gain Based Feature Selection." *Indonesian Journal of Electrical Engineering and Computer Science*. https://doi.org/10.11591/ijeecs.v18.i3.pp1494-1500

Qiu, Shilin, Qihe Liu, Shijie Zhou, and Chunjiang Wu. 2019. "Review of Artificial Intelligence Adversarial Attack and Defense Technologies." *Applied Sciences* 9(5):909. https://doi.org/10.3390/app9050909

Raj, Chahat, Ayush Agarwal, Gnana Bharathy, Bhuva Narayan, and Mukesh Prasad. 2021. "Cyberbullying Detection: Hybrid Models Based on Machine Learning and Natural Language Processing Techniques." *Electronics (Switzerland)*. https://doi.org/10.3390/electronics10222810

Rastati, Ranny. 2016. "Forms of Cyberbullying in Social Media and Its Prevention for Victims and Perpetrators Forms of Cyberbullying in Social Media and Its Prevention for Victims and Perpetrators." *Jurnal Sosioteknologi*. https://doi.org/10.5614/sostek.itbj.2016.15.02.1

Ratama, Niki, M. Kom, and M. Munawaroh. 2019. *Artificial Intelligence Concept with Fuzzy Logic Understanding and Application Application*. Uwais Inspirasi Indonesia.

RizkyFitransyah, Retha, and Ema Waliyanti. 2018. "Cyberbullying Behavior with Instagram Media in Adolescents in Yogyakarta." *Indonesian Journal of Nursing Practice*. https://doi.org/10.18196/ijnp.2177

Rosa, Hugo, Nádia Pereira, Ricardo Ribeiro, Paula Costa Ferreira, Joao Paulo Carvalho, Sofia Oliveira, Luísa Coheur, Paula Paulino, A. M. Veiga Simão, and Isabel Trancoso. 2019. "Automatic Cyberbullying Detection: A Systematic Review." *Computers in Human Behavior* 93:333–345. https://doi.org/10.1016/j.chb.2018.12.021

Rusdy, Marhamah, and Fauzi Fauzi. 2020. "Digital Literacy and Cyberbullying Behavior of Youths in Instagram." *KOMUNIKE*. https://doi.org/10.20414/jurkom.v12i2.2699

Russell, Stuart J. 2010. *Artificial Intelligence a Modern Approach*. Pearson Education, Inc.

Rusyidi, Binahayati. 2020. "Understanding Cyberbullying Among Adolescents." *Jurnal Kolaborasi Resolusi Konflik* 2(2):100–110. https://doi.org/10.24198/jkrk.v2i2.29118

Saelan, Athia. 2009. "Logika Fuzzy." *Program Studi Teknik Informatika, Sekolah Teknik Elektro Dan Informatika*. Institut Tekologi Bandung.

Sari, Dian Nurvita, and Abdul Basit. 2020. "Instagram Social Media as Educational Information Media." *PERSEPSI: Communication Journal* 3(1):23–36. https://doi.org/10.30596/persepsi.v3i1.4428

Selkie, Ellen M., Rajitha Kota, Ya-Fen Chan, and Megan Moreno. 2015. "Cyberbullying, Depression, and Problem Alcohol Use in Female College Students: A Multisite Study." *Cyberpsychology, Behavior, and Social Networking* 18(2):79–86. https://doi.org/10.1089/cyber.2014.0371

Silva, Yasin N., Christopher Rich, Jaime Chon, and Lisa M. Tsosie. 2016. "BullyBlocker: An App to Identify Cyberbullying in Facebook." In *Proceedings of the 2016 IEEE/ACM International Conference on Advances in Social Networks Analysis and Mining, ASONAM 2016*. IEEE. https://doi.org/10.1109/ASONAM.2016.7752430

Smith, Peter K., and Georges Steffgen. 2013. *Cyberbullying through the New Media: Findings from an International Network*. Psychology Press. https://doi.org/10.4324/9780203799079

Sterner, Glenn, and Diane Felmlee. 2017. "The Social Networks of Cyberbullying on Twitter." *International Journal of Technoethics*. https://doi.org/10.4018/IJT.2017070101

Suryanti, Made Selly Dwi, and M. Zaenul Muttaqin. 2023. "Online Gender-Based Violence in Indonesian Context: The Shadow Pandemic Study." *Violence and Gender*. https://doi.org/10.1089/vio.2022.0057

Tokunaga, Robert S. 2010. "Following You Home from School: A Critical Review and Synthesis of Research on Cyberbullying Victimization." *Computers in Human Behavior* 26(3):277–87. https://doi.org/10.1016/j.chb.2009.11.014

We Are Social. 2021. "Social Media Users Pass the 4.5 Billion Mark." *We Are Social* 23:2021. We retrieved December 24, 2022 (https://wearesocial.com/us/blog/2021/10/social-media-users-pass-the-4-5-billion-mark/).

Yadav, Satya Prakash, Dharmendra Prasad Mahato, and Nguyen Thi Dieu Linh. 2020. *Distributed Artificial Intelligence: A Modern Approach.* CRC Press. https://doi.org/10.1201/9781003038467

Yang, Feng-Jen. 2018. "An Implementation of Naive Bayes Classifier." Pp. 301–306. In *The 2018 International Conference on Computational Science and Computational Intelligence (CSCI).* IEEE. https://doi.org/10.1109/CSCI46756.2018.00065

Yuvaraj, Natarajan, Victor Chang, Balasubramanian Gobinathan, Arulprakash Pinagapani, Srihari Kannan, Gaurav Dhiman, and Arsath Raja Rajan. 2021. "Automatic Detection of Cyberbullying Using Multi-Feature Based Artificial Intelligence with Deep Decision Tree Classification." *Computers & Electrical Engineering* 92:107186. https://doi.org/10.1016/j.compeleceng.2021.107186

Zhu, Chengyan, Shiqing Huang, Richard Evans, and Wei Zhang. 2021. "Cyberbullying among Adolescents and Children: A Comprehensive Review of the Global Situation, Risk Factors, and Preventive Measures." *Frontiers in Public Health* 9:634909. https://doi.org/10.3389/fpubh.2021.634909

Zukhrufillah, Irfani. 2018. "Symptoms of Twitter Social Media as Alternative Social Media." *Al-I'lam: Jurnal Komunikasi Dan Penyiaran Islam* 1(2):102–109. https://doi.org/10.31764/jail.v1i2.235

12 Methods of Complex Network Analysis to Screen for Cyberbullying

Santhosh Kumar Rajamani
MAEER MIT Pune's MIMER Medical
College and DR. BSTR Hospital

Radha Srinivasan Iyer
SEC Centre for Independent Living

12.1 INTRODUCTION

12.1.1 DEFINITION OF CYBERBULLYING

Cyberbullying is defined as using electronic forms of communication to bully someone. Examples include sending unwanted messages, spreading rumors online, hacking into someone's social media accounts, impersonating another person online, and posting embarrassing photos or videos without permission (Wright & Wachs, 2023). Cyberbullying Research Centre redefines the act of cyberbullying as "wilful and repeated harm that is inflicted through the use of computers, cell phones, and other electronic devices" (Hinduja & Patchin, 2014).

The definition of cyberbullying as stated by American National Crime Prevention Council is as follows: "online bullying, often known as cyberbullying, occurs when someone utilises the Internet, a mobile phone, or any other device to email or upload text or images meant to harm or humiliate another person" (Zhu et al., 2021).

Cyberbullying is the deliberate use of some form of technology to annoy, threaten, or hurt other people. The following are some of the prevalent examples of the menace of cyberbullying, sending threatening or hurtful messages, disseminating untrue information, sharing humiliating or private images or videos without the individual's permission, or removing someone from online social networks without the consent of the user (Zhao & Yu, 2021).

12.1.2 CURRENT CYBERBULLYING STATISTICS

The reported incidence of cyberbullying from various studies latest up to 2023 ranges from 6.3% to 32% of adolescent internet users. About 10%–20% adolescent users report bullying someone online (Zhao & Yu, 2021). To better understand the experiences and opinions of 1,316 U.S. teenagers, Pew Research Center conducted

DOI: 10.1201/9781003393061-16

a survey in 2022. The results showed that name-calling (32% of the time) was the most common cyberbullying behavior experienced by 46% of teenagers ages 13–17 (Vogels & Atske, 2022).

Unlike traditional bullying that can be found in school premises, cyberbullying can become a 24×7 harrowing experience for the victim, with the victim being bullied in the security of homes, through several electronic devices, like cell phones (web forums, groups, chats, messages) desktops, and laptops. The anonymity offered by the social media with peer approval encourages the more aggressive behavior of the bully (Camacho et al., 2023).

12.2 PATHOLOGY OF CYBERBULLYING

People who are the victims of cyberbullying may have depressive disorders, anxiety, low self-esteem, and even suicidal thoughts (Tozzo et al., 2022).

12.2.1 PATHOLOGY OF CYBERBULLYING

Cyberbullying can have a variety of effects, from mild distress to serious psychological and social issues like poor academic performance, an increase in absences from school, a sense of danger at school, mood disruption (anxiety), and despair. This form of harassment can even have serious negative effects on an individual's mental health, self-esteem, and even their physical safety (Schodt et al. 2021). Victims may feel overwhelmed, anxious, and isolated because of these behaviors (Camacho et al., 2023). Cyberbullying in victims is linked to psychological depression and dysphoria, anxiety, loss of sleep, palpitations, poor academic performance, poor concentration in classroom, nightmares, loss of appetite or increased appetite, and suicidal tendency (Bitar et al., 2023). In addition, bullying victims have lower self-esteem, higher risk substance abuse, and cigarette or alcohol addiction. Boys are more likely to be victims than girls (Martínez-Valderrey et al., 2023).

Unchecked actions can, in certain severe cases, cause victims to suffer from serious mental illness or, even worse, to be killed. As a result, cyberbullying has drawn the attention of policymakers, educators, and parents (Shin & Choi, 2021).

12.2.2 PSYCHOLOGY OF CYBERBULLYING

As cyberbullying is a learnt conscious habit, psychology learning theories were applied to the phenomenon of cyberbullying. This has led to Barlett Gentile Cyberbullying Model (BGCM) which is considered as the most acceptable cognitive model of cyberbullying (Barlett, 2023). Cyberbullying aggressive behaviors are reinforced by a loop of peer and family approval, with bystander and supporter appraisal. This is essentially a community-approved and acceptable aggressive behavior in certain communities. In many cases, the aggressive behaviors are trivialized and even normalized (Wright & Wachs, 2023).

Individuals suffering from autism or autistic spectrum disorder were significantly more likely to be victims of cyberbullying. Traditional bullying victims were more likely to become victims of cyberbullying (Sampasa-Kanyinga et al., 2018).

12.2.3 KROHN'S NETWORK THEORY OF DELINQUENT BEHAVIOR

Marvin Krohn in 1986 advanced the "network theory of delinquency," as an explanation for delinquent behaviors (Krohn, 1986). Social control theories propose that weak social bonds especially in family, friends, school, community, etc. (support networks) are responsible for evolving of innate tendencies or genetic predispositions toward delinquent behavior. A lack of social control is at the heart of the problem (Hirschi, 1969). Differential association theory postulates that criminal and delinquent attitudes are learnt from peer groups and not innate (Edwin Sutherland et al., 1992). Peer influences are mainly responsible for nefarious attitudes and behaviors (criminal networks). Krohn's network theory of delinquency is a composite theory with elements of both social control theory and differential association theory (Armitage 2021). There are two levels in this combination approach. At the individual level, social acceptance and social bonding are balanced by (both criminal and anticriminal) acceptable behaviors in his personal network. At the community level, the levels of delinquency will be affected by number of such social networks which support the individual (support networks) or encourage delinquent behaviors (criminal networks). For example, Krohn found that young men who had strong support network of family, church, and friends were less likely to take up the habit of smoking cigarettes (Krohn et al., 1988).

12.2.4 SPECTRUM OF ONLINE BEHAVIORS THAT CONSTITUTE CYBERBULLYING

There are a variety of aggressive online behaviors that form the spectrum of cyberbullying like cyberstalking (stalking the victim online) excluding (removing a victim from a group against their wilk), doxing (revealing socially sensitive information about the victim like intimate photos, sexual orientation), fraping (maligning in the victim in a group, by posting negative content pretending to be the victim), masquerading (creating a false identity in a group using victims name or photographs), flaming (insulting the victim via comments and messages), ewhoring (pretending to be friendly females and sexually soliciting explicit/nude images from males or explicit chat conversations or explicit live video sessions, with main intend to blackmail and bully the male victim), and sexual harassment by sending explicit images to the victim (Aboujaoude & Savage, 2023; Floros and Mylona 2022).

12.3 COMMUNITY SUPPORT FOR PREVENTING CYBERBULLYING

Cyberbullying can have major repercussions for the kids who are subjected to it; it is crucial for instructors to adopt a proactive approach to preventing it. These are the mitigating steps that can be taken by parents, teachers, social media network administrators, and social media platform owners.

12.3.1 ROLE OF PARENTS IN PREVENTING CYBERBULLYING

A subfield of network cyberbullying can happen via a variety of online communication channels, including social networking, texting, and messaging applications

(Gabrielli et al. 2021). Parents must be vigilant about their ward's online behavior, particularly, their use of social media and messaging services. Parents must pay close attention to any modifications in their behavior, such as a tendency to withdrawn or get tense or signs of emotional disturbance.

Use monitoring software: There are many tools that can assist you in keeping an eye on your child's online activity and notifying you of any worrying conduct (Henares-Montiel et al. 2022).

Teach your child: Instill the value of online safety in your child and urge them to speak up if they encounter or see cyberbullying.

Use parental controls: Many gadgets and social media sites provide parental controls that let you limit your child's access to content or how much time they spend online.

Report cyberbullying: If you have reason to believe that your child is a victim of cyberbullying, you should inform the relevant parties, such as the school, the social media site, or police enforcement.

Cyberbullying can have serious social and psychological harm to the victims; it is vital for parents to take this seriously and to address cyberbullying as soon as possible (Alfakeh et al., 2021).

12.3.2 Role of Teachers in Preventing Cyberbullying

Teachers can take the following actions to stop cyberbullying.

Education of students: Students can be educated by teachers about the negative effects of cyberbullying and the value of showing kindness and respect online (Kim et al. 2021).

Encourage open communication: Teachers can promote open communication by establishing a secure, encouraging environment in the classroom where students feel at ease sharing their experiences and asking for assistance if they are being bullied. Teachers can keep an eye on their students' internet conduct and take appropriate action if they notice any worrying behavior.

Use of Software: Detect and prevent cyberbullying with the aid of monitoring software. Teachers can use monitoring software to do this.

Working with parents: To combat cyberbullying and promote online safety, teachers can collaborate with parents.

Report cyberbullying: Teachers should notify the proper authorities, such as the school administration or law enforcement, if they become aware of any cyberbullying involving students.

Teachers can make the internet environment safer and more encouraging for all students by putting these preventative strategies into practice (Ademiluyi et al., 2022).

12.3.3 Role of Social Media Network Administrators in Preventing Cyberbullying

Network administrators can take the following actions to stop cyberbullying on their social media networks or in their online communities.

Setup ground rule based on quality: Establish clear rules and guidelines that forbid cyberbullying and other forms of online harassment. Admins should implement these rules and guidelines. All community members should be made aware of these regulations in a straightforward manner.

Using AI-based moderation tools: Using moderating tools will help admins find and delete content that contains cyberbullying (Maheswaran & Rajamani, 2022). These tools include automated filters and human moderators.

Content promotion: Admins can promote content that encourages compassion and respect, and they can award users who uphold these principles. Admins can offer users who are experiencing cyberbullying resources and support, including reporting mechanisms and information on how to obtain help.

Liaison with other support groups: Admins can collaborate with outside groups to combat cyberbullying and advance online safety, such as schools and law enforcement.

Support and resources: Social media platforms can offer users who are experiencing cyberbullying tools for reporting incidents and information on how to receive assistance (Fazeen et al., 2011).

12.3.4 ROLE OF SOCIAL MEDIA PLATFORMS IN PREVENTING CYBERBULLYING

Social media platforms can make the online environment safer and more gratifying for all users by putting these prevention measures in place. Social media platforms can take the following actions to stop cyberbullying:

Adopt stringent community standards: Social media platforms should have explicit policies prohibiting cyberbullying and other types of online abuse.

Utilize moderating tools: To detect and delete information that promotes cyberbullying, social media platforms can make use of tools like automated filters and human moderators.

Encourage positive behavior: Social media platforms can promote content that encourages compassion and respect, as well as rewarding users that uphold these principles.

Collaboration: To combat cyberbullying and advance online safety, social media platforms can collaborate with outside entities like law enforcement and educational institutions.

Proactive attitude: Social media platforms and their admins must be proactive in combating cyberbullying since it can have major repercussions for those who are targeted (Huang et al., 2021).

12.4   GRAPH THEORY, COMPLEX NETWORK ANALYSIS, ARTIFICIAL INTELLIGENCE, AND MACHINE LEARNING

12.4.1   A BRIEF BACKGROUND IN GRAPH THEORY AND COMPLEX NETWORK ANALYSIS

In graph theory, complex networks are represented as graphs where nodes represent entities (such as individuals, organizations, or cities) and edges represent connections (such as friendships, business partnerships, or roads). By studying these graphs through techniques like centrality measures, clustering coefficients, and degree distributions, researchers can gain insights into how the system functions, who holds the most influence, and how resilient it may be under different conditions (Gongane et al., 2022; Rajamani & Iyer, 2022).

A graph is made up of a collection of nodes, also known as vertices, and a set of connecting links or edges or ties. The entities in the problem like webpages, cities, and molecules are represented by the vertices, and their connections are shown by the edges like HTML links in a web documents, roads between cities, and bonds between molecules. The discipline of mathematics that studies networks is called graph theory (Newman, 2010).

The difference between graph and network is that graph is an abstract mathematical object, existing on a paper or a computer, while network is the real-world analogy or application of a graph. Programmatically, a graph is represented by $G = (V, E)$, where V is the vertex set $V = \{v_1, v_2, v_3, v_4...\}$ and edge set $E = \{e_1, e_2, e_3, e_4, e_5...\}$. The number of edges connected to a node is called the degree of that node or vertex (Newman, 2010).

In many real-life networks like for example on social media, you can always find a group of people (groups) that are well connected to each other, like people who like gardening and follow specific gardening pages or posts or experts. They are referred to as clusters or communities. Networks can be visualized using several programming languages using libraries like Python, C++, and R language. There are many free software editors which can also be used by a nonprogrammer to visualize networks like yEd graph editor. Using computers, we can simulate complex or cybernetic networks and simulate dynamical processes on these networks. Visualization of a network helps in understanding the structure of a network and elucidating network connectivity and communities in an intuitive way. Analysis of complicated graphs or networks using a variety of algorithms and techniques is called complex network analysis. Optimization of paths and properties of vertices using algorithms is called graph optimization (Barabasi, 2002).

12.4.2 INTRODUCTION TO COMPLEX NETWORK ANALYSIS

A subfield of network science called complex network analysis studies the modeling and analysis of complicated networks. These networks frequently exhibit complex behavior and have a lot of nodes (also known as vertices) and edges (also known as connections) (Newman, 2003).

Understanding a network's basic structure and how it affects the behavior of its nodes is one of the key aims of complex network analysis. Analysts do this by spotting patterns and trends in the network using a variety of methods, including centrality metrics, network motifs, and community discovery algorithms (Butts, 2006).

Based on their connections to other nodes, centrality measurements are used to determine which nodes in a network are the most significant. For instance, because it has more links to other nodes in the network, a node with a high degree of centrality can be regarded as being more significant (Reda Alhajj & Jon Rokne, 2014).

Network motifs are connectivity patterns that show up more frequently than would be predicted by chance in a network. These patterns can disclose crucial details about the way the network works and how certain nodes interact with one another (Barabasi & Albert, 1999).

To find groups of nodes within a network that is more closely connected to one another than to the rest of the network, community discovery algorithms are utilized. These communities can be utilized to comprehend the overall structure and operation of the network (Lancichinetti & Fortunato, 2009).

In conclusion, complex network analysis is an effective method for comprehending the dynamics and behavior of complex systems and has applications in a variety of disciplines, such as biology, sociology, and computer science.

12.4.3 ARTIFICIAL INTELLIGENCE TO MITIGATE CYBERBULLYING

One potential use for AI in combatting cyberbullying is by implementing monitoring systems that flag suspicious behavior such as frequent unsolicited messages or posts. These algorithms could be trained to detect patterns associated with bullying tactics like harsh language or repetitive contact attempts (Milosevic et al., 2022). Another approach would involve using machine learning models to identify specific users who engage in abusive behavior through analysis of large amounts of data from sources such as chat logs or social media interactions. Once potential cyberbullies have been identified, they could receive automated warnings or notifications reminding them of proper online conduct standards (Rajamani & Iyer, 2023a). Additionally, AI technologies could aid in providing emotional support for victims of cyberbullying via text-based therapy systems or virtual reality exposure therapies designed to desensitize individuals to fearful situations like encountering threatening messages or images online (Sánchez-Medina et al., 2020).

12.4.4 MACHINE LEARNING ALGORITHMS TO MITIGATE CYBERBULLYING

Machine learning algorithms have been used in several approaches to identify and mitigate cyberbullying.

12.4.4.1 Content Analysis and Moderation

This approach involves analyzing text data from social media, online forums, chat rooms, emails, etc., using natural language processing (NLP) techniques and machine learning algorithms like topic modeling, sentiment analysis, and classification models (Rajamani and Iyer 2023b). These methods aim at identifying harmful content by detecting profanity, hate speech, racist, sexist, or discriminatory language among others (Martínez-Valderrey et al., 2023).

By using natural language processing and computer vision techniques, AIs can automatically detect and remove harmful content from platforms such as social media sites, forums, or chat apps, before human moderators review them. This speeds up the process, enabling quick removal of offensive posts or messages (Gongane et al., 2022).

12.4.4.2 Behavior Analysis

Another approach involves tracking users' behaviors, activities, and interactions across multiple online channels and sessions by building user profiles over time. By leveraging supervised learning techniques like decision trees, random forest classifiers, support vector machines (SVM), artificial neural networks (ANN), etc., researchers develop features, such as frequency of posting, number of followers/friends, type of messages sent/received, participation patterns in online communities, etc., serve as predictors for cyberbullying detection. Some works combine both content and behavior analyses to achieve better results (Rajamani & Iyer, 2023a).

12.4.4.3 Collaborative Filtering

Collaborative filtering-based systems analyze previous instances of identified cyberbullying cases; they recommend actions to other members of their community after comparing them against previous instances of cyberbullying hate text. Machine learning techniques can assist researchers and experts who develop interventions or educational materials aimed at reducing cyberbullying. These initiatives often involve identifying common risk factors, creating awareness campaigns, or training people in safer online practices.

12.4.4.4 Automatic Monitoring

With machine learning algorithms, platforms can track patterns of behavior among users. If someone frequently engages in harassing activities (e.g., sending abusive messages), they may receive a warning or have their account suspended.

12.4.4.5 Personalized Filtering

Some systems use machine learning models to analyze user preferences and behavior, filtering out unwanted or upsetting interactions. For example, Facebook allows individuals to hide certain keywords or topics they do not want to see in their news feed.

12.4.4.6 Sentiment Analysis

By analyzing the tone and context of messages or posts, machines can identify potentially hurtful language or behaviors before they cause harm. People responsible for these actions might then be approached by a counselor or offered resources to prevent future incidents (Milosevic et al., 2022).

Incorporating artificial intelligence into existing efforts against cyberbullying could make a positive impact. It is important to recognize potential risks associated with relying heavily on technology or automated decision-making processes (Neelakandan et al., 2022).

12.5 METHODOLOGY – GRAPH-OPTIMIZATION ALGORITHMS FOR ANOMALY DETECTION ON A NETWORK

For anomalous network activities, there are various kinds of graph-optimization techniques for detection as follows.

12.5.1 Shortest Path Algorithms

Algorithms that discover the shortest path between two nodes in a network are known as shortest path algorithms. Edgar Dijkstra's algorithm and A* search are two examples.

12.5.2 Minimum-Spanning Tree

The techniques known as minimum-spanning trees identify a subset of the edges in a graph such that all the vertices are connected, and the overall weight of the edges is kept to a minimum. Examples consist of the Kruskal and Prim algorithms.

12.5.3 Methods for Maximum Flow

These algorithms determine how much flow can be delivered from a source node to a sink node in a graph. Common examples are the Ford-Fulkerson algorithm and the Edmonds-Karp algorithm.

12.5.4 Network-Flow Algorithms

These methods locate a path through a network that satisfies a set of conditions, such as edge-capacity limitations. The simplex algorithm and the primal-dual algorithm are two such cases.

12.5.5 Algorithms for Finding Matches in Graphs

A matching in a graph is a subset of the edges where no two edges share an endpoint, namely: the Gale-Shapley algorithm and the Hungarian algorithm.

12.5.6 Classic "Traveling Salesman Problem" (TSP)

These methods identify the route that traverses every node in a network precisely once before retracing the steps to the origin. This paradigm determines the shortest path that stops at each node in the network, like a salesman who must tour all the customers but must use shortest possible path to save his time and gasoline/petrol. Two common examples are the nearest neighbor algorithm and the brute-force algorithm.

12.5.7 Algorithms for Finding Matches in Graphs

A matching in a graph is a subset of the edges where no two edges share an endpoint such as the Gale-Shapley algorithm and the Hungarian algorithm. There are other further graph-optimization strategies, including graph partitioning, graph coloring, and others.

There are several ways that complex network analysis can be utilized to find instances of cyberbullying in a network. The following are some detection paradigms using complex network analysis.

12.5.8 COMMUNITY-DETECTION ALGORITHMS

Since stalking act frequently involves a group of people cooperating, seeing communities inside a network can help spot possible nefarious activity. Communities inside a network can be found using algorithms like the Girvan-Newman algorithm and the Louvain approach. Girvan-Newman algorithm is the best-known method for this purpose which involves iteratively calculating the edge betweenness centrality of all the edges and then removes the edges with the highest value of centrality. This will increase the components and partition the graph (Lancichinetti & Fortunato, 2009).

12.5.9 ANOMALY-DETECTION ALGORITHMS

Cyberbullies frequently behave differently from other users in the network. Unusual network behavior that can point to fraudulent activities can be found using anomaly-detection techniques such as the isolation forest or the one-class support vector machine.

12.5.10 LINK-PREDICTION ALGORITHMS

Cyberbullies frequently use fictitious or deceptive links or names, inside a network to conceal their operations. You can utilize link-prediction algorithms to find connections in a network that might be cyberbullies, such as the Adamic-Adar index or the Jaccard coefficient.

12.5.11 EGOCENTRICITY OR CENTRALITY MEASURES OF NODES

A node's importance in a network is gauged by its degree centrality, which is dependent on the connections it has. High-degree centrality nodes are thought to be prominent or central nodes within the network. The most central nodes in a network can be found using centrality metrics such as degree centrality or betweenness centrality (Reda Alhajj & Jon Rokne, 2014).

It is worth noting that these are just a few examples of the ways in which network science algorithms can be used to detect nefarious activities. There are many other algorithms and approaches that can also be applied to this problem (Degenne & Forse, 1990).

12.6 PRACTICAL EXAMPLE OF DETECTING CYBERBULLYING USING NETWORK PARADIGM

Consider the scenario where we are social media network administrators, and we want to screen for personal accounts that may be involved in cyberbullying. First, we use community-detection algorithms to detect communities, which will essentially place the bullies and the victims in the same community. This happens because the stalker essentially tags or comments or harasses the victim and stays in close-network proximity to carry out nefarious activities. Second, we must determine degree centrality of accounts in the screened community, and we can then search for nodes with a particularly high-degree centrality.

12.6.1 Network Preprocessing

Preparation of network data for analysis if the first step is detecting cyberbullying using complex network analysis. Depending on the choice algorithm, we might need to clean up and prepare the data by deleting self-loops, eliminating nodes with low degree or less connectivity as they do not have much significance, or doing additional data preparation and cleaning (Rajamani & Iyer, 2022).

12.6.2 Community-Detection Algorithms

The principle of community-detection algorithms is to find nodes or groups of nodes, called communities, that do not fit in well with the rest of the network. This can be helpful for spotting cyberbullying, criminal activity, terrorists, hackers, fraudsters, cyberattacks, or other kinds of nefarious behavior within the network (Reda Alhajj & Jon Rokne, 2014).

Algorithms for community detection are used to locate communities or groupings within a network. They are frequently used to examine social networks, biological networks, and other networks in which the nodes stand in for people or other things and the edges signify the connections or relationships between them. Implementing the algorithm for community detection involves dividing the network into communities. Community-wise breaking-up the network can be done in a variety of ways, as follows.

12.6.2.1 Modularity-Maximization Algorithm

A graph-partitioning community-detection approach called modularity maximization can be used to bullying and stalking in a network. This is the process of finding the communities that maximize the percentage of intracommunity (links inside a given community) edges while minimizing the percentage of intercommunity edges (links between the communities). The network is split up into communities that increase the percentage of intracommunity edges while minimizing the percentage of intercommunity edges to achieve its desired results. Because nefarious networks frequently have a high degree of intercommunity connectivity and a low degree of intracommunity connectivity, this can be helpful for spotting such activities.

A graph's modularity can be increased using a variety of approaches. The Louvain algorithm, a heuristic algorithm that iteratively optimizes a graph's modularity score by shifting nodes between communities, is one popular technique. The Louvain algorithm begins with each node in its own community, combines communities iteratively based on the modularity score, and then starts over. The leading Eigenvector approach, the Infomap methodology, and the Map Equation are other examples of modularity maximization algorithms which can be used to detect communities.

It is crucial to remember that modularity maximization may not always work as a cyberbullying-detection strategy and can sometimes result in false positives or false negatives. As a result, it is crucial to verify any suspected fraudulent communities and to carefully consider the algorithm's limitations when interpreting the findings (Degenne & Forse, 1990).

12.6.2.2 An Example of Community-Detection Using Python 3.5′s NetworkX Module

A method in the *NetworkX* package called *"nx.community. modularity_max. greedy_modularity_ communities(Graph)"* can be used to identify communities in a network that maximizes the modularity score. The modularity score is a measure of the density of connections within a community compared to the density of connections between communities. A high modularity score indicates that the communities in the graph are well-defined and distinct from each other. This function takes a graph as input and returns a list of sets, where each set represents a community in the graph. The function works by iteratively merging communities based on the modularity score, starting with each node in its own community. Imagine a community or network of crime depicted by Figure 12.1. You must import the *NetworkX* library and create a graph before you can use *"max.greedy_modularity_communities."* The function can then be called with the graph as an argument (Hagberg et al., 2008) (Figure 12.2).

For instance, we could use this function to find communities in a graph using NetworkX.

The output of this program will be *"person: Suresh in community: a,"* indicating that all the nodes or accounts *"suresh"* in the graph belong to the same community of bullies with our assigned label *"a"* (Hagberg et al., 2008).

You can also use the *community.label_propagation* function to find communities in a graph using label propagation. This function takes a graph as input and returns a dictionary, where the keys are the nodes in the graph and the values are the labels (communities) assigned to each node (Reda Alhajj & Jon Rokne, 2014).

This will output *"person: Rudra in community: b"* mapping each node or account (*"rudra"*) to our label or community *"b,"* indicating that all the nodes or accounts in the graph have been assigned to the same community (Reda Alhajj & Jon Rokne, 2014).

FIGURE 12.1 Spectrum of online behaviors that constitute cyberbullying and cause trauma to the victims; author's original illustration made using Canva Pro (Hinduja & Patchin, 2014; Aboujaoude & Savage, 2023).

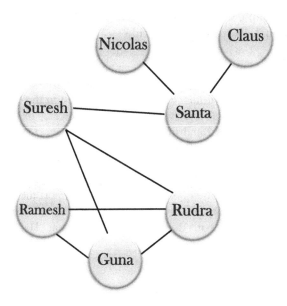

FIGURE 12.2   A simple example of seven individuals, who are segregated into two communities; we can create such a graph using NetworkX and delineate the communities using various complex analytical algorithms such as modularity maximization and label propagation. The working code for drawing this graph is also provided in Table 12.1.

TABLE 12.1

Creating a Simple Network Graph Using NetworkX and Matplotlib Modules

```
#Install these modules in python 3.5 and above python -m pip install
#network, and python -m pip install matplotlib
#Import network, matplotlib modules
import networkx as nx
import matplotlib.pyplot as plt
# Create a graph
G = nx.Graph()
#Initilalize options for the graph plot
options = { 'node_color': 'yellow','node_size':
 700,'alpha':0.9,'width': 1,
'edge_color':'red',}
# Add edges to the graph, create the community shown in figure 12.1
G.add_edges_from([('Santa', 'Claus'), ('Santa', 'Nicolas'), ('Suresh',
 'Santa'), ('Suresh', 'Guna'), ('Suresh', 'Rudra'), ('Ramesh',
 'Guna'), ('Ramesh', 'Rudra'),('Rudra', 'Guna'),])
nx.draw_circular(G, with_labels=True,**options) #font_weight='9')
```

TABLE 12.2
Simple Community Detection Using NetworkX Module greedy _modularity_ communities Function

```
import networkx as nx
# Create a graph
G = nx.Graph()
# Add edges to the graph, create the community shown in figure 12.1
# Add edges to the graph, create the community shown in figure 12.1
G.add_edges_from([('Santa', 'Claus'), ('Santa', 'Nicolas'), ('Suresh',
 'Santa'), ('Suresh', 'Guna'), ('Suresh', 'Rudra'), ('Ramesh',
 'Guna'), ('Ramesh', 'Rudra'),('Rudra', 'Guna'),])
nx.draw_circular(G, with_labels=True,**options) #font_weight='9')
# the number of edges incident to Santa is 3 Claus, Nicolas, Suresh
print(G.degree['Santa'])
# Find communities in the graph using the greedy modularity
 maximization algorithm
communities = nx.community.modularity_max.
 greedy_modularity_communities(G)
#Chr value of lower case "a" which is our assigned label for first
 community.
#This can be any label, but this code does automatic assignment.
#So next label is community is "b" then "c","d","e","f".. so on for
 any size
i=97
for persons in communities:
    print(f'====Community {chr(i)} By modularity maximization
algorithm ====')
    for person in persons:
        print(f' person: {person} in community:   {chr(i)}')
    i+=1
```

12.6.2.3 Hierarchical Clustering

Periodically separating the communities with the highest intercommunity edge density, the network is divided into a hierarchy of increasingly fine-grained communities is a process called hierarchical clustering. By treating the communities as network compressions, this probabilistic approach aims to determine the network's minimal description length.

12.6.2.4 Louvain's Method

The Louvain method is a quick, greedy optimization procedure (Table 12.2) that includes incrementally enhancing the network's modularity.

12.6.2.5 Label-Propagation Algorithm

A semisupervised machine-learning approach called label propagation presented in Table 12.3 spreads a limited set of labeled data points' labels across the remaining data points in the data set. Label propagation is based on the community membership of

TABLE 12.3

Simple Community Detection Using NetworkX Asynchronous Label _ propagation Algorithm

```
import networkx as nx
# Create a graph
G = nx.Graph()
# Add edges to the graph, create the community shown in figure 12.1
# Add edges to the graph, create the community shown in figure 12.1
G.add_edges_from([('Santa', 'Claus'), ('Santa', 'Nicolas'), ('Suresh',
 'Santa'), ('Suresh', 'Guna'), ('Suresh', 'Rudra'), ('Ramesh',
 'Guna'), ('Ramesh', 'Rudra'),('Rudra', 'Guna'),])
nx.draw_circular(G, with_labels=True,**options) #font_weight='9')
# the number of edges incident to Santa is 3 Claus, Nicolas, Suresh
print(G.degree['Santa'])
# Find communities in the graph using the greedy modularity
 maximization algorithm
communities = nx.community.label_propagation.asyn_lpa_communities(G)
#Chr value of lower case "a" which is our assigned label for first
 community.
#This can be any label, but this code does automatic assignment.
#So next label is community is "b" then "c","d","e","f".. so on for
 any size
i=97
for persons in communities:
    print(f'====Community {chr(i)} By Asynchronous label propogation
 algorithm (async_lpa) ====')
    for person in persons:
        print(f' person: {person} in community:   {chr(i)}')
    i+=1
```

nearby nodes; this straightforward, effective technique spreads labels or community membership information throughout the network. It operates by initially giving each node in the graph a distinct label, which is then iteratively updated based on the labels of the nodes around it. When there is a small amount of labeled data available but a huge amount of unlabeled data, this straightforward and effective approach can be utilized. A weighted average, where the weights are determined by how similar the data points are to one another, can be used to do this. Till the labels of the data points converge or attain an acceptable level of accuracy, keep iterating. For a variety of tasks, including classification, clustering, and regression, label propagation can be utilized. It is predicated on the notion that close data points' labels are probably going to be similar.

This involves the following steps: 1. Pick a sizable collection of unlabeled data points and a small collection of labeled data points. 2. Initialize the unlabeled data points' labels to match those of the labeled data points to which they are most comparable. 3. Update each node's label to reflect the label that is most frequently used by its neighbors by iterating across the graph's nodes. 4. Keep iterating, until the labels of the nodes converge or attain an acceptable level of accuracy (Everett, 1985).

12.6.2.6 Stochastic Block Model Method

This probabilistic model proposes that the network is constructed by connecting nodes more frequently inside communities than across communities once nodes are randomly assigned to communities.

12.6.2.7 Spectral Clustering

Spectral clustering is a mathematical technique that includes locating the eigenvectors of the graph's Laplacian matrix and using them to group the network's nodes.

There are other additional community-detection techniques suggested in the literature, each with distinct advantages and disadvantages (Al-Harigy et al. 2022). The specific properties of the network and the investigator's study objectives frequently influence the community-detection algorithm that is chosen.

12.6.3 EGOCENTRICITY-DETECTION ALGORITHMS USING PYTHON 3.5'S NETWORKX MODULE

After isolating the communities in a network, we examine the network to check if any nodes or clusters of nodes or communities do not seem to fit in with the rest of the network. These nodes could be revealing signs of nefarious behavior.

12.6.3.1 Degree Centrality

Degree centrality can be used to pinpoint nodes that may be implicated in staking in the context of cyberbullying detection. A network's central nodes can be used to identify probable cyberbullies activity because cyberbullies frequently play a central role in a network. Due to their greater number of connections to other nodes in the network, these nodes may be more inclined to engage in nefarious activities. It is important to keep in mind that degree centrality is merely one indicator of a node's importance and may not necessarily be the most useful indicator for spotting fraud. In this situation, other metrics such as betweenness centrality or eigenvector centrality may also be helpful. To effectively identify cyberbullying activity, it is also crucial to consider additional elements, such as the type of connections between nodes (Reda Alhajj & Jon Rokne, 2014).

12.6.3.2 Radial Measures of Centrality

Radial measures of centrality are measures of a node's centrality by examining routes that begin from a node and span outward toward other vertices in a radial fashion. These are degree, closeness, and eigenvector centrality (Borgatti & Everett, 1993). Degree of a node, explained in the introduction section, is the simplest radial measure. Closeness of a node is the sum of the shortest path of a given node to all remaining nodes on a network. This measure does not increase with size of the network making distinction between the nodes a difficult prospect. Eigenvector centrality of a node is the measures of the extent to which a node is connected to other well-connected nodes. This is computed by finding the principal eigenvector of the adjacency matrix of a graph. There are many computationally efficient algorithms for large sparse matrices. Eigenvector centrality remains stable for large networks and hence a usable measure of centrality in case of large networks (Figure 12.3).

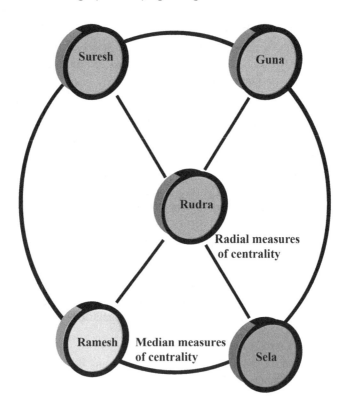

FIGURE 12.3 Radial measures of centrality and median measures of centrality are two measures of centrality of a node on a network. These are measure relative to a given node "Rudra" in this sample. Betweenness measures the connectivity of node to its neighbors and radial measures, degree, closeness, and eigenvector centrality of the radial distance to other nodes.

12.6.3.3 Median Measures of Centrality

Median measures of centrality are measures of a node's centrality by its longitudinal connectedness with other nodes (Borgatti & Everett, 1993). The most used medial measure is betweenness. Betweenness is number of times a vertex is found on the shortest route that connects any two other vertices. This can be computed using Ulrik Brandes algorithm. Cohesion is the extent of connectedness of whole network as opposed to a node. Cohesion matrix is the measure of cohesion. The adjacency matrix of a graph is the measure of cohesion in the simplest form. Connectedness and compactness are two more measures of cohesion of a network (Reda Alhajj & Jon Rokne, 2014).

12.6.3.4 Betweenness Centrality

The percentage of all shortest paths that pass through a node is thus considered to represent its betweenness centrality. The term "betweenness" in network analysis refers to a measurement of a node's significance (or vertex) in a network based on its capacity to link other nodes. Betweenness centrality counts the instances in which a node spans the shortest distance between two other nodes. A node with a high betweenness centrality is frequently referred to as a key connector or hub since it has a significant impact on how other nodes in the network communicate (Longobardi et al. 2021). To determine betweenness centrality, we first list every shortest path in the network between any two nodes. Then we count how many times each node appears on the shortest pathways for each node.

To understand the function that nodes play in the communication and information flow inside a network, such as gatekeepers or major influencers, betweenness centrality is frequently employed to identify significant nodes in a network. To construct effective communication and transportation networks, it is also used to locate network bottlenecks or weaknesses.

It may be feasible to find patterns of nefarious behavior that are hidden when examining isolated transactions or nodes by identifying nodes with high betweenness centrality. Due to the high betweenness centrality of the criminal networks, it may be simpler to trace the flow of resources or information through the network and spot any irregularities in situations where the crime involves the manipulation of resources or information moving through the network (Barabasi, 2002).

12.6.3.5 An Example of Centrality Detection Using Python 3.5's NetworkX Module

A method in the *NetworkX* package called "*nx.eigenvector_centrality*" can be used to calculate eigenvector centrality of a node or account in a network. The following code presented in Table 12.4 creates a path graph of alphabets from A to P, then proceeds to calculate the eigenvector centrality of each node, and plots the values in a bar graph (Hagberg et al., 2008).

The output of the code is an image which is depicted in the figure; it can be observed from the plot that the nodes 'G,' 'H,' and 'I' have highest eigenvector centrality as these lie at the center of the circular path of the graph and inferred to have maximum reach to all the nodes.

12.6.4 CONTINUE INVESTIGATION AND NETWORK SURVEILLANCE

It is vital to remember that these algorithms may result in false positives or false negatives because they are not perfect. As a result, it is crucial to confirm any abnormalities found and to carefully consider the algorithm's limits when interpreting the outcomes. These methods are not fool-proof methods as they are based on stochastic methods. There can be many instances of false-positive detections using the previously outlined steps. False-positive detections can entail compiling more information, conducting further research, or speaking with subject matter experts. Further, many cyberbullying instances may also go undetected using these methods (or false-negatives), which maybe be curtailed by repeating steps 1, 2, and 3. Thus, continued surveillance of network and optimization of our choice algorithms based on given network is essentially day-to-day activity of a network administrator in detecting and weeding out cyberbullying (Vasudev, 2006).

TABLE 12.4

Eigenvector Centrality Detection, Graphing Centrality Measures and Using *Python 3.5's NetworkX* Module

```python
#Imports Networkx, string, and matplotlib modules. String is built-in
 Python module does NOT need installation
import networkx as nx
from matplotlib import pyplot as plt
import string
#initialize plot options
options = {'node_color': 'yellow','node_size':
 700,'alpha':0.9,'width': 1,  'edge_color':'red',}
# load A to P in a list
list_vertex=list(string.ascii_uppercase)[0:16]
#Initialize networkx Graph
G = nx. path_graph(list_vertex)
# compute eigenvector centrality of each node
centrality = nx.eigenvector_centrality(G)
#converting input dictionary values to a list
y = list(centrality.values())
x = list(centrality.keys())
fig = plt.figure("Degree of a random graph", figsize=(8, 8))
# Create a gridspec for adding subplots of different sizes
axgrid = fig.add_gridspec(5, 4)
ax0 = fig.add_subplot(axgrid[0:3, :])
nx.draw_shell(G, with_labels=True,**options) #font_weight='9')
ax0.set_title("Connected components of G")
ax0.set_axis_off()
ax1 = fig.add_subplot(axgrid[3:, :2])
degree_sequence = sorted((d for n, d in G.degree()), reverse=True)
dmax = max(degree_sequence)
ax1.plot(degree_sequence, "b-", marker="o")
ax1.set_title("Degree Rank Plot")
ax1.set_ylabel("Degree")
ax1.set_xlabel("Rank")
ax2 = fig.add_subplot(axgrid[3:, 2:])
ax2.bar(x,y)
#*np.unique(degree_sequence, return_counts=True))
ax2.set_title("Eigenvector Centrality")
ax2.set_xlabel("Vertex")
ax2.set_ylabel("Centrality")
fig.tight_layout()
plt.savefig("Centrality.png", dpi=300)
plt.show()
```

It should be noted that these are only a few instances of how network science algorithms might be applied to uncover cyberbullying. There are other additional methods and strategies that can be applied.

12.7 NETWORK MOTIFS TO HIDE CRIME

Network motifs are connectivity patterns that appear more frequently than would be predicted by chance inside a network. They have been employed in many disciplines, including biology, economics, and social networks, and can be used to pinpoint functional modules or paths within a network (Ranney et al. 2021). Network motifs have the potential to be employed in the context of fraud detection to find unusual patterns of activity or interactions within a network that might signify fraudulent behavior (Vasudev, 2006).

12.7.1 AN EXAMPLES OF NETWORK MOTIFS TO HIDE CRIME

A network motif known as a "feed-forward loop," for instance, consists of three nodes connected in a specific fashion, with the output of one node acting as the input for the following node. This kind of motif, which has been seen in biological and social networks, can be employed to boost signals or carry out computational operations. A feed-forward loop may be used to amplify or hide fraudulent transactions; therefore if one is seen in a financial network, it may be possible to utilize it to spot fraud (Reda Alhajj & Jon Rokne, 2014).

Other network patterns, such as "bistables," which are structures that may transition between two stable states, and "oscillators," which are structures that can produce periodic signals, may be helpful for detecting fraud.

12.7.2 MECHANISMS OF A FEED-FORWARD NETWORK MOTIF

A feed-forward network motif consists of three nodes connected in a specific way. The "input node," the initial node, is where inputs from outside sources are received. The second node, sometimes known as the "output node," takes inputs from the first node and bases its output on those inputs. The third node, known as the "regulatory node," uses the inputs it gets from both the input node and the output node to control the information flow between the two nodes (Rajamani & Iyer, 2022). Figure 12.4 depicts the feed-forward loop motif.

According to this motif, the regulatory node receives its input from the regulatory node's output node and its output from the output node. The regulatory node modulates the information flow between the input and output nodes using the inputs it receives (Alsawalqa, 2021).

Networks of all kinds, such as social, biological, and economic ones, contain feed-forward loops. They have been seen in a wide range of devices and can be employed to boost signals or carry out computations. Feed-forward loops may be used to amplify or mask illegal transactions in the context of fraud detection, and they may also be used to spot fraudulent activities within a network (Gomez et al., 2022).

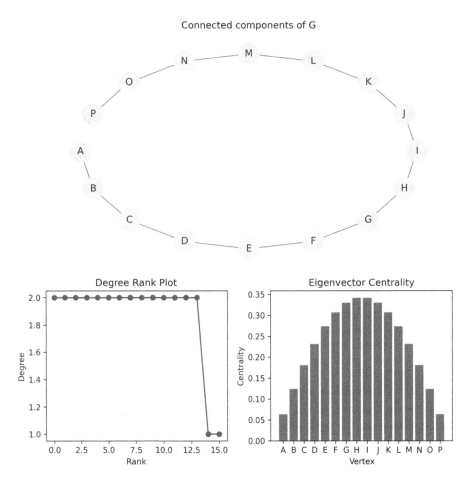

FIGURE 12.4 A simple example of path network from A to P ($N = 16$), shown above with measures plot of measures of centrality, namely, degree and eigenvector centrality. Plot of rank of node versus degree on left; it is to be noted that most nodes except "A" and "P" have degree of 2, and the bar plot of eigenvector centrality versus nodes, middle nodes "H" and "I," have maximum eigenvector centrality as they have access to maximum nodes being in the middle of the path graph.

12.7.3 FEED-FORWARD NETWORK MOTIF FOR CRIME AND EVASION OF DETECTION

By amplifying or hiding illegal transactions, a feed-forward network pattern may be used to hide criminal activities within a network. As an illustration, if a group of people were involved in a fraudulent operation, they would utilize a feed-forward loop to magnify the signals connected to their illegal transactions, making it harder for outsiders to identify the fraud (Everett, 1985) (Figure 12.5).

As an alternative, the feed-forward loop could be utilized to mask the fraudulent activity by generating a "smoke screen" of lawful transactions to hide the

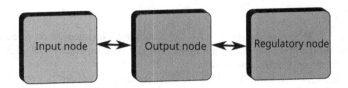

FIGURE 12.5 Network motifs can be tell-tale signs of nefarious activities and crime networks, a motif called feed-forward loop could be sign of fraud on a network. This picture illustrates the schema of such a network motif.

illegal activity. The regulatory node could be used to regulate the information flow between the two nodes, allowing the illicit transactions to be masked within the greater volume of legitimate transactions, for instance, if the input node of the feed-forward loop represents legitimate transactions and the output node represents illicit transactions. It is important to note that the potential employment of feed-forward loops or other network motifs to hide criminal conduct is completely conjectural, and there is no proof that such a plan has ever been successfully carried out. These kinds of motifs might be utilized to spot recurring patterns of conduct that might point to fraud (Lloret-Irles et al., 2022).

12.8 LIMITATIONS OF THIS REVIEW

This systematic review information and recommendations should be interpreted within a limited framework. Perceiving cyberbullying as a phenomenon is related to peer interaction and anonymity is an oversimplification. In contrast, the problem of cyberbullying arises due to a complex interaction of personal psychology, internet access, social media validation, social perception, family, and social media peer approval.

12.9 CONCLUSION

Cyberbullying is a modern menace and a misuse of technology to intimidate, harass, humiliate, and dehumanize others. As the technology of criminals evolves, so must the tactics and strategies to deal with such nefarious activities. In this compilation, a brief overview of cyberbullying is provided and followed by an account of steps to curb cyberbullying by network administrators, social media community administrators, teachers, and parents.

Complex analysis is the use of established and well-known network-analytical techniques to identify cyberbullying activities (Ngo et al. 2021). This is accomplished by establishing communities in the complex network and computing several centrality measures of offending node or account. To illustrate the actual process of complex network analysis, a few NetworkX working program samples are also included. These are based on simplified networks for the ease of comprehension. This is followed by continuous network surveillance to identify future culprits.

REFERENCES

Aboujaoude, E., & Savage, M. W. (2023). Cyberbullying: Next-generation research. *World Psychiatry : Official Journal of the World Psychiatric Association (WPA)*, *22*(1), 45–46. https://doi.org/10.1002/wps.21040

Ademiluyi, A., Li, C., & Park, A. (2022). Implications and preventions of cyberbullying and social exclusion in social media: Systematic review. *JMIR Formative Research*, *6*(1), e30286. https://doi.org/10.2196/30286

Alfakeh, S. A., Alghamdi, A. A., Kouzaba, K. A., Altaifi, M. I., Abu-Alamah, S. D., & Salamah, M. M. (2021). Parents' perception of cyberbullying of their children in Saudi Arabia. *Journal of Family & Community Medicine*, *28*(2), 117–124. https://doi.org/10.4103/jfcm.JFCM_516_20

Al-Harigy, L. M., Al-Nuaim, H. A., Moradpoor, N., & Tan, Z. (2022). Building towards Automated cyberbullying detection: A comparative analysis. *Computational Intelligence and Neuroscience*, *2022*, 4794227. https://doi.org/10.1155/2022/4794227

Alhajj, R. & Rokne, J. (2014). *Encyclopedia of Social Network Analysis and Mining* (1st ed.). Springer. doi:10.1007/978-1-4614-6170-8

Alsawalqa, R. O. (2021). Cyberbullying, social stigma, and self-esteem: The impact of COVID-19 on students from East and Southeast Asia at the University of Jordan. *Heliyon*, *7*(4), e06711. https://doi.org/10.1016/j.heliyon.2021.e06711

Armitage, R. (2021). Bullying in children: Impact on child health. *BMJ Paediatrics Open*, *5*(1), e000939. https://doi.org/10.1136/bmjpo-2020-000939

Barabasi, A. L. (2002). *Linked: The new science of networks*. Perseus Books Group.

Barabasi, A. L. & Albert, R. (1999). Emergence of scaling in random networks. *Science*, *286*, 509–512.

Barlett, C. P. (2023). Cyberbullying as a learned behavior: Theoretical and applied implications. *Children (Basel, Switzerland)*, *10*(2). https://doi.org/10.3390/children10020325

Bitar, Z., Elias, M.-B., Malaeb, D., Hallit, S., & Obeid, S. (2023). Is cyberbullying perpetration associated with anxiety, depression and suicidal ideation among lebanese adolescents? Results from a cross-sectional study. *BMC Psychology*, *11*(1), 53. https://doi.org/10.1186/s40359-023-01091-9

Borgatti, S. P. & Everett, M. G. (1993). Two algorithms for computing regular equivalence. *Social Networks*, *15*, 361–376.

Butts, C. T. (2006). Exact bounds for degree centralization. *Social Networks*, *28*, 283–296.

Camacho, A., Runions, K., Ortega-Ruiz, R., & Romera, E. M. (2023). Bullying and Cyberbullying perpetration and victimization: Prospective within-person associations. *Journal of Youth and Adolescence*, *52*(2), 406–418. https://doi.org/10.1007/s10964-022-01704-3

Everett, M. (1985). Role similarity and complexity in social. *Social Networks*, *7*, 353–359.

Fazeen, M, Dantu, R, & Guturu, P. (2011). Identification of leaders, lurkers, associates and spammers in a social network: Context-dependent and context-independent approaches. *Social Networks*, *1*(3), 241–254.

Floros, G., & Mylona, I. (2022). Association of cyberbullying and internet use disorder. *Current Addiction Reports*, *9*(4), 575–588. https://doi.org/10.1007/s40429-022-00440-9

Gabrielli, S., Rizzi, S., Carbone, S., & Piras, E. M. (2021). School interventions for bullying-cyberbullying prevention in adolescents: Insights from the UPRIGHT and CREEP projects. *International Journal of Environmental Research and Public Health*, *18*(21). https://doi.org/10.3390/ijerph182111697

Gomez, C. E., Sztainberg, M. O., & Trana, R. E. (2022). Curating cyberbullying datasets: A human-AI collaborative approach. *International Journal of Bullying Prevention : An Official Publication of the International Bullying Prevention Association*, *4*(1), 35–46. https://doi.org/10.1007/s42380-021-00114-6

Gongane, V. U., Munot, M. V., & Anuse, A. D. (2022). Detection and moderation of detrimental content on social media platforms: Current status and future directions. *Social Network Analysis and Mining, 12*(1), 129. https://doi.org/10.1007/s13278-022-00951-3

Hagberg, A. A., Schult, D. A., & Swart, P. J. (2008). Exploring Network Structure, Dynamics, and Function using NetworkX. In G. Varoquaux, T. Vaught, & J. Millman (Eds.), *Proceedings of the 7th Python in Science Conference* (pp. 11–15).

Henares-Montiel, J., Benítez-Hidalgo, V., Ruiz-Pérez, I., Pastor-Moreno, G., & Rodríguez-Barranco, M. (2022). Cyberbullying and associated factors in member countries of the european union: A systematic review and meta-analysis of studies with representative population samples. *International Journal of Environmental Research and Public Health, 19*(12). https://doi.org/10.3390/ijerph19127364

Hinduja, S., & Patchin, J. W. (2014). *Bullying beyond the schoolyard: Preventing and responding to cyberbullying.* Corwin press.

Hirschi, T. (1969). *Causes of delinquency.* University of California Press.

Huang, J., Zhong, Z., Zhang, H., & Li, L. (2021). Cyberbullying in social media and online games among chinese college students and its associated factors. *International Journal of Environmental Research and Public Health, 18*(9). https://doi.org/10.3390/ijerph18094819

Kim, Y. J., Qian, L., & Aslam, M. S. (2021). Cyberbullying among traditional and complementary medicine practitioners in the workplace: Protocol for a cross-sectional descriptive study. *JMIR Research Protocols, 10*(8), e29582. https://doi.org/10.2196/29582

Lancichinetti, A & Fortunato, S. (2009). Community detection algorithms: A comparative analysis. *Physical Review E, 80*(5), 056117.

Lloret-Irles, D., Cabrera-Perona, V., Tirado-González, S., & Segura-Heras, J. V. (2022). Cyberbullying: Common predictors to cyber-victimisation and bystanding. *International Journal of Environmental Research and Public Health, 19*(23). https://doi.org/10.3390/ijerph192315750

Longobardi, C., Thornberg, R., & Morese, R. (2021). Editorial: Cyberbullying and Mental Health: An Interdisciplinary Perspective. *Frontiers in Psychology, 12*, 827106. https://doi.org/10.3389/fpsyg.2021.827106

Martínez-Valderrey, V., Gil-Mediavilla, M., Villasana-Terradillos, M., & Alguacil-Sánchez, S. (2023). Editorial: Bullying, cyberbullying, and dating violence: State of the art, evaluation instruments, and prevention and intervention proposals. *Frontiers in Psychology, 14*, 1119976. https://doi.org/10.3389/fpsyg.2023.1119976

Marvin, Krohn. (1986). The web of conformity: A network approach to the explanation of delinquent behavior. *Social Problems, 33*(6), S81–S93. Marvin, Krohn, Massey, J. L., & Zielinski, M. (1988). Role overlap, network multiplexity, and adolescent deviant behavior. *Social Psychology Quarterly, 51*(4), 346–356.

Milosevic, T., Van Royen, K., & Davis, B. (2022). Artificial intelligence to address cyberbullying, harassment and abuse: New directions in the midst of complexity. *International Journal of Bullying Prevention : An Official Publication of the International Bullying Prevention Association, 4*(1), 1–5. https://doi.org/10.1007/s42380-022-00117-x

Neelakandan, S., Sridevi, M., Chandrasekaran, S., Murugeswari, K., Pundir, A. K. S., Sridevi, R., & Lingaiah, T. B. (2022). Deep learning approaches for cyberbullying detection and classification on social media. *Computational Intelligence and Neuroscience, 2022*, 2163458. https://doi.org/10.1155/2022/2163458

Newman, M. (2010). *Networks: An introduction.* Oxford University press.

Newman, M. E. J. (2003). The structure and function of complex networks. *SIAM Reviews, 45*(2), 167–256.

Ngo, A. T., Tran, A. Q., Tran, B. X., Nguyen, L. H., Hoang, M. T., Nguyen, T. H. T., Doan, L. P., Vu, G. T., Nguyen, T. H., Do, H. T., Latkin, C. A., Ho, R. C. M., & Ho, C. S. H. (2021). Cyberbullying among school adolescents in an urban setting of a developing country: Experience, coping strategies, and mediating effects of different support on psychological well-being. *Frontiers in Psychology, 12*, 661919. https://doi.org/10.3389/fpsyg.2021.661919

Rajamani, S. K., & Iyer, R. (2022). Development of an android mobile phone application for finding closed-loop, analytical solutions to dense linear, algebraic equations for the purpose of mathematical modelling in healthcare and neuroscience research. *NeuroQuantology*, 20, 4959–4973. https://doi.org/10.6084/m9.figshare.c.6156024.v1

Rajamani, S. K., & Iyer, R. S. (2023a). A Scoping Review of Current Developments in the Field of Machine Learning and Artificial Intelligence. In D. Samantha (Ed.), *Designing and developing innovative mobile applications* (pp. 138–164). IGI Global. https://doi.org/10.4018/978-1-6684-8582-8.ch009

Rajamani, S. K., & Iyer, R. S. (2023b). Machine Learning Based Mobile Applications Using Python and ScikitLearn. In D. Samanta (Ed.), *Designing and developing innovative mobile applications* (pp. 282–306). IGI Global. https://doi.org/10.4018/978-1-6684-8582-8.ch016

Ranney, M. L., Pittman, S. K., Moseley, I., Morgan, K. E., Riese, A., Ybarra, M., Cunningham, R., & Rosen, R. (2021). Cyberbullying prevention for adolescents: Iterative qualitative methods for mobile intervention design. *JMIR Formative Research*, 5(8), e25900. https://doi.org/10.2196/25900

Sampasa-Kanyinga, H., Lalande, K., & Colman, I. (2018). Cyberbullying victimisation and internalising and externalising problems among adolescents: The moderating role of parent-child relationship and child's sex. *Epidemiology and Psychiatric Sciences*, 29, e8. https://doi.org/10.1017/S2045796018000653

Sánchez-Medina, A. J., Galván-Sánchez, I., & Fernández-Monroy, M. (2020). Applying artificial intelligence to explore sexual cyberbullying behaviour. *Heliyon*, 6(1), e03218. https://doi.org/10.1016/j.heliyon.2020.e03218

Schodt, K. B., Quiroz, S. I., Wheeler, B., Hall, D. L., & Silva, Y. N. (2021). Cyberbullying and mental health in adults: The moderating role of social media use and gender. *Frontiers in Psychiatry*, 12, 674298. https://doi.org/10.3389/fpsyt.2021.674298

Shin, S. Y., & Choi, Y.-J. (2021). Comparison of cyberbullying before and after the COVID-19 pandemic in Korea. *International Journal of Environmental Research and Public Health*, 18(19). https://doi.org/10.3390/ijerph181910085

Sutherland, E., Cressey, D. R., & Luckenbill, D. F. (1992). *Principles of criminology* (11th ed.). General Hall.

Tozzo, P., Cuman, O., Moratto, E., & Caenazzo, L. (2022). Family and educational strategies for cyberbullying prevention: A systematic review. *International Journal of Environmental Research and Public Health*, 19(16). https://doi.org/10.3390/ijerph191610452

UmaMaheswaran, S. K., Deivasigamani, S., Joshi, K., Verma, D., Rajamani, S. K., & Ross, D. S. (2022). Computational Intelligence Approach to Improve The Classification Accuracy of Brain Tumor Detection. In *2022 11th International Conference on System Modeling & Advancement in Research Trends (SMART)*, pp. 1192–1196. https://doi.org/10.1109/SMART55829.2022.10047792

Vasudev, C.(2006). *Graph theory with application*. New Age International Publication House.

Vogels, E. A., & Atske, S. (2022, December 15). Teens and Cyberbullying 2022. *Pew Research Center: Internet, Science & Tech*. https://www.pewresearch.org/internet/2022/12/15/teens-and-cyberbullying-2022/

Wright, M. F., & Wachs, S. (2023). Cyberbullying involvement and depression among elementary school, middle school, high school, and university students: The role of social support and gender. *International Journal of Environmental Research and Public Health*, 20(4). https://doi.org/10.3390/ijerph20042835

Zhao, L., & Yu, J. (2021). A meta-analytic review of moral disengagement and cyberbullying. *Frontiers in Psychology*, 12, 681299. https://doi.org/10.3389/fpsyg.2021.681299

Zhu, C., Huang, S., Evans, R., & Zhang, W. (2021). Cyberbullying among adolescents and children: A comprehensive review of the global situation, risk factors, and preventive measures. *Frontiers in Public Health*, 9, 634909. https://doi.org/10.3389/fpubh.2021.634909

13 Cyberbullying and Social Media
Implications for African Digital Space

Basil Osayin Daudu
Kogi State University

Goddy Uwa Osimen
Covenant University

Kennedy Shuaibu
Kogi State University

13.1 INTRODUCTION

With regard to the gradual development and increasingly progress of technologies, the way and manner underage and adults handle digital communication network devices is appalling. A good number of them at first are technologically limited to e-mail and word processing, and this technologically limitation makes the concerned computer users to crave more by exploring into new discoveries of digital technologies. As such, some children and adults loss control, becoming Internet addicts, thereby breaching the ethics of Internet or online communication policies.

Anyone can fall victim of cyberbullying irrespective of gender, religion, education, social status, institutional affiliation, creed, among others; not everybody is a cyberbully. Even with technological advancement in developed countries, the problem of cyberbullying has not been dealt with completely. Although their case is far better than developing and underdeveloped countries who are lagging behind in terms of technological advancements, the case of cyberbullying in Africa digital space is quite alarming as a lot of people have suffered from the hands of cyberbullies, which weakens the Afrocentric society. The various communication means adopted by cyberbullies to carry out their nefarious online activities are in themselves devastating let alone their devastating effects on victims, digital space, and nations at large.

African leaders have been battling with the problem of cyberbullying but with little success, reason due to Africa's lukewarm in the use of technologies let alone artificial intelligence (AI) as they are capital expensive. This COVID-19 pandemic had proved in the year 2020, as well as exposing Africa's helplessness to the world,

DOI: 10.1201/9781003393061-17

243

although some African nations (South Africa for instance) are more technologically inclined than the others, making good use of technologies to boost their economies. The introduction of social media into the digital space is to enhance communication, networking among individuals, organizations, states, nations, countries, and continents. Cedillo et al. (2022) buttress that "the use of Internet, social networks, and platforms allows for people of all ages to have constant communication." But to cyberbullies, social media networks are just avenues to prey on their victims, and this undermines the fundamental dignity and rights of the affected persons. And this cannot continue. No wonder that cyberbullying is a vital "part of policy-making for social media platforms because of its harmful effect. Cyberbullies hack and threaten online users anonymously without concealing their identity" (Azeez, Idiakose, Onyema and Der Vyver, 2021). In the same vein, Chukwuere, Ebere, and Adom (2021) are of the opinion that cyberbullying is "an electronic bullying with mixed effect on the bullied."

Therefore, it is absolutely necessary for African leaders to put an end to cyberbullying by crippling the nefarious online activities of cyberbullies as it is not only victims that do suffer but also the image of African digital space. When the integrity of the African digital space is compromised, its economy suffers greatly; once the economy suffers, every other thing falls apart leading to a failed state or continent. A 2018 survey by Ipsos Global Advisor revealed that South Africa had the highest reported rate of cyberbullying among 28 countries surveyed, with 54% of South African Internet users reporting having experienced online bullying. According to a 2019 study conducted by UNICEF across 30 countries, approximately 1 in 3 young Internet users (aged 15–24) have experienced online bullying. In a 2020 survey conducted by the African Union Commission, 59% of African children reported experiencing online violence, including cyberbullying. The number of the bullied is on the rise till date (AI Language Model, ChatGPT 2023). What then is cyberbullying? How is it different from traditional bullying? What is social media? How is it instrumental in promoting cyberbullying? These and many more questions is what this chapter seeks to address.

13.2   THEMATIC REVIEW OF CYBERBULLYING AND SOCIAL MEDIA

Cyberbullying and social media are two distinct, popular concepts in the world today. Despite their distinctive nature, they are connected in terms of communication means and users. But it is quite disturbing that cyberbullies have abused social media networks and used them in negative ways. Ige (2022) writes: "while the era of Internet had brought in tremendous innovation and improvements to our daily activities and overall way of life, it had also opened floodgates to cyberbullying." In this regard, cyberbullying is a modern-day version of 1959 Golding's book *Lord of the Flies* (Shariff, 2009). Cyberbullying is "the use of information and communication technologies to support intentional, repeated, and hostile behavior by an individual or group that is intended to harm others" (Belsey, 2004).

Cyberbullying is known by different euphemisms such as "online buying," "online abuse," "online social cruelty," "electronic bullying," "digital harassment," "a social terror by technology," and "emotional wilding and going for the emotional jugular" (Diane Sawyer, quoted by Ross, 2006). Cyberbullying takes place without physical contact between the cyberbully and the victim (Ezeonwumelu et al., 2022). Cyberbullying shares similar traits with conventional bullying as it involves a cyberbully intending to exercise control over the bullied. Belsey (2004) noted that Internet "anonymity" clearly differentiated cyberbullying from traditional bullying. This anonymity empowers cyberbullies to release hurtful remarks to their victims without remorse or fear of being caught (Juvonen and Gross, 2008). Pseudonyms and well-disguised Internet protocol address shed the identities of cyberbullies (Shariff, 2009). Further, cyberbully is characterized by anonymity, an unknown identity who is passionate in digging out facts that may be sexually unhealthy or morally bankrupt (Shariff, 2009). Aggressive act, power imbalance, and repeated behavior can be identified in cyberbullying and traditional bullying (Hunter, Boyle and Warden, 2007). According to Campbell (2015), cyberbullying depicts "forms of bullying that use technology, which is the phenomenon that children and adolescents seem increasingly to be using to harm others" (cited in Shariff, 2009). Cyberbullying is considered to be a dangerous phenomenon as anyone can practice it without a physical contact with the victim. All that is needed is an electronic gadget to carry out the intention of hurting the victim.

Aftab (2006) differentiated direct cyberbullying from cyberbullying by proxy (indirect). The former is a direct operation while the latter is an indirect operation. In the first one, direct messages are sent to the victim, while in the second one, the cyberbully uses others to do the dirty work even with or without their knowledge. The cyberbully might reset the password of the victim's account to deny the victim access to his/her account. Also, the difference between playful teasing and cyberbullying lies in the aggressive intent behind cyberbullying. To McQuade III, Colt and Meyer (2009), cyberbullying involves "using computers or other information technology devices such as personal digital assistants or cell phone to embarrass, harass, intimidate, threaten, or otherwise cause harm to individuals targeted for such abuse." Thus, cyberbullying is getting more serious on social media platforms or networks.

The second concept of interest is social media. It refers to "a tool that boosts communication, interaction, and connection among different racial groups, gender, and families across the world" (Brewer, Massey, Vurdelija and Freeman, 2012). It refers to "dwellings where people act out their lives" (Trottier, 2012). Social media is "a dynamic area wherein structures and utilization practices are situation to constant modifications in an established culture of connectivity with multi-directional information flow" (Anderson and Jiang, 2018). In the same vein, social media is seen as a "computer-mediated communication in which people create their content, see, and interact with content created by friends or other consumers online" (Kaupe, 2019). Unlike cyberbullies, social media influencers see social media as a tool for positive transformation that benefits netizens (Internet users) and humanity at large. This is one of the bright sides of putting social media for good use. On this note:

> The rapid increase in the use of digital technology has brought about the digitalization
> of learning, globalization and literal compression of the world into a global village.
> With a click on a device, messages, content and information can be shared to every part

of the world in a fraction of a second. As a result, young people now embrace social media as a channel through which they express themselves, seek out entertainment and advertise their creative ideals.

(Ezeonwumelu et al., 2022)

Ige (2022) stressed on the positive and negative impacts of social media networks. He writes:

The impact of social media such as Instagram, Facebook, Twitter, WhatsApp etc. on daily basis cannot be over emphasized as they had greatly influence modern way of communication as useful as social media is, it is a medium for promoting hatred, harassment, racism, etc. which is currently affecting millions of people across the globe.

(Ige and Adewale, 2022)

Social media platforms or networks also help in promoting online businesses and ventures for efficient online buying and selling of goods and services. Little wonder Brewer et al. (2019) submit that social media is "a tool that opens several opportunities for e-commerce, e-learning, e-banking, and e-government to thrive. This is achieved through advertisement, governance, provision for learning and research tools, sharing of ideas with broad audience, professional skills acquisition, among its users." Thus, it is obvious that there is a logical connection between cyberbullying and social media in spite of their distinctive peculiarities. However, this chapter sees "cyberbullying" as an online abuse having variants; "cyberbully" as anyone (adult or teenager) who takes online bullying as a lifestyle or hobby and "social media" as an online tool of communication having variants. Thus, the next phase of this chapter is African digital space and the nightmare of cyberbullying.

13.3 AFRICAN DIGITAL SPACE AND THE NIGHTMARE OF CYBERBULLYING

"Unless and until our society recognizes cyberbullying for what it is, the suffering of thousands of silent victims will continue" (Anna Maria Chavez, cited in Ige, 2022).

African digital space is not totally free from cybercrimes and cyberbullying, in particular. Cyberbullying manifest itself in various forms such as strolling, cyber stalking, identity theft, callout/cancel culture, among others. Strolling is an intentional attempt at upsetting someone by sending the person offensive messages or using demeaning picture memes on the person's social media wall. Social media trolls use sarcasm to upset their victims. Direct response from the victims energizes trolls to continue with their nefarious activities repeatedly which may cause the victims to suffer from psychological distress or depression (Swenson-Lepper and Kerby, 2019).

In cyber stalking, cyber stalkers use electronic communication devices often to threaten their victims. They follow the victims from one online platform to another, keeping tabs on them (Ezeonwumelu et al., 2022). Adolescents are both perpetrators and victims of cyber stalking. Identity theft is a form of cyberbullying which involves impersonating or stealing of the victim's identity on social media in order to perpetuate fraud or embarrassing the original user or the victim (Ezeonwumelu et al., 2022). In some cases, identity theft may lead to blackmail. Callout/cancel culture is a new trend identified with social media ostracism directed at a victim in order to ridicule or embarrass him/her. Romano (2020) argues that cancel culture is "often targeted at popular individuals with the aim of derailing their careers."

Cyberbullying is associated with impersonation and cyber threats. According to Willard (2006a,b), cyberbullying manifests itself in different forms, viz. flaming, harassment, denigration, impersonation, outing, trickery, exclusion, and cyber threats. Flaming is an online contention by which distasteful messages are conveyed via electronic communication means (Aune, 2009). It takes place in public setting such as chat rooms or discussion groups (Kowalski, Limber and Agatston, 2008). Under the context of harassment, the cyberbully repeatedly intimidates the bullied with hurting comments via Internet. For *Black's Law Dictionary* (2004, p. 733), harassment is "a word, conduct, or an action (usually repeated or persistent) that is being directed to a specific person, annoys, alarms, or causes substantial emotional distress in that person." Cyber harassment occurs among "a special group of online bullies known as griefers, individuals who deliberately harass other players in multiplayer online games" (Kowalski, Limber and Agatston, 2008). Denigration is disrespecting someone online by posting rumors about the person in order to discredit the person. Impersonation is a form of cyberbullying in which a cyberbully steals another person's identity with the intention of destroying the person's integrity. If care is not taken, this may lead to the victim losing his/her life by some hate groups who may see the online victim as a cyberbully. Happy slapping or hopping is known by some scholars to be a form of cyberbullying. It is direct assault of the victim captured on camera phones (Kowalski, Limber and Agatston, 2008).

Outing is sharing someone's secrets or personal pieces of information online with or without the person's consent. Trickery shares similar trait with outing, in which the cyberbully deceives the victim to reveal his/her secrets that will be shared with others by the cyberbully online. Exclusion is an intentional removal of someone from an online group. Cyber stalking is a reoccurring, extreme embarrassment to instil fear in the victim. In other words, it is the "use of electronic communications to stalk another person through repetitive harassing and threatening communications" (Kowalski, Limber and Agatston, 2008). *For Black Law Dictionary* (2004, p. 1440), stalking is "the act or an instance of following another by stealth; the offense of following or loitering near another, often surreptitiously, with the purpose of annoying or harassing that person or committing a further crime such as assault or battery." Cyber threats are either threats or distressing material which depicts the writer as being emotionally upset and may lead to harming someone else (Willard, 2006a,b). In all these forms of cyberbullying, there are three key issues present, viz. addiction problem, suicide, and self-harm method.

E-mail, instant messaging, chat rooms/bash boards, small text messages to the victim (possible to trace but difficult to know who sent it), instant messaging, and voting or polling booths are some of the communication means used by cyberbullies to get to their online victims (Beale and Hall, 2007). As such, online platforms such as "Facebook, Telegram, Snapchat, Instagram, and Twitter have facilitated efficient real-time communication among millions of people around the world, cutting across political and geographical boundaries" (Whittaker and Kowalski, 2015). Present in them is a certain level of anonymity which makes it possible for cyberbullies to send violent, sexist, and discriminating harmful comments, posts, and exchanges to their online victims in order to intimidate, embarrass, or blackmail them (Whittaker and Kowalski, 2015). Factors responsible for cyberbullying, to mention but a few, are revenge; recreation, reward, and rage (Baldry et al., 2017); the need to belong (Zimmer-gembeck and Webb, 2017); dominance (Lou, Chaffee and Lascano, 2018); and jealousy, anger, boredom, and pure entertainment (Balakrishnan and Norman, 2020). In addition, "proliferation of technology exposes many youths to cyberbullying activities, thereby making them obsessive" (Makori and Agufana, 2020).

Cyberbullying finds its way into African digital space. First and most importantly, what does "cyberspace" mean? The concept "cyberspace" was first invented in a science-fiction novel *Neuromancer* authored by William Gibson to depict "his vision of a three-dimensional space of pure information, moving between compute and computer clusters that make up this vast landscape" (Kizza, 2014). Cyberspace infrastructure comprises "hardware nodes as sourcing, transmitting, and receiving elements; software as protocols; human-ware as users of information, and finally pure information that is either in a state of rest at a node or in a state of motion in the linking media" (Kizza, 2014). Simply put, cyberspace is networks between computer systems. As such, African digital space is a microcosm of global cyberspace that aid youthful and adult interactions—activities, experiences, and associations which may be unregulated resulting to a matter of concern.

The African digital space is strengthened by the African Digital Rights Network founded in 2020. Its headquarters is located in Brighton, East Sussex, UK. The network provides online democratic space, rights to privacy, and freedom of speech. It has the following set objectives: "expansion of digital access, social media activism, civic technologies, and legislation that extends digital rights and digital security technologies" (Roberts, 2021). There are numerous users (individuals, organizations, and government) of African digital space. We have digital openings and digital closings consisting of political, social, and economic report documents. We have social media campaign reports of the following African countries: #BringBackOurGirls (Nigeria), #RhodesMustFall (South Africa), #FreeBobiWine (Uganda), etc., then advocacy campaign reports: Amandla.mobi (South Africa), monitoring government online spending, for example, BugIT (Nigeria). In the case of digital closings, we have reported document of digital legislation online, for example, data protection and privacy (Uganda), criminalizing hate speech (Cameroon) (Roberts, 2021). Government of various African nations also makes use of social media to checkmate excesses of its citizens and for security purposes. However, the intent of using social media differs from individual, group, organization, country, and government.

Cyberbullying has negative impact on individuals (Internet users—cyberbullies and victims alike) and African digital space. Starting with cyberbullies, their actions for using social media on African digital space are not justifiable. Before the law, they are criminals, irresponsible, irresponsive, and unpatriotic people whose actions are detrimental to the progress of constituted authority and the society at large. In a way, they are technological terrorists, and when wanted by security personnel, they become fugitives, thereby losing their fundamental freedom of movement as citizens.

For instance, the case of one, Rachel Iyonmana, a Canada-based Nigeria lady wanted by the Nigerian Police over allegations of cyberbullying and the Police, is ready to compensate anyone with the sum of 5 million naira for useful pieces of information that will lead to her arrest (*Peoples Gazette*, 2023). Another instance is the misunderstanding between the People Democratic Party (PDP) and the Supreme Court of Nigeria where Justice Inyang Okoro pleaded with the People Democratic Party members to stop using social media to bully the court over the election of President-elect Bola Tinubu's running mate, Kashim Shettima who PDP members believed is guilty of double nomination (Inyang, 2023).

There are so many online hobbies or projects one can engage himself or herself in, certainly not cyberbullying. On the part of the victims, their fundamental rights as persons are being undermined, which may lead to psychological distress, depression, mistrust, anxiety, self-harm, mental breakdown, low self-esteem, suicide, etc. (Skilbred-Fjeld, Endresen and Mossige, 2020; Juvonen and Gross, 2008). An instance is the case of 19-year-old Bongekile Ngantweni from Qombolo in Centane, Eastern Cape, who was bullied by her school mates by creating counterfeit profiles to destruct her reputation. Also, a 15-year-old focus group participant asserts, "Unless you have been bubbled, you really cannot understand what it is like and how hard it is to forget. It really leaves a scar that even time cannot heal" (cited in Kowalski, Limber and Agatston, 2008).

African digital space reflects the image of Africa, its people, and nations. Cyberbullying gives a negative impression of Africa as a continent to the world, by doing so, leading to cyber security threats to online commerce, online banking, online learning, and online government in African digital space. This could lead to loss of Africa's integrity and robust resources paving way to hunger and starvation, diseases and sicknesses, wars and insurgency, illiteracy, unstable government, economic hardship, among others. So, how best can cyberbullying be dealt with?

13.4   COMBATING CYBERBULLYING VIA AI KNOWLEDGE PRODUCTION AND APPLICATION

It is no news that several studies have been done on cyberbullying and scholars have proffered varied recommendations as well as provisions for international and national cyber laws [The Malicious Communications Act 1998 and 2003 (UK), Education Act (Canada), The Cybercrimes Act 19 of 2020 (South Africa) and Cyber Laws and other related offences: Prohibition and Prevention Act of 2015 (Nigeria)] to tackle the menace of cyberbullying. Lending our voice to theirs, but in different way, we endorse AI knowledge production and application as a solution to combating cyberbullying especially in African digital space and Africa at large. Here, two things are involved: first, AI knowledge production, and second, AI application. The best legacy any government can give to its citizen is education, and next to education is technology. In fact, technology now permeates every core area of the human society by digitalizing them as seen in e-governance, e-commerce, e-learning, e-banking, e-research, e-medicine, among others. It is unfortunate that most African leaders are yet to come to terms with this truth of technology, and that is why technology is the least in their country's budgets.

The world's current technology is AI. AI refers to "the introducing of intelligence in machines to provide the capability of performing tasks which would normally require the human mind. It can be a technique for using data in an efficient manner to allow understanding to the human providing the data" (Ghosh, Chakra and Law, 2018). It is the "ability of digital computers or computer-controlled robots to solve problems that are normally associated with the higher intellectual processing capabilities of humans" (Ertel, 2017). Thus, AI has the capacity to improve network communications. Equipping the African society with AI knowledge production and skills tackles cyber security challenges with ease. The "technical know-how" of AI can enhance the visibility of African digital space and detect any forms of cybercrimes or cyberbullying in particular. AI machine learning and deep learning algorithms such as Artificial Neural Network (ANN), support vector machine, and k-nearest neighbor (James and Osubor, 2022) detect cyberbullying with ease, and cyber security challenges are best tackled with cyber counter measures and software applications. All these are embedded in AI.

13.5 CONCLUSION

Cyberbullying is a cybercrime against humanity. No digital space is totally free from its influence. Cyberbullying manifests itself in various forms, and its impact on the human society is worrisome. Cyberbullies use social media networks (WhatsApp, Facebook, Twitter, among others) via communication means or modalities (text messages, e-mail, web sites, among others) to prey on their victims which may lead to horrible experiences. Cyberbullies are now technologically inclined and are very cunning in their mode of operation. African victims and African digital space have suffered greatly from the activities of cyberbullies.

With anti-cyber laws and security personnel on ground, African leaders have been battling with the problem of cyberbullying but with little success. The nefarious activities of cyberbullies must not go undefeated as the image and resources of African digital space and Africa at large are at stake. African government, not putting much resources in technological knowledge production and applications, especially in the area of AI, is an error that needs to be corrected with immediate effect. AI knowledge production and application have what it takes to put an end to the activities of cyberbullies in particular and cybercrimes in general.

Further, the findings in this chapter are summarized as follows:

   i. The cyber security of African digital space is too weak, which makes it vulnerable to cyber criminals or offenders.
  ii. African leaders pay little attention to the acquisition of information computer technology and AI in particular. This misplacement of priorities on the part of the government has largely affected African economies badly.
 iii. Communication means or modalities used by cyberbullies, since they are not well managed, have caused more harm than good to Internet users and Africa at large.

13.6 RECOMMENDATIONS

As noted above, this chapter, thus, came up with the following recommendations to combat cyberbullying in African digital space and Africa at large:

i. Through frequent sensitization programs, African government and anti-cyberbullying organizations should enlighten Africans on the dangers of cyberbullying.

ii. African government should budget more on AI knowledge production and application so as to tackle the problem of cyberbullying with ease.

iii. African government should have zero tolerance for all forms of cyberbullying, and as such, stringent anti-cyber laws should be made and implemented while existing ones should be reformed to effectively tackle present-day cyber challenges.

iv. Cyberbullies should be brought to book or face the wrath of the law to serve as a deterrence for others to learn.

v. Security personnel should be empowered with sophisticated arms and ammunitions for an effective policing as well as provisions of modern technologies to effectively act as a watchdog to checkmate cyberbullying in particular and cybercrimes in general.

vi. The African Digital Rights Networks should intensify its efforts to make African digital space solid.

vii. All Internet users (netizens) should imbibe some digital literary skills such as collaboration, creativity, critical thinking, self-improvement, digital ethics, and personal information management.

REFERENCES

Aftab, P. 2006. Pobrano Z. https://www.wiredsafety.net

Anderson, M., and J. Jiang. 2018. Teens, social media and technology. Pew Research Center. 1–9. https://pubservicesalliance.org/wp-content/uploads/2018/06/teens-social-media-technology-2018-PEW.pdf

Aune, N. M. 2009. Cyberbullying. A Research Paper, School Psychology. The Graduate School, University of Wisconsin-St Menomonie, WI.

Azeez, N. A., Idiakose, S. O., Onyema, C. J., and C. V. Der Vyver. 2021. Cyberbullying detection in social networks: artificial intelligence approach. *Journal of Cyber Security and Mobility* 10, no. 4: 745–774.

Balakrishnan, V., and A. Norman. 2020. Psychological motives of cyberbullying among Malaysian youth adults. *Asian Pacific Journal of Social Work and Development* 00/00: 1–4. https://doi.org/10.1080/02185385.2020.177.2101.

Baldry, A. C. et al. 2017. School bullying and cyberbullying among boys and girls: roles and overlap roles overlap. *Journal of Aggression, Maltreatment and Trauma* 00/00: 1–15. https://doi.org/10.10810926771.2017.1330793

Beale, A. V., and R. R. Hall. 2007. Cyberbullying: what school administrators and parents can do. *The Clearing House* 81, no. 1: 8–12.

Belsey, B. 2004. What is cyberbullying? www.bullying.org/external/documents/ACF6F8.pdf

Black's Law Dictionary. 2004. 8th edition. B. A. Garmer (ed.) West Group.

Brewer, B., Cave, A., Massey, A., Vurdelija, A., and J. Freedman. 2012. Cyberbullying among female college students: an exploratory study. *California Journal of Health Promotion* 12, no. 1: 40–51.

Brewer, B. et al. 2019. Exploring and Learning Suicidal Ideation Connotations on Social Media with Deep Learning. In *Proceedings of the 7th Workshop on Computational Approaches to Subjectivity, Sentiment and Social Media Analysis*, 167–175.

Campbell, M. 2015. Cyberbullying: an old problem in a new guide. *Australian Journal of Guidance and Counselling* 15: 68–76.

Cedillo, P. et al. 2022. A Systematic Literature Review on Technological Solutions to Fight Bullying and Cyberbullying in Academic Environments. In *Proceedings of the 14th International Conference on Computer Supported Education* 1: 413–420.

Chukwuere, P. C., Ebere, J., and D. Adom. 2021. The psychological effects of social media cyberbullying on students in selected African countries. *Acta Informatica* 5, no. 2: 62–70.

Ertel, W. 2017. *Introduction to artificial Intelligence*. 2nd edition. Springer.

Ezeonwumelu, V. U., Okenwa-Fadele, A., Ijeoma, N., Nneka, M., Oparaugo, U. I., and C. C. Okoro. 2022. Students' and teachers' perception of cyberbullying and its influence on the academic grit of senior secondary school students in Onitsha South LGA, Anambra State. *Asian journal of Education and Social Studies* 37, no. 3: 28–38.

Ghosh, A., Chakra, B. D., and A. Law. 2018. Artificial intelligence in internet of things. *CAAI Transaction on Intelligence Technology* 3, no. 4: 208–218.

Hinduja, S. and J. W. Patchin. 2008. Cyberbullying: An exploratory analysis of factors related to offending and victimization. *Deviant Behavior* 29, no. 2: 129–156.

Hunter, S. C., Boyle, J. M., and D. Warden. 2007. Perceptions and correlates of peer-victimization and bullying. *British Journal of Educational Psychology* 77, no. 4: 797–810.

Ige, T. and Adewale, S. 2022. AI-powered anti-cyberbullying system using machine learning algorithm of multinomial naïve Bayes and optimized linear support vector machine: bit perception of cyberbully contents in a messaging system by machine learning algorithm. *International Journal of Advanced Computer Science and Applications* 13, no. 5: 5–9.

Inyang, Ifreke. 2023. Stop using social media to bully us - Supreme Court warns PDP. *Daily Post*. httpd://dailypost.ng/2023/05/27/stop-using-social-media-to-bully-us-supreme-court-warns-pdp/?amp=1

James, I. I., and Osubor, V. I. 2022. Hostile social media harassment: a machine learning framework for filtering anti-female jokes. *Nigerian Journal of Technology* 41, no. 2: 311–317.

Juvonen, J., and E. F. Gross. 2008. Extending the social grounds? Bullying experiences in cyberspace. *Journal of School Health* 78, no. 9: 496–505.

Kaupe, M. 2019. A content analysis of caregiver's computer-mediated communication on loneliness. Master's thesis 555. https:/epublication.marquette.edu/theses_open/555

King, L. 2006. No hiding from online bullies. http://www.news leaders.com/apps/pbcs.dill/articles?Dates=20060815.

Kizza, J. M. 2014. *Computer network security and ethics*. 4th edition. McFarland & Company, Inc., Publishers.

Kowalski, R. M., Limber, S. P., and P. W. Agatston. 2008. *Cyberbullying: bullying in the digital age*. Blackwell Publishing.

Lou, N. M., Chaffee, K. E., and D. I. V. Lascano. 2018. Complementary perspectives on autonomy in self-determination theory and language learner autonomy. *TESOL Quarterly* 52, no. 1: 210–220.

Makori, A., and P. Agufana. 2020. Cyberbullying among learners in higher educational institutions in Sub-Saharan Africa: examining challenges and possible mitigations. *Higher Education Studies* 10, no. 2: 53–65.

McQuade III, S. C., Colt, J. P, and N. B. Meyer. 2009. *Cyberbullying: protecting kids and adults from online bullies*. Praeger Publishers.

Peoples Gazette. 2023. Cyberbullying: police place N5 million bounty on wanted Canada-based Nigerian. April 3. https://gazettengr.com/cyberbullying=police-place-n5-million-bounty-on-wanted-canada-based-nigerian

Rashid, F. H. A., Omar, S. Z., Bolong, J., and W. A. W. Abas. 2022. Is it because of I'm famous, success or rich: Why social media influencers become a victim of cyberbullying on social media? *International Journal of Academic Research in Business and Social Sciences* 12, no. 1: 1192–1211.

Roberts, T. 2021. Digital rights in closing civic space: lessons from ten African countries. https://www.ids.ac.uk/opinions/digital-rights-and-closing-civic-space-lessons-from-ten-african-countries.

Romano, A. 2020. Why we can't stop fighting about cancel culture. https://www.vox.com/culture/2019/12/30/20879720/what-is-cancel-culture-explained-history/debate.

Ross, S. 2006. (Executive Producer). *Prime time television broadcast.* American Broadcasting.

Santrock, J. W. 2016. *Adolescence.* 16th ed. McGraw-Hill Education.

Shariff, S. 2009. *Confronting cyberbullying: what schools need to know to control misconduct and avoid legal consequences.* Cambridge University Press.

Skilbred-Fjeld, S., Endresen, R. S., and S. Mossig. 2020. Cyberbully involvement and mental health problems among late adolescents. *Cyberpsychology* 14, no. 1: 1–17.

Swenson-Lepper, T., and A. Kerby. 2019. Cyber bullies, trolls and stalkers: students perception of ethical issues in social media. *Journal of Media Ethics* 34, no. 2: 102–113.

The South African. 2020. The many forms of cyberbullying: Bongekile's story. https://www.thesouthafrican.com

Trottier, D. 2012. *Social media as surveillance.* Ashgate.

Whittaker, E., and R. M. Kowalski. 2015. Cyberbullying in social media. *Journal of School Violence* 14, no. 1: 11–29.

Willard, N. E. 2006a. *Cyberbullying and cyber threats responding to the challenge of online social cruelty, threats and distress.* Eugene.

Willard, N. E. 2006b. Educators guide to cyberbullying: addressing the harm caused by online social cruelty. www.asdk12.org/middle.ink/AvB/bully-topics/educatorsguide_cyberbullying.pdf

Zimmer-Gembeck, M. J., and H. J. Webb. 2017. Body image and peer relationships: unique associations of adolescents' social status and competence with peer-and self-reported appearance victimization. *Journal of Adolescence* 61 (October): https://doi.org/10.1016/j.adolescence.2017.10.002

14 A Study on the Impact of Social Media and Cyberbullying on Teen Girls in India

Swapna M. P.
Centre for Cyber Security Systems and
Networks, Amrita Vishwa Vidyapeetham

G. Satyavathy
KPR College of Arts Science and Research

14.1 INTRODUCTION

Technological advancements are a testament to human ingenuity, aimed at simplifying tasks and enhancing the quality of life. However, every innovation that enhances and sustains human existence carries both positive and negative consequences. The Internet serves as a prime illustration of this phenomenon. It effectively bridges global connections and democratizes access to information, yet it also provides a platform for individuals to shield themselves through the veil of anonymity. The proliferation of cyberbullying is a growing concern, highlighting one of the negative aspects of the World Wide Web (Donat et al., 2022). The introduction of smartphones has revolutionized communication, making it more convenient and sophisticated. Almost everything is now accessible with a simple touch on the screen, including social interactions that have become increasingly digitized. The advancements in gadgets and seamless remote connections have significantly boosted the smartphone industry. These devices have not only captured the attention of young people and the working class but have also captivated the interest of toddlers and senior citizens. This emerging trend has exerted a profound influence on the younger generation, similar to other societal revolutions.

The influence of smartphones permeates every aspect of human life, encompassing areas such as corporate business, education, health, and public engagement. This multifaceted innovation has fundamentally altered social norms and behaviors. Its impact is characterized by both positive and negative effects (Peker and Kasikci, 2022). On the one hand, smartphones empower individuals to create and engage in communities that may foster activities considered detrimental to society. On the other hand, they also enable continuous connectivity, allowing people to stay in touch at all times.

DOI: 10.1201/9781003393061-18

Social media serves as a global platform for the exchange of thoughts, opinions, and ideas. It encompasses Internet-based services where individuals create public or semi-public profiles to connect with others. In the 21st century, social media has rapidly evolved as a web application. Notably, children, especially teenagers, dedicate significant amounts of time to the Internet based on the study by American Psychological Association. The usage of social media is continuously rising worldwide, becoming one of the most popular online activities for Internet users. Recent global statistics indicate that by 2023, there will be approximately 4.59 billion social media users, accounting for 57.5% of the world's current population. This number is projected to significantly increase in the forthcoming years as per the report from Statista in 2022.

14.1.1 METHODOLOGY

Social media platforms and smart gadgets have emerged as the primary means of communication for a wide range of activities, including education, shopping, work, personal relationships, and leisure. In light of these concerns, a research study was conducted to investigate the usage and abuse experienced by teen girls in India through social media. To gather accurate information about the challenges faced by young girls in the country, a well-structured questionnaire was designed. This digital questionnaire was distributed among female students, resulting in an impressive response rate of over 1,600 participants from different states.

14.1.2 CHAPTER ORGANIZATION

The rest of the chapter is organized as follows—Section 14.2 gives an insight into the aspects of social media, like the addiction factor, the detrimental effect, and the impact on girls. Section 14.3 is an eye-opener on cyberbullying, types of cyberbullying, facts and statistics, and the cyberbullying scenario with relevance to India. Section 14.4 represents the implementation method of the research work. Section 14.5 describes the results and findings of the research. Section 14.6 emphasizes the summary and implications of the results. Section 14.7 concludes the chapter.

14.2 SOCIAL MEDIA—THE UNCOMPROMISING ADDICTION

While social media presents new opportunities and career prospects for students, it also poses a threat to their physical and intellectual well-being (Nazir, 2014). Platforms such as Facebook, Snapchat, Instagram, TikTok, and others may not directly impact teenagers, but studies suggest that they can reduce the time adolescents spend on healthy activities. It is widely acknowledged that social media has negative implications for psychological health, as multiple reports have consistently highlighted these concerns. Furthermore, certain creators within the realm of social media have raised alarms regarding the addictive nature of specific features and their impact on user behavior.

Over the past decade, there has been a significant increase in addiction to social media. While many users engage with social networking sites without issue, a portion of individuals has developed addictive tendencies, displaying excessive or compulsive use. This behavioral dependency revolves around an intense preoccupation with social media posts and comments, an uncontrollable urge to utilize social media platforms, and a significant investment of time and effort into these platforms, leading to impairment in crucial areas of life. Social media platforms employ similar neural circuitry as seen in gaming and recreational drugs to keep users engaged and repeatedly using their products. Surveys have revealed that the constant stream of re-tweets, likes, and shares on these platforms can stimulate the brain's reward center, triggering chemical reactions akin to those induced by substances like cocaine. Neuroscientists draw parallels between social media activity and the injection of dopamine into the human system via a syringe. Figure 14.1 illustrates the global usage of social media.

14.2.1 SOCIAL MEDIA—THE DETRIMENTAL EFFECT

Social media usage becomes problematic when individuals rely on social networking sites as a means to alleviate stress, loneliness, or depression. For these individuals, engaging with social media provides a constant source of validation

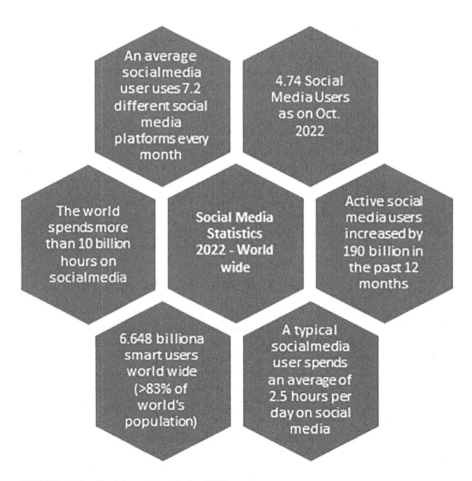

FIGURE 14.1   Social media statistics 2022.

and recognition that may be lacking in their offline lives, leading them to repeatedly turn to social media for fulfillment. However, this incessant reliance on social media can have detrimental effects on various aspects of their lives, including neglecting real-life relationships, work or school responsibilities, and physical well-being. Consequently, as users continue to rely on social media as a mechanism for alleviating negative emotions, their level of psychological dependence on these platforms increases.

One of the psychological effects associated with social media is the negative impact on sleep patterns. The use of technology, particularly smartphones, keeps teenagers awake late into the night. The artificial blue light emitted by smartphones stimulates neurons in the brain, disrupting the production of melatonin, a hormone responsible for inducing sleep. As a result, sleep deprivation becomes prevalent among teenagers, leading to increased physical and psychological stress. Prolonged sleep deprivation can heighten the risk of teenage depression, substance abuse, and engaging in risky behaviors while diminishing emotional regulation skills.

Friendships play a crucial role in the lives of adolescents, and the psychological effects of social media heavily influence their interactions with peer groups. In a survey conducted by the Pew Research Center in 2018, 743 teenagers were assessed, revealing that 81% of respondents aged between 13 and 17 believed that social media made them feel more connected to their friends' lives. Additionally, 66% of these teenagers reported that online social connections made them feel supported during difficult times. However, the survey also highlighted a distinction between genuine friendships and "fake friends," referring to social media connections with whom teenagers did not spend time in real life. Interestingly, many respondents had unfriended or disconnected from social media connections due to experiences of cyberbullying or digital harassment.

14.2.2 SOCIAL MEDIA AND GIRLS

Adolescent girls are particularly vulnerable to the detrimental effects of social media, leading to psychological issues. The researchers at The Lancet Child and Adolescent Health have established a compelling connection between the use of social media, mental health, and overall well-being. The study reveals that online media usage has a more negative impact on young adolescent girls compared to boys. Out of a total of 1,000 individuals surveyed, 210 of them were girls. Numerous academic studies have highlighted a significant increase in psychological problems among young girls over the past decade, coinciding with the exponential growth in their use of social media.

Dr. Bernadka Dubicka, a prominent psychiatrist at the Royal College of Psychiatrists, has identified a growing crisis in the mental health of children and adolescents, particularly in the form of increased mental distress and depression among young girls and young women. According to Dubicka, social media platforms such as Instagram and Snapchat can have a significantly harmful and even catastrophic impact on the psychological well-being of young girls. These negative consequences can stem from factors such as disrupted sleep patterns, cyberbullying, and, to some extent, a lack of physical activity.

Investigators conducted a study at London University College, which supervised the online media usage of about 13,000 teenagers with the age group of 13, and concluded that three main factors induce the consequences of online media on girls, but on the other hand, boys were not the victim of these factors, which are as follows:

- **Inadequate sleep**—Young girls keep awake until late, browsing through their social media posts, a practice known as vamping.
- **Disclosure to cyberbullying**—Damaging, fabricated, or personal matter posted about them on social media.
- **Lack of physical activity**—Having online media on their mobiles or other gadgets forces young girls to sit for longer time frames, and thus, they lack physical activity. Consequently, they lose the favorable effects of physical activities on emotional wellness.

The fear of missing out (FOMO) on social media poses a significant danger to young people worldwide. FOMO refers to the feeling of anxiety or apprehension that arises from the perception of missing out on the recognition and experiences that others are receiving. This FOMO sensation, particularly among young girls, drives their constant engagement with social media, thereby significantly impacting their psychological well-being (Franchina et al., 2018). Social media has detrimental effects on emotional well-being. Individuals who spend more time on social media are more likely to experience psychological issues such as loneliness, anxiety, depression, and FOMO compared to those who spend less time on these platforms (van der Schuur, Baumgartner, and Sumter, 2018). Examining the top eight online platforms based on monthly active users, TikTok, Twitter, and LinkedIn show higher utilization by male users (Table 14.1), while Pinterest, Instagram, and Facebook are predominantly used by female users.

TABLE 14.1
Usage of Social Media Gender Split

Platform	Male	Female
Facebook	63	75
Instagram	31	43
Twitter	24	21
LinkedIn	29	24
Pinterest	15	42
Snapchat	24	24
YouTube	78	68
TikTok	56	44
Reddit	15	8
WhatsApp	21	19

Sources: Statista, Brandwatch, Statista, Statista, Worldometers, OurWorldInData, Data Portal, Social media platforms & Kepio's Analysis.

14.3   CYBERBULLYING

Cyberbullying is the torment being executed using digital gadgets like computers, laptops, smart phones, and tablets, through the platforms like social media, chat rooms, etc. It primarily dwells inside the concealed realm of cyberspace, cell phones, social networking sites, information and communication technology (ICT). Frightening or blemishing communications posted via ICT publicly, or anonymously by using fake identity, is called as cyberbullying.

Surveys have shown that social media is currently the favored platform for digital bullies. They're progressively part of a "bedroom culture." Gadgets like smartphones and tablets are changing how and where youngsters go on the web (Esquivel et al., 2023). Smart phones empower children to access the web in the privacy of their bedrooms or from a companion's house, prompting to web access that is more personal, more confidential, and less supervised.

14.3.1   TYPES OF CYBERBULLYING

- **Cyber harassment:** A digital tormenting strategy that includes passing frightful and slanderous messages to a target child that is phrased in a serious, persevering, or pervasive manner.
- **Cyber threats:** Cyber threats is a strategy where a cyberbully is actively involved in passive-aggressive methodologies of informing the target child that they are in danger from undisclosed or felonious assailants.
- **Exposure:** It incorporates the public showcase, posting or sending of individual communication, pictures or video by the digital harasser that is confidential and private to the target user.
- **Interactive gaming harassment:** Here, cyberbullies orally abuse others through the swapping of data with gaming adversaries and fellow companions, use threatening and profane language, lock others out of games, or pass bogus data about others.
- **Sexting:** Sexting is the idiom addressing the utilization of a smartphone or other digital devices to pass images or videos of a sexually explicit nature. It also includes text messages of a sexually levied theme.
- **Sextortion:** Sextortion is another cyberbullying strategy where targets are abused for sex and sexually themed actions in exchange for not revealing humiliating and embarrassing information about the target child.
- **Social media bullying:** In this situation, the cyberbully demands the target user to add them to their "friends" or "buddy" lists and then starts approaching the target child's friends, peers, and loved ones dispersing undesirable wrong information about the target child.
- **Trolling:** Trolling is a childish cyberbullying procedure called Internet Troll. Internet Trolls are regularly formed by adults who slander and harass unidentified web-based users, but the cyberbullying troll knows the identity of the target child. They show up in all types of online mediums like forum discussions, online video gaming gatherings, chat rooms, etc.

- **Twitter pooping:** Twitter pooping is an informal articulation regularly used to define the cyberbullying act of using tweets to embarrass a target child.
- **YouTube channelling:** Being the objective of a slanderous YouTube channel, the target victim is haunted by both the subject of the videos posted and by the number of online views. Aside from the number of opinions used to humiliate the victim, the remarks made by others can be very malicious.

As computerized technology continues to advance and the Internet becomes more prevalent, cyberbullying has reached epidemic levels among young people and has become a devastating weapon. Bullying, whether it takes the form of cyberbullying or traditional bullying, involves the exploitation, defamation, and mistreatment of targeted individuals. Figure 14.2 depicts certain terms related to cyber bullying.

14.3.2　CYBERBULLYING FACTS AND STATISTICS

Cyberbullying is on the rise worldwide. Comparitech.com have collected global cyberbullying statistics, trends, and facts through a survey, which illustrates the fear of this growing problem. The effects of cyberbullying are illustrated in the figure 14.3. Some of the cyberbullying data from 2018 through 2022 are as follows:

- According to the survey conducted by Comparitech with over 1,000 parents, 60% of them reported that children within the age group of 14–18 are being bullied.
- One-fifth of all cyberbullying is through social media—Albeit a vast majority of parents reported the bullying occurred in school, 19.2% stated

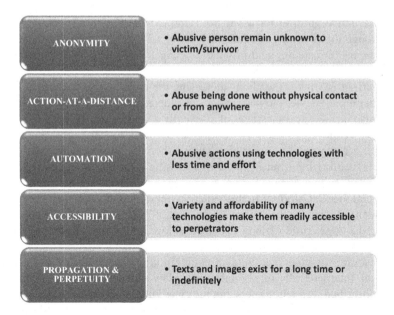

FIGURE 14.2　Terms related to cyberbullying.

that bullying occurred through social media sites and apps. Eleven percent indicated that bullying occurred through text messages, while 7.9% identified video games as a source. Meanwhile, 6.8% reported bullying occurred on non-social-media websites, while 3.3% indicated the bullying occurred through email.

- Most parents respond proactively after their children are cyberbullied—Comparitech found 59.4% of parents had a talk with their children about Internet safety and safe practices after cyberbullying occurred. Parents may need to take more steps to intervene; however, as only 43.4% identified adjusting parental controls to block offenders, only 33% implemented new rules for technology use.
- One out of four students who are victims of cyberbullying has harmed themselves as a solution to cope up. Twenty-four percent of the victims attempted suicide after continuous bullying.
- Students who face bullying are three times more likely to participate in violence and delinquency.
- Only 38% of the bullied victims openly discuss it with their parents.
- 71% of the participants in the survey feel that social platform is not taking serious action to overcome the problem.
- Cyberbullying is most prevalent in India, Brazil, and USA.
- More than 6% of global users had their accounts hacked, while 4% lost access to their devices.
- A survey on 3,000 Asian students reveals that 48.4% had embarrassing videos posted online and 47.3% were the victim of hate speech.
- The most common victims of cyberbullying are children, women, and people with non-traditional sexual orientation.

14.3.3 CYBERBULLYING AGAINST WOMEN AND CHILDREN (SCENARIO IN INDIA)

According to the Director of CDAC India, there has been a significant surge in cyber abuse against women in India during the pandemic. The speakers at a webinar organized by APCID and Cyber Peace Foundation discussed how the lockdown has emboldened cyber stalkers, making them more powerful. The National Commission for Women in India revealed that there were 412 valid complaints of cyber abuse reported between March 25 and April 25, 2020. During a webinar titled "Harassment of Women in Digital Space," Superintendent of Police Kiran Sivakumar from the Central Bureau of Investigation highlighted how rapidly advancing digital technology has become a nightmare for women instead of a safeguard. Chandramukhi Devi, a member of the NCW, emphasized the importance of victims coming forward, seeking help from cybercrime cells, and raising awareness about strict laws to prevent the abuse of women and children in the digital realm. At the same event, Pavan Duggal, a Supreme Court advocate and cyber law expert, suggested that amendments are needed in the IT Act to address the pervasive role of social media in people's lives. He also pointed out that the COVID-19 pandemic, with its increased reliance on technology, has made women and children more vulnerable to online abuse. Online abuse has a strong impact in women as presented in figure 14.4

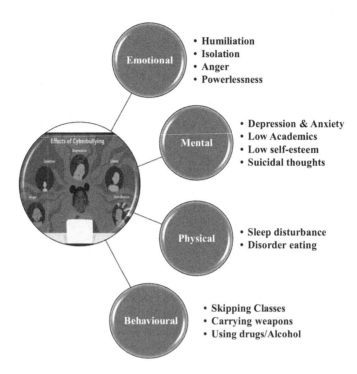

FIGURE 14.3   Effects of cyberbullying.

14.4 IMPLEMENTATION—ONLINE SURVEY TO ASSESS THE INFLUENCE OF SOCIAL MEDIA AND CYBERBULLYING ON TEEN GIRLS

The impact of social media on young teenage girls is profoundly negative, as evidenced by a survey conducted by Plan International, an NGO dedicated to promoting gender equality in India. The survey revealed that over 58% of women have experienced online abuse. Given the prevalence of social media platforms in today's digital age, it is nearly impossible to avoid their influence, regardless of age. However, ensuring the safe and effective use of these platforms has become a growing concern, particularly due to the rising threat of cyberbullying and online abuse. To address this issue, a survey was conducted online specifically targeting teenage girls. A total of 1,600 girls from various states in India participated in the survey, the questionnaire consisted of three sections designed to gather relevant information.

Section I—Basic information

- You Belong to (State)   _____
- Your State   _____
- Your area (Category)   *Urban*   *Rural*
- You belong to age group   *13–15*   *16–18*   *19–21*
- Educational Status   *10th or below*   *10th*   *HSE*   *UG*

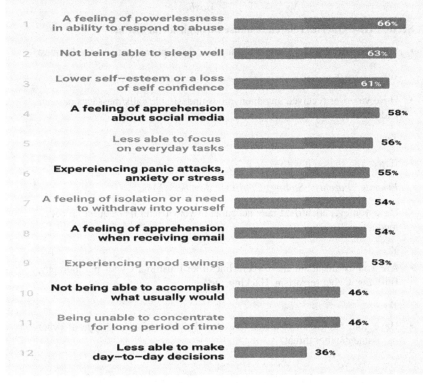

FIGURE 14.4 Data on the psychological impact of women experiencing online abuse or harassment worldwide.

Source: Statista.com.

Section II—Queries related to the usage of Smart gadget and Social media

- How much time do you spend on your gadget
  <1 hour   2–5 hours   5–8 hours   >8 hours

- You use gadget for   *Educational purpose   Entertainment*
                            News/Awareness   Online Shopping

- You own an account in   *Facebook   Twitter   Instagram*
                            Tiktok   LinkedIn   Whatsapp

- How often do you use Social Media sites in a day?
  Onceaday   2–5 times/day   5–10 times/day   >10 times   Noteveryday

- How often do you post on Social Media?
  Many times a day   Daily   Weekly Monthly   Never

- What type of content do your prefer to post in Social Media sites?
  *Personalpiscs   Occasionwithfriends   Occassionwithfamily
  Newsfeed   Trolls/Videos*

- Is checking the social media, your last task before going to bed?
  Yes   No   Maybe

Section III—Queries related to abuse through social media

- If you possess a Social Media account, do you accept anonymous friend request

  Yes   No

- Have you ever received any anonymous undesirable calls/messages on your gadget

  Yes   No

- If yes, you shared it with your......

  Friends   Parents   Siblings/Cousins   Teachers None

- Have you ever identified fake accounts in your friend list/request on social media?

  Yes   No

- Are you aware about the Cybercrimes like Phishing, Cyber pornography, Bullying, Cyber terrorism, Hacking, etc?

  Yes   No

- Have your friends or relatives (particularly girls) faced any type of cyber harassment/cyber threat?

  Yes   No

- If yes, has any action been taken against the harasser?

  Yes   No

- If no action is taken, the reason is (Select more than one option, if applicable)

  Ignored it   Felt Nervous/Apprehensive   Lack of resources   None

- Are you aware about the Cybercrime investigation cell nearby you or about online cyber-crime registration?

  Yes   No

- How frequently does your educational institution provide awareness sessions about Cyberattacks on girls?

  Yearly   Twice in an academic year   When specific issue happens Never

14.5   RESEARCH FINDINGS AND IMPLICATIONS

The detrimental effects of media usage on children, especially young girls, have become a pressing concern. This issue has been further exacerbated during the pandemic, as smart devices have become an indispensable part of people's lives, almost like a necessity. Social media platforms and smart gadgets have emerged as the primary means of communication for a wide range of activities, including education, shopping, work, personal relationships, and leisure. In light of these concerns, a research study was conducted to investigate the stress and abuse experienced by girls in India due to their social media usage. To gather accurate information about the challenges faced by young girls in the country, a well-structured questionnaire was designed. This digital questionnaire was distributed among female students, resulting in an impressive response rate of over 1,600 participants from various states. The survey's implications and findings are presented as figures.Table 14.2 illustrates the details of the research methodology.

14.5.1   AGE GROUP OF THE RESPONDENTS

The survey primarily focused on teenage girls, with a majority of the respondents falling into two age groups. From Figure 14.5 it is evident that among the participants,

TABLE 14.2
Research Details

Type of Research	Descriptive
Methodology adopted	Online questionnaire
Sample size	Total sample collected: 1,648
	Samples with disorders: 340
Statistical tools applied	SPSS—frequency and mean score

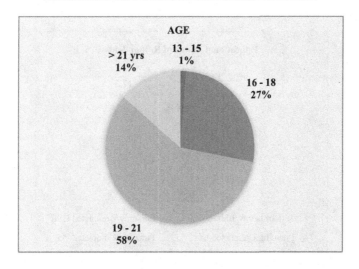

FIGURE 14.5   Age group of respondents.

there were 351 girls aged 16–18, while 764 girls belonged to the age group of 19–21, making up 58% of the total respondents.

14.5.2 Educational Status of the Respondents

Figure 14.6 reveals that majority of girls who participated in the study were under-graduate students, accounting for 66.4% of the total respondents. Following closely behind were higher secondary students, comprising 17.3% of the survey participants.

14.5.3 Assessment of Time Spent on Smart Gadgets

The survey revealed that most of the respondents spend around 2–5 hours in a day on their smart gadget. Around 315 girls spend almost 5–8 hours on the smart device as specified in Figure 14.7.

14.5.4 Purpose of Using Smart Gadgets

When examining the utilization of smart devices, a majority of the participants indicated (Figure 14.8) that they employ their gadgets for educational purposes, entertainment, and staying informed through news and awareness. It is noteworthy that the respondents were allowed to select multiple options.

14.5.5 Type of Entertainment through Smart Gadgets

To analyze the impact of entertainment through smart device, the respondents were asked about the type of entertainment they cherish through smart gadget. Most of the teen girls have their online entertainment as social media. Spending time on various social media platforms is a major activity for the as represented in Figure 14.9.

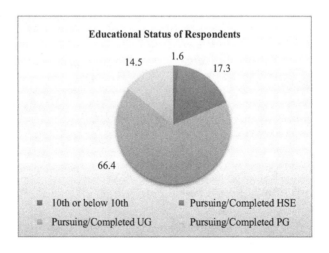

FIGURE 14.6   Educational status of respondents.

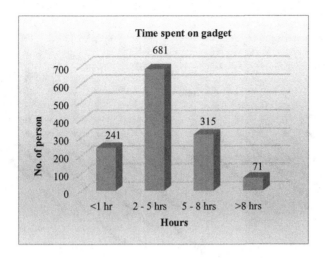

FIGURE 14.7 Time on smart gadgets.

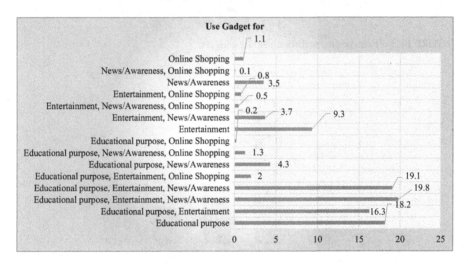

FIGURE 14.8 Use of smart gadgets.

14.5.6 FREQUENCY OF VISITING SOCIAL MEDIA SITES

When examining the frequency of visiting social media sites on a daily basis, it was found that a significant number of respondents displayed a high level of curiosity in checking posts and their responses. Majority of participants (37.5%) reported visiting social media platforms between 2 and 5 times a day (Figure 14.10).

14.5.7 TYPE OF SOCIAL MEDIA ACCOUNTS

Among the respondents, it was found (Figure 14.11) that a significant portion (35%) owned a WhatsApp account, indicating its popularity among the participants. Additionally,

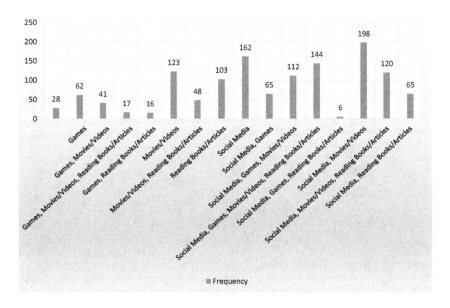

FIGURE 14.9   Entertainment through smart gadgets.

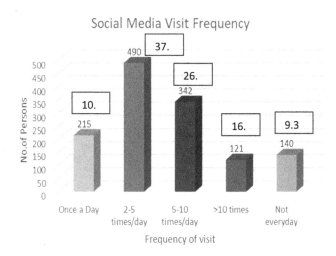

FIGURE 14.10   Frequency of visiting social media sites.

the majority of users (more than 50%) reported owning multiple social media accounts, highlighting the widespread presence of individuals across various platforms.

14.5.8   AWARENESS OF ANONYMOUS IDENTITIES IN SOCIAL MEDIA

When analyzing the receipt of anonymous calls or messages (Figure 14.12), a majority of the respondents (58.6%) indicated a positive response by selecting the option "No," implying that they did not receive such calls or messages.

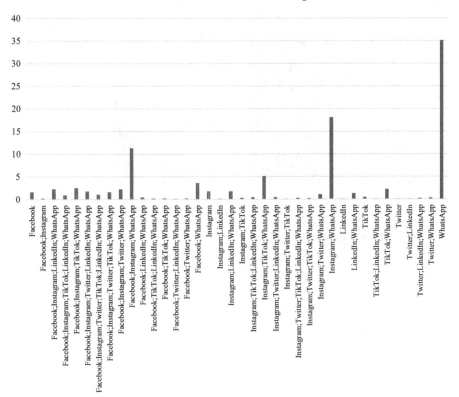

FIGURE 14.11   Social media accounts of respondents.

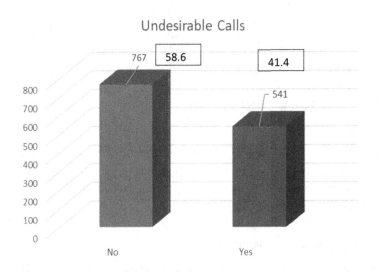

FIGURE 14.12   Anonymity in social media.

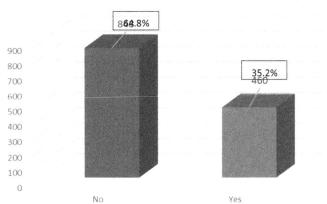

FIGURE 14.13   Recognizing fake accounts.

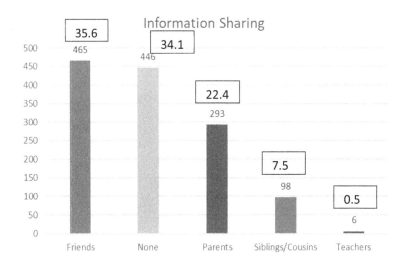

FIGURE 14.14   Sharing of bullied experience.

14.5.9   Awareness of Fake Accounts in Social Media

The survey findings revealed that a significant majority of respondents (64.8%) were unable to recognize or identify fake accounts within their social media friend list or requests (Figure 14.13).

14.5.10   Cyberbullied Experience

Approximately 35.6% of the respondents have chosen to confide in their friends about their experiences with bullying, while 34% didn't share with anybody (Figure 14.14).

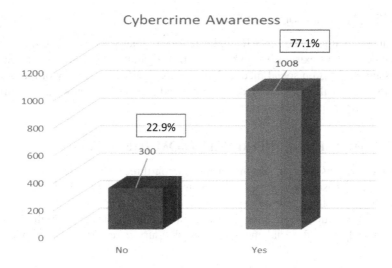

FIGURE 14.15   Awareness on cyber hazards.

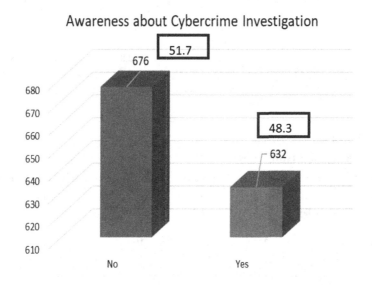

FIGURE 14.16   Awareness of cyber investigation cell.

14.5.11   AWARENESS ON CYBER HAZARDS

The analysis (Figure 14.15) clearly indicates that a substantial number of respondents, specifically 1,008 individuals (77.1%), possess awareness regarding the potential hazards they may encounter on digital platforms. Furthermore, these respondents expressed their intention to exercise caution in navigating these platforms.

14.5.12 Awareness of Cyber Cells

The survey findings (Figure 14.16) indicate a lack of awareness among the respondents regarding the existence of cybercrime investigation cells, which are crucial for addressing hazards on social media platforms. A significant majority of the participants (51.7%), totaling 676 individuals, expressed their lack of knowledge regarding crime investigation in the context of cybercrimes.

14.6 SUMMARY OF INFERENCES FROM THE SURVEY

The survey results provide significant insights on three crucial aspects, serving as eye-openers. These key findings (highlighted in bold in Tables 14.3–14.5) can be summarized as follows:

The aforementioned analysis highlights a concerning trend of high addiction to smart gadgets and social media among the survey respondents. Despite their

TABLE 14.3
Time Spent on the Smart Gadgets

Time	Frequency	Percent	Valid Percent	Cumulative Percent
<1 hour	246	18.8	18.8	18.8
2–5 hours	**703**	**53.7**	**53.7**	**72.5**
5–8 hours	**298**	**22.8**	**22.8**	**95.3**
>8 hours	61	4.7	4.7	100.0

TABLE 14.4
Frequency of Posting in the Social Media Sites

Period	Frequency	Percent	Valid Percent	Cumulative Percent
Daily	132	10.1	10.1	10.1
Many times in a day	25	1.9	1.9	12.0
Monthly	392	30.0	30.0	42.0
Weekly	214	16.4	16.4	58.4
Never	545	41.7	41.7	100.0

TABLE 14.5
Awareness on Cyber Cell/Supporting System

Period	Frequency	Percent	Valid Percent	Cumulative Percent
No	**676**	**51.7**	**51.7**	**51.7**
Yes	632	48.3	48.3	100.0
Total	1,308	100.0	100.0	

awareness of cyberbullying on social media platforms, the findings reveal a disturbing lack of knowledge regarding the existing laws and support systems in place to protect individuals from cyber assaults. Given the indispensable nature of smart gadgets and social media in today's digital era, it is imperative to prioritize awareness campaigns and frequent reminders about the different forms of bullying and the necessary measures to safeguard oneself.

14.7   CONCLUSION

Cyberbullying refers to the act of tormenting or harassing individuals through digital devices such as computers, laptops, smartphones, and tablets. This form of bullying takes place on various platforms, including social media networks, chat rooms, and other online communication channels. The research is an attempt to understand the impact of smart gadgets and social media among teen girls in India. The research employed a questionnaire consisting of three sections to gather comprehensive information. The first section aimed to collect basic participant details, while the second section focused on understanding smart device and social media usage patterns. The third section aimed to assess the respondents' knowledge and awareness regarding abuse targeted at girls through social media.

Upon analyzing the collected data, several noteworthy insights emerged. It became evident that teenage girls exhibit a strong addiction to smart gadgets and are significantly influenced by social media platforms. One concerning outcome of this influence is the inclination to publicly share personal and family events through status updates and posts, thereby inadvertently providing an opportunity for cyber stalkers to identify potential targets.

However, when examining the responses to the third section of the questionnaire, it appears that the girls are relatively safe as they tend to avoid accepting or responding to fake requests or accounts on social media. Additionally, approximately 70% of the respondents stated that they had not received any anonymous calls or messages on their devices. These responses could be attributed to either a lack of awareness regarding the hidden threats of smart social media platforms or the introverted nature of the respondents.

However, the survey also highlighted a concerning fact that more than 50% of the participants lacked awareness regarding the existence of cybercrime investigation cells. This emphasizes the urgent need to educate girls about the potential threats, consequences, and available measures during emergencies. It is imperative to enforce this awareness through educational institutions and the media. Organizing frequent awareness campaigns on cyberbullying and methods of protection should be systematized to ensure the safety and well-being of individuals in the digital realm.

BIBLIOGRAPHY

S. Bano, A. Mohammad, "An analysis of social media use and its impact on mental health of female students", *European Journal of Physical Education and Sport Science*, 5(6), (2019), pp. 66–76.

V.K. Bhonsle, J.K. Sony Krishnamurthy, "Cyber bullying in India during Covid-19 pandemic", *Law Audience Journal*, 3(1), (2021), pp. 71–79.

S. Cook, Cyberbullying facts and statistics for 2018–2020 (2020). Available online at: https://www.comparitech.com/internet-providers/cyberbullying-statistics/ (Accessed on 12 January 2019).

M. Devmane, N. Rana, "Usability Trends and Access of Online Social Network by Indian Population and Its Analysis," In *International Conference on Nascent Technologies in the Engineering Field (ICNTE'15)*, IEEE, 2015.

M. Donat, A. Willisch, A. Wolgast, "Cyber-bullying among university students: concurrent relations to belief in a just world and to empathy", *Current Psychology*, 42(10) (2022), pp. 7883–7896.

eMarketer, "Slowing Growth Ahead for Worldwide Internet Audience" (2016) (available online at https://www.emarketer.com/Article/Slowing-Growth-Ahead-Worldwide-Internet-Audience/1014045, accessed on February 28, 2018).

F.A. Esquivel, I.L.D.L.G. López, A.D. Benavides, "Emotional impact of bullying and cyber bullying: perceptions and effects on students", *Revista Caribeña de Ciencias Sociales*, 12(1) (2023), pp. 367–383.

A. Franchina, A.J. van Rooij, G. Lo Coco, L. De Marez, "Fear of Missing Out as a Predictor of Problematic Social Media Use and Phubbing Behavior among Flemish Adolescents", (2016), "Social media 'likes' impact teens' brains and behaviour".

V. Franchina, M. Vanden Abeele, A. J, Van Rooij, G. Lo Coco, & L. De Marez, "Fear of missing out as a predictor of problematic social media use and phubbing behavior among Flemish adolescents." *International Journal of Environmental Research and Public Health*, 15(10) (2018), p. 2319.

Hindustan Times, Lucknow, March 22, 2018, "Social media misused as a tool for sexual predation" https://www.thchindu.com/news/cities/Delhi/aiims-looks-to-tackle-internet-addiction-eyond the-walls-of-clinics/article17688685.ece

O. Jain, M. Gupta, S. Satam, S. Panda, "Has the COVID-19 pandemic affected the susceptibility to cyberbullying in India?", *Computers in Human Behavior Reports*, 2 (2020), p. 100029.

H.S. Lallie, L.A. Shepherd, J.R. Nurse, A. Erola, G. Epiphaniou, C. Maple, X. Bellekens, "Cyber Security in the Age of COVID-19: A Timeline and Analysis of Cyber-Crime and Cyber-Attacks during the Pandemic", (2020), arXiv preprint arXiv:2006.11929

Y.C. Lee, W.L. Wu, "Factors in cyber bullying: the attitude-social influence-efficacy model", *Anales De Psicología/Annals of Psychology*, 34(2) (2018), pp. 324–331

M. Leiner, A.K. Dwivedi, MW.M. AlRahmi, N. Yahaya, M.M. Alamri, N.A. Aljarboa, Y.B. Kamin, F.A. Moafa, "A model of factors affecting cyber bullying behaviors among university students", *IEEE Access*, 7 (2018), pp. 2978–2985.

V. Manjula, "A Study on the Usage of Mobile Phones for Cyber Bullying Among Tweens & Teens of Chennai, India", In *International Conference on Communication, Media, Technology and Design*, May 2015.

H.N. Mischel, & W. Mischel, The Development of Children's Knowledge of Self-Control Strategies. In: Halisch, F., Kuhl, J. (eds) *Motivation, Intention, and Volition*. Springer, Berlin, Heidelberg, 1987. https://doi.org/10.1007/978-3-642-70967-8_22

T. Nazir, "Use of social networking sites by the secondary and higher secondary school students of Srinagar, Kashmir", *International Journal of Digital Library Services*, 4(3) (2014), pp. 231–242.

A. Peker, F. Kasikci, "Do positivity and sensitivity to cyber-bullying decrease cyber- bullying?", *Acta Educationis Generalis*, 12(2) (2022), pp. 90–111.

D.A. Prathima Mathias, B. Suma, "A survey report on cybercrime awareness among graduate and postgraduate students of government institutions in Chikmagalur, Karnataka, India, and a subsequent effort to educate them through a seminar", *International Journal of Advanced Research in Engineering and Technology*, 9(6), 2018, pp. 214–228.

K. Radha, S. Kewalramani, "Cyber bullying through smart phones & other electronic devices-a theoretical perspective", Scope, 13 (2023), pp. 276–279.

N.R. Ramesh Masthi, S. Pruthvi, M. Phaneendra, "A comparative study on social media addiction between public and private high school students of urban Bengaluru, India", *ASEAN Journal of Psychiatry*, 18(2) (2017), pp. 206–215.

L.A. Reed, R.M. Tolman, L.M. Ward, "Snooping and sexting: digital media as a context for dating aggression and abuse among college students", *Violence Against Women*. DOI: 10.1177/1077801216630143.

S. Sankhwar, A. Chaturvedi, "Woman harassment in digital space in India", *International Journal of Pure and Applied Mathematics*, 118(20) (2018), pp. 595–607.

W.A. van der Schuur, S.E. Baumgartner, S. R.Sumter, & P. M. Valkenburg, "Media multitasking and sleep problems: A longitudinal study among adolescents." *Computers in Human Behavior*, 81(2018), pp. 316–324.

World Stats-Usage and Population Statistics PopulationPyramid.net https://www.internet-worldstats.com/asia/in.htm

WEBLINKS

https://www.statista.com/topics/257/internet-usage-in-india/
https://www.thelancet.com/journals/lanchi/article/PIIS2352-4642(19)30323-2/fulltext
https://blog.securly.com/2018/10/04/the-10-types-of-cyberbullying/
https://kids.kaspersky.com/10-forms-of-cyberbullying/
https://www.comparitech.com/internet-providers/cyberbullying-statistics/
https://firstsiteguide.com/cyberbullying-stats/
https://www.firstpost.com/tag/cyber-bullying
https://statusbrew.com/insights/social-media-statistics/

Index

Note: **Bold** page numbers refer to tables and *italic* page numbers refer to figures.

Printed in the United States
by Baker & Taylor Publisher Services